Praise for
The Art of Teaching Children

"Done mines his 33 years of experience for colorful stories and sound advice in this spirited teacher's survival guide. . . . Well-crafted examples and pithy prose drive his points home. Done's experience will hearten those in the trenches and be a tonic for young teachers."

—*Publishers Weekly*

"After three decades teaching elementary school, Done has amassed hundreds of interesting stories about his students, and he demonstrates a strong grasp of what works (and doesn't) in the classroom. . . . Given the author's highly successful career, it's clear that his methods are proven to work. For teachers seeking inspiration, Done provides numerous stimulating concepts that can be incorporated into any lesson plan; for prospective or aspiring teachers, the author has plenty of insights into the ups and downs of teaching young children. All readers will have no doubt that Done chose the right profession. . . . A well-rounded, satisfying look at the daily life of a teacher."

—*Kirkus Reviews*

The Art of Teaching Children

All I Learned from a Lifetime in the Classroom

Phillip Done

AVID READER PRESS

NEW YORK LONDON TORONTO SYDNEY NEW DELHI

Avid Reader Press
An Imprint of Simon & Schuster, Inc.
1230 Avenue of the Americas
New York, NY 10020

Author's Note: As teachers, one of our most important responsibilities to our students is to protect them. For that reason, throughout this book, I have altered names, timeframes, and in some cases specific details, while simultaneously striving to capture the true spirit of the stories I wish to pass along.

First Avid Reader Press trade paperback edition July 2023

AVID READER PRESS and colophon are trademarks of Simon & Schuster, Inc.

For information about special discounts for bulk purchases, please contact Simon & Schuster Special Sales at 1-866-506-1949 or business@simonandschuster.com.

The Simon & Schuster Speakers Bureau can bring authors to your live event. For more information or to book an event contact the Simon & Schuster Speakers Bureau at 1-866-248-3049 or visit our website at www.simonspeakers.com.

Interior design by Carly Loman

Manufactured in the United States of America

10 9 8 7 6 5 4 3 2 1

Library of Congress Cataloging-in-Publication Data has been applied for.

ISBN 978-1-9821-6566-6
ISBN 978-1-9821-6567-3 (pbk)
ISBN 978-1-9821-6568-0 (ebook)

Contents

The Craft

Colleagues, Parents, and Mentors

The Challenges

Closing Thoughts

I have come to believe that a great teacher is a great artist and that there are as few as there are any other great artists. Teaching might even be the greatest of the arts, since the medium is the human mind and spirit.

—JOHN STEINBECK

The Art of
Teaching Children

Introduction

One, two, three, four, five . . . I continued counting on my fingers. When I stopped at thirty-three, I shook my head. *It can't be that long.* Disbelieving my own fingers, I recounted them. Then my hand rose to my forehead and rubbed it. *Yep, it's thirty-three.* I had just counted the number of years I'd taught children.

Teaching plays tricks with time. As the school years come and go, you don't realize that you're getting any older. Your students are always the same age. Their parents are always the same age too. The book characters you read about to your kids never age either. And then one day, as happened to me not too long ago, time holds its mirror in front of you when one of your third graders announces, "You taught my mom!"

I never thought about getting old—probably because *my* world was always young. *Where did the time go?* Children who once played soccer at recess are playing on high school teams now. Boys and girls who sang their hearts out during music time are performing in the high school musical. Kids who could barely write a sentence are writing essays to get into college.

I remember the very first lesson I gave when I was a student teacher. I was pretty nervous, even though I'd practiced the night before in front of the bathroom mirror. I can recall my first interview for a teaching position, wearing my dad's tie and trying to act confident while answering questions such as "What's your teaching philosophy?" when I really didn't have a clue. Or a philosophy. I can also recall the day I was offered my first teaching job: a third-grade class in Sunnyvale, California—my hometown. The pay was $19,300 a year. I thought I was rich. The advice I got from a colleague at my new school was: "Don't worry. The first twenty years are the hardest." And I remember my first year of teaching, tiptoeing at night into the classroom next to mine and reading Mrs. Gonzales's plan book to see what she was teaching that week. Mrs. Gonzales had been teaching forever. She claimed to have taught Abraham Lincoln.

Over time, I didn't need to sneak into Mrs. Gonzales's classroom anymore. I learned my craft. For the past thirty-three years, I have taught in public and private schools in the United States and internationally. I've coached teachers on different continents, taught adults, and was even an on-set teacher for child actors in television and film. I've had good teaching years, bad ones, and years I wanted to quit. All in all, it has been a rich and rewarding career. For most of it, I taught grades three and four—my sweet spot. Third and fourth graders can do so much more than the little ones, aren't as sassy as the older kids, and they still love their teacher. As the years passed by, I attended graduations and weddings and baby showers of students I had in elementary school. I guess I've come to the place where I can say that I taught Lincoln too.

I always wanted to be a teacher—ever since I was in second grade with Miss Greco. I used to bring home my papers from her class and trace over them so that I would have worksheets for playing school. I loved to play school. I always insisted on being the teacher and would make my younger brother be my student. Sometimes I'd get the whole neighborhood gang to play school too. I'd set up a classroom in my garage and pass out my worksheets. But they didn't like this. Once, they all mutinied and walked out.

I have come to the conclusion that playing school as a child is one thing that all grade school teachers have in common. One afternoon when I was in the staff room at lunch, I asked my colleagues how many of them played school when they were kids. They chuckled and nodded and raised their hands. Then I asked, "And how many of you insisted on being the teacher?" All hands went up again. In my Back to School Night talks, I used to ask the parents if their children liked to play school. To those who raised their hands, I'd smile and say, "Your child is going to be a teacher."

This year is an important one for me. I have just finished my last year in the classroom. After thirty-three years, I have decided to retire. It's time. I am happy to report that I am retiring while I still love my work. I never wanted to be one of those teachers who holds on long after they've lost their love for it.

When I packed up my classroom for the last time, I had thirty-three lesson planners, thirty-three class lists, and thirty-three years of paint on my smock. I had sixty-six class photos too—thirty-three with me fake smiling in the back row while saying "Stand still" between my teeth, and the other thirty-three with several pairs of bunny ears above my head because the photographer had just said, "Okay. Now, let's take a silly one." I also had all of my own individual school portraits from my first year of teaching to my last. Looking through them felt like I was seeing one of those time-lapse videos you find online where people who take snapshots of themselves for years become older before your eyes. As I thumbed through the images, I watched my hair get thinner, my wrinkles deeper, and my ties get narrower, then wider, then narrower again. I laughed at my most current photo. My new eyeglasses were exactly the same style as the ones I wore in my first school picture in the '80s.

I am looking forward to retirement. I'm looking forward to having more than ten minutes to eat lunch. I'm happy about being able to use the bathroom when I want to and not having to hold it till recess. I'll enjoy not having to take the 7 a.m. dentist appointment and make up a year's worth of doctor visits during my summer break. I'm looking forward to going to the dry cleaner without pointing out the glue and marker on my clothes. It'll be nice to watch TV without a stack of papers on my lap. I will like sleeping in. I'll admit—I won't miss the paperwork and the politics. I won't miss the grading, report writing, or all the meetings either. I know I'll miss the kids.

Now that I'm retired, I wonder if my teacher muscle memory will kick in, and I'll find myself doing certain things just because I've done them for so long. I wonder if, come August, I'll be itching to buy school supplies, and if, around Halloween, I'll be hankering to carve a pumpkin. I'm curious if I'll still collect cottage cheese containers and egg cartons for class projects. I wonder if, when I drive by a group of students walking on a field trip, my first instinct will be to check that the stragglers in back aren't too far behind. And if I see a new children's book in a store, will I have the urge to read it aloud to a group of kids?

My teacher friends at school gave me a nice send-off. One colleague got me a T-shirt that said "School's Out—Forever!" Another bought me a mug that read "Retired Teacher—Every Child Left Behind." A third wrote in her card:

"You realize that you can never really get out of here. You know too much." And one of my friends gave me three bottles of wine, each with a tag. The first said "To enjoy when we have to go back to school, and you don't." The second: "To have while we're holding conferences, and you're not." And tied on the third: "To drink when you are home, and we're still in the staff meeting."

But the best retirement gifts were the ones from the children. In my last year of teaching, when one of my third graders named Gabi learned that I would not be returning, she wrote me notes begging me to stay and vowing to kidnap me. These notes were usually accompanied by drawings of me suspended on a hanger in her bedroom closet. At the end of the school year, the secretary posted photos of the teachers who were leaving outside the office. One day, mine was gone. Gabi had swiped it. Around the same time, Gabi handed me a folded piece of paper and asked me to sign it. I played along. After I wrote my name, she gleefully unfolded the paper and showed me what I had signed. Above my signature were the words "I promise I won't leave," followed by seventeen exclamation marks.

There's no question that teaching is one of the most demanding professions. And it's not your imagination. It *is* getting harder—exponentially so. Every year, our students come to school with more and more challenges, and the bar for achievement is continually being raised. More is added to our plates, and rarely is anything removed. Each year, the job takes more out of you. Enrollments are up. Funding is down. Stress is at an all-time high. There's a tremendous sense of overwhelm. When the coronavirus pandemic hit in 2020, and millions of teachers were thrown into virtual classrooms, that overwhelm only intensified. For teachers, sometimes it feels like we work in a pressure cooker set on high—for nine months. Today many teachers are feeling like they're barely keeping their heads above water. One colleague of mine put it this way: "I feel like a three-legged hamster on a nonstop hamster wheel." For this reason, teachers need all the help, support, and guidance they can get. *That's* the reason I'm writing this book. Over three-plus decades in the classroom, I learned a lot about teaching, learning, and children. Now that I'm retired, I've decided to write it all down.

Throughout my career, I saw enormous changes in education. The education pendulum is always swinging. I taught when basal readers were in, then they were out; when phonics was emphasized, and then it wasn't; when skills-based learning made way for the whole language movement, then back to skills again. I observed textbooks come and go, standardized tests and classroom management programs pushed aside for new ones, and No Child Left Behind replaced by Common Core. I witnessed the jargon in education change too. *Groups* are now called *cohorts*. *Challenging work* is referred to as *rigor*. And some of the new terms can be deceptive. Nowadays, we don't *change* something, we *pivot*. Learning that brings about deep understanding is now *robust*—as if we're drinking a fine French cabernet. Also, we don't just *look* at standards anymore. We *unpack* them, as though we're opening our suitcases on vacation.

In this book, I won't write about the educational policies and programs composed in ivory towers. Instead, my aim is to share the universal truths of teaching. You know the old saying "Don't throw the baby out with the bathwater." It means, of course, not to throw away what's favorable along with the unfavorable. In today's world, when education is changing so rapidly, it's important to remember this, or as I like to say: Don't throw the third grader out with the bathwater. That's *also* what I will share with you—those teaching truths that should never change.

The Art of Teaching Children is for anyone who has wrestled with butcher paper when putting up a bulletin board or pried staples out of a stapler that isn't working because one of your students thought it was a sledgehammer. It is for anyone who has borrowed a library book for the whole year, found dry erase markers in your pocket at the end of the day, or searched the bottom of dozens of little shoes to see which one has dog poo on it. It's for anyone who has asked their students if they had any questions, gotten zero responses, then thirty seconds later had a line of kids at your desk. This book is for anyone who has jammed the copier and then walked away, or called a kid "sweetie" because you couldn't remember the child's name, or picked through a plate of food in the staff room that was left over from a previous day's event. It's for anyone who has forgotten to take attendance, gotten a reminder from the school secretary, then said you'd get to it right away but forgot again. It's for anyone who has heard a child say, "Are we doing anything today?" "How long does it hafta be?" or "Did we do anything while I was absent?" It's for

all teachers who need a quick pick-me-up, a long heart-to-heart, or just a reminder that you're not alone. This book is for those who played school when
they were young and grew up to have real classrooms of their own.

In the following pages, my goal is to encourage, enlighten, and empower—
to offer advice, guidance, and maybe even a little wisdom from the perspective
of an experienced teacher. You might not agree with everything I write, and
that's okay. I don't pretend to have all the answers. I acknowledge that in
teaching one size does not fit all. There is no magic formula. But I do know
what worked for me—and more importantly, what works for children. If you
are a teacher, or learning to become one, my wish is that you also will have a
rich and rewarding career—one that is so long that someday a student of yours
will announce that you taught his mom too.

The Children

Children

A few weeks after my last day of teaching, I settled into a chair at home and began thinking back on my career. As I sat there quietly, I decided to conduct a little experiment on myself: In all my years in the classroom, what had my mind held on to? What images were imprinted in my memory? What, after all this time, would pop into my head? I closed my eyes and just let my mind wander.

Immediately my thoughts took me to my former classrooms. I saw desks and rabbit cages and walls covered with student work. I recalled student libraries and messy cubbies and wires strung across the room like clotheslines, drooping with children's art. And then, like a carousel on an old slide projector, my mind flooded with the faces of children. I thought of Patrick from my first year of teaching and Sarah from my last. I remembered Hannah from one school and Bradley from another. I could see Hector in grade three and Chiara in grade five. I saw children working at their desks and under tables and behind the piano in newly constructed hideouts that required a password to get in.

As I pondered over the children, I pictured exactly where they used to sit in the classroom. I wondered: *Do all teachers remember their kids this way?* I saw Fiona in the corner (an independent worker) and John in the front (he tended to get off task). I could see Bryce by the classroom library (he needed his space) and Aaron way in the back (I needed my space). I saw Kayla far from the window (too distractible) and Grant seated between two girls (to cut down on the talking). I recalled Juliana (new to the school) seated by Bianca (a little mom), Elaine in the front (wore glasses), and Jared right beside me (needed drawing out). I thought about Katie on the opposite side of the room from Lana (best friends), Louisa close to my desk (required a lot of one-on-one), Matthew right under my nose (a pistol), Conner where I could see his shoes (liked to hide the soccer ball between his feet), and Amelia—first in the back of the room, then in the center, and finally next to my desk (a huge chatterbox).

As my mind drifted, I remembered children waiting in line for the photographer on Picture Day while I smashed down bed head. I saw kids excitedly wrapping up their teacher with rolls of toilet paper at the Halloween party because the room moms thought it would be a good idea to turn him into a mummy. I recalled boys and girls holding hands as tightly as they could during a game of Red Rover while a classmate raced toward them at full speed to break their grip. I pictured children scurrying away from a bee that had gotten inside and pretending to be scared, when the truth was that they were happy to be running inside the classroom. I thought back to stages full of Munchkins and Lost Boys and Oompa Loompas bowing at the end of school plays in multipurpose rooms packed with moms and dads holding up phones. I saw children lined up for hugs on the last day of school.

I had a feeling that I would remember things this way. It made sense that my thoughts took me back to my students. That's why I became a teacher. Ask any teacher why they went into the profession, and they will tell you that they wanted to work with children. They have a heart for kids. When I started teaching, I never imagined that my heart could hold so many. Teachers don't just teach subjects or grade levels. We teach young human beings. We aren't just experts in what we teach. We are child experts.

Teachers know that kids love pizza parties, Stuffed Animal Day, and crazy thingamabobs on the end of their pencils. We understand that children enjoy talking about their moms, their pets, and their sleepovers. We know that they like to laugh at funny stories, goofy voices, and seeing their teacher make math mistakes on the board, but they don't like homework, bread crust, or eating food that's green (unless it's lime Jell-O). We realize that kids aren't very good at cleaning paintbrushes, closing caps on glue bottles, rolling up measuring tapes, and throwing away the wrappers after putting on a Band-Aid.

Teachers know that some children don't want to be called on, while others will shoot their hands up and wave at you with both arms like the person on the tarmac who taxis in airplanes (Robert). Some kids can work at their desks, whereas others prefer to lounge on the beanbag chair as if it's one of those big inflatable pool donuts you can float on while holding a piña colada (Sawyer). Some students can stand still, but some can't stand beside you without twirling like the inside of a washing machine or bending their legs up to their bottom like a flamingo (Mia). Some children walk quietly in line, when other kids can't walk under a door frame without jumping up to touch it as if shooting a layup (Michael). Some students look at you as they are listening, and some listen while fiddling with paper clips, rubber bands, or staples that they just pulled out of the carpet (Benjamin). Some children keep their desks tidy, but others' desks look like they belong on an episode of *Hoarders* after Hurricane Harvey swept through (Jacob). Some kids are more like cats (skeptical and observant), while others are more playful and attention seeking, like doggies (Brandon). Some students are absolute angels, and some like to hold the bathroom door handle tightly with both hands so that their friends can't get out (Robert, Sawyer, Michael, Benjamin, Jacob, and Brandon).

All children are different, of course, but all classes are pretty much alike. It's funny how that works. In every class, you have the shy kid and the talkative one; the student who needs extra help and the one who is independent; the overachiever and the child who needs a nudge; the serious student and the one who is waiting to laugh; the book lover and the child who needs help finding one; the kid who loves to hold a ball and the one who loves to hold a marker. It's always the same.

And every year, you also have *that* kid. All your colleagues know *that* kid. The secretary, the principal, and the yard supervisors know *that* kid. Your significant other knows *that* kid by name too. Once, the husband of a teacher friend of mine walked into her classroom during the school day. He spotted a student sitting right next to his wife's desk, put two and two together, and said, "Hi, Seamus," to which Seamus shouted out, "How did you know my name?" The man just smiled. Usually *that* kid can't stay seated, doesn't get along in groups, gets into squabbles on the playground, has a messy desk—and never misses school. *That* kid takes up a great deal of your time and energy and thoughts. But—and I don't know how they do it—he or she somehow always manages to take up a big space in your heart too.

When working with children, you will find yourself asking questions you never imagined you would ("Why is your backpack moving?"). You will be asked questions you never expected to hear ("Teacher, how fast do ants travel—not just regular ants, really fast ones?"). You will give answers you never dreamed you'd say ("The Statue of Liberty is *not* holding an ice cream cone" and "No, I don't know how long T-Rex poop is"). And there will be times when you witness things you never believed you would see, such as children squeezed into lockers to see if they can fit, students sucking juice out of markers, and kids licking their shoes—and their desks and computer screens too. Whenever any of these things occur, teachers often respond with one of their most popular comebacks—the "We do not": "We do not cut our friend's hair." "We do not bark in the classroom." "We do not ride our yardsticks." For children, I'd imagine that the "We do not" response sounds pretty funny. A child knows that teachers do not do these things.

I've heard some teachers insist that kids have changed over the years, but I disagree. Yes, their toys, gadgets, and slang have changed. Their haircuts, clothing, and what's printed on their backpacks have changed as well. But children still need love and comfort and routine. If they're standing with you at the copier, they will still take the copies out of the machine, put them against their cheeks, and exclaim how warm the paper is. They still push the stapler hard with two hands, then turn over the paper to see if the staple went all the way through. When using a ruler to draw a straight line, kids still don't press down hard enough, so the line ends up crooked. They still have their favorite color marker and still scramble for it in the marker basket when you ask them to grab one. They still push the tape that hangs over the serrated metal edge of the dispenser straight down, until you show them that it comes off more easily if you pull it from the side. And they still love to clean the whiteboard.

Children still measure time by holidays, tell you how many days until their birthdays, and raise their hands eagerly when you say "I need a volunteer." If you catch them running in the hall and send them back to walk, they still speed walk. They still ask you to bring your dog to school and beg you to read each letter in *icup* so they can laugh. They still ask what's written on the back of your hand if you wrote yourself a reminder that you have recess duty. When playing bingo, kids still announce how many squares they need to complete the row and still shake and bounce and squeal if they only need one more square. They still like to show you that they can curl their tongues, stick their earlobes in their ears, or balance a pencil on their upper lips. They still lean back in their chairs too far, then crash onto the floor. If a student gets the hiccups during class, and you say to get a drink of water, the child still hopes that the drink doesn't make them stop because it's fun to hiccup in class. Kids still tell you your future with their origami cootie catchers by pinching and pulling the paper pockets that cover their thumbs and index fingers. And when it is time to read your fortune, they still crack up when the cootie catcher says that you are going to marry Justin Bieber.

When selecting a sticker from your sticker book, children still look at every sticker on every page, as though you both have all the time in the world to wait for them to find the perfect sticker. If you tell them a story about your childhood, they still listen more raptly than if you were teaching them how to write a topic sentence. When passing out papers, if you accidentally hand a student an extra one, the child will shout "I got two!" as if you have done something terrible. If, after sitting with your kids on the carpet, you say, "You may go back to your seat if you are wearing stripes," one wise guy will still yank up his underwear to show you that there are stripes on it. They still ask why we grade A, B, C, D, and F, then tell you that it makes no sense to leave out the E. They still say, "When's lunch?" "My mom forgot to put my homework in my backpack," "Do we have to write in complete sentences?" "Is this a real fire drill?" and "He cutted." The second you begin speaking with another adult, children still listen to every word. And when you turn to them with a pretend-mad expression and say, "Did you all catch that?" they still smile and shout, "Yes!"

Love

The week before Valentine's Day, I asked my third graders to write sentences to include in the valentine cards for their parents. Each sentence was to start with "Love is." After I shared some examples, the children spread out all over the classroom and started writing. I walked around and smiled as I read their sentences.

Megan wrote, "Love is when I'm sad, and my mom starts crying just because I'm sad." Jovanna described love as "the lipstick marks my grandma leaves on my cheek." Mason penciled, "Love is when my hamster climbs on my back." Jack wrote, "Love is when my dad lets me watch the Disney Channel even though he doesn't really like it." Griffin came up with "Love is when I give my dog a treat without him doing a trick." Gigi had written, "Love is when I practice the piano for one hour without being told." And one of Riley's sentences made me pat my heart: "Love is when my teacher writes Great Job! on my spelling test."

When I looked at Christopher's paper, I was surprised by what I saw. Every one of his sentences began with: "_ _ _ _ is."

"What's this?" I asked, pointing to the dashes.

Christopher didn't answer. He stared straight ahead.

"Why didn't you write *love*?"

Silence.

"He won't say it," Danny volunteered.

"Why not?" I said.

Christopher remained frozen.

And then a smile spread across my face. I realized why. For Christopher, writing *love* was in the same category as watching two people smooch in a movie, and he wanted nothing to do with it. I decided to have some fun.

I walked to the front of the room and wrote *love* on the board. "Christopher," I announced so that everyone could hear, "could you please read this word for me?"

Christopher shook his head.

By then, all eyes were on him. You could sense what his classmates were thinking: *Will he say it? He's not answering the teacher! What will he do?*

"Come on, Christopher," I coaxed. "You can say it."

He slammed one hand over his mouth.

I leaned into him and gave a sly grin. "What if I said you have no homework tonight? *Then* would you say it?"

Someone squealed.

"Say it!" Luke cried.

Christopher shook his head again. His hand was still covering his mouth.

I leaned in closer and made my voice more enticing. "What if I said you have no homework for a *week*?"

"*I'll* say it!" Henry shouted.

I looked at Henry. "This is just for Christopher." I turned back and improved my offer. "How about no homework for the rest of the *year*?"

A couple of kids shot out of their chairs. "Christopher, say it! *Say it!*"

I glanced at the clock. "Christopher, you have ten seconds to say it. After that, the offer is over." I started counting down. "Ten, nine, eight, seven . . ."

"*Say it!*" the kids were begging.

Christopher slapped his other hand over his mouth as the class joined me in a loud countdown. "Six, five, four, three . . ."

At the last second, he uncovered his mouth and blurted out, "The *L*-word!"

Love. In the field of pedagogy, rarely do you hear the word. In my own teacher training, it was never discussed. I've never heard it addressed at a workshop or a conference, or read about it in a professional journal. For some reason, academics are just like Christopher. They're afraid to say the *L*-word too. And yet teachers know that love is a vital part of education. Good teaching is infused with it. The most successful classrooms are brimming with it. Love is the reason people go into teaching—love for a subject and love for children. It's what keeps them in the profession too.

One of my favorite lines from the classic children's book *The Velveteen Rabbit* is about a child's love. It goes like this: "When a child loves you for a long, long time, not just to play with, but really loves you, then you become real." Children have an enormous capacity to love. A child's love is blind to race, gender, and disability. And sometimes the love from children shows us what this world is supposed to be.

Once, on the first day of school, I walked into my friend Jill's kindergarten classroom after the final bell rang to see how her day had been. She was talking with Colin's mom. Jill had taught Colin the year before in pre-K and kept him again for kindergarten. Everyone in the school knew Colin, a sweet child with severe language delays. As I stepped into the classroom, Jill was wiping her eyes with a tissue.

"You okay?" I asked.

"Oh yes," she answered. "Yes. These are happy tears." And then she proceeded to tell me what had happened. That morning before school started, Jill was standing on the blacktop with Colin and his mother. Colin's head was down. He was crying. Both Jill and his mom had tried to comfort him, but it didn't stop the tears. As the three waited for the bell to ring, a boy named Daniel—he had been Colin's classmate the previous year—walked up to Colin and saw that he was sad. Without saying a word, Daniel took Colin's hand and held it.

"It was precious," Jill said, clearly moved. "Daniel held on to Colin's hand till the bell rang and all the way into class. Then he helped Colin find his cubby and his chair."

Colin's mom turned to me. Her eyes were wet. "Every day I fear that someone is going to laugh at him because he doesn't speak correctly or blurts out or doesn't sit still. I'm always afraid that kids will be mean to him. He doesn't have friends." There were tears in her voice. "I never expected kindness."

I gave her a tender smile. "Daniel sounds like a little angel."

Jill nodded. "But that's not all," she said. "During naptime, Daniel asked me if he could lie down beside Colin. I said yes, of course. After all the children were settled on the floor and the lights were out, I saw . . ." Jill covered her mouth. If she'd continued speaking, she would have started to cry. Then, after a shake of the head, she got out the rest of her sentence. ". . . I saw Daniel cover Colin with his blanket."

"Whoa," I said, touched by the story. "*That's* the world I want to live in."

Colin's mom smiled at me. "Actually, you do."

Oftentimes, a child's love is directed at the teacher. Kids give us signs all the time. That's why they shout our names from monkey bars and slides and jungle gyms. That's the reason they follow us around when we have playground duty and stop by to visit after school. They want to be around us. Children also show their love by bringing gifts. That's what motivates them to give us daisy-chain necklaces they put together at recess and handmade napkin rings made out of toilet paper rolls for Christmas. That's the reason they leave half-eaten Pop-Tarts and Oreos from their lunches on our desks, even though they love Oreos. That's what causes children you taught years before to visit you on their birthdays with a cupcake. That's why, if you happen to mention that the coffee machine in the staff room is broken, a little while later, a child will hand you a drawing that she just made for you in secret of a mug full of steaming coffee—and a donut covered with icing and tropical marker sprinkles.

One time the mom of a student I'd had several years earlier dropped by my classroom and said she had a bone to pick with me. Her son, who was now in middle school, had made a pair of wooden candlesticks and given them to me. It was the first thing he'd made out of wood. The mom said, "I told him that I'd like to have them, but he wouldn't hear of it. He insisted they be yours."

Some students express their love by trying to get your goat. Kids tease the teachers they love. When it's your birthday, they will guess you're the age of your grandmother. When teaching them about the Civil War, they will ask with a grin if you remember the sound of the cannons. One day, as I was giving my students a math quiz, one of my pistols grabbed the answer sheet, wrote his name over the word *key*, then handed it back to me with a flourish. "Here," he said, "I'm finished." And once, when I was trying to impress upon my kids—for the millionth time—to begin their sentences with capital letters and end them with periods, I joked to one of my fourth graders, "Listen, if you don't put in capitals and periods, I'm going to have a heart attack." With a huge smile on his face, he quickly started changing all his capital letters to lowercase ones and erasing every period.

Sometimes children just tell you how they feel outright. A friend of mine who teaches grade one had a student tell her that she needed to stop getting older and wait for him to grow up because *he* was her Prince Charming. He also told her that he loved her hair more than spaghetti. In my last year of teaching, I had an eight-year-old student named Zoe, who had no problem telling her teachers that she loved them. It was pretty darling. Zoe would leave notes on my computer keyboard or inside my coffee mug with messages such as "I love you Mr. Done but clean your desk!" Once, before leaving for the day, she and her friend wrote, "We love you Mr. Done!" on the whiteboard. But instead of using a dry erase marker, they accidentally used a permanent one. When I pointed this out, Zoe replied—without missing a beat—"Then our love for you will stay forever."

As a kid, I was like Zoe. I used to fall in love with my teachers too. When I was in first grade, I confided in my buddy, Art Newell, that I loved my teacher, Mrs. Ranada. Big mistake. Later that day, as I was sitting in the cafeteria with my friends, Mrs. Ranada was on lunch duty. When she walked past our table, Art yelled out, "Mrs. Ranada, Phillip loves you!" I turned beet red, and everyone at the table started laughing. Then Mrs. Ranada said the worst thing possible. She smiled at me and said, "I know."

If you're a single teacher, children are very concerned about your love life. Kids do not want their teachers to be alone, which is sweet. If students find out that you are single, they will try to hook you up with other teachers on the staff—single or not. Sometimes they will even suggest their parents. If you are not married, and you teach the little ones, they will come right out and express their concerns: "Who's gonna lift your heavy things?" "Who's going to kiss you good night?" "Who's gonna rub your feet?" A single friend of mine had a first grader tell her, "If you're not married by the time I'm an adult, *I'll* marry you. Okay?" If you tie the knot during the school year, it could confuse your students. I knew one teacher who got married in January and changed her last name from Harris to Carpenter. Not long afterward, one of her kindergartners looked at her and said, "Ms. Carpenter, you sure look an *awful* lot like Ms. Harris."

Of course, teachers love their students too. How do we show it? We greet our kids at the door when the morning bell rings and give them smiles and big thumbs-ups at the end of the day. We give up our breaks to work with children who need extra help. When walking across the blacktop, we stop to watch students perform back bends and crazy fast hand-clapping routines because they asked us to. We retrieve balls that get stuck in basketball hoops and listen to kids play "Three Blind Mice" on recorders that the music teacher just handed out too. We attend dance recitals and ball games and funerals for class pets. We check foreheads for fevers, laugh at jokes we've heard a hundred times, and let children keep the stuffed Birthday Bear at their desks to celebrate their big day. For kids with summer birthdays, we use their half birthdays. We make late-night runs to the store to buy snacks and treats and chocolate coins wrapped in gold foil that we will set out all over our classrooms on Saint Patrick's Day to show that the leprechauns were there, and then we read the notes that the leprechauns left behind with magnifying glasses because their writing is so small. We never allow put-downs or bring up past mistakes. We ask children their opinions. We keep our promises. We take kids on the field trips and put on the plays and jump into games on the blacktop and wear our PJs on Pajama Day because we understand that these things bring children joy and that one day, when our students are older, *these* are the moments they will remember when they think back on their days in school.

The Cute Factor

It has always fascinated me how teachers have different favorite grade levels. Some want to teach young children, while others prefer the older kids. Naturally, teachers who are just starting out don't know yet what their favorite grades to teach will be. A colleague of mine has a theory that would help them out. He claims that it comes down to bathrooms. If you want a bathroom in your classroom, teach kindergarten. If you enjoy giving the "Peeing Talk" to young boys ("Stand close and aim straight"), teach grade one. If you prefer shooing girls out of the bathroom at recess, choose grades two through five. If you don't mind crawling under stalls to unlock the doors, work in middle school.

I always knew I wanted to teach younger children and not the older ones. I wanted thirty-two students, not one hundred thirty-two. I didn't want to have to refer to the Urban Dictionary to figure out what my kids were saying. I didn't want to go to the prom thirty years in a row. I did not want to walk through the parking lot and see that the students had nicer cars than mine. I didn't want to work in a classroom that reeked of Axe body spray. And I didn't want to spend my days saying: "Yes, it's for a grade"; "If you can access Tik-Tok, you can access Google Classroom"; "Nobody looks down at his lap and smiles. Put the phone away"; "You need to clean the drawing off your desk. It only shows that you need to take classes in both art and anatomy"; and (after hearing a Snapchat tone) "So, whose phone am I selling on eBay today?"

One of the reasons I chose to teach elementary school and not middle or high was the "cute factor." In an elementary teacher's life, not a day goes by without children saying or doing something charming. Kids sneak dandelion bouquets onto the teacher's desk, talk about the presents they got from Santa, ask if they can include their dogs in their family trees, or applaud every time you take a sip of coffee. I remember the day that three of my third-grade girls walked into the classroom after lunch wearing hats, purses, and jewelry made from paper plates and napkins. The girls explained that their new hats were Versace; their purses, Dolce & Gabbana; and their jewelry, Donna Karan New York. After I told them how lovely they looked, they asked if I would be interested in some pieces too. Soon they'd be starting a men's line.

I recall another day when I crouched beside one of my third graders and noticed that she hadn't capitalized the first letter of a sentence. I tapped on it and said, "Do I see a lowercase letter here?" Immediately she reached over, took off my glasses, and said, "No." I remember a descriptive writing lesson where I passed out a bunch of those paint sample cards you can pick up for free at Home Depot. Usually the colors on these cards are given catchy names like Ocean Mist or Desert Sunset. I asked my kids to think of their own names for the colors, and they were pretty charming: Green became Grass Stains; brown turned into Root Beer Float; and pink, Mom's Lipstick. And I remember one year, a few days before Valentine's Day, I explained to my third graders that if they wanted to bring in valentines, they needed to have one for everybody. Well, one of my students had just recently moved to the States from France and didn't understand the concept of passing out valentines. He made one for himself.

Of course, those who teach the youngest children get extra doses of cuteness. My friends who teach the little ones are always sharing adorable things their students say. Jill, who teaches kindergarten, had a student who told her in all seriousness that her aunt, who was also her "fairy godmother," would be taking her to *Disney on Ice*. Another one of Jill's kids called the student teacher "the step teacher." When Beth, another kindergarten teacher, was putting a Band-Aid from the first aid box on one of her youngsters, the child asked if there was such a thing as a "second aid box." Lucy, who teaches grade one, said one of her first graders told her that his mom had bought his dad online. It turned out that they met on Match.com. Audrey, also a first-grade teacher, was in the middle of a math lesson when one of her kids asked her to please stop teaching because he didn't have any more room in his brain. Dana, who teaches second grade, was reviewing the days of the week with her students when one of them launched into "Sunday, Monday, happy days!" Another time, Dana was helping one of her boys look up something online when the question "Will you accept cookies?" appeared on the screen. The child, who was standing beside her, grinned broadly and said, "Always."

When children know that babies are coming, the cute factor is especially high. When my friend Jessica was expecting her first child, she told her first graders that the baby was in her stomach and that's why she was getting bigger. A few days later, one of Jessica's boys asked if the baby was still in her stomach, and Jessica answered yes. The child, looking very concerned, yelped, "But what if the stomach acid gets her?" Another youngster in Jessica's class must not have been paying attention for about six months, because, just weeks before the baby was due, she came up to Jessica and said, "No offense, Mrs. Lewis, but you sort of look like you're going to have a baby." Jessica affirmed that she was, and the child spouted, "You *are*? Since *when*?" And one afternoon when her little ones were asking a lot of questions about the upcoming birth, Jessica told them that it takes nine months for a baby to be born and (in age-appropriate language) what would happen when it was time to deliver the child. As she explained, a boy shouted out, "I didn't want to hear about any of this until I'm in college!"

When students say cute and funny things, delight in these moments. Have a laugh and enjoy their "kid-ness." It sounds simple, but I've met many a teacher who doesn't do this. Delighting in your students will help you to stay focused on them and keep you positive. Also, when your kids say something sweet, write it down in a journal. It's impossible to remember all the charming things children say. On the tough days, this journal can be a lifesaver, and it will help you get back on track. A friend of mine calls her teacher journal her "Why Binder" because it reminds her why she's teaching. The husband of another teacher I know calls her journal the "Bad Day Book." If he sees it out, he knows his wife had a rough one.

I began keeping a journal when I started teaching. A veteran teacher had recommended it. Over the years, the journal was always good for a chuckle and a pick-me-up. Now that I'm retired, I'm glad I kept it. It's a nice reminder. I didn't write a lot, just a sentence or two so that I wouldn't forget. Here are some entries:

"Today I had a good laugh. My kids and I were walking on the blacktop when Jordan stepped out of line and started walking alongside of us about ten feet away. I asked him what he was doing, and he said that he had to fart."

"Today, as Elijah walked up to my desk, I heard a clicking sound but couldn't figure out what it was. When I asked where the noise was coming from, Elijah yanked up his shirt to reveal a step counter on his belt."

"Today we were playing Multiplication Bingo. When Itai lost, he announced, 'I got a bad hand.'"

"Today Molly, who loves country music, pointed to an atlas that was sitting on my desk and cried, 'I didn't know Tim McGraw and Faith Hill wrote a book together!' I looked at the atlas and laughed. On the cover was the name of the publisher: McGraw-Hill."

"Today Isabel walked in late. I asked her why she was tardy, and she said her mom didn't know it was Monday already."

"Today I taught the class a new song and wrote the lyrics on the board. After singing it through, I erased a couple of the words to see if they would remember them. We sang it again, and I erased a few more. After singing it a third time, one of my kids called out, 'Take it all off!' I lost it."

In my early days of teaching, I used to tell my students about my teacher journal. If they said something cute or funny, I'd stop whatever I was doing and say, "Wait! That's darling." And the kids would wait as I scribbled it down. But one year I stopped being so open about writing in it. That was the year I had Ricky. For some reason, this kid always wanted to be in my journal and would say silly things in hopes that I'd write them down. One day when Ricky got into a scuffle on the playground, which he often did, I took him into the hallway to talk with him. Normally, Ricky wasn't very apologetic, but this time he said he was sorry and that he wouldn't do it again.

"Ricky," I said, "I have to tell you I'm very impressed with how you're handling this." He looked up at me with an eager smile and asked, "Are you going to write this down?" My eyes widened. *So that's why he's being so agreeable! This little rascal is trying to get into my journal again!* I shook my head and told him no. But later, I did write it down. It *was* pretty cute.

The Fourth *R*

We all know the three *R*s: reading, writing, and arithmetic. But I contend there is a fourth—one that is vitally important. You need it to teach the other three. In fact, you need it to teach everything effectively. It touches on all teaching and learning. The fourth *R* is *rapport*.

Rapport is an especially harmonious connection. It is trust, affinity, and respect all put together. In school, rapport is the invisible classroom glue that binds teacher and student. It cannot be forced or rushed. It develops. Rapport takes commitment on the part of the teacher and emerges as the result of many little things that teachers do.

Rapport impacts every aspect of your teaching: your classroom management, your room environment, your work with kids. It has a profound effect on a teacher's ability to reach, motivate, and inspire children. All boys and girls are eager for connection. They seek it. The rapport between teachers and students compels children to want to do well, to behave, and to please you. When a rapport has been established, kids are more apt to buy in to what you are trying to achieve. In classrooms where there is trusting rapport, everything just goes smoother. Rapport also increases students' comfort and satisfaction. It's what brings satisfaction to teachers too. For most teachers, it is our rapport with children where we find our greatest pleasure in teaching.

Think back to your own days at school. We have all experienced classrooms where rapport existed and those where it did not. We've all encountered teachers or professors who didn't establish any kind of relationship with us, perhaps didn't even bother to learn our names. And we've all enjoyed committed and caring teachers who gave us that wonderfully special feeling of being believed in by someone whom we believed in too. When recalling our favorite teachers, *these* are the ones who immediately come to mind. These are the men and women whose names we remember. Oftentimes, it is one of these teachers who inspired us to become teachers ourselves.

So how do teachers build and nurture rapport with their students? Certainly your kindness, gentleness, and consistency go a long way. But there are other things you can do to strengthen those relationships. What follows are a few rapport-building approaches that always work:

Get to Know Your Students

Teachers spend a lot of time learning about curriculums and programs, strategies and technology. It's important to "learn" your kids too. Take a genuine interest in them. It tells children that you're interested in them as people. Ask your students about their families and hobbies, their dreams and aspirations. Don't just collect the information on interest inventories and questionnaires, then file them away. And ask them about their world outside of school: "How was your baseball game?" "How did your ballet recital go?" "How was your piano lesson?" "I read in your paper that you love *Fortnite*. Why's that?" Well, maybe skip that last question. If you ask it, half your class will start talking all at once, and it will be hard to get them back to work.

Ask About Their Pets

All children have their "light-ups": those topics that cause their faces to break into smiles. One light-up that all kids share is when you ask them about their pets. Children adore their dogs and cats, guinea pigs and hamsters, and if you express an interest in them, they will love you for it. Pets connect. And kids love to talk about them. It's not just the little ones. A teacher I know has periodic Pet Days at school where her students share pictures of their beloved four-, two-, and non-legged friends on their phones—a pause for pets. The kids get mushy over seeing their classmates' photos. And these are *eighth graders*. Many teachers will tell you that when schools were shut down during the pandemic, one of the best parts of remote learning was seeing the animals. Cats sat on the back of chairs. Dogs snored in the background. Lizards and gerbils and parakeets joined Zoom classes. In the crazy world of distance learning, the pets were calming. When teaching virtually, one wise friend of mine included her students' animals while taking attendance: "Jason? Snowball? Amanda? Fluffy?"

Understand Children's Individual Needs

Some kids crave attention and others don't. Some are social; others, more reserved. Some students love you from day one, whereas others take more time to warm up. Some children respond to overt praise. For others, private praise is more effective. Observe your students and pay close attention. Figure out what they need. The more you understand how your kids tick, the better you can serve them.

Say These Three Words

When teaching children to write compound sentences, we tell them about the three "connecting words": *and*, *but*, and *or*. However, these aren't the only connecting words teachers use in school. There are three others that are much more important. These words don't connect sentences, they connect people. And when you put them together to form a question, they carry enormous power. The words are *how*, *are*, and *you*. We all desire to be seen and heard. Kids are no different. Every day, in hundreds of small ways, our students ask us: Do you see me? Do you hear me? Do I matter? By looking children in the eye and saying "How are you?" you answer them. I'm not talking here about the quick "How are ya?" that so many people toss out without waiting for an answer. I'm speaking of the sincere "How are you?" that requires slowing down and being fully and completely present.

Interact with Kids Outside of the Classroom

One sure way to establish rapport with children is to spend a little time with them outside your classroom. Chat with them on the blacktop briefly before the first bell rings. Greet them by name in the hallways. Jump in a game of kickball or hijack a game of hopscotch. You don't have to spend a lot of time doing this, just a minute or two every now and then. We all know the phrase "thinking outside the box." Interacting with kids outside of the classroom is teaching outside the box.

Eat Lunch with Your Students

For children, eating with the teacher is always a special treat. Once in a while, join your kids in the cafeteria for lunch. Don't tell them ahead of time. Just show up unannounced with your lunch in hand and squeeze in next to them. If you teach little ones, some will be so happy you are there that you'll have to remind them to eat.

From time to time, also invite your students to eat lunch with you in the classroom. I always found it cute when kids would walk into their classroom with their cafeteria trays and act all excited to see you, though they just saw you a few minutes earlier when you excused them for lunch. Periodically, I would invite small groups of kids into my room at lunchtime, usually four or five at a time. During these get-togethers, we'd just eat and chat. The rule: No talking about school. One year I had a group of third-grade girls who would have had lunch with me weekly if they could. After our first lunch together, they'd ask me every week when we were going to have the next one, and I'd repeat that they had to wait until everybody else had their turn. When the day finally arrived for them to eat lunch in the classroom again, they brought in decorations for the table, including homemade placemats and goody bags. *Cute.*

Write Home When Children Are Absent

If students are out sick, email them saying that you hope they're feeling better and that the class misses them. The children will feel valued. Their parents will see that you care too.

Cook with Your Kids

When we think of a teacher's tool kit, we don't often think of rolling pins, mixing bowls, and measuring cups, but cooking with children offers a smorgasbord of benefits. Cooking with kids brings everyone together and always creates a joyful atmosphere. And it's a cinch, really. To make applesauce, just set up a hot plate in the back of the room, ask your students to bring in some apples, and hand them peelers. Young children will use the peeler upside down and wonder why the peels aren't coming off the apples. To cook spaghetti, just boil some pasta and pour in a few jars of sauce. On Spaghetti Day, some students will act as if they have never been fed. Your picky eaters will just want plain noodles. To make your own butter, pour heavy cream into baby food jars and let kids shake them till the cream turns into balls of butter. Children always start off shaking their jars with great enthusiasm. After a few minutes, though, they will complain that their arms are sore.

When cooking with kids, here are my top six tips: (1) Keep it simple and safe; (2) Expect a mess; (3) Invite a parent or two to come in and help; (4) Before you begin, check that your students' sleeves are pushed up; otherwise you'll spend a lot of your time pushing them up; (5) As you're cooking together, verbalize what you're doing, pose questions, and talk about the foods and where they're from. Many kids don't know; and (6) If you cook anything that involves a hot plate, make sure that you ask the secretary to turn off the smoke alarm in your classroom so that you don't end up setting it off. I did that once. On a rainy day.

Let Your Students Overhear You

After you've excused your kids for the day, if you see the mom of one of your students and want to tell her something positive about her child's day at school, call the child over first. *Then* tell the mom. If the principal steps into your classroom when your students are there, say—in a loud voice so that all the children hear—that you're sure someone switched out your students when you weren't looking because they're behaving so well. When you email parents with good news about their kids, write the messages in front of your students and read them aloud as you type. Let the children click Send. The next day, when you ask them what their parents said about the messages, they will grin as they answer.

Give Students a Special Task

Kids like to be asked to run errands all by themselves. It makes them feel grown up and special. If you need something from the office, send a child. But don't ask the student privately. Say it in front of the whole class. The child will beam because all his classmates know that you trust him. You'll find that this strategy works particularly well for the challenging student who has never been tasked with a special job before. The child will take the assignment very seriously. Once, I had a student named Ralph who needed some TLC, so I asked him to go to the classroom next door and borrow a box of paper clips. (I'd arranged this with the teacher ahead of time.) Well, Ralph was gone a long time. Finally, after almost a half hour, the door swung open and in came Ralph carrying an armload full. "What took you so long?" I asked. "And why do you have so many boxes?" Ralph explained that he hadn't just gone next door. He took it upon himself to walk around the entire school, knocking on all the doors, interrupting lessons, and announcing that Mr. Done needed paper clips.

Apologize When You've Done Something Wrong

When building rapport with students, it is also important to be mindful of the things *not* to do. Never scold, argue with, or yell at a child. Never pull a student aside for a lecture, use sarcasm, or respond emotionally if a child misbehaves. And never send children to the principal for anything but dangerous behavior. Any one of these creates friction, weakens trust, and damages rapport. If *you* have done something wrong—perhaps you raised your voice or lost your cool (we've all been there)—find a moment to tell the student that you're sorry. Children are quick to forgive. They are willing to look past your mistakes, especially if you already have a rapport with them.

Visit Some Children Off Campus

At times, you will have students who require some extra care. If they are involved in an after-school activity like Little League, gymnastics, soccer, and so on, consider showing up at one of their practices or games. I'm suggesting that you visit only those kids who really need it. You know who they are. Don't tell the children ahead of time. Surprise them. They'll be all smiles when you're there. Some kids will bring it up to you the following day. Some will not. But none will ever forget that their teacher made the effort to come see them. Once, I attended a soccer game that a few of my students were playing in. I had to keep running from one side of the field to the other to cheer because I had kids on both teams. The parents got a kick out of it.

Make a Choice to See the Best in Them

Sometimes teachers have negative thoughts about a particular student. It happens. Maybe a kid gets under your skin or tries your patience. If a teacher has these thoughts, the child will always pick up on it. Children are keenly aware of how adults feel about them. The problem is that if kids sense that you are irritated or frustrated with them, you will never develop a good rapport. So choose to think positively about all of your students, including the ones who are disrespectful or misbehave. Let go of any resentment and set aside your negative thoughts. Decide that no matter how much they irk you, you are going to see the best in them. It's not always easy to do, but it's the only way to establish genuine rapport with children.

In my last year of teaching, I had a third grader named Jonathan who presented a big challenge. A nine-year-old with spiky, gelled hair and temporary tattoos on his arms (usually superheroes), Jonathan had the energy of three kids. On some days, it felt like ten. Jonathan wouldn't follow directions and was often doing what he shouldn't be doing. He touched everyone and everything and would get into trouble everywhere. Pretty much every week, I was contacting his parents about something. I don't like to admit this, but after a while, Jonathan started to get on my nerves. I tried not to show how I felt, but I was sure he sensed it.

And then one day I had a big aha moment. I realized that I'd been holding negative thoughts about a student and that this was keeping me from establishing the rapport we both needed. I had allowed negativity to creep in. I hadn't been careful. That day, I gave myself a serious talking to, and it started like this: "Phil, you know better."

In teaching, there's an old adage that if a student is having difficulty, before looking at how the child can improve, look at yourself. Well, that day I shone a bright spotlight on *my* attitude toward Jonathan and knew that I needed to change it. I had a choice to make. I could think negatively or positively about this child. And so, from that day on, I made a concerted effort to throw away my irritation toward Jonathan and focus on the positive. What we see in children depends on what we look for—and I was determined to see the best in this kid. When I changed my attitude, a funny thing started to happen. Jonathan suddenly became less taxing. In fact, I began to enjoy him. I noticed little improvements in his behavior too. It wasn't perfect—not by a long shot. He still required a lot of my energy, but things were better. We both were happier. I'd gotten myself back on track.

During that year with Jonathan, I practiced several of the rapport-building strategies that I've just shared with you. I typed positive email messages home as Jonathan read them over my shoulder. If he was out sick, I emailed saying we missed him. When I was outside on recess duty, I'd kick the soccer ball with him once in a while. A couple of times, I invited Jonathan and his buddies into the classroom for lunch. During those lunches, Jonathan showed me his favorite singers on YouTube. He demonstrated how he could dance like them too. I hadn't known he could dance. In addition, I often asked Jonathan how he was doing and inquired about his parents, his siblings, and his grandparents, whom he adored. I asked about Max, his beloved dog, and hung Max's photo on my file cabinet so that he could be with Jonathan at school. More than once, I sent Jonathan out to get paper clips.

On the last day of the school year, after I had excused the kids and was alone in my classroom, the door flung open, and in came Jonathan. Without a word, he hurried over to me and gave me a hug. He'd never hugged me before. Then, in a flash, he was gone. In teaching, it is said that the children who challenge you the most need you the most. It is also said that your most difficult students become your favorites. It's true—*if* you have a rapport with them. Jonathan is my proof.

Melt

At home, I have a drawer full of teacher ties. A lot of man teachers do. Most of them were chosen lovingly by children and delivered the week before winter break. One tie is shaped like a crayon, another like a pencil, and a third like the face of a reindeer. When you press the reindeer's nose, it lights up, and the tie starts singing "Rudolph the Red-Nosed Reindeer." I have ties covered with math problems, globes, punctuation marks, rulers, science equipment, paper airplanes, and cursive letters too.

One morning, one of my third graders named Melina asked, "Mr. Done, why do you always wear a tie?" I decided to seize the teachable moment. "Well," I said, "children respect their teachers, right?" Melina nodded. "It's also true that teachers respect their students." I smiled at her. "And one of the ways I show respect for my students is to dress nicely for them. You see, by wearing a tie, I'm sending you a message. I'm letting you know that you're important to me." I paused a beat. "Does that make sense?"

She nodded.

The next day, Melina walked into the classroom all gussied up. Now, Melina was known to dress up occasionally, but on this day, she was especially decked out. Her ensemble included a shiny leotard, turquoise cowboy boots, a leopard-print scrunchy, and a tiara from her *Frozen* costume.

As she took her seat, I commented, "My, don't *you* look nice today. What's the occasion?"

Melina sat up bright and straight. "I wanted to send *you* a message," she said. "You're important too."

Melt.

* * *

Sometimes the cute and charming things that kids say hit you at your core. I call them melt moments. They are the extra special moments that, like fingers on a harp, pluck the strings of our teacher hearts. Every teacher experiences them. They're part of our rewards. People in other professions get stocks and bonuses and company cars. We get moments like Melina's. Some melt moments pull our heart strings gently—like when a child slips her hand into yours as you're walking in line. Other melt moments tug harder, such as when your class cheers after you return from being out sick, or a former student finds you on Facebook to let you know that he wants to be a teacher "just like you." Melt moments can make you smile or laugh or cry—or all three. A melt moment can remind you of why you chose this profession. It can restore your faith in humanity. Sometimes it can put you in that lovely place where, for a second, all is right with the world.

I've been fortunate. In my long career, I melted a lot. I remember one melt moment when I was planting seeds with my third graders. I had just explained to the children that the seed coat protects the seed and that a plant must break through the coat when reaching for the sun. As most of the kids were filling their Dixie cups with soil, I saw Logan carefully removing the coat from a seed. When I asked him what he was doing, Logan said he was helping it out so it wouldn't have to work so hard.

Another melt moment occurred one afternoon when a mom dropped by to see me. The school year was almost over. Her daughter, Elena, was in my class. The whole family had emigrated from Argentina a few years earlier. When they arrived in the States, Elena's mom spoke very little English, and Elena, none at all. In our meeting, Elena's mom told me something I hadn't known. Every day when Elena came home from school, she would teach her mom the lessons she learned in class. Elena had taught her mother English!

A third melt moment arose one day in June after giving my third graders their final spelling test of the year. I'd told the children that the words on the test were ones they should know for fourth grade. At recess, I began correcting the papers. When I started looking over Elizabeth's, I was surprised. She'd misspelled almost every word, which didn't make sense. Normally she was a good speller. When the kids came back to class, I called Elizabeth over and asked what happened. She put her head down and whispered, "I thought if I got them wrong, maybe I could stay in third grade."

Among my many melt moments, there is one I could never forget. I wrote it down in my teacher journal, but I didn't need to. I have something else to remind me of what happened that day. I pull it out every Christmas.

For many years around the holidays, I used to teach my students how to draw nutcrackers, like the one in Tchaikovsky's famous ballet. I'd walk the kids step-by-step through the art lesson till their blank pieces of white construction paper were filled with tall black boots, tasseled uniforms, and rosy-cheeked faces topped with fancy, wide-brimmed hats. After completing the drawings, the children would color them any way they wanted with chalk pastels. When they finished, I'd hang our army of multicolored nutcrackers around the room until the day before winter break; then we'd wrap them in white butcher paper covered with red and green handprints, tie them with school yarn, and send them on home as gifts for their moms and dads.

One year, while my fourth graders were working on their nutcrackers, and the music from the ballet played softly in the background, I explained to the kids that someday these paper soldiers would become very special to their parents.

"Do any of your moms cry when they look at your old baby shoes or your baby blanket?" I asked the class as they colored.

"Oh, yeah!"s and big nods filled the room.

"And do any of them save your artwork?"

More "Oh, yeah"-ing and nodding.

"Well," I continued, "someday when you're older and out of the house, your parents will look at these nutcrackers and cry happy tears over them. Parents—moms, especially—do this when their children grow up. Do any of your moms ever cry happy tears?"

"Yes!" the kids chorused.

"My mom cries all the time!" Julian declared.

"Mine too," Cameron echoed. "At Hallmark movies."

I didn't expect the children to fully understand what I was talking about. They were young. But one child did.

It was the last day before winter break. I was standing at the front of the classroom, opening the pile of gifts that had been growing on my desk all week long. Hanging on my chest was my Rudolph tie. As the children looked on, I picked up a large, lidded box and read the tag. It was from Olivia, a small, soft-spoken nine-year-old who was mature beyond her years—an old soul. She sat near the back of the room, by the door.

I held the box up to my ear, gave it a shake, and smiled at her the way all teachers do when they open presents from their students. Then, with wide, excited eyes, I removed the paper carefully so as not to tear it. (It's an unwritten rule that teachers never tear wrapping paper. Grandmas have the same rule.) When I finished unwrapping the box, I set it on the table and lifted the lid. Immediately my lips pressed together the way lips automatically do when one's heartstrings are tugged. Smiling up at me was an upturned mustache circling two rosy cheeks. Olivia's nutcracker. On his shoulders sat two gold epaulets; around his waist, a matching sash. Beside his boots: "To Mr. Done, from Olivia." His uniform was turquoise, my favorite color. Olivia had learned this when she'd cupped her hand over my ear earlier in the week and whispered, "What's your favorite color?"

I looked over at Olivia—she was waiting for me to   and gave her another smile. She returned it. No words were spoken, but I understood why she had given me this gift that was supposed to be for her parents. Olivia knew that I had no children of my own. I'd told the class I didn't. And because I had no sons or daughters, this little old soul understood that I would have no baby shoes or baby blankets or children's artwork to hold and tear up over one day when I am old. Olivia wanted me to have something to cry happy tears over too.

Recess and Lunchtime and Field Trips, Oh My!

"Mr. Done, my arm hurts," Stephen, my fourth grader, whimpered from his seat. I looked over at him. His arm was covered with old reel-to-reel recording tape.

"What did you *do*?" I asked, stepping toward him.

"I wrapped my arm up."

"I can see that." I bent down to take a closer look. He'd wrapped it pretty tightly. "Where did you get this tape?"

"I found it on my way to school. In a garbage can."

I looked heavenward, let out a sigh, and shook my head. All at the same time. It wasn't the first time something like this had happened with Stephen. A few weeks earlier, I'd moved him away from the supply table after he decided to clip an entire jar of clothespins into his hair and onto each earlobe. Once, at lunchtime, I found him trying to suck milk from the fingers of a plastic glove as though it were a cow's udder. Quickly I started cutting off the tape before his arm turned blue. As I cut, I thought, *When I dreamed of becoming a teacher, I never imagined I'd be doing this.*

Like all teachers in training, when I was a teacher candidate in my university's education department (Teacher School, I like to call it), I took courses in childhood development, educational philosophy, classroom management, and classes in how to teach all of the subjects. I remember that my Instructional Technology class consisted of decorating bulletin boards and making overhead projector transparencies. After I landed my first teaching position, I realized that there were several topics my instructors hadn't covered. I have a theory about this: If they had told the truth about the profession, there'd be an even bigger teacher shortage.

If I were an instructor at Teacher School, I would offer a class called The Truth About Teaching, in which I'd divulge all the things teachers should be warned about. Topics would include: recess duty, lunch supervision, field trips, and Spirit Days. Following is my partial syllabus:

Recess Duty

When I looked up the definition of *recess duty* in Webster's dictionary, I discovered that there wasn't one. Webster's, I surmised, is in cahoots with the Teacher Schools. It doesn't want you to know the truth either. So, here's my definition: *recess duty*—the act of walking around a blacktop and field covered with children who are running around and playing games, as you try not to get hit in the head by flying balls. Unless you've handled this duty, you can't understand what goes on. A bell rings. Hundreds of kids dash outside at the same time. A couple of teachers walk around while desperately needing to use the bathroom.

When on recess duty, also known as yard duty in some parts of the country, you wear several hats. When you stand by the soccer cage, you're the referee. ("No, I didn't see that. Take over.") When it starts to drizzle, you are a meteorologist. ("It's only a little water. You're fine. Go play.") When you walk past the play structure, you're the traffic cop. ("No running up the slide!") If you watch kids hanging upside down on the bars or performing cartwheels, your role is the spectator. ("I'm looking! I'm looking!") And when you are dragged by the hand to look at a poor worm, snail, or ladybug that has just been discovered by a group of young children, you're the bodyguard. ("Okay, everyone, stand back. Leave him alone.")

When on duty, you also become a child magnet. Kids will run up to you with crowns made out of dandelions and wait for you to put them on. They will jump on your shadow and, after you send them away, run back to jump on it some more. While you are walking around the blacktop, one child will follow you the whole time, talking his head off and asking you personal questions such as whether or not you've ever gotten any speeding tickets and how much your wedding ring cost, until you shoo him away to play. You will also be the base in kids' games of tag. When you try to pry off a first-grade girl's arms wrapped tightly around your leg because she refuses to let go of the base, you will feel like you're using an ice scraper.

As you walk around the playground, you will recognize some of the children's games, like soccer and basketball. Some you will not. Take the game of Bowling Alley, for example. At my last school, the fourth-grade boys were crazy about it. To play Bowling Alley, children stand close together on the grass in a triangle formation. Another child rolls a ball toward the triangle. When the ball reaches the human pins, they go flying. Then the "pins" quickly reassemble so they can fly again. Some games that you think you understand, you won't—like four square. When kids play this game, they have their own words for everything. Don't even try to figure them out. It's part of children's secret language. Speaking of kid talk, once, when I was out on yard duty, I spotted a little girl crying in the tanbark. I walked up to her and asked what was wrong. She whimpered, "They won't let me play on the up down." *Up down?* I had no clue what she was talking about, so I asked her to point to it. "Oh," I said, smiling, "that's a slide."

After you've done yard duty for a while, the crazy games that children play will start to seem perfectly normal to you. The last time I was on duty, I witnessed a group of kids running backward on the blacktop while chanting that they were in reverse; a bunch of boys with red rubber balls under their shirts slamming into one another like sumo wrestlers; and a group of girls doing a rain dance with banana peels on their heads. Didn't faze me a bit.

Lunch Supervision

Lunch supervision, also known as cafeteria duty, is the bane of most teachers. For teachers, *duty* can be a four-letter word. If you have to be out from school, you pray that it falls on a day when you have lunch duty. I've known teachers who begged colleagues to swap. ("I'll do your bus duty for a week if you take my lunch.") If I ever get an Alexa, Amazon's virtual assistant, I will say, "Alexa, do my duty."

The first thing you will notice when entering the cafeteria for lunch supervision is the noise. How can I describe it? Think of jet engines, rock concerts, space shuttle launches, then put them together at the same time. *That* is a school cafeteria at lunchtime. You know how glass can break when it comes in contact with high decibels? Well, I wouldn't be surprised if the windows in school cafeterias have to be shatter resistant. If you share lunch duty with colleagues, do not bother trying to have a conversation with them. They won't hear you. The funny part about all of this is that on most cafeteria walls hang posters that say "Thank you for using quiet voices."

During lunch supervision, you will walk around rows of long tables and repeat the same four things: "Eat your lunch," "Sit down," "Stop playing with your food," and "Don't karate chop your sandwich." Words will come out of your mouth that you never predicted you'd hear yourself say, such as: "Please stop licking the table" (when a child wants to get every last bit of orange dust from his Cheetos), "Caterpillars don't eat peas" (when a youngster tries to feed them to one that she found at recess), and "Don't point your banana gun at the teacher." One time, after I said this, the second grader blew on the top of his banana like a cowboy, then holstered it in his pocket.

For many kids, lunchtime is playtime. Pretzel sticks morph into daggers. Orange peels become mouth guards. And children place cucumber slices over their eye sockets like they're getting a facial. While on lunch supervision, your main job is to open things. Kids will hand you juice boxes they can't poke their straws into, bananas they can't unpeel because there's no stem, oranges with skins too tight for small fingers to get under, and ketchup packets that are too difficult to tear open with baby teeth.

As you patrol the cafeteria, you will witness all kinds of eating habits. Some children eat only white food: noodles, rice, saltine crackers, and hot dog buns after they have picked off all the crust. Some kids steer clear of certain colors. I've seen a child not touch her entire meal because there was a pickle on her plate (it was green!), another kid refuse to eat anything orange because she hated carrots, and a first grader have a complete meltdown after he bit into a tuna sandwich and discovered there was celery in it. You'll also encounter children who stick with one thing. Take Harry as an example. For an entire year, I never saw him eat anything but frozen waffles.

Some kids' dietary habits make absolutely no sense. I knew a girl who was crazy about strawberry applesauce, strawberry jam, and pretty much everything strawberry—except actual strawberries. She hated those. And I remember one boy who would not eat hot food. If his mom gave him a hot dog, she had to call it a "cold dog," otherwise he wouldn't touch it. And then there are those children who like the strangest combinations. I've observed kids eat banana, mayo, and Pringles sandwiches; dunk pizza crust in Coke; roll up Kraft American cheese singles filled with ketchup; and prepare Skittles milk: Drop a whole pack of Skittles into a thermos of milk, shake well, and drink.

Field Trips

Children love field trips. Teachers? Not so much. It doesn't matter what grade you teach. Certain things always happen on a field trip: Even though you sent out permission slips weeks ahead of time, you will get the last few back on the morning of the trip. Wherever the destination, you will spend most of your time corralling kids to listen to the docent. When children have to use the bathroom, you will stand guard to make sure they don't play "toaster" with the paper towel dispenser to see how many towels will pop out. If the bathroom has one of those powerful hand dryers, you will stand by that as well to make sure your little weasels don't stick their heads under it while pretending to dry their hair. At lunchtime, you will share your lunch with a child who forgot to bring it. If you let your students play for a few minutes during a break, some will behave as if they've never been outdoors before. If there's a tree nearby, they will want to climb it. If there's a fountain, they'll want to play in it. If there's a duck, they will chase it. Many of your parent chaperones will not notice any of these things, though, because most will be on their phones. Occasionally, you will have one rookie chaperone who has never been on a field trip before (usually a dad), looking dazed because he had no idea what he was in for. That night, on his Facebook page, he will post a shell-shocked selfie that he took on the bus ride home.

Spirit Days

At my last school, we had Spirit Days about every month or so. On Crazy Hair Day, the children walked around with paint, glitter, and Christmas bows on their heads. On Crazy Sock Day, kids would lift your pant legs to see how wild your socks were. If the socks weren't crazy enough to meet their standards, they would let you know. On Twin Day, children dressed like someone else.

Whenever my school had Twin Day, a couple of boys would always dress up like me. They'd walk around sporting their dads' ties, carrying pens in their shirt pockets, and holding large coffee mugs. Once, a little smart aleck who was dressed like me stood over my messy desk and cried, "Has anyone seen my keys?" (I tended to misplace them.)

And then there was Opposite Day. This one nearly did me in. On Opposite Day, kids sit in the wrong chairs and line up in the incorrect order. They stand when asked to sit. During math, they subtract when they're supposed to add. A lot of children wear their clothes inside out. On my first Opposite Day, I kept forgetting to say the opposite of what I meant, and the kids would laugh at me. By the end of the day, however, I finally got it right. When it was time to assign homework on the board, I wrote, "Do not do your math page and your spelling," then turned to the class with a smirk. I was quite pleased with myself. Unfortunately, it backfired. The next morning, as I collected the homework, I saw that several children hadn't done it.

"Why didn't you do your homework?" I asked Owen, one of the kids who didn't have it. "I wrote the opposite."

"Because," he answered, grinning, "Opposite Day ends right when the last bell rings. At three thirty, it goes back to normal."

The Hat

There is one special feeling that all teachers experience. It doesn't come often, but when it does, our mouths turn up, our chins lift slightly, our chests expand, and our shirts feel a little tighter. If this feeling is especially strong, our eyes well up and our hands rise to wipe them. What I'm describing here is teacher pride: that pleasant mix of satisfaction and delight that comes from working with children. Teacher pride is similar to parent pride, which certainly makes sense, since teachers are often the third parent. Ask any teacher to share a moment when they felt it, and they will always be smiling when they tell you.

Teacher pride reveals itself in different ways. It comes at high school graduations when you see former students who once wore Disney princess costumes in the Halloween parade now in caps and gowns. It turns up when young men and women who were in your class many years before find you online to let you know that they got into college. It appears when a mom contacts you because she wants you to know that the third grader whom you read with before and after school because reading didn't come easily to him just completed his MBA. Teacher pride visits at the time you run into pupils you had long ago who are now all grown up, and you see how well they turned out. It shows up when your whole class does well on a test or when you've assessed your students in reading and see that they've improved. It emerges as you witness children work hard to meet a goal, face a fear, accomplish something they didn't know they could do, or have a breakthrough at school. When I think back on my own moments of teacher pride, there is one that stands out, because when it happened, I witnessed both the loving act of a child *and* a breakthrough at the same time. Double the pride.

It started on Halloween. Sutton, one of my third graders, dressed up as the Cat in the Hat, complete with his famous tall red-and-white-striped hat. Sutton wore the costume all day. During recess and lunch, a second grader named Noah, a freckle-faced boy with a mop of red hair, followed Sutton around. He was fascinated by Sutton's hat. As he tagged behind Sutton, Noah would point at the hat and make sounds. He was trying to say "hat," but it didn't come out that way. You see, Noah could not speak. He was severely autistic and attended a special class on campus. Sutton didn't mind having Noah follow him like this. He was a good sport about it.

The next morning, Sutton came to me and said that he'd like to give the hat to Noah. "That's very kind of you," I said. Sutton had asked his mom, and she'd said it was okay. I told Noah's teacher, Linda, what Sutton wanted to do, and during lunch recess, she brought Noah over to my classroom. I stepped outside to get Sutton, and, when I spotted him, called him over and told him Noah was here.

Sutton came inside, where he went straight to his cubby, grabbed the hat, and presented it to Noah. "It's for you," he said. Noah opened his mouth wide and made a loud, happy sound. Linda placed the hat on Noah's head, and we all laughed when it fell over his eyes. When Noah pushed up the hat, his face was one giant smile. Then Linda and I took photos of the boys, their arms around each other's shoulders. I felt proud of Sutton, proud of what he had done, proud that he had such a big heart. The smile on my face was as big as Noah's.

All of a sudden, Noah started patting Linda's bag. She always carried it when she was with him. In it was an iPad with a special app that helped her nonverbal students to communicate. The app had a grid of pictures, each with a corresponding word. When you tapped on a picture, a voice would say the word aloud. Noah pulled the iPad out of the bag and opened the app. Then he leaned over the pictures on the screen, searching intently for a word. When he found the one he was looking for, he started tapping on it. *Tap, tap, tap. Tap, tap, tap.* Over and over, a voice said, "Thank you. Thank you. Thank you. Thank you." Everyone was smiling. Linda's eyes had tears in them. Proud ones.

After we excused the boys back to recess, Linda leaned against the wall and let out a sigh. "I'm so happy," she said, wiping her eyes. "You see, Noah's never done that before. We've always had to prompt him to say thank you and help him with the iPad. He's never been able to do it by himself. This was the first time."

A victory.

Linda and I stepped outside. It would soon be time to collect the kids. Out on the field, I spotted a tall red-and-white hat bouncing up and down. "Somewhere under that hat," I said, "there's a very happy little boy."

Linda chuckled. "I don't think I'll ever be able to look at that hat again without thinking of those two."

"Me neither."

Then, as Linda and I waited for the bell to ring, we both stood there in silence, enjoying what had just happened and how we felt about it. Our mouths were turned up, our chins slightly raised.

The Classroom

The Only Perfect Moment

There is one moment in teaching that is like no other. It happens every
year, the moment right before your new students walk in on the first day
of school. It's a moment when everything is in its place. Everything is organized and tidy. Your classroom is perfect.

Around the room, the bright red, yellow, and blue butcher paper that you
just stapled onto the bulletin boards waits for the new group of self-portraits
with buzz cuts and ponytails, as well as the new batch of autobiographies announcing favorite foods, sports, and subjects in school (the latter of which will
surely include recess). Your birthday board awaits the paper cakes that your
new students will write their names on and place above the month they were
born. Your file cabinet awaits a whole new crop of drawings from children
too. The whiteboard is clean except for your name and "Welcome!," which
you wrote in large letters with colored Expo markers. You drew a happy face
inside the o.

The sink is shiny, the tile floor around it has a new coat of wax, and the
ball box is full of newly pumped-up balls ready for play. In the box, there are
no baseball caps, hairbands, or scrunched-up balls of paper that were shot
like free throws but missed the garbage can. Your classroom door is decorated with a new slogan and dozens of construction paper birds ("Welcome
to our nest!"), bees ("Welcome to our hive!"), crayons ("Welcome to our new
pack!"), or smiling whales ("Whale-come!"), on which you wrote your new
students' names because children like seeing their names on smiling whales
on the front door.

On the rug, there are no mud tracks, spilled paint, or wet grass brought in on sneakers that just played on the field. In the closets, packs of markers, index cards, colored pencils, and sticky notes still in their wrappers sit in new baskets that you recently purchased at Target. On the students' desks, the name tags are crisp and clean. So are the cards you've taped underneath them, each with a number line and a row of perfectly formed letters surrounded by little arrows that show kids how to make them. On each desktop sits a stack of new folders, a set of markers, and a pencil box with a freshly sharpened pencil. On your desk, the stapler has a complete bar of staples. The new yellow pencils are all exactly the same height. And in the tape dispenser, the end of the roll of Scotch tape rests just as it should over the serrated metal edge and isn't stuck to the roll so that you have to pull the whole thing out and hunt for the end with your fingernail.

On the center of your desk, your new lesson planner lies open to the first page. In its empty squares, you've written the first few days' activities and marked them with different colored highlighters. In those squares that indicate when your students will be away at PE and library, you've drawn smiley faces. None of the pages in your planner have brown rings on them yet from the bottom of your coffee mug. On your desk or nearby table, you have the first week's work for the children: stacks of papers, thirty in a pile, all paperclipped and ready to go. Your treat jar is full. Your wastebasket is empty. Your correcting basket is empty too.

On the supply table, none of your markers lay dead at the bottom of your marker basket because they don't have caps. None of the red markers have blue caps—or yellow or green caps either. The eraser tops on the kids' pencils are bright pink, not gray and rounded from rubbing out misspelled words and math mistakes. The glue in your glue sticks is still hidden in the cases like push-up ice creams that haven't been pushed up yet. And the orange-capped glue bottles are full, so you don't have to turn them upside down and wait for the glue to come out like you do with a bottle of ketchup. Over in the classroom library, the books about sharks are in the basket labeled "Animals" and not in the one for biographies.

As the clock ticks down to the start of school, outside you will begin to hear the chatter of excited children awaiting your arrival like the lucky golden ticket holders who anxiously wait for Willy Wonka to step out of his chocolate factory. There is always something so hopeful about a classroom ready for children to arrive on the first day of school. But before you open the door, look around your shiny new classroom. Enjoy this perfect moment. Savor it. You've worked hard to make it this way.

The Classroom Home

"**M**r. Done, please can I sit on the beanbag?" Dylan begged after I gave my kids their writing assignment.

"Why?" I asked.

"I get better ideas there."

Over the years, my students taught me much about their classroom: It is more fun to work under a table than to sit at one. Chairs, like wild horses, can stand up easily on their back two legs. The best seat in the house is by the ball box. The best places to hide from the teacher are behind the door and under his desk. Two third-grade boys can fit into a broom closet if they squeeze in really tight. If the teacher lets you sit in his chair to read, it's hard to concentrate on your book because you're so excited to be sitting in the teacher's chair.

We all know that teachers are doctors and dentists (for all those lost teeth), coaches and travel agents (for all those field trips), directors and handwriting analysts (for all the papers without names), and counselors and lawyers ("I'll cross-examine you in a second to find out what happened at recess"). But we're also interior designers. Come August, we arrange furniture, organize cabinets, and hide yardsticks so that they don't transform into swords. We hang welcome banners, posters, and charts with the scientific method, story elements, multiplication strategies, and giant smiling punctuation marks trying to convince children that punctuation is fun. We write our new students' names in our best teacher writing on notebooks and folders and cubbies and name tags and tongue depressors that we will pull out of cans when we want to call on someone. We plaster our desks with trains of bright pink and yellow and blue sticky notes reminding us to prepare, plan, file, sort, make, email, read, copy, and label everything short of the hamster.

I always liked setting up my classroom. For me, it was a little like Christmas. Instead of pulling out holiday decorations, teachers bring out our back-to-school decor. In place of opening presents, we open boxes that have been delivered to our rooms over the summer. Instead of writing lists of gifts we need to buy, we make lists of school supplies that we need to purchase. We fill goody jars instead of stockings.

For teachers, setting up our classrooms is similar to birds building their nests. Pretty soon both will be filled with loud little ones. And just as birds build different types of nests, teachers set up classrooms differently too. Some are elaborate. Some are no fuss. Some are meticulously put together. Some are more cluttered. My classroom nest was like a magpie's, full of a little bit of everything: string, twine, paper, you name it. The cupboards in my room were filled with seashells, sombreros, magnifying glasses, arrowheads, cowboy hats, old *National Geographics*, skeins of yarn, carnival tickets, empty cottage cheese containers, polished rocks, colored clay, rainy-day recess games, Halloween costumes, boxes of old papers that I'd inherited from a retired teacher and didn't have the heart to throw away, broken pottery for archeological digs, a jar of sand from a trip to Egypt, and yellow tape to tie around a pretend crime scene when we read mysteries. A lot of teachers are magpies. Our motto: You never know when you're going to need it.

I've always thought that the HGTV channel would have a blockbuster on its hands if it aired a show about classroom makeovers. For sure, millions of teachers would tune in to watch. I can totally picture it. In each episode, as the lucky teachers' blindfolds are lifted, the camera zooms in on their tears of joy when they see that there are no pencil shavings or sunflower seed shells on the carpet, no dried glue on the desktops, and no forgotten lunch bags in the cubbies. For that matter, HGTV could produce a makeover show about staff rooms too. Just imagine it! All the mismatched dishes and flatware would match. The inside of the microwave would be clean. The '80s sofa and chairs would be substituted with new ones from Ikea. And the old green paper cutter would be replaced by a new one that no longer sounds like a guillotine.

When setting up a classroom, teachers have two goals: The first is to create

a functional place for learning. The second is to make a positive and comfortable learning environment—to set a nice tone. One of the best ways to establish a pleasant atmosphere is to think of your classroom as a home. Teachers
and students spend thirty-plus hours a week at school. For most of us, it's
our second home. So why not make it feel like one? Think of your classroom
home as having different rooms. The area with your desk is your office. The
section with your children's books is your library. The cupboard beneath the
sink, crowded with glass jars, pie tins, and paper plates, is your kitchen, and
the cubby area is your walk-in closet. Jill, my kindergarten teacher friend, calls
this area "Baggage Claim."

Just as all homes have a living room, so should your classroom. If your
school district will allow it, and if you can fit it in, I suggest bringing in a
couch. Nothing cozies up a classroom more. And while you're at it, purchase
a used coffee table at a local thrift store—or, as I call it, the Teacher Design
Center. Stack some books on the coffee table and set some pillows and stuffed
animals on the couch. I loved having a couch in my classroom. That's where
I'd read with children, correct papers, and hold parent-teacher conferences.
Sometimes after school, when the kids were gone, I'd collapse into it for a few
moments of shut-eye. Once, when the custodian was cleaning in my room,
he didn't realize I was napping on the couch. I sat up, and his vacuum went
flying. If you do get a couch, be prepared. During silent reading time, all your
students will want to sit on it, and they'll argue over whose turn it is to hold
the stuffed animals.

Area rugs, like couches and pillows, also warm up a home. And the most
important one in any classroom home is the reading rug. On my reading rug,
I had an easel and my teacher's chair. Usually a stuffed animal kept the seat
warm till I returned. Scattered around the rug were some large pillows. I liked
to think of this area as the family room. Here's where teachers gather their
kids and read to them. It's also where you make your morning announce-
ments, have class discussions, and hold impromptu meetings about good
sportsmanship after the playground supervisor tells you that your boys got
into a scuffle on the soccer field.

Because you and your students are sitting together, it's also in the family
room that—if you're a man teacher—your kids will notice and comment on

the spot on your neck where you missed shaving, the sweat marks under your arms, the hair on your calves when you cross your legs, or the "$6.99" written on the bottom of your Oxfords that you picked up at the Teacher Design Center when you bought the couch. One day I was sitting in the family room with my students when Matthew said, "You're wearing your cookie socks." I looked down. So I was. The socks were blue with chocolate chip cookies. This group liked them. All of a sudden, Matthew got up and went to his desk, where he pulled out a notebook, flipped through a few pages, and stopped when he found what he was looking for. "You wore those . . ."—he looked up—"last week. On Wednesday."

Personal items are key to cozying up any home, so fill your classroom with lots of stuffed toys and framed photos and personal collections. A lot of teachers collect things to delight their students: Smurfs, trolls, Minions, plastic squishy toys, crazy pencils, bobbleheads. A teacher I know collects the teeny used pencils her kids have written with. One of them is so short that there is no pencil left, just a metal band and a pointed piece of graphite sticking out of it. Another is about one inch long and sharpened on both ends. No matter what you collect, you must set it on top of your file cabinet. It is an unwritten law that all teacher collections go there, along with all of your apple-shaped plaques, bells, ornaments, and paperweights. Naturally, in your classroom home, you also have to put out your favorite things. A lot of teachers have their most treasured classroom possessions: a favorite mug, a favorite poster, a favorite chair. One friend of mine who teaches high school would not allow any of her students to sit in her director's chair. She told them that they could do so only after they graduated. Many of them came back to sit in the chair. I'm sure my friend did this so she'd get to see her kids again.

All interior decorators will tell you that lighting is important in a home. The same is true at school. So, when you're at the Teacher Design Center, pick up some inexpensive lamps, set them around your classroom, and keep them on throughout the school day. It changes the whole tone. And, if possible, turn off those awful glaring fluorescent lights. Early in my career, I attended a workshop where the instructor told us about the negative effects of fluorescent light on children. She shared studies concluding that fluorescent lighting can cause hyperactivity. Well, I certainly didn't want that. So, I bought a half dozen lamps and placed them around my classroom. As I was plugging them in and screwing in the bulbs, one of my students asked what I was doing, so I explained.

"Well," I said, pointing to the ceiling, "those lights up there are called fluorescent lights, and I've learned that they can make people hyper." I held up a regular lightbulb. "These are different. They're what we call full-spectrum bulbs. They're more calming."

A few hours later, Justin, one of my live wires, got up from his desk and took a seat beside a lamp.

"Justin," I said with a raised eyebrow, "what are you doing?"

"I'm feeling hyper," he answered. "I need to calm down."

Nothing warms up a home quite like plants and flowers, so place some houseplants around your classroom and bring in some flowers once in a while. And invite your students to bring in flowers from home. Numerous studies show that plants in the home and workplace improve concentration, attention span, and memory. Plants also increase work productivity, boost energy, and reduce stress—everything teachers want. But if you do ask your kids to bring in flowers, emphasize that they get them from their *own* homes. I once had a third grader who kept coming in with flowers. When I thanked her mother for them, she didn't know anything about it. We discovered that her daughter was picking them on her way to school.

Whenever I move to a new place, it never feels like home until I hang up the pictures. This applies to classrooms as well. Remember: things on walls = home; bare walls = hospital. When it comes to wall decorating, here's where a teacher's design style really comes out. Some teachers set up more austere classrooms, hanging little on the walls. Some prefer a plastered look, covering every inch. Some like that glossy finish. Nothing goes up unless it has been laminated. (These teachers are also called laminator hogs.) Some opt for bold and bright. Their rooms are full of primary colors. And some go for cutesy. They decorate with bows and polka dots. My classrooms leaned toward plastered, bold, and glossy. Occasionally, I'd hog the laminator.

When hanging things on your walls, it goes without saying that you have to put up your bulletin boards. We all know the symbols for school: an apple, a red one-room schoolhouse, a bell. But those symbols never really worked for me. No one gives apples to the teacher anymore, and I've never seen a red school. If I had to pick one symbol that represents teaching, it wouldn't be any of these. It would be the bulletin board. It doesn't matter what or where you teach. Putting up bulletin boards is the one thing that teachers have in common. It binds us. It connects us to our heritage. For ages, teachers have been pulling colored butcher paper off of large rolls, stapling it onto boards, pressing out air bubbles, cutting around light switches, patching up spots because the paper wasn't long enough, and finishing the edges off with scalloped borders. In a hundred years, no matter how much education changes, teachers will still be putting them up.

There are countless bulletin board ideas, but every classroom should have these two: the student board and the teacher board. The student board is where you place all your children's work. Displaying kids' work is important. Teachers hang their students' work for the same reasons that parents put up their kids' art on the fridge. By doing so, you're saying, I'm proud of you. One teacher I know actually decorated her student board to look like a refrigerator. She plastered it with her kids' best papers and titled the board "The Fridge." On my student board, I'd put up one piece of red construction paper for each student. Below each piece was the student's name. In the center of the construction paper, I'd hang the child's work after I had drawn a big star or a happy face on it. Each month, I'd replace all the students' papers with new ones. Easy. If a child's paper wasn't ready to post on the board, rather than have a blank space, I'd just pin up a sign that said "Coming Soon!"

While we're on the topic of student boards, I have never understood why so many teachers stop hanging their kids' work after elementary school. I just don't get it. Yes, I understand that middle and high school teachers have a great many more students than grade school teachers do. But imagine how touched you would have felt in middle or high school, and what a boost to your self-confidence it would have been, if one of your teachers took the time to hang a piece of red construction paper on the wall with your work on it and drew a giant smiley face.

The second most important board in your classroom is the teacher board. This one is just for you. It's a place to display your personal photos, postcards from your travels, and funny sayings such as: "I can't believe how slowly summer is passing—said no teacher ever!" Be sure to include your teaching certificate too. Other professionals hang their certificates; why shouldn't teachers? On my teacher board, I'd put up photos of my family, my friends, and my dog, Roxie. There was a photo of me standing on the Great Wall of China and one of me pretending to push over the Leaning Tower of Pisa. I had snapshots of me walking in Halloween parades while holding plastic spears and lightsabers that I'd just confiscated and pictures of me stepping out of swimming pools fully clothed after being pushed into them at end-of-school-year parties. On my board, I also had photos from when *I* was in grade school, including one of me holding a metal *Peanuts* lunch box on my first day of third grade and another in fourth, where I'm sporting long hair just like teen idol David Cassidy from *The Partridge Family*.

At the beginning of each school year, I'd use my teacher board to introduce myself to my new students. Kids naturally want to know their teachers, and the board gives them a glimpse into your life. It shows them that you have a life outside of school. Some children can't fathom this. When I shared my board, it gave my students a chance to ask questions and to get to know me better. Of course, if you have a photo of your dog or cat, the children will ask more questions about your pet than you. Once, when a new girl joined the class midyear, I asked Melanie (she was the class greeter) to show her around the room. The first thing Melanie did was to take the new student to Roxie's photo and tell her all about my dog. It didn't matter where the pencils were; Roxie was way more important. At the beginning of the school year, you don't even have to point out the teacher board to your students. They will discover it. And when they spot the school photos from your childhood, they will ask, "Is that *you*?" Then at the end of the day, when their moms come to pick them up, they will pull them into the classroom to show them what you looked like on day one of third grade and laugh at your David Cassidy haircut in fourth.

Lastly, to set a pleasant tone in your classroom home, play classical music in the background. Background music can reduce tension and lower stress. Hotels use it to relax their customers. Starbucks plays it to create a soothing atmosphere. The same is true in the classroom. Have music playing when your kids enter in the morning. Put it on when they're working. Keep the volume low. Select music that is calming, such as Bach, Mozart, or Vivaldi, and avoid high-energy pieces like "The William Tell Overture," unless you want to see children galloping in their chairs like the Lone Ranger. And never play the frantic "The Flight of the Bumblebee." If you do, *your* little bees will start buzzing around the classroom too. I don't recommend letting your students select the music, though. Kids don't choose Mozart. Also, don't pick anything with lyrics. They'll sing along. And whatever you do, *do not* play opera! I have made that mistake.

"What's that music?" Nicholas announced as he walked into the classroom with his classmates after lunch. I was playing a CD of Puccini's *Tosca*.

"It's opera," I answered with a smile. "You like it?"

"No!" he exclaimed, screwing up his face.

Alex covered his ears. "It's breaking my eardrums!"

"Turn it off!" Rodney shouted.

"How can you kids not like this?" I asked.

I was answered by a room full of barfing noises, cringing faces, and thumbs turned downward.

"Don't *any* of you like it?"

One lone hand went up. Marco's. He was Italian.

"*Aha!*" I exclaimed. "My *Italiano*! Of course! Good for you, Marco." I crossed my arms and smiled triumphantly. "Marco," I said, gesturing to the rest of the class, "would you be so kind as to explain to your classmates just *why* you like opera?"

"Well . . ." Marco said hesitantly, "my dad listens to it all the time."

I nodded. *There's a cultured child.*

"And if I don't interrupt him, he gives me money."

The First Day of School

At the start of the school year, sometimes parents would forward me their kids' first-day-of-school photos, and some of them were pretty creative. One year a mom sent me a shot of her son holding a small whiteboard with the words: "Help me! I have ten more years of these pictures!" Another year a dad shared a photo of his backpacked kids standing beside their pool and pretending to cry while he floated on a raft, cocktail in hand. My favorite first-day photo wasn't a kid's. It was a colleague's. In it, he held a handwritten sign with the date and the number of years he'd been teaching. The sign said: "I can't believe I let my wife take this."

Without a doubt, the first day is *the* most important day of the school year. It's the day teachers begin to introduce rules, establish routines, practice procedures, and learn which kids need to be moved to a different seat. Of course, it's the day you meet your new students. I liken the start of school to an arranged marriage. You don't know whom you're going to meet. The difference is that in an arranged marriage, you get only one new set of parents. At school, you get dozens.

The first day of each new school year, my morning routine was always the same. I'd wake up before the alarm clock went off because I was excited. I'd put on the freshly ironed dress shirt and slacks that I hadn't seen in two and a half months. I'd slip on dress shoes that I hadn't set eyes on since June. And every year I would have to knot my tie a couple of times till I got it right because I was out of practice.

I like first days of school. I like their freshness: the new clothes and school supplies, the new backpacks and haircuts. But most of all, I like the first-day buzz. All schools have different kinds of excitement: field trip excitement,

Friday-before-break excitement, snow day excitement, school play excitement. My favorite is day-one excitement. Every start of school has a palpable wish-I-could-bottle-it excitement in the air. In most jobs, there's only one first day. In teaching, you get one every year.

As much as I enjoy the first day of school, it's always a shock to the system. One day it's summer, and the next, it's *Bam! Pow! Wham!* You feel like you've been thrown into a Marvel comic. In twenty-four hours, your brain goes from summer mode to overdrive. There's no transition, no easing into it. It's like relaxing on a peaceful beach one minute, then getting slammed by a tsunami. One of the reasons the first day is such a shock for teachers is because we're not in teacher shape yet. When the new school year begins, it will have been months since we ran to a copier, speed-walked to a bathroom, blew a whistle, raced to the blacktop because we forgot we had yard duty, or bolted across campus because we were late for a staff meeting. Even our teacher look is rusty.

Over my career, I had several student teachers, and during our time together, they always asked about the first day of school. They were unsure about what to do on this most important day. I guess Teacher Schools don't devote a lot of time to day one. And so I will share with you the same first-day tips that I shared with them. Most of the suggestions are for the elementary grades, but many can be modified for middle and high school.

Before I begin, I'd like to say one thing to the veteran teachers who are reading this chapter. Whenever I speak to large groups of teachers, I often begin my presentation by asking how long they have been teaching. "Please stand if you've been teaching for ten to fifteen years," I will say. Many teachers rise. "Now stand up if you've taught between sixteen and twenty years." The first group sits and a different one gets up. This goes on until I ask who has taught for more than thirty-five years. When these teachers stand, the rest of the audience always gives them a round of applause. Some of the teachers who are seated will shake their heads with wide-eyed expressions because they can't fathom making it that long. Before the last group sits back down, I smile at them and say, "To all of you who are standing right now, there is nothing I am about to say that you don't already know. You may go to the back of the room and get a cup of coffee." Well, the same applies here. If you're a veteran teacher, you have many first days under your belt and will already know what I am about to explain. You wouldn't have made it this long if you didn't. So you have permission to skip the next few pages. Or, you may just want to keep reading so you can nod in agreement and say to yourself, "Yep, that's how you do it."

Guidelines and Goals

To start, I'd like to say that there is no one right way to run the first day of school. There are, however, things you can do to get off to the right start. Generally, on the first day, it's best to be organized, clear, confident, and, if possible—a little funny. Kids like funny. It sets them at ease. It's also important that you do what works for you. Don't do what someone else does because you think you're supposed to. On the first day, a teacher should have two goals. The first is to make your new students feel relaxed and comfortable. The second is this: When the children leave school, and their parents ask them if they like their new teacher, you want them to say yes.

Planning Your Start

Before the first day of school, plan the whole day thoroughly. So much will happen that you don't want to be worrying about your plans. Leading up to the first day, it's a good idea to keep a checklist, so that you don't leave anything out. (A friend of mine has a T-shirt with the following back-to-school checklist: "Pens. Check. Paper. Check. Sanity—No Check.") And it's always better to overplan than to not have enough. What you don't use on day one, you can use the next. Also, have all your materials ready to go. You don't want to be scrambling during your breaks. You'll need those to sit in the staff room and eat the donuts that the principal (hopefully) brought in. Before day one, try to have all your plans and materials ready for the second day of school as well. The last thing you'll want to do at the end of the first day is have to make plans for the next one. When day one's over, you'll want to go home as soon as you can and crash.

Your First Meeting

If you teach grade school, chances are you will pick up your new students in line. Unless you're teaching kindergarten, I do not recommend leaving your classroom open before school on the first day. You need your time, and some parents will want to corner you. After the first bell rings and the kids have lined up, stand at the front of the line with a big smile and say, "Good morning!" to your new class. If you teach the little ones, lots of parents will be standing around. Smile at them too. They will also be nervous.

At the Door

After you've walked your students to the classroom, stand at the door and tell them to look for their desks with their name tags. Don't make children choose their desks. This makes kids anxious. Have their names already on them. As the children walk past you and into their new classroom, greet each child individually with a welcoming smile. After the last student is in the room and you start to close the door, turn to the parents who are still lingering and say, "I'll take good care of them."

Your Kids' First Task

As the children find their seats, have something on their desks for them to do. It can be as simple as coloring a name tag, completing a word search, or drawing a picture—nothing fancy. Leave the directions written on the board or placed on their desks. This gives you a little uninterrupted time to take attendance, find out who is buying lunch, and collect all the boxes of Kleenex that the kids will pull out of their backpacks because tissues were on the back-to-school supply list. Of course, your new students won't begin the activity that you set out for them until they have checked out their new desks, pulled out all their new school supplies from their backpacks, and figured out how far away their friends are seated.

Introductions

Once the children are settled, it is time to introduce yourself. Tell them your name and write it on the board. I'd say, "My name is Mr. Done. It rhymes with *phone*. It is not Mr. Dunn. And"—with a half smile and half don't-you-dare-call-me-this expression—"it is *not* Mr. Donut." It would get a laugh. Then tell the kids a little about yourself. There are many ways to make an introduction, of course. One compelling way is to pull items that represent you out of a bag and talk about them: a souvenir from a recent trip, a book you're reading, a photo of your dog doing something funny. An autobiography in a bag. It's also a nice way for your new students to acquaint themselves with one another later in the week. Another creative way to make your introduction is to write single words related to your life on the board and let your class guess what they mean. For example, if I wrote "three," "red," and "8:00," the kids would have to guess that I have three siblings, red is the color of my car, and eight o'clock is the time I would likely be in bed that night.

When your students are introducing themselves, instead of the standard "Share your favorite _____" kind of introduction, try having them tell the class two true things and one that is not. The children have to guess which is false. Or ask kids to share one "boring" fact about themselves. This takes the pressure off of trying to think of an interesting one. My boring facts: I sleep on my side. I keep the water running while brushing my teeth. When eating fried eggs, I save the yolks till the end. Later in the week, if you want your students to write about themselves, rather than the typical autobiography, ask them to write what they *didn't* do over the summer. Kids get a kick out of this. Examples: I didn't ride a unicorn. I did not win the lottery. I did not make a video with Taylor Swift.

Getting Their Attention

I suggest that the very first thing you teach your new students is how you will get their attention throughout the year. There are many ways to do this: turning off the lights, playing wind chimes, even ringing a classroom doorbell. The call-and-response attention grabber, also known as a callback, is extremely popular in primary grades. For instance, the teacher might say, "Spaghetti," and the children respond with "Meatballs." Or the teacher calls out, "Macaroni and cheese!" and the students shout out, "Everybody, freeze!" One of my favorites: teacher says, "Scooby-Dooby-Doo"; kids, "Where are you?" You can use just one attention grabber or several. Choose whatever works for you. Most of the time, I would just say, "Eyes on me, class," or "Eyes on the tie." Often I'd simply say, "Could I have your attention, please?"

No matter which attention grabber you pick, do not begin speaking until all your students are quiet and looking at you. This is key. The number one mistake I see new teachers make (and even some veterans) is to start teaching before they have everyone's attention. If your kids aren't listening, wait—as long as you need to.

After you tell the class how you will be getting their attention, practice it. Let the kids pretend to be working at their desks, then call out your attention grabber. Students should stop what they're doing, look at you, and freeze. Wait until all eyes are on you and every child is still. Then ask the children to stand up and walk around the classroom. Let them chat with their friends and have a silly conversation ("Peas and carrots," "Carrots and peas," "Peas and carrots?" "Carrots and *peas*!") till you give your signal. Again, do not continue until every student is looking at you and is quiet and still. Repeat this a couple of times. For fun, challenge the kids to stop, look, and freeze even faster: "Okay, boys and girls, it took you five seconds that time." Smile. "Can you do it in four?"

Play a Game

As soon as you can, get your students out of their chairs and moving. It gets the nerves out. I liked to play an icebreaker called People Hunting. It's an oldie but goodie. For this activity, give each child a piece of paper with a long list of questions such as: Can you play chess? Did you go to the beach this summer? Do you have blue eyes? Do you know how to hula-hoop? Are you left-handed? And so on. After you say "Go," the children scurry around the room with their papers, asking their new classmates the questions. If students answer yes, they sign their names beside the questions. (A child may sign the same paper only twice.) The purpose is to get as many signatures as they can within a certain amount of time.

A variation on this game is Back to School Bingo. Using bingo cards with the same type of questions written in the squares, kids find classmates who can sign their names in them. Of course, whatever game you choose, the teacher has to play too. (For the record: I can play chess. I have blue eyes. I can hula-hoop—a little.) When playing an icebreaker like this, you will already begin learning about your new students: who needs support, who's shy, who has trouble reading, and also who your new spitfires are. These kids will be easy to recognize. They're the ones standing on the chairs, shouting, "Is anyone here left-handed?"

Give a Tour of the Classroom

Sometime in the morning, give your students a tour of their new classroom and show them where things are: the student library, the computer cart, the supply table. Point out what they may touch and what they may not: marker basket, help yourself; goody jar, off-limits. When at the supply table, this might be a good time to give the Pencil Speech: "Pencils are for writing. We do not chew on them. We keep them out of our noses and ears. We do not write with pencils that are less than two inches long. You know those signs at amusement parks that say children must be a certain height in order to go on the ride? In our classroom, pencils have a height requirement too."

Explain the Rules

On day one, it's important, of course, to explain the classroom rules. There are two ways to establish them. One common strategy is to let students create them. The idea behind this is that by allowing kids to come up with them, there will be more buy-in. The second way is to set the rules yourself. I always chose to set my own. Doing so confirmed that I was the leader in the room. Children want their teacher to lead. Also, in my experience, students don't buy in any less if the teacher makes the rules. In fact, some children prefer it. Furthermore, I found that kids who can be challenging respond better if the teacher says, "Here are the rules of the classroom." Generally, I believe students should have plenty of opportunities to make decisions, just not when making the rules.

A great deal has been written about establishing classroom rules. The important thing is to set ones that work for you and your students. Keep them simple and positive. Emphasize what kids *can* do, not what they can't. Make sure the rules are clear. And don't have too many; I'd suggest no more than five. In my classroom, I had three main rules: (1) Be thoughtful to others (including the teacher); (2) Listen and follow directions; and (3) Raise your hand before speaking. (This applied to when I was working with large groups or the whole class.) We also had several supplementary rules for using the bathroom, sharpening pencils, and so on, but these three were the main ones. Children are generally good at following rules one and two. Rule three, not so much. Some years, if I had a really chatty group, I'd have to add rule 4: When I'm talking, you're not.

After setting the rules, it's very important that kids practice them. Let your students role-play what it looks like to be thoughtful and follow directions. Have the class practice raising their hands too. One fun way to go over this is to tell your kids that you're going to ask them a question and would like them to raise their hands. Next, ask a simple question such as "What's the name of the school?" All hands will shoot up. Make the children wait before calling on someone to answer. Then ask another question. This time when the hands go up, pause even longer. If you wait a really long time, the kids will look like they are going to explode.

When reviewing the rules, also allow students to demonstrate what *not* to do. To illustrate, have your kids show what being *un*thoughtful looks like by asking a few of them to form a line and let another student take cuts. Ask children to *not* follow directions too. To start, tell them that you're about to give a direction that you *don't* want them to follow. The kids will sit up brightly, excited about what's coming. Next, ask the children to get out their math books. The giggles will begin as they happily do not take them out. Pretend to be upset that they aren't following your direction. Then, once again, ask the kids to pull out their books. Say it more firmly this time. Listen to more giggles and watch shoulders bounce. In the same way, tell your students that you're going to ask a question and permit them all to blurt out the answer at the same time without raising their hands. On hearing this, your kids will again sit up straight like pages in a pop-up book. Delay the question. When you finally ask it, they will gleefully shout out the answer. For children, being able to call out an answer without having to raise their hands is like being allowed to stay up way past their bedtime.

Of course, don't think you're finished reviewing your rules on day one. You'll need to revisit them throughout the year. Good times to go over the rules are whenever you get a new student and when your kids return after a break. Actually, you will have to remind your students of the rules before most every break as well because children get squirrely before vacation. Don't ever feel bad for having to review the rules. Kids need reminders. It's normal.

Review Routines and Procedures

When you think about it, it's mind boggling just how many routines and procedures are necessary to run a classroom. We have routines for lining up, entering the room, getting supplies, hanging up backpacks, handing in work, transitioning from one subject to another, checking out books, and even using hand sanitizer (more commonly referred to as "hanitizer" in kindergarten). My hanitizer procedure: one pump, not seven.

Routines are vitally important for a smooth-running classroom. Be sure to have a system for everything children do repeatedly in class. On the first day, talk about a couple of important routines that your kids need to know right away. Then add more as they come up during the first two weeks of school. Two routines that you will want to practice on day one are lining up and walking in line. On the first day of school, the hallways can get pretty crowded with single-file lines led by teachers. Oftentimes, these teachers are walking backward (a teacher talent) to make sure that their kids are doing it correctly. When Jill would parade her kindergartners through the hallways on the first day, she'd announce, "Make way for ducklings!" Of course, when she said this, a couple of her wise guys would quack.

Whenever you're introducing a routine to children, practice the heck out of it. The more kids practice in the beginning of the year, the fewer headaches you'll have later on. Begin by modeling exactly what it is you want them to do. Let's say, for example, you are teaching your kids how to transition from their desks to the reading rug. Sit in a student's chair and show them what you expect: Stand up, push in your chair, walk quietly to the carpet, and sit down. Children enjoy seeing their teacher act like a student. While you're at it, have a child play the teacher and report how you did. Kids like that too. Next, ask one student to demonstrate the task as the rest of the class looks on. Then let a couple of children model it. Finally, invite the whole class. Kids don't mind practicing routines. They have them at home. Also, tell students why you are asking them to practice. Explain that it will help their classroom to run smoothly and thus help them learn. Children appreciate being let in on your reasons for doing things. As with classroom rules, if at any time during the year you feel that a routine could stand improvement, have your students practice it again. Classroom routines need to be brushed up now and then. To add a little fun, when the kids are practicing, give them a score between 1 and 10. They'll try to beat it.

Feed Them

As I mentioned, your goal on the first day is to make your students comfortable—and what's more comforting than food? On day one, consider bringing some in. Every first day with my new students, I'd pick up a couple of cartons of orange juice and some muffins on my way to school and set them on a table at the front of the classroom, so the kids could see. At some point in the morning, usually when the children were doing seat work, I would pass them out. But I wouldn't serve the whole class at one time. I'd invite the kids to the table individually and serve them. It was my way of connecting with each child, our little time together. During this time, I'd tell the children how nice it was to have them in my class and how happy I was to be their teacher. I understand that some teachers might not want to feed their students. I get that. For kids, though, there is something warm and calming about receiving a snack and a smile from their new teacher.

Teach Something

Some teachers like to ease into their teaching the first week of school, but I believe it's important to teach your new students a lesson on day one. By doing so, you're launching your classroom as a place for learning. Children want to get started on the first day. They've waited all summer to be in their new classroom and are eager to begin.

On the first day of school, I would teach my students how to draw their self-portraits. After giving all the children white construction paper, I'd guide them step-by-step. I would teach an art lesson for a number of reasons. For most kids, art is nonthreatening. I knew it was an activity in which all children could succeed. The lesson also allowed me to start learning about my new students: who had good fine motor skills and who didn't, who worked quickly and who took their time, who followed directions well and who did not. An art project also gave me something to put up on the walls in time for Back to School Night, which always came too soon. Plus, when the children finished their portraits, they could color them. Coloring, like having muffins and juice, is also calming.

Read a Picture Book

At some time during the day, gather your kids on the reading rug and read them a back-to-school-themed picture book. After lunch is always a nice time to read. Of course, before you do, explain exactly how you would like them to move to the carpet and practice it. The first few weeks of school, prop up lots of books around the room and read one a day. Some favorites of mine included: *The Teacher from the Black Lagoon*; *Miss Nelson Is Missing!*; *A Fine, Fine School*; *Officer Buckle and Gloria*; *How I Spent My Summer Vacation*; *First Day Jitters*; *School's First Day of School*; and *Please Don't Eat the Teacher*. I would choose these books for three reasons: They make kids laugh, which calms and relaxes. I knew most of the kids had heard them before, but familiar books are comforting. Also, children like to hear stories about their teachers being eaten up.

Send Home a Letter

At the end of the first day, send a welcome letter or email to all the parents. They'll expect it. Tell them a little about the grade and how excited you are about the upcoming year. Let them know how to get in touch with you and when Back to School Night is. Also, share something about yourself: your favorite food, drink, book, subject, and hobby. Just like kids, parents like learning about the teacher too.

Don't Go Overboard

One day when I was online, I clicked on an article about back-to-school gifts and almost fell out of my chair. I thought the piece was going to be about things to give the teacher on the first day of school, but instead, it was about gifts that teachers can make for their students! Yes, the first day should be motivating and engaging, but you do not need to give children bottles of bubbles with tags that say "I've been bubbling with excitement to meet you!" It's school, not a birthday party. This applies to the holidays too. There's nothing wrong with handing kids a new pencil or a candy cane before winter break, but you don't need to give them presents. Once, a colleague of mine received an email from a parent that said it all: "You show up. You plan. You teach. You love. You worry. You care. You buy supplies. You do not need to give my kid a present!" Signed: "A grateful mom."

Wrapping Up the Day

If you think about it, the first day of school is really a microcosm of a good school year: a little reading, a little art, a little fun. Both the first day and the school year, if done well, are carefully planned, lovingly taught, and solidly managed. By the end of the first day—and, in many cases, by first recess—your new students will have bonded with you. Most will be at ease in their new classroom. It never takes long. Some of them will already have a new favorite teacher.

Before you excuse your kids, gather them on the carpet and reflect on the day together. Have them share their favorite parts. Acknowledge their feelings by asking how they felt at the beginning of the day and how they feel now. They'll be honest. Tell them you were nervous too. During this carpet time, I would ask my students what their parents said to them in the morning before sending them to school. Every year, the children's answers were always the same: "Be good." "Do your best." "Work hard." One year, after my kids shared their answers, a child asked, "Mr. Done, what did *your* mom tell you?" She was serious. "Well," I replied, charmed by the question, "I didn't talk to my mom this morning, but if I had, I'm sure she would have told me the same things that your parents said to you." A thought popped into my head. "Oh yes—and she would have reminded me to keep my desk neat too." Immediately my whole new flock looked over at my already cluttered desk and laughed.

My Final Tip

On the first day, most likely you will talk a lot. We all do. Keep in mind that you do not have to get through everything on day one. One September, at the end of the first day, I walked outside with my students and overheard a mom talking with her son.

"How do you like your class?" she asked.

"It's pretty good," her son answered. "I like it."

"And how do you like your teacher?"

"He's nice—but he sure does talk a lot."

Door Time

One day I asked my third graders to write how-to papers. These are step-by-step instructions on how to do something. It's a good writing activity for the young ones. My students could write about whatever they wanted. After I gave some examples, the children shared their ideas. Ian wanted to write about how to make a paper airplane. Natalie decided to give instructions for making cinnamon toast. Sebastian would explain how to ride a skateboard. And Anthony, one of my sparkplugs, announced that his title was "How to Bug Your Sister." I gave him a look. "Can we write on the back of the paper?" he asked. I said yes. "Good!" exclaimed Anthony, rubbing his hands together with a devilish expression. "I will have *lots* of steps."

As the kids started writing, I looked over at Madison and asked what she was going to write about. Madison picked up her paper and read out her title: "How to Be a Teacher." I chuckled and said, "I look forward to reading it." A few minutes later, as I was walking around the classroom, I smiled when I leaned over Madison's shoulder. She had written her first sentence: "Step one: In the morning, stand at the door and smile really big."

Greeting students at the door each morning is not just a pleasant-sounding idea. It's an important part of a teacher's day. It has an impact. When I speak of greeting children, I'm talking about standing in the doorway of your classroom and welcoming your students individually by name. It's not always easy to find the time to greet kids in this way. Mornings at school can be crazy. Parents stop by unannounced. Copiers break. Early meetings go all the way up to the first bell. For children, the school day begins after they've hung up their backpacks and taken their seats. But to me, it begins at the front door.

When you greet students at the door, you're starting the day on a bright note. You're creating a positive climate and fostering a sense of belonging. You're modeling good social and communication skills and giving children a chance to practice them as well. Teachers greet their kids before school for the same reason that orchestras play overtures before a show. It sets the tone. Through your posture, expression, and voice, you're showing children that you care. Your message is: I value you. In fact, I value you so much that I've stopped everything else to take the time to be with you right now.

One of the greatest benefits of greeting students is how it makes them feel. Think of how you feel when a boss or coworker meets you in the morning with a smile and a friendly hello. It warms you up. The same is true for children. There is great power in "Hello." That's the reason so many stores and banks and restaurants have greeters. It's why flight attendants say hello as you enter a plane. It feels good, relaxes you, and makes you want to come back—all things we want for our students. All children deserve to start their day with an adult saying: I value you.

Greeting your students also allows you a brief check-in with each one of them. Do they seem happy, sad, or tired? If a child had a behavior problem the day before, the morning greeting reassures that student that today is a fresh start. For children who have difficult lives at home, a cheerful smile and hello from their teacher can be a lifeline. During class, a teacher's one-on-one time with students is limited, so welcoming them at the door gives you another opportunity to make those all-important personal connections. Don't skip door time.

One year my friend Doug, who teaches high school, added door time to his routine. He told me that he started seeing a difference almost immediately. Fewer kids were late to class. His students were more involved. There were fewer behavior problems. For Doug, it was a game changer. Now, I'm not saying that greeting kids is going to turn your class around, but it does set it in a good direction. And it's not just children who benefit. Teachers do too. A funny thing happens when you welcome kids as they enter the classroom. It also makes *you* feel good. In those moments at the door, you're aware that you are connecting with your students. You know that you're setting a positive tone. You're teaching well. And that is satisfying.

Early in my career, I worked with a veteran teacher named Eleanor, whose third-grade classroom was next to mine. Eleanor had been teaching for more than thirty years and had only a couple more years until retirement. She used to joke that when she retired, her eyebrows would be permanently raised from years of giving the "teacher look," and that the little eleven between her eyes would probably never go away either. Eleanor was not the type of teacher to welcome kids at the door. In fact, she used to give me and another young teacher a hard time about it. She called us "softies." But one morning, as I was standing in front of my classroom while my students stepped inside, I was surprised to notice Eleanor standing outside of hers. At lunch, I ran into her in the staff room and asked, "Are my eyes playing tricks on me, or did I see someone in the hallway this morning?"

Eleanor made a face. "You young'uns were making me look bad."

But I knew that was a cover.

"Is someone becoming a *softy*?" I sang with a smirk.

"Shut up."

Eleanor continued door time until the day she retired.

When welcoming children, the important thing is to do what's comfortable for you. Be yourself. Be authentic. There are certainly a variety of ways to greet kids. Some teachers let their students choose the greeting. I remember one boy who liked to greet me at the door with a salute. He wouldn't enter the classroom till I said, "At ease, Sergeant." Before the Covid-19 pandemic, one colleague of mine used to have a special handshake for each child in her class. There was no way I could have done that; I wouldn't have been able to keep them straight. My friend Diane, who teaches grade one, plops a chair in the doorway of her classroom each morning and takes a seat. This way, she can look directly into her students' eyes when she says good morning. Diane calls her chair "the tollbooth"—no passing till you say hello.

Whatever type of greeting you choose, I'd recommend some general guidelines. In fact, if I were writing my own how-to paper on welcoming children, I would list the following ten steps. They're in no particular order. I'm sure Madison would approve of the list.

How to Greet Children at School

1. Stand in the doorway, or, if you have little ones, sit in a chair.
2. Look each child in the eye.
3. Smile.
4. Use your kids' names.
5. Give each student your full attention.
6. Say something encouraging, such as: "Nice to see you," "I'm glad you're here," or "We're going to need your good math skills today."
7. Use a nonverbal greeting: a wink, a wave, a thumbs-up, or an elbow bump.
8. Notice something about the child and comment on it: "You got your hair cut!" or "Just how many key chains are on that backpack?"
9. Ask a question about something they're learning in class: "In order to get inside, what's three times three?"
10. Ask questions about their lives: "How was your soccer game?" "We missed you yesterday. Are you feeling better?" "So, Anthony, what did your sister have to say about that how-to paper?"

The Box

If I were to ask you which things you are most likely to find in a grade school classroom, what would you guess? I'll give you a clue. It's not pencils. It's not markers. It isn't World's Greatest Teacher mugs. Give up? It's boxes. Look around the classroom of any elementary school teacher, and you will see boxes everywhere—on the counters, in the cupboards, on top of the cabinets, under the sink, in the desks, on the tables. In our classrooms, we have storage boxes, pencil boxes, theme boxes, costume boxes, and, in December, boxes with cans of pork and beans and Campbell's soup for the food drive. There are lunch boxes, ball boxes, recycling boxes, and prize boxes that students can pick from on Fridays if they did all their homework. We have boxes for science supplies, math manipulatives, holiday decorations, and Pokémon cards and other contraband that will be returned to kids at the end of the day because Pokémon was more interesting than math. And we also have plenty of shoeboxes on hand to turn into dioramas, valentine mailboxes, bunny cage houses, and emergency homes for caterpillars that were brought in with love after recess.

There was one box in my classroom that was just mine. It was my treasure box. A painted wooden box with a metal clasp, it sat on the table behind my desk. In it, I kept treasures that I had collected over the years at school: cards from parents, messages from the principal, drawings that children had made for me, and cute notes from the kids, including one that had been slipped into the pocket of my suit jacket on the last day of school: "I will miss you," it said simply. Another child wrote, "Mr. Done, you are almost my favorite teacher I ever had." My treasure box also held some gifts I'd received from students: a bracelet with those little plastic letter beads spelling out my name, a small stuffed animal that had once been a student's favorite, and a half-used candle that a third grader brought from home because she thought I'd like the smell.

Sometimes when I was having a rough day at work, I would open my box and look at my treasures. It always cheered me up. Oftentimes, the kids' notes were filled with hearts drawn with pink and red Magic Marker, lots of exclamation points (a child's favorite punctuation mark), scribbled-out words, and plenty of misspelled ones ("Mr. Done, you are the beast teacher!").

Some of the notes from parents were special too. Alexandra's dad wrote, "My daughter calls me your name by accident." A note from Wyatt's grandma read "During vacation, Wyatt said he didn't miss his friends. Just you." Isabel's mom tried to bribe me: "What do I have to do to get my son into your class? What kind of wine do you like?" One note came the day after a school shooting in another state: "Thank you for keeping my son safe while he is in your care." Another arrived after a parent chaperoned on a field trip: "I don't know what you make, but it's not enough!" I saved a note from one mom because it sounded like a missing person's report: "Hailey's father will be picking her up today. His name is Ed. He drives a Bronco and will be wearing a baseball cap." A card from Cleneisha's mom was a real surprise: "Thank you for helping me learn how to read." I found out later that she was reading all the books I sent home each week with her daughter. And one note completely choked me up: "You were a parent to my son when I couldn't be there. Cancer sucks."

Not everything in my treasure box was written to me. It also contained love notes I had found from one student to another: "Will you be my girlfriend? Please circle yes, no, or maybe." There were Mother's Day messages that I'd copied because they made me smile: "Dear Mom, you are special because you clean the dog throw-up." And I even had a few notes written to my teacher friends that I had asked to copy because they cracked me up, like the one a first grader wrote to my colleague Laura Schmidt: "Ms shit is buytufl." Laura said that this particular child wrote her lots of notes and often left out the *m* in her last name.

The children's drawings of me always put a smile on my face. In them, my legs and arms were often pencil thin. My neckties were full of stripes or polka dots. My head was frequently as round as a bowling ball. On my face, I'd usually have a banana-shaped smile, button-blue eyes, and a backward-C nose. A couple of years back, I noticed a change in the way my students drew my hair. In my early years of teaching, the kids would draw me with a full head of hair. Toward the end of my career, the top of my head looked more like Charlie Brown's. Only once did a student draw me with big muscles. It was the week before report cards came out, and I had told my students I was finishing up their grades. Nick, who was worried about his math grade, drew a picture of me with huge Popeye arms. When I asked him if he was trying to butter me up, he grinned and giggled. One year, when I sported a mustache and a beard, the drawings of me were pretty funny. I looked either like an apostle, a druggie, or a werewolf. Whenever I put a drawing or note into my treasure box, I'd always try to write the name of the child and the date on the back so that I wouldn't forget.

Children like to draw their teachers. And when they do, we are usually depicted standing in one of two places: either in front of the classroom beside a desk with a math problem behind us on the board or outside under a giant sun (often with a dimpled face, sometimes wearing sunglasses) and a Lucky Charms rainbow swooping over our heads. No matter where the teacher is standing, we always wear a giant smile that stretches from ear to ear. Once in a while, kids' drawings of their teacher will end up on the whiteboard in the staff room or on a teacher's Facebook feed because they made her laugh. Jill posted a drawing that one of her kindergartners had made of her. Jill colors her hair blond. Her student drew Jill's hair bright yellow, and in the middle of her head added her dark roots.

One day I referred to my treasure box as my "love box," and the name stuck. It made sense to call it that. *That's* what it was full of. Over the years, I filled up my love box several times. When it was full, I'd take the contents home, then start another.

Every teacher should have a love box. Whenever I had student teachers, I'd always give them one like mine at the close of our time together. My last student teacher was Kathy. The children called her Miss Kathy. At the end of her assignment, my third graders and I held a little party for her in the classroom. After our cookies and juice, it was time to give Miss Kathy her present. The children and I clustered around her, and two of my girls presented the gift.

"Excuse the taping job," I said to Kathy with a wink. "I had some help."

My presenters had also wrapped the box. They used masking tape instead of Scotch.

"It's beautiful," she declared, peeling off the tape. Soon Kathy uncovered her gift and held it up. "What's this?"

"A love box!" the class chorused. They knew what a love box was. I'd shown them mine. And I'd told them that I was going to give Miss Kathy one. Kathy also knew what a love box was. We'd laughed together at my Charlie Brown hair.

"Oh, thank you," Kathy half sang. She opened the lid. In it was a card from me with her name on it.

"That's to start you off," I added. "You can read it later."

"Thank you," she said again. Then she smiled at the kids and gave the box a hug. "I will cherish it."

I looked at the children, who were all smiling, and grinned at them. Then I looked back at Kathy. "Now we have a surprise for you." I turned to the kids. "Are you ready?"

"Yes!" they chirruped.

"Okay . . . *Go!*"

The children dashed to their desks, pulled out what they'd been hiding, then hurried back holding pieces of paper that they handed to Miss Kathy. In her hands, she held thirty-two drawings—all of her. In some of them, suns were wearing sunglasses. In others, Miss Kathy stood under rainbows. In every drawing, her huge smile stretched from one ear all the way to the other.

Pinterest Perfect

When preparing for a new school year, it's fun for teachers to visit online sites such as Pinterest and Instagram and look at all the ideas for setting up a classroom. On these sites, you'll find circus-themed rooms with pennants and bunting, jungle classrooms full of desks wrapped with butcher paper and painted to look like jeeps, and pirate-themed rooms with the teacher's desk renamed The Captain's Quarters. Though a lot of these ideas are clever and inspiring, looking at them can also leave you feeling discouraged and that you don't measure up. These sites can make already tired teachers feel like they have to do more and be more. Whenever I scrolled through those Pinterest-perfect classrooms, I'd think, *Where did these teachers get the money to buy all this stuff? How did they find the time? Where did they hide the mess?* Another problem with these sites is that once you start checking them out, they never leave you alone! After going on Pinterest a few times, I received regular email notifications from it with titles such as: "Classroom Makeovers Picked Just for You" and "Discover Your Desktop Today!" It felt like Pinterest was spying on me.

Before the internet, teachers obviously didn't have to deal with sites like Pinterest. We didn't have to contend with Instagram featuring before and after classroom shots, or bulletin board "reveals," or posts followed by dozens of hashtags: #myclassroompics, #schooldecor, #lookatallthemoneyIspentonmyroom! The only classrooms that teachers would typically see were the ones in their own schools. So, there wasn't much to compare yours to. In the old days, all teachers set up their rooms in pretty much the same way. You'd put up a few posters that you had laminated. If the laminating machine wasn't hot enough, the plastic on the corners of your posters would peel off, so you tried (not too successfully) to repair it with Scotch tape. The titles on everyone's bulletin boards had the exact same construction paper letters because the dye-cut machine in the staff room cut letters in only one font. On your desk, your pencils sat in frozen orange juice cans that you had rinsed out and covered with contact paper. If you wanted to get fancy, you'd turn empty laundry detergent boxes into file boxes and cover them with the same paper.

The key to not getting discouraged when looking at Pinterest-perfect classrooms is to remind yourself of what's really going on. There's a reason those images look so flawless. Have you figured it out? *There are never any children in them!* As soon as kids enter those pristine classrooms, the empty cubbies will be stuffed with backpacks, the supply table will become messy, and by the end of the day, the clean carpet will end up covered with scraps of paper, stray supplies, and the tiny paper circles from the hole punch. The children will not match the decor! Also, bear in mind that those perfect photos never show you the whole picture. They do not reveal the piles of correcting that are just out of sight of the camera or the ones that the teachers shoved into the closet right before the photo shoot. Remember: Those Pinterest pins do not represent typical classrooms. Regular classrooms have clutter on the counters, stains on the rug, and poop in the hamster cage.

My classroom was certainly never Pinterest worthy. There were plenty of times that it looked like the Cat in the Hat had just let out Thing 1 and Thing 2. I did not keep my supplies in Mason jars tied with raffia. I never lined my bookshelves with fabric or trimmed my file cabinet with washi tape. I didn't color coordinate my books, put up burlap wreaths, or hang giant paper pompoms from the ceiling. My pencil baskets were not labeled with cute tags that said "Sharp," "Dull," and "New." If I labeled them at all, they would have read "With Teeth Marks" and "Without." My desk usually resembled the return counter at Target the day after Christmas. In fact, my desk was always covered with homework that needed to be graded, tests that ought to have been corrected, papers that should have been filed, and school flyers that I'd forgotten to pass out. Under all those papers would be a thumb drive, a whistle, the stapler, a sheet of stickers, a whiteboard eraser, the remote to the projector, my lesson planner, several to-do lists, the school calendar (with all the holidays highlighted), and a sticky note reminding me to clean my desk. The desktop on my computer didn't look much different.

I tried to keep my classroom tidy. I just wasn't very good at it. Those books on getting organized don't work for classrooms anyway. Take the popular *The Life-Changing Magic of Tidying Up,* for example. The author recommends discarding anything that doesn't spark joy. Well, teachers can't do that! If we did, our kids wouldn't get any papers returned because we all would have tossed out our correcting baskets. The author also suggests that when organizing your home, you consider your things' "feelings." She asks: "Are your clothes happy being squashed on the shelf?" "Are your socks really thrilled to be balled up?" When I read this, I thought, *Is she kidding?* If I had considered the feelings of the things in my classroom, my wall-mounted pencil sharpener would deserve a vacation. The chewed-up pencils would have grounds to file a class-action suit for harassment. And my poor stapler that had been banged on for decades would need therapy.

All teachers want their classrooms to be inviting, but that doesn't mean you have to spend more than your student loan fitting it out with new items from Lakeshore, Ikea, and Amazon *and* take up weeks of your hard-earned summer decorating it. You do not need to spend your free time building jungle huts. Teachers have more important things to do. And remember: It's not about the *stuff.* I once worked with a teacher whose room was an absolute showplace. Her windows had gingham curtains that she'd made herself. The spines of her books all lined up perfectly. Her stickers were organized by season. Nothing was ever out of place. If I opened her desk, I'm sure that none of her thumbtacks would have been mixed up with her paper clips. I bet that none of the circles in her watercolor trays looked like mud puddles either. Despite all this, this woman's teaching was just mediocre. She used a ton of worksheets. Her students hardly ever got out of their seats. She rarely smiled. Yes, organized and colorful classrooms loaded with goodies are nice, but far more important are classrooms full of children who feel cared for and special. And what's important is *you*: your passion, your enthusiasm, your creativity, and your connection with kids. These are the things that matter most.

Baseball, Hot Dogs, Reading Rugs, and Show-and-Tell

It was the week of Halloween. I was sitting in my classroom at the American School in Budapest, Hungary, sharing some Halloween poems with my fourth graders, when I read the words *trick or treat.*

"What's *that*?" Tamás called out.

Oh, yeah, I thought, *I'm not in Kansas anymore. European children don't go trick-or-treating.* I closed my book and began to explain. "Well, in America, the children dress up in costumes on Halloween. And when it gets dark, they go outside with bags, walk up to a home, and knock on the door or ring the doorbell." I stood up and pretended to ring one. "*Ding-dong!*" I sang. The American kids smiled and nodded. The non-Americans, including Tamás, sat round eyed and open mouthed.

I continued. "Then someone opens the door." I pantomimed opening one. "Usually this person has a big bowl of candy." I held up my hands as if I were holding a giant bowl. Tamás clutched his head with both hands. "The children open their bags and shout 'Trick or treat!' and the person with the bowl drops a piece of candy into each one. After that, the kids run to the next place and do it all over again. This goes on all night until their bags are full."

"Did *you* do that?" a child called out.

"Oh yes," I said. Then I grinned. "But I used a pillowcase. You can get more candy in a pillowcase than in a bag."

"What kind of candy do you get?" one of the kids asked.

"Oh, everything." I started listing them. "Starburst."

Squeals.

"Kit Kats."

Cries.

"Reese's Peanut Butter Cups."

More squeals and cries. Tamás started banging his fist on his desk.

Then I lowered my voice and grinned again. "And sometimes they might even give you *two* pieces of candy."

Tamás couldn't take it anymore. He covered his ears, collapsed on his desk, and cried, "Americans have all the fun!"

It is said that when you move out of your country, you learn to see things from a different perspective. It's true. When you teach in a different country, you also become aware of aspects about your profession that you took for granted or never noticed before.

When I was teaching in Hungary, one day I visited a country school to see what it was like. A teacher named Eszter took me around the campus, showing me different parts of the school: the library, the cafeteria, and the computer lab with those crazy Hungarian keyboards. The Hungarian keyboard has two different *a*'s, four different *u*'s, and the *z* is where the *y* should be. Believe me, they need all those letters. A lot of Hungarian words are so long that they look like winners in a tongue twister tournament. *Bye* is *viszontlátásra*, *plane* is *repülőgép*, and *car* is *személygépkocsi*. Try saying that one five times fast.

At the end of our tour, Eszter and I ended up in her classroom, where she pointed out her new reading rug and said, "It's American."

"It came from America?" I asked.

"No, not the rug itself. The *idea*."

I looked confused. "What do you mean?"

"Reading rugs are new to Hungary," Eszter explained. "The whole idea of having children sit on a rug while their teacher reads to them is from *your* country."

"Really?" I said, delightfully surprised. "I've never thought about it before. I just assumed elementary classrooms all over the world have reading rugs." I smiled. *What a nice thing to be associated with.*

While working in Hungary, I discovered something else about an American education that I had never considered. Actually, it is something that parents in other countries admire and respect. I learned it from a mom named Eva.

Eva and her family were from the Netherlands. Eva's daughter, Sophie, was one of my fourth graders in Budapest. Sophie had attended the American School since she was in kindergarten. As the name of the school suggests, we followed an American program. Sophie's family would soon be moving back to the Netherlands, where she would begin attending a Dutch public school. One afternoon, Eva dropped by my classroom to say good-bye. I took the opportunity to ask what she had liked best about the school and the American system. Eva didn't even have to think about it. Her answer: "You teach children how to speak." I was surprised by her response. "Don't all schools?"

"Oh no," Eva said. "Not in Europe. In European schools, kids are not taught how to speak. They aren't given those opportunities. I didn't learn to get up in front of a group and address an audience until college. In the American system, it's different. Children are talking in front of the class from the time they're little." She shook her head. "When Sophie goes back home, she won't have this anymore."

I thought about what Eva had said. She was right. In American schools, students get up in front of their peers and give presentations all the time. They share their reports, their writing, their projects. From kindergarten on up, children are bringing in half their bedrooms for show-and-tell. It was the same when I went through the system. I guess I'd taken it for granted.

"And," Eva continued, "you don't just teach kids to speak, you teach them to speak with humor."

I didn't expect her to say that either. "What do you mean?"

Eva explained. "Once a month, I attend the meetings of the International Women's Association and listen to women give speeches. These women are from all over the world. The Americans stand out. They begin their talks with humor and inject it into their presentations. The European women don't do this." I was smiling as she spoke. "And I'm not the only one who feels this way. My husband agrees. Several moms I know think as we do." Eva nodded. "Yes, without question, *this* is what I will miss most about your American way of teaching."

Gone with the Overhead Projector

Years ago, I brought in an old rotary phone and showed it to my third graders. They were entranced. Few had ever used one before. The children lined up, and I let them put their fingers in the dial holes, wind the plastic wheel, and wait for it to return all the way back to its original position before dialing the next number. As one of my girls dialed, she announced, "It takes so *long*!"

Another time in class, I was explaining how manual typewriters work. My kids could not grasp that as you're typing and come to the end of a line, you have to push a lever in order to bring the carriage back to the left side of the page so that you can type the next line. A few days later, I brought in my dusty old Remington that I had used in college and watched my students type words, push the return lever, and lock up the keys. They loved it. *I*, on the other hand, felt like that old Remington. Like a relic. I had a similar relic moment when I was walking with my class on a field trip, and a child pointed to a phone booth at a gas station and asked what it was.

But my most surprising relic moment occurred the day my students and I were reading a story, and a child asked what a chalkboard was. *You're kidding me.* I ended up showing the kids a YouTube video of a teacher writing on one. I also played them a clip of how we used to clean the chalkboard erasers in the old days by banging two of them together while standing in Pig-Pen-like clouds of dust. Of course, after that, every child wanted to bang erasers.

The longer you teach, the age gap between you and your students keeps widening, and sometimes you forget just how much time has passed. Today's children have never known a world without smartphones, Netflix, Instagram, and YouTube. They've never known KFC as Kentucky Fried Chicken or when

Legos were just rectangular blocks of various sizes. Today's kids will never understand the fun of spotting the name of someone you know on the library checkout card in the back of a book or the thrill of walking into class and seeing that the teacher has rolled in the TV cart. Today's children will never know what it's like to fold an actual map the correct way, cover a textbook with a brown grocery bag, do their homework without Google, search the Yellow Pages, drive to a movie rental store, drop off film at the drive-through, or sit through commercial breaks on television. They'll never experience using tiny strips of white correcting tape for typing mistakes, texting on a non-smartphone and having to press a key four times till you get the letter you want, standing in a line with nothing to do but chat with the person next to you, or rolling down a car window. Once, I was overseeing a student car wash for a school fund-raiser and watched two girls cleaning a car window that was rolled up. One girl was outside the car and the other in it. The girl who was outside wanted the window lowered, so she tapped on it and said, "Scroll down!"

The world is changing quickly—it has advanced since I started typing this page—and the teaching profession has changed dramatically right along with it. When I started teaching, there obviously were no classroom computers. Teachers kept track of absent and tardy kids in attendance registers and recorded grades in grade books, which we averaged by hand at the end of each quarter. The report cards, which we also handwrote, usually came in triplicate: the top copy for the parent, the second copy (generally pink) for the teacher, and the third copy (blue) for the office, which you could never read very well if you didn't push down hard enough with your pen. When computers first arrived, we had Apple IIs, floppy disks, and dot-matrix printers. We didn't use the computers for much more than playing the video games *The Oregon Trail, Number Munchers, Reader Rabbit,* and *Where in the World Is Carmen Sandiego?* Needless to say, there was no such thing as email. Every morning, you'd go to your mailbox and pick up the daily bulletin with the news of the day that the secretary had typed and copied before the start of school. On Valentine's Day, the paper was pink.

There were no phones in the classrooms either. If you wanted to call the office, and you didn't send a lucky student with a note, you pressed a button on the wall to ring the secretary. She or the school clerk would speak to you through the intercom while the whole class listened. If you needed to contact a parent, you waited in line for the one phone in the staff room. To make copies, you used a mimeograph machine that teachers called "the ditto machine." The ink smelled faintly sweet. Your dittos came out slightly wet. To play music in class, you counted the rings on the record to find the right song. Filmstrips were shown on projectors accompanied by cassette tapes that dinged to tell you when to advance the frame. If the recorder ate the tape, you untangled it gently and then used a pencil to wind it back into place.

When you wanted to show your students a video, you rolled in the large TV that you had checked out on the audiovisual calendar in the library. If you wanted to use the TV the day before Thanksgiving or winter break, you raced to the library on the first day of school to sign up for it because everyone wanted it on those two days. Movies were delivered to the school in tin canisters from the county office. If you wanted to project something onto the screen, you put a plastic transparency on the glass plate of the overhead projector, and when you wrote on it, you ended up with Vis-à-Vis marker on the side of your hand. Maps were something that you pulled down, then tugged on to get back up. If you yanked on it just right, it rolled up on the first try. When kids asked for calculators, we'd say, "You won't have a calculator wherever you go." Boy, were we wrong.

But it's not just the *things* in classrooms that have changed. Since I started teaching, the whole system has seen sweeping changes: The coursework to become a teacher has grown significantly. There are more requirements. In elementary school, the lower grades have become increasingly academic. Thirty years ago, teachers pretty much worked in isolation. We closed our doors and did what we thought was right. Now teachers collaborate in teams. There's far less autonomy. Today's students work in groups much more than they used to. Nowadays, we see tables and chairs on wheels to make classroom seating more flexible. We've seen the incorporation of innovative learning methods developed by tech companies, such as Google's Genius Hour. When I began teaching, standardized testing was minimal. Now it's high stakes. Schools were not data driven. Now it's all about the data.

Without a doubt, the number one change in schools has been technology.

Schools have embraced the digital revolution, and technology is redefining the way we teach. Screens and LCD projectors have replaced whiteboards. Laptops have taken the place of textbooks. iPads have supplanted notebooks. The internet has ousted those heavy sets of encyclopedias, cloud storage has usurped file cabinets, and Google Drive has displaced hard copies. Today the three Rs have gone digital. Children read, write, and do arithmetic on their devices. Lessons are delivered on interactive Smart Boards. Instead of taking notes, kids snap photos with their phones. Students complete assignments and take tests online, and they send their work to their parents to view in their digital portfolios. If a child is home sick, he can watch the whole class in real time. If teachers need a chaperone on a field trip, they contact parents through an app. If a parent can't make it to a school performance, not to worry—they're livestreamed. No longer do students rely on getting information from just the teacher. Now they can google anything in seconds, then watch three YouTube videos on the subject. Technology is moving so quickly that some things that aren't even old, like those Smart Boards, are becoming obsolete. So much is virtual in this day and age that it wouldn't surprise me if in the future teachers will be holograms like Princess Leia in *Star Wars*.

Despite the gargantuan transformation in education, not everything has changed. I'm happy about that. At the end of the day, teachers still plan, prepare, and deliver lessons. We just have more tools now. We still think about, care for, and worry about our charges. In today's world, there is much more to worry about. Despite the ever-increasing challenges of our profession, we still aim to engage, motivate, and inspire our students. And after work, we still go home and talk about our kids.

The Curriculum

Smart

L essons. They're at the core of what teachers do. Day in and day out, we take the words from our plan books and give them life. In our lessons, we grab kids' attention, state our objectives, teach skills and concepts, check for understanding, provide guided and independent practice, review what they've learned, then clean up before the bell rings.

Out of all the lessons I ever gave, there was one that I considered to be most important. No matter what grade I was teaching, I'd give it at the beginning of each school year. I recommend that you do too. It doesn't matter what age level or subject you teach. The lesson is this: Teach your students that there are different ways to be smart. Here is how the lesson went with a class of third graders:

I'd begin by asking my kids what they thought it meant to be smart. The children would reply, "When you read fast." "If you're good at math." "Being a good speller." Most of their answers would involve reading and math, which made sense. This was their experience. Reading and math receive the most attention in elementary school. Students practice these two subjects a great deal for the standardized tests. To most kids, there are two ways to be smart: if you're good in math or you're a good reader.

Next, I would write the following words on the board: "number smart" and "word smart." "These are two ways to be smart," I'd explain. "We say that people who are good with numbers are *number smart*, and those who are good in reading and writing are *word smart*." I'd tap the words as I said them.

Now would begin the important part of the lesson. I'd take a step toward my students and pause. "But," I'd say, "what if I were to tell you that there are *other* ways to be smart?" This question would always pique the children's interest. You could see it on their faces. Most had never heard a teacher talk this way.

"How many of you like to sing?" I'd ask. Hands would rise and heads would nod. "How many of you sing all the time? You even sing in the shower." Kids would giggle. The nods would get bigger. I'd look at the nodders. "*You* boys and girls are most likely what we call *musically smart*." I'd write the two words on the board—not under *number smart* and *word smart*, but beside them, so that they appeared equal in importance.

"And how many of you are good at playing chess or making models or putting things together?" More hands would shoot up. "*Ah*," I'd say, stretching out the word, "*you* children may well be what we refer to as *spatially smart*." I would pronounce the new word slowly as I wrote it on the board. When finished, I'd turn back to the kids and ask, "And how many of you are good at art? You like to draw and paint and color." Lots of hands would go up this time. "*Aha!*" I'd exclaim. "*You* kids with your hands up are what we would call *visually smart*." I'd then write *visually* on the board, sounding out each syllable as I wrote it.

The next question would always elicit the biggest reaction. That's why I'd save it for the end. "And . . . how many of you are good at jumping and running and climbing, and you like to move around?" Before I could even finish, boys and girls all over the room would start popping out of their seats, shouting, "Me! Me! Me!" *Right on cue*. Smiling, I would tell them, "The term we use to describe you kids is *body smart*." And I'd add it to our list.

At this moment, I'd explain that another way to say *body smart* is *kinesthetically smart*, and I'd write *kinesthetic* on the board too. Immediately the word-smart children, delighted to see such a long, spiffy word, would begin mouthing it to feel it on their tongues. I'd also point out that kids who are kinesthetically smart like to fiddle with things, take objects apart, and touch everything in front of them. When I said this, I'd stare square at a child who happened to be fiddling with his name tag. He'd grin, happy to have been caught.

By now, most of the body-smart kids would be smiling. For some of them, this would be the first time they had ever thought of themselves as smart. Once, after hearing that someone can be body smart, one of my third graders, who struggled in reading but excelled in athletics, sprang out of his seat, threw up his arms like Rocky Balboa after the winning knockout, and cried, "I'm smart! I'm *smart*!" He'd never considered it before. "You *are*!" I replied, pointing at him. Then I looked out at the whole class. "You *all* are.

"You see, boys and girls," I'd continue, "it's not just children who are strong with numbers and words who are smart. Kids who are good in music, sports, dancing, and building things are smart too." To underscore my point, I made eye contact with the children that I knew were good at these things.

At this point in the lesson, I'd explain that people can be smart in more than one way. To give an example, I'd tell my students that I considered myself visually and musically smart, as well as smart with words. But I was definitely not spatially smart. I was never good at putting things together. I wasn't body smart either; I could never run very fast or throw a ball very far. I'd also share that I wasn't particularly math smart, but the kids would never believe this. To children, anyone who can add and subtract big numbers on the board is smart in math.

"And you know what?" I'd add, pointing to the words on the board. "All these different kinds of smart are equal. No smart is better or more important than the others. For instance, a person who is musically smart is just as smart as a person who is number smart, and someone who is body smart is no less smart than one who is smart with words. You see?" Whenever I'd tell my kids this, you could see relief on some of their faces.

I'd say all this not just for those children who hadn't considered themselves smart before but also for the students who excelled in school and to whom reading and math came easily. It's good for these kids to hear that their classmates who might not read and solve math problems as well as they do are just as smart as them. Many of your top students will not have considered this.

I would not be finished with the lesson just yet. I wanted the children to keep thinking about what I had taught them. "In school," I'd ask the class, "which kinds of smart do you think are *not* valued highly?" The kids would call out, "Spatial!" "Body smart!" "Musical!" Even third graders understand this already. Then I'd lean in to them and soften my voice the way teachers do when they want to make sure that everyone is listening closely. "What if schools tested running and jumping, dancing and singing, drawing and building things? What would you say to *that*?" Immediately the classroom would fill with cheers. It always did.

After the lesson, I'd give each child a paper listing the six different kinds of smart. Their task was to circle the types of smart they thought they were. Now, you'd think that young students would circle all six terms, but they don't. Children take this kind of activity very seriously. Even at a young age, they know their strengths and weaknesses. And they're honest about it too. When the kids were finished, I'd collect the papers, and we'd tally the results together on the board. I would do this so that everyone could see just how different we all really are.

At the end of the day, I'd ask my students to take their papers home and explain to their parents what they had learned. (One of the best homework assignments is to have kids teach what they learned that day in school.) I'd also give the children a second copy for their parents to fill out. The following morning, everyone in the class would share what their parents circled on *their* papers. I'd tally the parents' answers beside the kids' to again make the point that everyone is different. The children were always excited to share their findings, and the discussion was always lively.

One morning, as we went around the room listening to the parents' responses, it was Zeke's turn to share.

"And what did your mom and dad say?" I asked him.

"Well," Zeke answered, looking down at his paper with a cringe, "it didn't go so well."

I looked surprised. "Why not?"

"Well," he repeated slowly, "my mom and dad got into a fight."

"Oh, my," I said. "What happened?"

Zeke made an embarrassed face. "My dad said he was visually smart, and my mom said there's no way in—" He stopped. "Well, you know."

"Go on."

"My mom won."

"How so?"

"She pointed to her desk—it's really neat—and said, '*This* is a visual person's desk.' Then she pointed to my dad's desk—it's really messy—and said, '*This* is not!'"

Note to teacher: If you'd like to give this lesson, here's a simple refresher on learning styles to help you out: Verbal/linguistic learners, or word-smart kids, like to go on and on when sharing about their weekend, tend not to raise their hands, and can convince you to buy multiple rolls of wrapping paper for the school fund-raiser even though you don't need any. Logical/mathematical learners, or number-smart children, are the first ones to discover your math mistakes. They are the ones you call on when you can't get your computer to work too. Bodily/kinesthetic, or body-smart students, press down so hard on their pencils that you can read their writing through to the other side of the paper. These kids also like to connect Magic Markers into one giant marker and make happy faces on their pink erasers by stabbing them with their pencils.

Words

"Does anyone know what *micro* means?" I asked my third graders as I wrote it on the easel. The children were seated around me on the rug. I was starting to teach the kids about prefixes.

"Small," Claire answered.

"Very good. Can anyone give me a word with *micro* in it?"

"Microphone!" someone volunteered.

"Microwave!" another offered.

"Microsoft!" Dominic chimed in.

"But Microsoft isn't small," Jackson countered. "It's huge."

Claire turned to Jackson. "But they make small things."

"Thank you, Claire," I said. Next, I wrote "tele" on the easel. "Now, can any of you give me a word beginning with *tele*?"

"Television!"

"Telephone!"

Blake shot up on his knees. "*Telepathetic!*"

I suppressed a laugh. "That's tele*pathic*, Blake. But close." I continued. "Here's a new one," I said, adding "trans" to the board. "Who knows a word starting with *trans*?"

"Transportation!"

"Transformers!"

"Transmission!"

"Trans fat!"

Everyone laughed.

"What's *that*?" Aiden asked.

Derek raised his hand and shouted, "I know! I know!"

I called on him.

"It's bad fats," he explained. "My mom says there are good fats and bad fats, and trans fats are bad fats, and that's why she doesn't buy Girl Scout cookies, because they have trans fats in them."

"Thank you for the explanation, Derek."

After discussing several more prefixes and their meanings, I wrote a list of root words beside them, and we talked about those too. Then I explained the assignment. The children would take a couple of the prefixes and attach them to a root word to invent their own new words. The kids could use as many prefixes as they wanted. As examples, I explained that they could create a micro-tele-graph, or a terra-trans-mobile, or a sub-aquatic-cycle. After coming up with their new words, they were to write them down, and I would check them. Then they could illustrate them any way they liked. The children excitedly got to work.

A few minutes later, Kevin skidded up to me, holding his paper against his chest. I was seated at my desk with a couple of other kids. When we were alone and the coast was clear, Kevin showed me his paper as if we were playing cards and he didn't want anyone else to see his hand. I smiled when I saw it. Under his drawing, he'd written: "super-sonic-mono-micro-photo-aquatic-trans-tele dog bowl."

"Wow," I said with a chuckle, "that's some word. I think your dog will love it."

Kevin's cheeks dimpled. "Thanks." Then he pointed out various parts on his invention. "It also has a hovercraft, a helicopter, and a pizza oven."

"Very nice," I said. "Maybe you should really invent one."

Kevin gasped, then quickly leaned over his paper and added a c with a circle around it. He'd copyrighted it.

Teachers are word champions. We teach phonograms and sight words in reading, describing words in writing, and patterned words in spelling. On our walls hang posters with the parts of speech, figurative language, story elements, literary terms, as well as "word walls" with commonly used words that kids can refer to if they forget how to spell them. On our easels, magnets hold up large pieces of lined chart paper with the vocabulary for science, social studies, and math units. Beside these words are little pictures that we've drawn with colored markers to help our kids understand them. All day long, teachers are explaining, defining, clarifying, pointing out, breaking down, spelling out, and over-enunciating words so that students hear the *v* in *leaves*, the *r* in *library*, and the second *e* in *sincerely*. When children ask us how to spell, sometimes it feels like we are walking dictionaries. Actually, dictionaries have it way easier than teachers. They get to rest on a shelf all day. Teachers don't rest.

If you distill a teacher's job down to its simplest form, it all comes down to words. Words are the atoms, molecules, and electrons of teaching. We know that the more words kids have, the better they are at being able to read, write, and speak. We understand that students' success in school is linked to the words they know. We also know that words bring beauty and richness to our lives. The right word can create understanding, spark a laugh, and tug at a heart. Personally, I have always loved words. I like the music in them. Even as a child, I remember being captivated by words like *crimson*, *vermilion*, and *aquamarine* on the side of my crayons.

Children are word sponges. They gobble them up. They love to take compound words such as *football* and *playground* and find the smaller words inside of them. They laugh at palindromes like *kayak* and *noon*, which read the same backward and forward, and delight in tongue twisters that they can repeat for you really fast. Kids have fun writing alliterative sentences like "Big baby bunnies bounce backward" and get a charge out of funny-sounding onomatopoeia such as *beep-beep*, *glub-glub*, and *arf-arf*. Children enjoy clapping out the syllables in words to see how many there are, especially if the words have lots of them, like *kindergartner* (four), *metamorphosis* (five), and *encyclopedia* (six!). They delight in taking two words that can be used to make a contraction—say, *he* and *is*—killing off the *i*, replacing it with an apostrophe, then squishing the *he* and *is* together to make one word. They like learning that the plural of *sheep* is *sheep* and *deer* is *deer*, then testing their parents to see if they know this too. Kids enjoy learning abbreviations because it is much more fun to write *Mon.* than *Monday*, *Dec.* than *December*, and *CA* than *California*. They do not like the abbreviations for pound (*lb*) and ounce (*oz*), because these spellings are completely nutty.

Children also love big, juicy words. Just listen to any five-year-old rattle off the names of all his plastic dinosaurs or an older child tell you some of the terms used in his video games. My teacher friend Lucy had a first grader once tell her that she was being "a little overzealous." Lucy still laughs about it. Sometimes kids get so excited about learning a big new word that they want to teach it to anyone who will listen. One time, after teaching my third graders the word *environment*, a student named Rebecca was so proud to know it that she would ask every adult in the school—the secretary, the librarian, the noon supervisor—if they knew what the word meant. When Rebecca asked the principal, he scratched his head and said he couldn't remember (smart principal), so she taught him.

Of course, teaching new words to children can be highly entertaining. When introducing my kids to right angles, one of them wanted to know if there are left angles too. When reading a story to my students, I came to the word *inquire* and asked if anyone knew what it meant. A child answered, "When you sing." And once, when I pointed to an exclamation point on the board and checked to see who knew what it is called, one of my boys announced, "An excitement point!" Ever since, I've called exclamation marks excitement points. It's just better.

Teaching words to children who are learning English can be a lot of fun as well. ELL students (English language learners)—also referred to as EL (English learners), ESL (English as a second language), and EAL (English as an additional language)—crack up when hearing idioms like "It's raining cats and dogs" and "He has ants in his pants." When I was teaching in Europe and told my kids that in America frogs say *ribbit*, pigs say *oink*, and roosters say *cock-a-doodle-do*, the children used to fall out of their chairs in hysterics. Frogs, pigs, and roosters don't say these things in their first languages. From time to time, ELL students will come up with cute new words and phrases when they can't think of the correct way to say something. When one of my kids didn't know the word *eel*, he called it an "electric snake." When a student couldn't remember the word *adjective*, she renamed it a "dress-up word." After a child had been out sick, she said she'd had "Shrek throat." Occasionally, English language learners ask questions that you've never thought about before, like the day one of my girls asked me why *chilly* means cold if *chili* is hot, and the time another asked, "If you rake with a rake, saw with a saw, and hammer with a hammer, why don't you broom with a broom?" Good question.

Sometimes these children get annoyed with their new language. Once, I was reading with a group of ELL students when the word *vomit* appeared in the text. I explained that *vomit* was the more adult way to say *throw up*. To that, one of my girls exclaimed, "Why do people change the words when they grow up? I want to say *throw up*!" I said she could. And every so often, an English language learner will get downright mad at English: "Why don't you say the *k* in *know*?" "How come *ph* sounds like *f*?" "*Bologna* should end with an *e*!" And: "Wait! *Read* sounds like *reed* and *red*? This is crazy!" And don't even get me started on words ending with -*ough*. When explaining to ELL kids that *through*, *rough*, and *cough* all sound different, sometimes they squeeze their skulls and scream because it makes no sense.

All teachers know to have word-rich classrooms with well-stocked libraries filled with biographies and fantasies, nonfiction and graphic novels, picture books and every single edition of *Diary of a Wimpy Kid*. But in addition to word-rich classrooms, children need word-rich teachers. How do you become one? The key is to talk about words. All. The. Time. Introduce your students to famous quotations, idioms, and proverbs. Talk about collective nouns such as a "school of fish" and a "cache of jewels"; easily confused words like *desert* and *dessert* (teacher trick: one *s* = sand, two *s*'s = soup and salad); words that go together, like *salt* and *pepper* and *black* and *white* (you would never say these in reverse); words with alternative spellings like *theatre* and *colour*; and words that we borrowed from other languages, including *boulevard* from French, *mosquito* from Spanish, and *karate* from Japanese.

Once, after a student handed in his homework late, I shouted, "Hallelujah!" Surprised, a Hebrew-speaking student called out, "Where'd you learn *that*?" I told him it's an English word, to which he responded, "You stole it from us." When introducing a new word to your class, treat it as if you're giving them a present. Be excited to share it. Give it a bit of a buildup and, with a twinkle in your voice, say, "I have a new word I'd like to teach you today."

When speaking with children, use a rich vocabulary. If the sky is dark and gray, say *ominous*. If you hear birds in the morning, use *mellifluous* (a personal favorite). If a student is super social, tell her she's *gregarious*. She'll teach the word to all her friends. If a child reads everything in sight, call him a *voracious* reader. If your hair is a mess, say it's *disheveled*. (On second thought, maybe not. After you've explained what it means, your students will use it to describe the state of your desk as well.) And don't shy away from using vocabulary that might be considered too difficult for children. It's okay if kids don't understand a word right away. Children need to hear new words multiple times before they learn them. Sometimes it takes hearing a word five, ten, or fifteen times before they really know it. Words are like seeds. They need time to take root. Also, whenever possible, don't just *say* a new word. If you can, *show it*. Draw a picture or act it out. As an example, when teaching a snazzy word like *scrumptious*, rub your tummy and pretend that you're eating something absolutely delicious. Ask your kids to show you *scrumptious* too.

When you can, also try to use the specific names of things. Specificity adds richness to children's writing, thinking, and speech. Teach students the names of rocks, minerals, and precious stones such as *emerald*, *ruby*, and *amethyst*. Start with your kids' birthstones. Point out patterns in clothing: *plaid*, *checked*, *paisley*, and *herringbone*. Teach them the names of trees too: *oak* and *maple*, *sycamore* and *birch*. Begin with the trees around your school. Acquaint them with the specific names of colors and fabrics, flowers and birds. Why say "*blue*," if you can say "*teal*"? Why use *cloth* when you can use *velvet*, *silk*, or *cashmere*? Why choose *flowers* when you can choose *alyssums* and *azaleas*, *calla lilies* and *chrysanthemums*, *foxgloves* and *forget-me-nots*? These words are beautiful to the ear. In my experience, most young children can give you the names of only a couple of flowers: *rose*, *daisy*, and *tulip*. That's usually about it. Consider teaching your students a flower a week. Bring in a single flower from the supermarket, put it in a bud vase on your front table, and make that the week's flower. By the end of the year, your kids will have learned the names of dozens of them. It's pretty darling to read an eight-year-old's writing sprinkled with words like *daffodils*, *jasmine*, and *gardenias*.

Once in a while, be a little crazy with your word love too. Share your favorite words with your students and ask them theirs. Children have favorite cursive letters (it's never *Z*) and favorite multiplication facts (it's never 9 x 7—too hard). Everyone has a favorite food, book, and movie. Why shouldn't we all have favorite words too? When you encounter one in a book, shout, "I love that word!" When you write a word that you adore on the board, declare that you love it, then give the word a loud smooch. Your kids will say "Yuck!" but they will see that their teacher is a word nut—which is what you want. Big word nuts help make smaller word nuts. When you come across a great, zippy word, announce, "That's a hundred-dollar word!" If it's a really good one, say it's worth a thousand. Sample price list: eat = $5; devour = $100; brave = $5; courageous = $100; talkative = $5; loquacious = $1,000!

One way to drench children in words is to collect them. You read that correctly. Introduce a Word of the Week. Every week, ask your kids to bring in a word that they like. Have them write it down. It can be a word that they read or heard. They don't even have to know what it means; they could just like the sound of it. When it's Word of the Week time, go around the room and ask students to share. Children enjoy this time—no papers to fill in, no definitions to look up—just talking about words. I remember one day during our Word of the Week sharing, a student named Sam brought in the word *boisterous*. I asked him if he knew what it meant, and he said his mom had told him. She also said that *he* was boisterous, and that's why the word starts with *boy*.

Another way to collect words is to go on a Simile Search. Before you begin, review similes with your students so that they understand what they are. Then, using a book that you know has lots of similes, have kids hunt for them as they read. Roald Dahl's books are excellent for this. The author is a master of simile. Suppose, for instance, you're reading Dahl's *The BFG* with a group of students. Ask them to be on the lookout for similes in the text. Whenever they find one, they call out, "Simile!" Children love Simile Searches. Something wonderful happens when kids forage for similes in a book. They will root them out in other books as well and use them in their writing. Once, when scouting for similes in *James and the Giant Peach*, my students asked if they could get a minute of free time for every ten similes that they found in the book. It sounded like a good deal, so I agreed. *Teacher alert*: Do not do this! It will backfire. Children are expert simile detectives. They find every one—especially if it means getting free-time minutes.

One of the reasons kids are so good at finding similes is because they naturally speak in simile, particularly when talking about their teachers. One of Lucy's first graders noticed her laugh lines and said she had "gills like a shark." Another student of Lucy's told her that her glitter nail polish looked like sprinkle cookies. A boy in Dana's class hugged her and said, "You smell like a big ol' sausage, and I love sausage!" The same kid told Dana that her hair looked like curly fries. I had a third grader tell me that I smelled just like her dad. I found out later that we both wore the same aftershave. One of Jill's kindergartners said he loved her because she looked like his grandma. Jill was thirty-four at the time. And another one of Jill's kids said she smelled "like five luscious rainbows," then called the rest of the class over to smell her.

Every spring, I would take my class outside on a Simile Search. We'd walk around the campus to see how many we could find. I'd point to clouds and blossoms and dandelions, and the kids would come up with similes for them: "The white blossoms look like popcorn," "The clouds are as fluffy as cotton candy," "The yellow dandelions look like little suns." Or "lollipops."

On one of our simile hunts, Tyler pointed to a large spiderweb and yelled, "Look!" The children ran over to it. The strands were covered with dew. *Aha!* I thought. *There's a simile here.*

"Boys and girls," I said, pointing to the web, "look at those dew drops. What do they remind you of?" I was thinking of pearls. No one volunteered, so I decided to help them out. "I'll give you a clue. Your mom might have them."

The children scrunched up their faces. Still no answers.

"She probably keeps them in her bedroom," I added. "Maybe on her dresser or in a drawer."

"I know!" Tyler shouted.

I was sure he had it. "What is it, Tyler?"

"Pills!"

One of the best ways for children to focus on words is to have them write lists, and I suggest they write several of them at the beginning of the school year. For children, making lists is a good way to get the summer writing cobwebs out and the writing juices flowing. It's also not as intimidating as writing a paragraph or a story.

One list that my kids and I would write together in the first few weeks of school was of words that should be capitalized. All children benefit from a review of capitalization. For this lesson, I'd put a large piece of butcher paper on the whiteboard and write "Words We Capitalize" in the center of it. Then we would brainstorm all the words we could think of that should be capitalized, including the beginning of sentences, titles of books and movies, names of people, bridges, landmarks, and so on. The kids would throw out ideas, and I'd write them down as fast as I could. Under each category, I'd also give an example like this: Below "Names of Statues" (written in one color) I'd write "The Statue of Liberty" (different color). This would go on for about twenty minutes or so until I would casually say, "Okay. Nice work. We can stop now. You almost beat last year's class."

Immediately a few children would holler, "What do you mean?"

"Well," I'd continue, "last year's class made this list too, and they came up with more words to capitalize than you did. But you did great. We can stop now." Then I'd turn to the board and start taking down the paper. Instantly every child in the room would shout *"No!"* and plead with me to continue. I always enjoyed this moment. Children do not normally beg their teachers to review capitalization. As you can see, what I did here was introduce some friendly competition. When brainstorming with children, a little fun competition creates excitement. It turns up the heat on any lesson.

Of course I would continue. I never planned to stop. I'd tell the kids how many words the previous year's class thought of (if I couldn't remember, I'd make up a number), and my students would not let me finish the activity until they beat it. And when they did, they would jump out of their seats and cheer and hoot as if they had just won the World Cup. Their prize? An old trophy I picked up at a garage sale. On it, I'd written: "The Word Cup."

Another list I always made with my kids was titled "Synonyms for *Said*." This is a list of words such as *yell* and *scream*, *whimper* and *wail*, *giggle* and *grumble*—any way to say something. Many teachers brainstorm synonym lists with their students, but oftentimes they just write the words. By only listing the words, you're missing out on a lot of the fun. When creating a list of *said* synonyms with children, every time you add a word, you or your students should also demonstrate how it sounds. Let your kids snicker and boom, brag and mumble, growl and talk back (a child's favorite). Begin this activity with your whole class, just like I did for the capitalization lesson, brainstorming the words together on a large piece of butcher paper. After a while, let the children get into groups of two or three and spread out around the room to continue their lists together. Expect it to get noisy. All around the classroom, your students will be howling and moaning, sighing and sobbing, whispering and cackling. For a word to count on their lists, I had one rule: You have to be able to say the word when expressing it in the manner described on the paper. I'll explain. Take *groan*, for example. You can groan while voicing a word, so *groan* counts, but you cannot whistle as you're speaking, so *whistle* doesn't. I had final approval on whether a word counted or not. One year when my kids were writing their synonyms, I vetoed *sneeze*, *burp*, and *gargle* because, as I explained, you can*not* articulate words while doing any of these things. In all three cases, however, I had to reverse my decision after the children happily demonstrated that they could indeed sneeze, burp, and gargle while speaking.

Among all the lists my students wrote, my favorite was the Happy List. A Happy List is quite simply a list of everything that makes you happy. Children really get into this activity. Some will write pages. Once, when my kids' Happy Lists were on the wall outside of my classroom, a dad came by to pick up his daughter and started reading them as he waited. He was so charmed by the lists that he told me he was going to ask all his employees to make them at work.

To begin this activity, tell your students that each of them will be writing his or her own Happy List and explain what they are. Let them know that they do not have to write sentences, just words. Children like hearing this. They also don't have to worry about spelling—just try their best. They like hearing this too. Give them more than one class period to write the lists and also assign it as homework. Allow them to work with a buddy if they wish. Set a minimum number of words. I would require a minimum of a hundred, which to kids always sounded like a lot at first. But I'd assure them that once they got going, they'd come up with a hundred words quickly.

Encourage your students to use specific language. To illustrate, kids shouldn't just write *sports*. That counts only as one word. They should write *baseball* and *hockey* and *football*, which count for three. Some students will include all of their friends on their lists. That was fine with me—as long as they made them happy. Most children include their favorite teachers, which is sweet.

When giving this assignment to a group of third graders, right after explaining the instructions, I would rub my chin and *just happen* to mention: "I think the world record for third grade is two hundred words." (Note the competition.) This would, of course, cause the kids to shout: "I'm writing two hundred and fifty!" "I'm writing five hundred!" And "I'm writing a thousand!" It always happened.

By this point, your children will be eager to get started. They will have already made eye contact with the friends they'd like to work with (some will have hooked arms) and scoped out where in the classroom they want to hide and write. As soon as you say go, they will grab their clipboards, papers, and pencils and scurry off to start.

One year after starting my kids on their Happy Lists, I stopped at Elliot's desk and looked at his. He had already written: *lasagna, secret codes, watermelon, cookie dough, puddles, meatballs, popping bubble wrap,* and *Harry Potter 1, 2, 3, 4, 5,* and *6.*

"Have you really read all six?" I asked, skeptically.

He erased the last three numbers.

Next, I read Grace's. She'd listed: *waterfalls, kayaks, Frisbees, Tom and Jerry, trampolines, the sound that crickets make, marbles, unicorns, mermaids,* and *not taking out the trash.*

I smiled. "You don't like taking out the garbage?"

She shook her head.

"Neither do I."

Chloe was scribbling away when I kneeled beside her. She had dashed off: *my birthday, hummingbirds, sharp pencils, Easter egg hunts, snow globes, allowance, pennies, nickels, dimes, quarters, one-dollar bills, five-dollar bills, ten-dollar bills,* and *twenty-dollar bills.*

She looked up at me. "Is there a fifty-dollar bill?"

"Yes."

"Good." She wrote it down.

Kevin's list (the boy who made the copyrighted dog bowl) was already long. It included: *staying up late, roller coasters, Cocoa Pebbles, my baby blanket, milkshakes, tooth fairy money, pie eating contests, beating my mom in Monopoly, seeing class pictures for the first time, microphones, sparklers, the last ten minutes of the school year,* and *Mr. Done's coffee cup.*"

I smiled. "Mr. Done's coffee cup? Why does *that* make you happy?"

"I don't know," he said with a shrug. "It just does?"

Then he dived back into his list to beat the world record.

A Word About Reading

It was my first year of teaching, and my third graders and I were in the school library for our weekly visit. I'd been teaching for only a couple of months. The children had a half hour to choose their new books. After they checked them out, they could sit on the floor by the library door and read quietly until it was time to leave.

As the children looked for their books, I watched Oscar wandering around the library, dragging his fingers along the spines of the books but never choosing one. A Lost Boy. I walked over to him and reminded him that we would be leaving soon. It was a familiar scene. Oscar and I went through it every week. Pretty soon library time was over, and I announced that it was time to go. Oscar grabbed something off the shelf and quickly checked it out.

As the kids and I walked back to class, I thought about what had just happened. Here was a child, a reluctant reader, who couldn't find a book, and I hadn't helped him. All I'd done was hurry him along. In my teacher training, I'd learned all about how to teach reading. I knew how to teach phonics and sight words and how to ask higher-level-thinking questions using Bloom's taxonomy. But I didn't know how to help an eight-year-old find a book that he would enjoy. I had failed a student and felt badly about it. From that day forward, I was determined to not let that happen again.

And so I began to learn. I asked the school librarian what the kids were reading. I visited the city library and spoke with the children's librarians. I checked out stacks of kids' books and dedicated myself to reading them. I found out which books had waiting lists. I reacquainted myself with the classics and learned the new titles. I also went to the children's bookstore in town and picked the brains of the men and women who worked there. That's where

I met Mary. A retired grade school teacher with white hair and twinkly blue eyes, she had worked in the shop for years.

Beside Mary's desk stood a post with arrows pointing to different destinations in children's literature: Neverland and Narnia, Treasure Island and the Emerald City, Wonderland and the Hundred Acre Wood where Winnie-the-Pooh and his gang live. On one wall of the bookshop, Mary had set up a cardboard fireplace. On the mantel sat framed pictures of Paddington Bear and Amelia Bedelia and Babar the Elephant, which gave you the sense that they were members of her family. On the path leading up to the front door, Mary had put a row of stakes, each with large, illustrated pages from classic children's books to draw kids in as they approached the store.

When I visited the shop, I would watch Mary in action. She knew children. She knew books. And she knew how to put the two together. Mary could spot a child who needed help finding a book. She recognized those lost, overwhelmed looks on kids' faces when they didn't know which ones to pick. I wanted to be like Mary. I needed to be.

One Saturday afternoon, I was in the store talking with Mary at the counter when something across the room caught her eye. She spotted a Lost Boy. "Excuse me a minute," Mary said, stepping out from behind the counter. I followed her.

The boy was with his mother, who explained that her son was looking for a book but couldn't seem to find one he liked. Mary smiled at the child and asked his name and what grade he was in. His name was Andrew. He was in fourth grade. From then on, Mary spoke directly to Andrew. Mary understood that children wish to be engaged with directly, even when a parent is willing to speak for them—a lesson she'd surely learned from being a teacher.

"And what kinds of books are you interested in, Andrew?" Mary asked.

He shrugged.

"Well, let me see," Mary said. Andrew watched her pucker her lips the way grown-ups do when they're thinking of something. "Do you like books about real things or make-believe?"

"Real."

"Me too." She puckered again. "Do you like books about animals?"

"No."

"How about books about people?"

He shook his head.

"What about books about catastrophes?" She intentionally made the word sound catastrophic. "Like earthquakes or volcanic eruptions or shipwrecks."

Andrew didn't respond. But Mary could detect by his expression that he was considering it. She knew she was onto something.

"Have you heard of the ship called the *Titanic*?" she asked.

"Yes."

"Of course you have." Suddenly Mary snapped her fingers, and her face broke into a smile. "*I* know a book you might like. What about Pompeii? Have you ever heard of the great volcano eruption near Pompeii?"

Andrew shook his head.

"It destroyed the whole city," Mary added. Then she made a face. "It's pretty gruesome. A lot of people died. It's a true story." She paused. "Do you think that might interest you?"

He nodded.

I smiled at Andrew's mother, and she smiled back.

"Follow me," Mary announced. Then she turned and led Andrew through the shop. His mother and I lingered behind, allowing Mary to perform her magic. Once they reached the shelf that Mary was looking for, she bent over, cocked her head, and ran her index finger along the spines. "Aha!" she cried. "Here you are!" She sounded as though she had just found a friend in a game of hide-and-seek. Mary pulled the book off the shelf and handed it to Andrew. "How does this look?"

Andrew eyed the cover. "Good."

Mary asked Andrew to open the book, which he did. "Think you can read that?" Andrew nodded. Mary glanced up at his mother, who gave her a nod too. "Great," Mary said. "I think you'll enjoy it." Then, after giving his mom a smile, Mary left Andrew with his new book, and she and I returned to the register.

A few minutes later, Andrew appeared at the counter. Mary turned to him and asked, "Anything I can do for you, Andrew?"

"Where's that other book you were talking about?" he asked. "The one about the *Titanic*."

Mary didn't give the slightest hint that she was delighted by the question. She understood that Andrew was stepping out of his comfort zone to ask about the book, and that whenever a child is taking a risk, one must never make light of it. Another lesson she'd learned from teaching.

Mary looked at me and said, "Excuse me, please." Then she slipped out from behind the counter and chimed, "Follow me, Andrew."

When teaching children to read, teachers use different strategies and methods. There are different views regarding the best way to teach it. But no matter what your philosophy or teaching practices, there is one thing that every teacher of reading agrees on. We all aim to instill a love of reading in our students. It is one of the most important things we do.

Unfortunately, the reality is that a lot of children don't like to read. Today's kids can find the main idea and supporting details in a text and analyze passages on a standardized test, but these things do not create lovers of books. In today's schools, the emphasis is on reading skills because these can be tested, not on developing lifelong readers. Reading for pleasure, though encouraged, takes a backseat. It doesn't help that books have an enormous amount of competition these days. Smartphones and video games, computers and TV—they all cut into reading time.

So how do teachers help students to become lifelong readers? How do we help the Andrews and Oscars in our classrooms? It's not that complicated, really. A lot of it is common sense. Through the whole of my career, I taught countless children how to read, and here's what I've found works best to help them love it:

Become an Expert

A teacher of reading is like a search engine. Both can help you find a book. But where a search engine will give a child merely a list of reading options, a teacher can help find the perfect one. To do so, though, teachers have to become experts in children's literature—to know the literature inside and out, particularly for the age level you teach. To start, review lists of recommended books. There are so many wonderful reading lists online. Pick librarians' brains. Look at what your colleagues have propped up on their whiteboard trays in their classrooms. And ask your students what they are reading. Kids are one of the best resources. Of course, visit the bookstores and explore the new titles. If there's one that strikes your fancy, ask your school librarian to order it. If you think about it, teachers really are matchmakers. We are constantly trying to match children with books and hoping it will be a good fit. Keep honing those skills. Never stop learning the literature. Learn it so well that when your kids don't know what to read, you know just the right book to put into their hands. For me, one of the greatest joys of teaching is introducing a book to a student and seeing the child fall in love with it. Nothing better.

Reading Time

Reading, like everything else, improves with practice. The more kids read, the better readers they become. When children practice reading, they grow their vocabularies, fluency, stamina, and comprehension. Kids learn about authors and genres and what kind of books they like. The problem is that during many a reading period, children aren't reading. Instead, they're busy completing worksheets, answering questions, and participating in discussion groups. It's reading that makes readers—not activities. So make sure you give students plenty of time to practice. My kids had thirty minutes of uninterrupted independent reading a day, usually after lunch. This time was sacred. There were no worksheets, no discussions, no reflections in their reading notebooks. Just reading. A fellow teacher would do the same. He referred to his silent reading time as "church."

The Classroom Library

If you think about it, the libraries in our classrooms are similar to some of the books we put into them. Like the candy house in "Hansel and Gretel," classroom libraries also lure children. Like the small furniture in "Snow White and the Seven Dwarfs," our reading corners have little furniture as well. And like the mess that Goldilocks makes in the Three Bears' home, after children go through books in a classroom library, it often needs to be tidied up too.

Most primary teachers set up their classroom libraries the same way. First, they separate their books by author or genre. Next, they put the books into plastic baskets that they bought at Dollar Tree. Then they print out labels, laminate them, and attach them to the baskets. Sometimes teachers will have an extra basket for the books that are falling apart. This one is labeled "Book Hospital." Finally, beside the *Clifford*, *Olivia*, and *Curious George* books, teachers put stuffed Cliffords, Olivias, and Curious Georges because a stuffed animal beside a book always makes it more enticing.

When setting up your classroom library, have the book covers facing out if you can. Covers are more inviting than spines. Also, don't label the baskets by reading level. It used to be common practice for teachers to organize their classroom books this way, but I don't recommend it. Doing so limits children in what they can select and places an emphasis on reading levels, not a love for reading. No child ever fell in love with a book because of its level. Reading is a journey, not a race. Above all, make the space as inviting as you can. Basically, you want your classroom library to become a child magnet. If you're allowed, add some pillows and lamps or even some twinkle lights. If you want to go all out, give your library a theme. My friend Dana once decked out her reading corner to look like a campsite, complete with camping chairs that circled construction paper logs and flames made out of red and yellow tissue paper. She also hung a clothesline. Jill begins her year with beach chairs, beach balls, and giant jellyfish made out of paper plates and streamers. Once, I set up a small inflatable pool in my reading corner and let my kids sit inside it while wearing snorkeling gear. The pool didn't last long. It popped in three days, which was just as well. Third graders *cannot* concentrate on their reading when dressed in snorkeling masks and flippers.

My first classroom library consisted of a stack of *National Geographic*s, a few Little Golden Books, and a couple of Berenstain Bears books with torn covers. A lot of new teachers begin this way. To grow your classroom library, visit garage sales, library sales, and, of course—the Teacher Design Center. Request books for your birthday. Find out who is retiring and see if they're getting rid of any. Ask your school librarian for the discards. Order a lot from the Scholastic Book Clubs so that you can get free books with all your bonus points. Around Christmastime, let your students and parents know that you are looking to build the library. It will cut down on the coffee mugs, candles, and bath sets.

Favorite Authors

Rather than help a student find one particular book, assist the child in finding an author. That's how I fell in love with books. I was in fourth grade. My teacher, Mr. Jacobs, read us *James and the Giant Peach*. After that, I had to read more by the man who wrote about boys who fly in peaches.

Reading Spaces

When it's time for quiet reading, let your kids sit where they want—behind the furniture, on the couch, in the beanbag chairs. One kindergarten teacher I know has a couple of heavy-duty plastic tubs, each large enough to hold one child. On the side of each tub is a sign that says "Book Boat." When reading inside their boats, the young sailors may bring along stuffed animal first mates. I used to keep a big tub full of stuffed animals in the corner of my classroom. We called them our "Book Buddies." During silent reading time, the tub was often empty.

The Three Types of Books

This tip is more for parents than teachers, as most teachers are already well aware of this. For children, books can be broken down into three levels—easy, challenging, and just right. Think of those three chairs that Goldilocks sits on. Another way to think of it is like riding a bike. "Downhill books" are a breeze. "Uphill books" can be a struggle. "Just right" books might have a bump or two, but, for the most part, the ride is pretty smooth.

To figure out if a student will be able to read a particular book, pick a section from it that is about one hundred words in length and ask the child to read it aloud. If the reader makes zero to two errors, it's probably pretty easy. The student can handle something harder. (Errors include mispronounced words, reading words incorrectly, omitting words, or adding them.) If the child makes around four to six errors, the material is most likely just right. If the student makes close to ten errors or more, the book is probably too hard at this time. (*Note*: If a child mispronounces a character's name multiple times, I would count this as only one error.) Generally, you want children to read with around 95 percent accuracy or higher when reading independently.

Another way to check if a book is at the correct level for a student is to use what teachers call the five-finger rule. Again, select a text of about one hundred words. Put your fist behind your back and ask the child to read the text aloud. Every time the student makes a mistake, extend one finger. If you've extended five or fewer fingers, the material is probably at the right level for the child. But don't get too hung up on all of this. It's just a guide. If a student finds a book that is challenging, but really wants to tackle it, let the child try. It's okay to dip into a difficult book once in a while. I've seen plenty of kids get through books that I would have considered too challenging, because they were interested in them. Oftentimes, if books are too hard for children, they will stop on their own. Once, I had a student beg to check out a book about video games. The book was definitely a challenge, but I let him. When I asked why he wanted to read it so badly, he said he wanted to learn how to beat his brother.

Book Talks

One of the best ways to connect kids to books is to give a book talk. These talks, also known as book commercials, are short teasers. To give one, hold up a book and pitch it. Share a summary, say what you liked about it, and read an excerpt. It's key that *you* have read the book. Children are much more apt to want to look at a book that you have read than one you haven't. When you've finished your talk, hold up the book and say, "Any takers?" You'll see a wall of hands. One year I was just about to begin a book talk when a child put his hand up. I thought he had a question, but he said he was raising it early to beat the crowd.

First Chapters

This strategy allows you to expose kids to many more books and authors than you would normally have time for. Pick a book that you think your students would enjoy and read just the first chapter. When you're done, prop it up on your whiteboard tray and watch it get whisked away during silent reading time. A friend of mine who does this at the end of each week calls it "First Chapter Friday." If her students beg for more, sometimes she'll cheat and read chapter 2.

Reading Conferences

Reading conferences are mini check-ins between teacher and student about the child's reading. These chats are key to building readers. When holding a reading conference, you'll want to check the student's understanding of the material, ask if the child needs any help, and see how their reading is coming along. During your meeting, keep a list of questions handy so that you can refer to them easily. Questions might include: What has happened so far? How are you enjoying the story? Who's your favorite character? What do you think of the writing?

Make notes as you talk. Aim to keep the conversation casual and relaxed. Stay away from "stumper" questions such as "What's the theme of the book?" This kind of question can cause students to feel anxious. Typically, I'd hold reading conferences a couple of times a week, often during silent reading time. That chunk of time worked well for me. Some experts suggest that the teacher read during silent reading time to be a good role model. It sounds nice, but it's not realistic. Teachers don't have that kind of time. Use this time to conference with your kids instead.

Choice
In school, teachers often pick their kids' reading material. Just like children want to choose what they watch on TV or what music they listen to, they prefer to decide on their own reading material too. So, whenever possible, allow your kids to select their books. And if a student finds that he doesn't like one, don't make him keep wading through it. Let the child put it down and try something else. That's what good readers do.

Add These to Your Reading Arsenal
Teachers know to offer children a variety of reading materials besides books: magazines and comics, maps and scripts, menus and travel brochures. Heck, every spring one teacher I know has her kids read seed packets! To add a little whimsy to your classroom library, consider adding cereal boxes. Just bring in your empty ones from home and ask your students to do the same. Flatten them out, put them in a basket, and let the children pore over them during silent reading time.

Class Picks
You know how bookstores will sometimes have a shelf of "Staff Picks"? Do the same in your classroom. Once a month, ask your students to select a favorite book. It doesn't have to be one they read recently. It can be any book they

think the class would like to know about. Have your kids attach index cards to their books explaining why they chose them. Set the books on a special shelf, like they do at Barnes & Noble, or in a basket labeled "Class Picks."

Reading Killers

When my brother Steve was a kid, he loved to play soccer, so my parents put him in a Saturday soccer league. One Saturday morning, Steve came home from practice and said he wanted to quit because it wasn't fun anymore. All they did was drills, and they never played a game. Steve said the grown-ups had ruined it. The adults had killed his joy.

As teachers, we need to be careful not to kill our students' joy of reading. One of the reasons that kids do not like to read is because teachers give them so much to do after their reading. To prove that they have read and understood the material, we ask children to reflect in their notebooks, fill in study guides, complete worksheets, write book reports, and jot down connections on sticky notes. If taken too far, all this dissecting can destroy a story. It can also turn reading into a chore and cause struggling readers to dislike it. Choose your assignments thoughtfully. There is such a thing as over-teaching. I'm not proposing that you eliminate all reading activities, only that it's okay to not have kids *do* something every time they finish reading.

For Parents

Parents are instrumental in raising readers and always want to know how they can help. Here are some of the pointers that I would share with them: (1) Read in front of your children. Kids learn from modeling. When children see their parents read, they want to read too; (2) Don't stop reading to your kids once they've learned to read themselves. Read to them as long as they'll let you; and (3) Support your child's reading choices. Occasionally, parents will inform you that they aren't too happy with what their children are choosing to read. When this happens, sometimes it's necessary to give the Reading Speech: "If your child wants to read *Calvin and Hobbes* or graphic novels or *Sports Illustrated* or *Ripley's Believe It or Not!*, let him. If he prefers picture books to ones with chapters, that's okay. If he chooses to pore over *Captain Underpants* right now, that's fine too. It may not be high literature or what *you* would want to read, but he's reading. Yay! And all reading is good." When you're finished, promise that he won't read *Captain Underpants* forever.

Future Reading Lists

This idea I picked up from reading expert Nancie Atwell, and I loved it. One thing that strong readers do is to keep a running list of books they'd like to read. Some people write this list down. Some keep it in their heads. Ask your students to log the titles that they wish to read in the future. When you talk about a book, and your kids want to read it, have them write it down. Then when they're looking for a new book, they can refer to their future reading lists to see what they'd like to pick up next. Keeping a list like this also provides children with an authentic reason to write.

Genres

It has been said that there are no reluctant readers—just children who haven't found the right book yet. I believe that some kids don't like to read because they haven't discovered the genre they like either. Adults have their genre preferences, and children do too. So help your students find out what these are by exposing them to all kinds of books: fantasy, mystery, biography, history. A perfect time to get this in is during your book talks or First Chapter Fridays. One friend of mine who teaches grade two holds what she calls a "genre challenge" with her kids. After a student reads a set number of books in a particular genre, the child gets a "badge," which is really a sticker. Of course, the children try to get all the badges. It's sort of like being in the Scouts and working for patches. When talking about genres with kids, share your favorites. I'd tell my students that I like biographies but am not too crazy about fantasy or science fiction. Whenever I said this, my *Harry Potter* and *Star Wars* fans would just shake their heads at me. Once, when discussing genres with my third graders, one girl announced that she only reads books that are pink. Smiling, I explained that pink is not a genre.

Book Tastings

This is another way to expose your kids to a lot of different books quickly. It's also an excellent way to familiarize children with different authors and genres.

You can hold a "book tasting" in the library, cafeteria, or classroom. Here's how to set it up: Before the event, prepare tables or desks as though you're setting them for a meal. Include plates, napkins, and silverware. If you want to get fancy, pull out some tablecloths, candlesticks, and salt and pepper shakers. Place one book on each plate. You can use picture books or chapter books. When the tasting begins, turn on some music and invite your students to take a seat and "sample" the books. After about ten minutes or so, depending on the age of your kids, have them rotate to another seat. If children want to continue reading a book later, they record the titles in their future reading lists. Invite the principal, librarian, and reading specialist. Be sure to take lots of photos. During the tasting, your little hams will tuck their napkins into their shirts, pretend to sprinkle salt and pepper onto their books, and ask if there's any ketchup. One wise guy will ask for the wine menu.

Reading Aloud

In his famous song "You're the Top," Cole Porter lists those things in our world that are just the best: the Colosseum and the Louvre Museum, the Tower of Pisa and the smile on the *Mona Lisa*—even Mickey Mouse. Well, if Porter were writing a song about teaching "tops," reading aloud would be number one on the list. In fact, it is so important that if you knew you were going to be stranded on a desert island with a bunch of kids and could take only one thing with you to teach them (I understand it's a scary example, but you get the point), I'd say bring your read-aloud. Nothing sparks a love of reading in children more than this. Since reading aloud is so important, it deserves its own chapter. I'll cover it in greater detail in the next piece.

For the Lost Boys (and Girls)

If you spot a Lost Boy or Girl in the school library, follow these steps that I learned from Mary: (1) Walk up to the child and offer some assistance; (2) Learn what the student is interested in; (3) Lead your youngster to the books on that topic—because you know right where they are; (4) Pull out a couple of books and give each a little commercial; (5) Smile when you see the student check out the book you recommended; and (6) Smile again the following week when you spot this same child checking out the next one in the series.

Reading Aloud to Children

"Boys and girls, please join me on the carpet," I announced to my third graders after picking up my copy of *The Cricket in Times Square*, the classic children's book about a cricket's adventures in New York City. The kids pogoed out of their chairs and raced to the reading rug. Those in front sat on their bottoms, the children in back on their knees. After they were all settled, I began where I'd left off the day before. As I read, the kids smiled and laughed and fiddled with their shoelaces. When I got to the end of the chapter and closed the book, the children shouted, "No!" I glanced at my watch. "Sorry," I said. "We're out of time." I was just about to send the kids back to their seats when Garrett, who always sat right in front of me and wouldn't allow anyone else to take his spot, raised his hand. "Mr. Done," he asked innocently, "is the cricket book a true story?"

J. K. Rowling once said that she would defend the reading of bedtime stories till her dying breath. I feel the same about reading aloud to children at school. As educators, we've all heard the words "classroom magic." While this may sound like nothing but a fanciful phrase found on inspirational calendars and Hallmark mugs, such magic does exist. And in elementary classrooms, the place where it occurs most often is on the reading rug. It is here that teachers, through their voices and eyes and gestures, can entrance, enthrall, and hypnotize their young audiences. It's here that children can sit spellbound, riveted, and enchanted. There is something truly extraordinary that takes place between a child, a teacher, and a book.

As I mentioned, reading aloud to kids is one of the most valuable things a teacher can do for them. Every time you read to your students, you improve their learning advantage. Reading aloud stimulates the imagination and lets children explore people, places, times, and events beyond their own experience. It builds motivation and curiosity. When you read to kids, you are conditioning them to associate print with pleasure, whetting their appetite for reading, and fostering a lifelong love of books. Reading aloud also increases kids' attending and listening skills. And it helps grow children's vocabularies. You are pouring words into their ears. The average number of words in a picture book for children is around a thousand. There are approximately 185 days in a school year. If you read one book a day to your students, at the end of the school year, your kids will have heard 185,000 words. By the end of fifth grade, students will have heard close to a million.

There's much research to support the value of reading aloud to children. A great deal has been written on the subject. But teachers don't need research articles to know the benefits. They know that when you pick up a book and announce, "Please join me on the carpet for a story," children immediately behave just like puppies that see you holding a treat.

The read-aloud time was definitely one of my favorite parts of the school day, one of my joys of teaching. I imagine it is for most teachers. It's a time when we bond with our students. Teachers and students experience a similar connection during story time as parents do when they read to their children before bedtime. When I would read to my students, I liked hearing their reactions: giggles, chuckles, gasps, and hoots. I'd be heartened by their faces too—bright eyes lost in a story, chins slightly elevated, upturned mouths waiting for a laugh. *Beautiful.*

When reading aloud, you are not just teaching students how to read. You're teaching them how to write. When listening to a book, children hear perfectly chosen words and finely crafted sentences. They take in the richness of metaphor and simile. They hear descriptions and dialogue. They pick up phrasing, tempo, melody, timing, and rhythm—an author's music. When hearing the language spoken correctly, children begin to imitate the patterns in their own speaking and writing. Grammar, as they say, is more caught than taught.

When I was a young teacher, I taught a summer school class for third and fourth graders who needed support in writing. The principal's name was Barbara. This was her first principal position, and she wanted everything to be just right. Barbara stopped by regularly to check on things. The first day she popped in, I was reading Roald Dahl's *Matilda* aloud to my students. The next week, Barbara dropped by, and once again I was reading *Matilda*. A few days after that, when she stepped into my classroom, it just so happened that I was reading the same book. Later that day, as I was standing at the copier, Barbara said, "Phil, I have to ask you something. Every time I come into your room, you're reading to your students." She paused. "You *are* teaching them to write, aren't you?" I decided to needle her a little bit. "Nope," I answered. Barbara's eyes grew large. Then I flashed a grin and said, "But Roald Dahl is."

Studies show that the older kids get, the less their teachers read to them. This seems backward to me. I contend that the older children get, the more important the read-aloud should be. Every year in the United States, more than a million students drop out of high school. That's seven thousand kids a day! I wonder: *Could there be a connection between the dropout rate and the read-aloud?* Would we have more students staying in school if they couldn't wait to hear what happens in the next chapter?

Teachers are often described as artists. To me, this is most evident when they read to their kids. Reading aloud requires the voice of an actor, the timing of a playwright, the expressions of a mime, and the rhythm of a musician. How do we achieve this? What follows are some of my favorite read-aloud tips to help you create your own classroom magic with children:

Making the Announcement

Before beginning a new read-aloud, hide the book in a bag or under your sweater. Do not let your kids see it. This creates excitement. Once the children are settled, pull out the book, show them the cover, give it a hug, and announce that it's one of your favorites. By the way, it's fine to choose books that are above your students' reading levels. Kids' listening comprehension is higher than their comprehension when reading by themselves. And it's okay if a child doesn't understand every word.

Gathering the Children

Some teachers let their kids sit at their desks during the read-aloud. I preferred to have mine sit with me on or around the reading rug. It was more intimate.

In the pre-pandemic world, sometimes I'd ask them to sit close to me like sardines. When I did, one sardine might pet my shoe.

Starting Out

Before you begin reading, scan the group and make sure that you can see every child and that they all can see you. Do not start until you have everyone's attention. For some reason, as soon as kids sit on a reading rug, they begin examining their fingers or shoes as though they're seeing them for the first time. Prior to reading, announce, "Okay, everyone, look at your fingers and say hi." Giggling, your students will play along. Then ask the kids to say so long to them. Giggling some more, they will say good-bye. Some children will wave. "Great," you can say. "Now look at me." This always does the trick. Now you can begin.

Changing Your Voice

When reading to your students, your job is to grab and hold your listener. One way to do this is to alter your voice. Change the volume, speed, length, pitch, and quality of your words. Speak with an accent. Shake your voice when you read *"shiver,"* stretch it out when you pronounce *"long,"* and talk quickly when you say *"race."* Read faster in the exciting parts and softer when it gets scary, so that your kids scoot back and grab their friends. And use different voices for different characters. Witches cackle. Ghosts moan. Pirates snarl. Big, friendly giants sound like . . . well, big, friendly giants. Aslan the lion should not have the same voice as the White Witch. Augustus Gloop must always sound different from Veruca Salt. Sometimes you will forget to use the right voice. If you do, your students will immediately point this out.

Using Your Body

Don't just read the words. Whenever possible, act them out. Frown if a character is sad. Yawn and stretch if someone's tired. Jump back in your chair when you come to a scary part. Give a big sigh when a character in the book does. And don't forget to stand up once in a while. The Grinch should stand when looking down at *Who*-ville. The giant in "Jack and the Beanstalk" should stand when booming, "Fee, fi, fo, fum!"

Adding Sound Effects

When reading a book, if there's a knock on a door, knock on the arm of your chair. If a character hears footsteps, make them with your feet. If the scene has thunder, lightning, or howling wind, sound like it. Don't just say the words *explosion*, *alarm*, or *siren*. Make the sounds. And invite the children to make the sounds too. Children are sound effect experts. I have never met a child who wasn't able to imitate a dog, ghost, motorcycle, witch, fire truck, thunderstorm, or chicken on command.

Leaving Out Words

If the final word of a sentence is predictable, stop right before you reach the end and let your students finish it. To give an example, when reading "The Night Before Christmas," say, "'Twas the night before Christmas, when all through the house, not a creature was stirring, not even a _____." The children will chant back, "Mouse." After doing this a couple of times, look at your students with a surprised expression and ask, "How do you kids know these words? Did *you* write this?" Smiling, they will say they did.

Holding the Book

When holding a picture book, you have two options: (A) Set it on your lap and read upside down (another teacher talent); or (B) Hold it next to your head and turn your neck as far as it will go, so you can read the words sideways. If you go to the doctor's office with neck pain, tell them you're a teacher. They'll understand.

Showing Pictures

When showing kids pictures in a book, hold it in front of you and sweep the book slowly from side to side. Repeat this every time you come to a new picture. When you think that you're finished sharing a picture, you'll have to show it one more time to the children who say they can't see. If you are reading a chapter book with occasional pictures, make sure you show every one of them. Don't skip any. If a student notices that you passed over one, the child will announce it, and from then on, your whole class will ask repeatedly if you're showing them all the pictures to make sure you don't skip anymore.

Turning Pages

After turning a page in a picture book, don't always show students the new picture right away. Delay it. Look at it yourself without letting the kids see. Enjoy the picture alone. The children will beg you to show it to them. Finally, look up from the book as though you didn't even realize your students were there and say, "Oh, I'm sorry. Would you like to see the picture too?" Pause for yelling.

Helping Children Visualize

When reading a book, good readers have a movie of it in their minds. Kids who struggle with reading often don't do this. If you're reading a chapter book aloud to your students, stop occasionally and ask them to close their eyes and form a mental picture of a scene or character. In doing so, you are strengthening their ability to visualize. When your kids' eyes are shut, ask them specific questions to help them create the images. Here's an example:

"Boys and girls, close your eyes and picture Charlotte writing the first word in her web. It's late at night, and all the other animals in the barn are asleep. Keep your eyes closed and raise your hand when you can see this." Wait. You'll notice that it takes some children longer than others to do this. After all hands are up, continue. "Now picture Charlotte scrambling over her web to make the letters. Watch her go up and down and back and forth." Again, pause for your students to visualize this. Some will be squinting hard. Others will be covering their faces. Some will be smiling as they watch the spider in their minds.

"Now, with your eyes still closed, look around the barn where Charlotte is working. What else do you see? A tractor? Some tools? The animals? Do you see any moonlight? If so, where is it coming from? Raise your hand when you have looked around the barn." Pause for hands. "Before I ask you to open your eyes, look back at Charlotte's web. What letters has she written in it so far? Is she almost finished? Where is she right now? When you have seen this image, open your eyes, but please do not talk until I say you may. We want to give everyone a chance to visualize the scene." After all eyes open, say, "Okay now, who'd like to share?"

Having Fun

When you come to a really good part in a book, stop and say, "Well, I'm afraid that's all we have time for today." Your kids won't like this. As they plead with you to continue, look at the clock and act like you're trying to decide if you should or not—even though you know you're going to. Hem and haw a little bit until you finally say, "Okay. I guess we have time to read just a little more." Your students will forgive you for teasing them. If your reading cuts into math time, they will love you forever.

Incorporating Hats and Maps
Hats add fun. When sharing a mystery, wear a Sherlock Holmes hat. As you're reading *Caps for Sale*, stack a couple of them on your head. When taking a ride through *The Mouse and the Motorcycle*, hold a helmet. While delivering Longfellow's "Paul Revere's Ride," don a three-cornered hat. For "Casey at the Bat," put on a baseball cap. And always read with a world map and a US map within pointing distance, so that you can show your kids where the story takes place. Then you're reinforcing geography too. Eloise resides in New York. Madeline lives in Paris. Strega Nona's home is in Italy. Harry Potter lives in Surrey, England. And the Little Prince crash-lands in the Sahara.

Teaching as You Read
While reading a book to children, sometimes teachers will stop and ask their kids to participate by, say, predicting what will happen next, or turning to a classmate and discussing something. There's nothing wrong with this, but be careful not to interrupt the story too much. When stopping and starting too often during the read-aloud, you interrupt the pictures that children are creating in their minds. You break the rhythm and flow of the text—and the spell that the writer is trying to cast. Of course, it's okay to explain vocabulary and ask questions as you read, but pull students away from a story as little as possible, so they can savor it.

Focusing Kids' Attention
There is a trend these days to let children draw or work on something quietly while the teacher reads to the class. It's probably to make more efficient use of time. I don't recommend this. It can rob kids of the benefits of being read to. No one can give his full attention to two things at once. Plus, it's disrespect-ful to the author. Authors deserve children's full attention. To me, working

on something while the teacher is reading is like talking on the phone with a friend when you're out having dinner with somebody else.

Showing Your Emotions

When reading something funny to your kids, enjoy a hearty laugh. A teacher's laugh is comforting to a child. If you read something sad, don't be afraid to let your students see you get teary. Once, when I was reading a heart-tugger to my kids, they decided we needed a new classroom job: Kleenex box holder. Remember, when you laugh and cry while sharing a book, you show children two of reading's greatest rewards.

Finishing Up

When selecting a place to stop reading for the day, pick one that leaves your students wanting more. You want kids to whine when you stop. As a rule, children shouldn't whine in class, of course—unless it's at the end of story time. Then it's okay.

Following Up

After you finish reading to your kids, do not send them back to their desks to write about the plot or the theme or the conflict in the story. It will defeat what you're trying to accomplish. As I touched upon earlier, not everything needs to finish with a writing exercise. For children, writing after a read-aloud is like looking up words in a dictionary. Not fun.

Remembering Your Purpose

All teachers know what happens when a substitute teacher continues your read-aloud while you're away. When you return, your students will tell you that the sub didn't use different voices or act out the story like you do. Kids want these things from their reader. Always put your heart into it. And always remember your purpose: to lure children into the wonderful world of the written word.

My Favorite Reading Strategy

Reading is the king of subjects. Math and science, writing and social studies—they all depend on it. It's the most important thing children learn in school. There are certainly countless reading strategies, and out of all of them, there's one that I would have to say is my favorite. It can be used at any grade level and is also highly effective for English language learners and remedial readers. Children make excellent gains when using it. And it doesn't even involve a book.

Here's how the strategy works: Select a text that you'd like your students to read—a story, a biography, a piece of nonfiction, or something you've written yourself—and type it out. Use a larger font size than your kids would typically find in a book. Larger text is less intimidating to read and easier to work with. For third graders, I liked to use a font size of around eighteen. The length of a text will vary depending on the age you teach. I'd aim to keep mine a page or two. Print out copies for all the children you are working with. This paper will be their reading material. And keep a copy for yourself, as initially you will be reading the text to your students. Each child should also have a pencil and different colored highlighters. Before you begin, tell the children that they should follow along as you read because you'll be stopping and starting a lot. Then begin reading aloud.

Now, here's where the fun begins. As you read, and your students follow, stop at words that you want to talk about. These could be new vocabulary words, difficult ones for them to decode, those you suspect children might not understand, or words you want to examine in greater depth. If you're pausing for only a moment, tell the kids to keep a finger on the word where they stopped so that they don't lose their place when you resume reading. When you want to bring your students' attention to a particular word, ask them to highlight it. Or have them circle the word with a pencil, then draw an arrow to the margin, where they can write a definition in their own words. When writing words, have kids use their pencils. It's cleaner than using a highlighter. If a word can be illustrated, let students make a quick sketch in the margin. Children enjoy drawing in the margins. To them, it's like doodling. Your artists will want to spend a lot of time on their drawings, so you'll need to nudge them along. As your students are marking up their papers, you're doing the same right along with them. This is important. Then you're not just directing the activity. You're one of the group.

Use the text to focus on all sorts of skills. If you're working on contractions, have the kids highlight them. If you're teaching students singular possessives, ask them to circle the apostrophes, which to children are better known as "flying commas," "commas in the sky," and "the thingies on top." If students are learning about proper nouns, let them draw boxes around all the capital letters. When you finish working through the text, your papers will be full of circles, boxes, highlighting, arrows, drawings, and scribbled notes. Basically, the kids will have marked the heck out of them. If your students discover a typo, tell them that you made it on purpose to see if they were reading carefully.

Delving into a text this way with children is like giving them a magnifying glass or a microscope, but instead of observing leaves and bugs, they're examining their reading. Studying reading material like this slows kids down and enables them to look more closely at the words, the writing, and the author's message. Interacting with text in this manner also enhances children's comprehension, which makes sense. Think about when you read in college. What did we all do to understand the material? We highlighted our textbooks and wrote in the margins. Kids in grade school don't usually get this opportunity.

There's no right or wrong way to implement this strategy. The point is to let students dig into the text and chew on it. And not all the marking needs to be led by the teacher. Sometimes let the kids decide. For example, I'd say to my third graders, "Okay, highlight all the words that you think are the most difficult," or "Circle those words that you suspect would be hard for a first grader to read." Children will be honest. Of course, when you see the words that your students have highlighted, be sure to review those.

When you're finished reading the text with your kids—and it might take more than one sitting—pair them up and let them spread out around the classroom. As each child holds a paper, the pairs read the text a second time together. This is known as partner reading. I liked to call it "buddy reading." Children benefit from more than one exposure to a text. It gives them another opportunity to practice. For buddy reading, one child reads aloud while the other follows along with his eyes, or his finger if you teach younger students. Every time they come to a new paragraph, the reader and listener alternate so that each child gets equal time to read. From time to time, you will have to remind the student who is not reading to follow along.

After the kids finish reading the text together, now it's time for them to play school. Children get a charge out of playing school at school, which I find cute. Starting back at the beginning of their text, the "teacher" asks the "student" questions just as you did when you first read the piece to them. For instance, the junior teacher might point to a highlighted word and ask her partner, "What does this word mean?" or "Can you read this?" Children are very good at playing the teacher. They don't need help. Many will mimic you. Some will be pretty tough on their "students." In this case, you will have to remind them that they are playing school, not "Let's Stump Our Friend." When the kids are halfway through their papers, have the "teachers" and "students" switch roles so that each child gets a chance to ask questions. When kids are playing school, the classroom teacher (the grown-up one) walks around and listens, encourages, and takes notes. As you do, also instruct your little teachers to say "Good job!" to their students, just like real teachers do. After this, you will hear "Good job!" popping up over and over from every nook and cranny in the room.

Once in a while, have your kids take the text home and play school with their parents too. Children can be teachers or students. Of course, most will choose to be the teacher because it's always more fun to make Mom and Dad play the student. I'd ask my kids to read their papers at home like this for a couple of reasons. First, it provided the children yet another opportunity to practice reading the text, which I wanted. Also, it gave the parents a chance to see what their kids were learning in school and hear how their reading was coming along.

I started using this reading strategy early in my career. At that time, we didn't have a name for it that I was aware of. It wasn't a common strategy. Nowadays, some would describe it as "close reading," but I prefer to call it something else. The name I use actually came from a nine-year-old. One day I asked my third graders to get out their reading papers (we'd started marking them up the day before), when one of them announced, "It's time for messy reading!" I started laughing. *Messy reading*. It was the perfect way to describe it. And from that day on, I never called it anything else.

Writing Time

"So boys and girls," I asked my third graders, "if you could travel anywhere in the world, where would you go?" We would soon be writing about our dream trips.

"Hawaii!" Maggie called out.

"Hollywood!" Emma volunteered.

"New York City!" Ivan trumpeted.

"Can we go to Mars?" Eduardo asked excitedly.

"Sure," I answered.

"I'm going to Mars too!" Jake exclaimed.

I continued. "Okay, everyone. Think about what you'd like to bring with you on your dream trips. What would you put in your suitcase?"

"A camera!" Katherine threw out.

"A computer," offered Matilda.

"Underwear," Eduardo announced with a smirk.

"Very important," I added amidst the giggling. I continued to toss out ideas. "Don't forget to bring money."

"How much can we bring?" asked Maggie.

"As much as you want," I answered.

A loud "Whoa!" sped around the room.

"Can I bring a million dollars?" Cecelia broke in.

"You *may*," I said, emphasizing the word.

She squealed.

Ivan picked up on my correction. "*May* I bring a billion dollars?" he wanted to know.

"Absolutely," I replied.

Another "Whoa!"

"May I bring my dog?" Alicia asked quickly.

"Of course," I confirmed. "It's *your* dream trip." I looked at the group. "What about your parents? Don't you want to bring them with you?"

"*No!*" they boomed.

When I finished chuckling, I said, "Well, if you don't bring your parents, you might want to bring a smartphone so you can speak with them."

"I don't have one," George grumped.

"It's a pretend trip," I reminded him. "You can bring whatever you want."

Frederick sat up straight. "Then I'm bringing an iPhone!"

"Me too!" Jake declared.

I squinted at him. "I'm not sure iPhones will work on Mars."

"Sure they will!" Eduardo proclaimed. "iPhones work everywhere!"

Immediately I had a thought. Apple should hear this conversation. I could picture the company's Super Bowl commercial in my head: A bunch of third graders plan their dream trips and choose to bring their iPhones over their moms and dads.

Teaching writing to children demands craft, enthusiasm, and a lot of stamina. When I was a student teacher, I remember my master teacher telling me that if I felt tired after writing with children, I was doing it right. Learning to write isn't easy, and teaching children to write isn't easy either. Teachers work hard at it.

We give lessons on expository, descriptive, and narrative writing. We teach persuasive and creative writing too. We instruct children in how to write engaging leads, use powerful verbs, incorporate dialogue, show don't tell, "stretch" sentences (My dog sleeps. My dog sleeps on the rug. My dog sleeps on the rug all day long), and also vary the length of them: "This sentence has five words. This one has the same. It sounds like a robot. Let's try to change them."

We hand out colored sticky notes so that kids can put them into books to identify topic sentences and supporting details. We pass out rubrics and worksheets and checklists to remind children to capitalize and punctuate and spell correctly, though we know that when they hand in their papers, they'll be missing capitals and periods and have lots of misspellings.

We draw giant fishhooks on chart paper to remind kids to "hook" their readers and huge hamburgers to show the parts of a paragraph (top bun: main idea; hamburger patties: supporting details; bottom bun: restate the main idea). We make construction paper tombstones with the words *RIP SAID* to remind our students that *said* is dead. Use a synonym.

We distribute lists of transition words and sentence starters and character traits so that children can cut them out and pound them into their writing notebooks after rubbing glue sticks all over the back. We cover our walls with posters of the writing process, editor's marks, and mug shots from Alcatraz outlawing the use of *LOL*, *OMG*, and *WDYT* in our kids' writing.

We use catchy terms such as "vivid verbs," "wow words," and "awesome adjectives" to make them more exciting. We create writing corners stocked with pencils, pens, markers, and trays with all kinds of paper: wide ruled, college ruled, newsprint, graph paper, sheets with dotted lines, bordered paper, and special paper with lines on the bottom half and big open rectangles on the top for children to draw pictures.

We hang up colorful anchor charts that we made in our fanciest teacher writing with funny acronyms like *OREO* to help kids with their persuasive paragraphs (state *o*pinion, give your *r*eason, provide an *e*xample, and restate your *o*pinion) and *COPS* to help them edit (*c*apitals, *o*rganization, *p*unctuation, and *s*pelling).

As springboards for children to write, we read them books about terrible, horrible days, and jolly postmen, and old women who swallow things. We cut out construction paper "books" to look like pumpkins, turkeys, mittens, hearts, and slices of bread (for writing directions on how to make a peanut butter sandwich) because we know that having books shaped like these things motivates children to want to write.

When our students have completed their final drafts, we put them into portfolios, thumbtack them onto bulletin boards, and tape them onto walls, hoping that when we take them down, we don't upset the custodian by also pulling off the paint. Sometimes, if it's an important assignment and a child wrote several pages, we slide them into the loud spiral binder machine in the staff room because we know that having your writing held together with a shiny plastic spiral makes it special.

* * *

For me, the writing period was one of the most enjoyable times of the day. I liked brainstorming ideas with my kids and hearing their ideas. I found it charming when children would link arms with their buddies like Barrel of Monkeys toys after I said they could write with a partner. I got a kick out of looking at little faces scrunch up when thinking of ideas—and then light up when they got one. I liked seeing kids scribble their ideas hurriedly on their papers so they wouldn't forget. It made me happy when children would read over their own writing and giggle at what they had just written. I enjoyed listening to them share what just made them giggle.

This might sound funny, but I actually like the way children's papers look. To me, there's something sweet about a child's slightly oversized letters and punctuation marks that fill up most of the space between the lines and the little hints of personal style already peeking through their penmanship: an extra loop here, a little flourish there. It's the *un*-adultness of their writing that charms me. Kids' papers are like baby animals. Their legs are still wobbly.

Over the years, I learned a lot about the teaching of writing from my students. The children taught me that it is more fun to write a story if you put yourself and your friends into it. It's fun to include your teacher in the story too. I discovered that when making a comma, if you start it off with a big thick dot and then finish it with a tail, it looks like a tadpole. A quotation mark looks like two tadpoles swimming together. I learned that making hyphens can also be fun, especially when you're in the middle of writing a word and you reach the pink line that runs down the right side of the paper. Then you get to karate chop your word with a hyphen before writing the rest of it on the next line. My students taught me that some kids like to write above the line—I call these "flying letters"—and some will write midway through them like their words are sinking. "*Titanic* letters." I found out that children don't like to indent paragraphs, to write in complete sentences, to make capital letters unless it's SOOOO or ZZZZZ or THE END, or to put in periods—except when you give them a paragraph to edit without any periods and ask them to fill in the missing periods with M&M's. If they know that they get to eat all the candy after they finish editing, they will find every period that is missing in record time. And I learned that there are three different ways to cross out a misspelled word: with a straight line, a squiggly one, or by scratching out the word with your pencil so many times that it ends up looking like top-secret, heavily redacted, highly classified material that must never be found out or else you will be killed.

After giving thousands of writing lessons and reviewing tens of thousands of kids' papers, I've learned what children need to be successful writers. The following is a list of general thoughts and strategies for helping your students learn to write successfully too.

Have Children Write Often

When I was a kid, my piano teacher, who was also my grandma, used to give me the Practice Speech when it was clear that I hadn't practiced for my lesson. It went like this: "If you miss one day of practice, *you* notice. If you miss two days, your teacher notices. Three days—and your audience notices." I didn't like to practice the piano, so I would get the Practice Speech a lot. Just like learning to play the piano, writing requires regular practice too. Writing is a craft—like carpentry, knitting, and cooking—and the more you practice, the better you become at it. So try to have your students write every day or almost every day. Play soft music in the background. Make it a routine.

Let Your Kids Write All Sorts of Things

Give children lots of different writing experiences. Have them write lists and sentences, stories and poems, paragraphs and wanted posters for the Big Bad Wolf. Ask them to write cards, brochures, reports, journal entries, and Mother's Day coupon books in which they promise to take out the garbage and go to bed without whining. Have them interview their parents to find out what life was like when they were young. Let them research the meaning of their names. Invite them to write to an author. They'll be excited when they receive a reply. Ask them to write notes to colors ("Dear red, I use you to draw apples and ladybugs. Please don't quit!") and messages from the Gingerbread Man ("Please don't eat me! Eat peppermints. They taste better!"). Have them compose letters to their future selves that they can slip into "time capsules" made out of empty plastic liter-sized bottles wrapped with large warnings to not look inside for twenty years and topped with caps covered with gobs of tape to make sure that no one does.

Allow Children to Write with a Friend

Some kids like to write alone, while others like to write with someone else. Give students the option of working independently or writing with a partner. Buddy writing. When you ask your kids to find a friend to write with, three girls will come up to you embraced tightly in a group hug, begging you to let them work together. Let 'em.

Let Your Students Spread Out All Around the Classroom

Personally, I don't like to write at a desk. When I'm writing, I prefer to sprawl out on my couch at home or on an overstuffed chair in a position that would make my chiropractor have a heart attack. Kids are the same. Some children like to write at a desk, but many prefer not to. During writing time, allow your students to work all over the classroom. For kids, writing is more fun when they are out of sight from their teacher. *Note*: Do not let children go outside to work on the jungle gym even if they promise that they will. It won't happen.

Explain What Writing Is Supposed to Look Like

Children do not like rewriting, so it's important to tell them why we ask them to. Explain to your students that writing is not like the other subjects. In math, for example, when you answer the problem *3 x 5*, you don't look at the *15* and try out different numbers to see if they might express more clearly what you're trying to say. The answer is *15*. Period. If you read a word in a book correctly, you do not linger over it, thinking of others that might sound better. You move on to the next one. But writing is different. Writing *is* rewriting. Teach your kids this. Get them used to writing more than one draft—a "sloppy copy"—and a final draft. For children, two drafts are enough. Kids needn't write two drafts of everything, but I would recommend that they write second drafts of their important papers.

To illustrate the writing process to my students, sometimes I would share a piece of needlework that my grandma had made. I'd explain that the front side of the needlework is like the final drafts of their writing. The mistakes have been corrected. It is pleasing to the eye. And then I'd turn the piece over. After the burst of "Whoa!"s—kids do not expect the back to look like this—I'd tell them that the back side, with all its crisscrossed threads and knots and loose ends, represents their first drafts full of crossed-out words and arrows and spelling mistakes. You can't create the beautiful side without the messy one.

Proofread with a Purpose

It's not easy for children to proofread their own work. One of the reasons is because they're looking for too much at once. So, have your kids go over their work in stages: one time for spelling (I'd just have them circle words they thought might not be correct) and a second time for missing periods and capitals. Kids do not want to check their papers more than twice. That's their limit. One of the best ways for children to proofread their work is to have them read it aloud. It slows them down so that they catch missing words and punctuation, clunky sentences, and parts that don't make sense. Before your students hand in their work, ask them to read their papers out loud with a pencil in hand. If the weather is nice, send them outside. On many days, the courtyard outside my classroom was filled with children talking to themselves.

Conference with Your Kids

One afternoon, I was sitting with my student teacher when she finished editing a batch of my kids' writing. "There!" she announced happily. "All done. Yay!" As she started filing away the papers, I looked at her and said, "I hate to break it to you, but you're not finished. Now you have to review the papers with each child." Her eyes got huge. It hadn't occurred to her.

After you have edited your students' work, hold short writing conferences with them. They needn't take long, sometimes just a couple of minutes. You won't be able to conference with children about all their work because of limited time. One middle school teacher friend of mine uses a deli-style format during her writing conferences. She passes out numbered "tickets" to all of her students. When she's ready for the next conference, she flashes a number on the screen along with the words "Now Serving."

When speaking to students about their writing, of course start by noting the positive. Then point out a few things for them to fix. Don't review all the errors. You do not want to overwhelm them. Just as reading conferences are important for developing readers, writing conferences are essential in helping kids grow as writers. It's also a nice time to have some one-on-one.

Share Children's Writing with Other Children
When your students complete a writing assignment, make copies of some of the better pieces and save them for the following year. Then, if you're repeating the activity, pass out the copies to your current students. Kids enjoy reading papers written by other kids. They connect to them in a different way.

Write the Room
This activity gets kids out of their seats and adds a little zip to their learning. Say, for example, you want your students to practice editing. Instead of having them edit at their seats, let them do it around the room. Just post a dozen or so cards on the walls and cabinets of your classroom. On them have sentences with spelling, punctuation, and grammar mistakes. The kids grab clipboards and recording sheets, then walk around and write the sentences correctly on their papers. Writing the Room can be used for anything, really—solving math problems, matching vocabulary with definitions, practicing spelling, and reviewing the content in any unit of study. Make one card a silly one. It adds to the fun.

Read a Child's Writing to the Rest of the Class
Can you remember when a teacher read your writing to the class? I can: grade two, Miss Greco; grade eight, Mrs. Watson; grade ten, Mr. Duncanson. And I can remember exactly where I was sitting when they read them. As you walk around your classroom during writing time, pick up a student's paper now and then and announce, "Boys and girls, sorry to interrupt, but I want you to listen to this." Then read a sentence or two to the whole class. The child whose paper you just picked up will never forget it. It makes that much of an impact. When teaching writing, you're not just building children's skills but also their confidence as writers.

Write—Don't Type—First Drafts

Some teachers have their students type their first drafts. I don't recommend this for children in elementary school. When kids type their first drafts, they're not focused fully on their writing. They're hunting for letters on the keyboard and thinking about what font they want to use. Every primary teacher knows that it can take a child five minutes to type one sentence on a laptop—ten on an iPad. On a good day. If you ask one group of children to handwrite their first drafts and another group to type theirs, the handwritten papers will always be superior. There's no comparison. Although laptops and iPads certainly have their time and place, you don't have to use them all the time.

Share Your Own Writing

A lot of teachers are closet writers. If you've written something that you think your students would enjoy, share it with them. It's one of the best ways to encourage kids to write. It also shows children what the process of writing looks like. A couple of times a year, I would bring my own writing into school and share it with my kids. I'd show them my multiple drafts of the same piece, so that they saw that grown-ups have to write more than one too. Inevitably, one child would ask how many drafts I had written, and I'd tell them that sometimes I revised a piece more than a dozen times till it was just right. To that, half the kids would collapse on the floor.

When I was working on my first book, *32 Third Graders and One Class Bunny*, I'd occasionally share some of it with my third graders—sort of like a tryout. All the stories were set in school. The children knew I was hoping to sell the manuscript. One morning, as I was reading one of the chapters, the kids began laughing. A good sign. I read them a second piece, and they chuckled some more. *This is going great*, I thought. The children asked me to read a third story, and even though it cut into our science time, I said, "Why not?" I picked another piece I knew they'd enjoy. But this time, no one laughed. Not even a giggle. When I finished reading, I looked at the kids and said, "Why didn't you laugh?"

One boy spoke up. "Mr. Done," he said hesitantly, "it's not funny."

"Not *funny*?" I said, ego bruised.

Heads shook.

And then a child shouted out, "You should start over and write about pirates! That will sell!"

"*Yeah!*" everyone agreed.

We started science.

Balance Your Writing Program

There are two main schools of thought regarding the teaching of writing. One focuses on the process of writing, emphasizing brainstorming, free writing, and journaling. The second is focused more on the basics, including sentence construction and the instruction of grammar and punctuation. Each has its place. I recommend a balanced combination of both. Children need to brainstorm and free write and journal. They also need to learn that verbs should agree with subjects and that not all sentences should start with *I*. Have you ever been at a restaurant and ordered the combination platter because a little of everything was better than having just one dish? Well, that's how I feel about teaching children to write. Give them the combo plate.

Remember Your Audience

Sometimes we ask kids to write things that aren't very fun for them. Take research reports, as an example. These days, many third and fourth graders are required to write research reports with evidence. But is this really necessary? Students will be writing research papers all the way through college. Do they really need to write them when they're nine? In all my years of teaching, never once did a child ask to write an extra research report with evidence. Children want to write about dream houses and pet rocks, magic hats and bicycles, the superpowers they would like to have, and what they would hide on top of their heads if they were wearing Abe Lincoln's hat (oftentimes a kitten). They like to write about funny things such as April Fool's Day pranks, how to catch leprechauns, the costume they think their teacher should wear for Halloween, and what they would do if they got trapped inside a snow globe. *These* are the kinds of things that excite children about writing. I realize that many teachers are required to follow a writing program. I did too. And I understand you have to cover all your standards. But that doesn't mean you can't supplement from time to time with assignments your children are excited to write about. In education, we often talk about cultivating a love of reading in children. Aim to make your writing activities lovable too.

Support the Reluctant Writer

Some students do not like to write. Actually, some are afraid of it. Once, I had a third grader named Joel who would cry all through the writing block. For weeks, he would sit with me at my desk, wiping away tears as he wrote, and I'd try my best to help him through it. *Poor kid.* Following are three strategies that work for students like Joel. Actually, they can help all of your kids.

The first strategy is to teach children that writing is talking on paper. I have a good friend named Debbie who teaches tap dancing. She tells her students to say the steps aloud as they make them with their feet. "If you can say the steps," Debbie claims, "you can tap 'em." Well, the same is true for writing. Saying the words helps you write them. If children are having trouble getting words onto paper, have them first tell you what they're thinking. "Joel," I'd say, "tell me one sentence. Just one. Nothing more." Through his sniffles, he'd give me a sentence. "Good," I'd remark. "Now, let's write that down." After he wrote the sentence, I'd ask him to tell me a second one, and he'd write that. We'd go on like this till Joel had written a whole paragraph. "Look what you just wrote!" I'd point out, running my finger under his sentences. "All these words just came out of your mouth. Writing is just talking on paper. You see? Now go blow your nose."

The second strategy to help reluctant writers is to give them some of the words. In teaching, we call this kind of support a scaffold. It's just like the ones that builders use to construct a house, but in this case, we're giving them to children to help construct sentences. When teaching students how to write a paragraph with transition words, for example, provide them with a scaffold that looks like this: "I love school for several reasons. First, _____. Second, _____. Next, _____. Also, _____. Finally, _____." Let the kids fill in the blanks. It's okay to start children off this way. As your students write more paragraphs and gain confidence, you will take away the scaffold. Think of scaffolds as training wheels. Eventually, children won't need them anymore.

The third strategy is to "chunk" the writing. Asking kids to write a whole story or multiple paragraphs at one time can be overwhelming. So, separate assignments into sections and spread the writing out over a couple of days. It's less daunting. When your students finish, they will be proud to see how much they have on their papers.

A footnote: Joel made it through third grade. He got through college too. Over the years, he kept in touch with me via Facebook. One day when he was in high school, he wrote to me and said: "Hey, Mr. Done! I'm working on a college essay this week and guess what . . . I'm not crying! Ha! Ha!" This was followed by a row of laughing emojis with tears pouring out of their eyes.

Provide Sentence Starters

Who doesn't like an appetizer? When writing, children appreciate starters too. One of my favorite ways to get kids writing was to provide them with the first few words of a sentence and let them finish the rest. Sentence starters, like scaffolds, relax students and allow them to focus on what they want to say and not stress about how to begin their sentences. Examples include: "Happiness is _____," "Every child should _____," and "I love my mom because _____." I'd ask the children to write a couple of sentences using the same starter.

Before your students write their sentences, teach them to use specific language: *Mac and cheese* is more specific than *food*; *freeze tag* is more specific than *game*. Also, to get kids writing longer sentences and to practice using commas, which all kids need, ask them to include three different examples in each sentence. When structured this way, the sentences are often rich and charming, as you will see from the following ones written by my third graders:

Happiness is pillow fights with my brother while jumping on the bed, smelling clothes when they come out of the washer, and my dog's wet nose when I come home from school (Mark). Happiness is seeing raindrops drop on the car window, looking at all my Halloween candy after I went trick-or-treating, and beating my mom in Uno (Tiffany). Happiness is hearing my hamster run on the wheel, handing in my no homework pass, and looking at the ground when I'm in an airplane (Galilea).

Every child should be the leader in follow-the-leader, play mini golf, and have a really special moment (Tim). *Every child should count down till New Year's, jump off a diving board, and make something you have never made before* (Bailey). *Every child should play in the rain (and the sun and the wind), decorate a Christmas tree, and have a cat wake them up* (Zoey).

I love my mom because she lets me stay up until 9:30 on weekends, cooks me soft things to eat because of my braces, and lets me lick the spoon after we make vanilla cupcakes (Mitchell). *I love my mom because she helps me with math like 3 x 7, lets me put my hand on the steering wheel when she is driving, and kisses me at night so I sleep really fast* (Danielle).

Hold an Authors' Tea

This is one of my favorite events of the school year. Long before the tea, ask your kids to write a story. I'd call their stories "manuscripts." Children like this grown-up word. After taking your students through the writing process of editing, revising, and rewriting, have them write their final manuscripts in hardback blank books, or let them type their stories and then cut and paste them into the books. Blank books can be ordered online in different sizes. I recommend ones that are 8 ½" × 11". Children prefer the larger books, and they are easier to manage. In kids' eyes, the hard covers are what make their books "real." When writing in the books, have students leave space for illustrations. Also, ask them to reserve a few blank pages in the beginning of the book for the title page and dedication—which might be to a gold fish. If, after finishing the book, the children end up with extra pages, just take them out with an X-Acto knife.

After they're done writing, let your kids illustrate their books, including the covers. Before they begin, discuss what makes a good cover design and share some examples. I suggest having students draw a mock cover first until they get it the way they want. On the back of the book, ask kids to write a short autobiography titled "About the Author." Some of your junior authors will include make-believe websites and Facebook pages where readers can "visit" them. Once, a student of mine drew a large O in the corner of her cover. When I asked her what it meant, she happily informed me that Oprah had picked it for her book club. If you wish, you can also have children create dust jackets, including summaries on the inside flaps. If your students make dust jackets, some will include pretend bar codes, as well as the price of the book in both US and Canadian dollars.

When the books are complete, ask your kids to write invitations for the tea. Invite the parents, the principal, the librarian, and any support teachers who helped your students during the year. Hold the tea around noon so that parents can swing by on their lunch breaks. On the day of the tea, prop up all the books on the children's desks, and set up a table or two for refreshments. Ask your room parents to bring in some cookies and punch, as well as tea and coffee for the adults. For the event, invite the kids to dress up. Dressing up, I'd explain to the children, makes any occasion more special. Some of my boys would bring in their dads' ties and ask me to tie them. And some would have put on the ties themselves with the back part of the tie hanging longer than the front. I wouldn't fix those. It was cute.

After you have welcomed your guests, let your students spread out around the classroom and read their books to them. All the kids will be reading at the same time. For a teacher, there is not much lovelier than seeing and hearing a room full of children read their writing to their proud moms and dads. When your kids are finished, direct them to serve the refreshments to the adults before having theirs. Practice this ahead of time. The parents will be charmed that their kids are serving them. Some will be speechless. A couple of them will look at their children and say, "Now you can do this at home." I suggest holding your Authors' Tea at the end of May or in early June. It's a lovely way to celebrate your students' writing and the end of the school year. Before the guests leave, have a grand book signing where all the kids sit at their desks and sign their books in their best handwriting while their parents hold up their phones to record the event.

Always Start Like This

No matter what the writing assignment, there is one very important thing that all teachers must do before asking children to write: Model exactly what you want your kids to do. If you ask students to write a story, compose one in front of them first. If you want them to draft a friendly letter, demonstrate how to write one. If you assign kids to pen a paragraph, show them how. When I speak of modeling, I don't mean giving students an example that you copied out of the teacher's manual. I'm talking about giving them your *own* example by standing at a blank board and composing a piece right in front of them. I'm talking about writing out loud.

We all know that one of the best ways to learn something is to watch someone else do it. Writing out loud is when you write something in front of children and verbalize your thoughts while you're constructing it. Let's say by way of illustration that you want your kids to write about those dream trips that I talked about at the beginning of this chapter. I'm suggesting that you stand at the whiteboard with your dry erase markers and describe *your* dream trip from start to finish. Let your students watch you struggle with that opening sentence. Talk out loud so they can hear your thoughts. Allow them to observe your scribbles and arrows. Let them see you scratch your head as you try to come up with the perfect word, then get excited when you think of it. By writing aloud, you demonstrate what real writers do. Kids don't know what goes into a piece of writing until you show them. When writing this way, you're pulling back the curtain to reveal what lies behind every piece of good writing.

This reminds me of a favorite story of mine. When film star Debbie Reynolds was still a teenager, she was cast in the classic movie musical *Singin' in the Rain*. It was one of her first films. In the picture, Reynolds would be required to dance, but the problem was that she wasn't a dancer. To get up to speed, she had to practice the dance routines sometimes up to fifteen hours a day. The young actress would cry every day in rehearsal. She thought she'd never be good enough. One day when she was whimpering under a grand piano, a man poked his head under it and asked what she was doing down there. The man was cinema's greatest dancer, Fred Astaire. Reynolds told him what was going on and said she wasn't going to make it. Then Astaire did something he never did. He invited Reynolds to his rehearsal. Astaire's rehearsals were always closed. And there, with just the two of them and a piano player in the room, Reynolds watched Astaire practice his steps over and over and over again. She saw the work and sweat that went into making a dance perfect, even for the great Astaire. Finally, after about an hour, he walked over to her

and said, "Okay, kid, you've seen what it takes. Now go out there and do it."
And she did.

Writing out loud is like that rehearsal. You're taking your students behind the scenes of writing. Something special happens when children see their
teacher writing aloud in front of them. It gives them the courage to try it
themselves. It shows them that mistakes really are okay. For kids like Joel, all
of a sudden writing isn't so scary anymore. So whenever you write with children, invite them to *your* rehearsal. And always, always, always model it first.

A Word About Math

"What's *that*?" Russell asked, pointing to the thick spiral-bound book that lay open on my desk, where I sat with a student. It was math time.

"The teacher's edition," I replied.

Russell leaned over it and looked more closely. "It has all the answers!" Immediately he grabbed the book and held it tightly to his chest. "I'll give you a million dollars for it!"

I laughed.

Then he shouted to his classmates, "Hey, look! This book has all the answers!" Instantly a half dozen kids sprang from their chairs and ran toward us. I yanked the book out of Russell's hands before things escalated into a full-blown game of hot potato, teacher's edition.

Math time: the period in every school day when children work with numbers and teachers cling to their coffee mugs. In fact, of all the "times" in a school day—math time, reading time, writing time—I wouldn't be surprised if researchers discover that math time is the one when teachers consume the most coffee. Why is this? For grade school teachers, the math period is almost always in the morning. Experts claim that children's minds are freshest then. Well, kids' brains might be fresh in the morning, but teachers' brains surely aren't. While many people begin their workdays at their desks with a coffee and a computer, teachers start their days with a coffee and a room full of children. During this time, we are expected to solve math problems on whiteboards without calculators when we still have sleep sand in our eyes.

I'm not complaining. I actually enjoyed teaching math. After all the years

I taught it, I wouldn't even venture to guess how many math problems I've written on the board or papers I have corrected or flash cards I've held up while waiting for children with cringed faces to try to remember the answer. In fact, sometimes I felt like a McDonald's marquee. Years ago, McDonald's restaurants used to post the number of hamburgers they had sold under the golden arches. As the years went by, the numbers would keep growing: "Over 5 Billion Sold." "Over 10 Billion Sold." "Over 20 Billion Sold!" Well, just change a few words, and you describe a grade school teacher to a T: "Over 20 Billion Math Problems Solved Here!"

After decades of playing Addition Fact Bingo (and fraction and decimal and multiplication fact bingo too), singing times tables, making stupid math jokes, and sucking in my stomach while wrapping a measuring tape around my waist so that my kids would understand circumference, I will share my thinking about math time. I won't offer specific strategies here—just some general thoughts on what works and what doesn't when teaching math to children.

Concrete Objects

When teaching kids any math skill or concept, begin your instruction using concrete objects. If you're a teacher, I understand that I'm preaching to the choir here and saying something that you already know, but it never hurts to be reminded of this point every now and then. Take the problem $3 + 5$ as an example. When children have three beans and add five beans to them, we call it "concrete" because they're manipulating tangible objects. When students solve $3 + 5$ on a piece of paper without anything to manipulate, we call this "abstract." When teaching math, it is always best to move from the concrete to the abstract. C to A. It's in the touching and holding and manipulating that the deepest understanding of math takes place. *This* is the reason elementary school teachers have closets packed with base ten blocks, Unifix cubes, geometric shapes, tangrams, number tiles, play money, geoboards, and pattern blocks. This is why we store plastic pizzas cut into slices that kids will pretend to eat while practicing fractions.

When introducing children to multiplication—an abstract concept for kids that requires a lot of work with real objects—have them build multiplication problems with all sorts of things before giving them a piece of paper with problems to solve. When teaching graphing, hand students a cup of different-colored Smarties or gummy bears or conversation hearts—heck, even the marshmallow shapes in Lucky Charms—and let them make their graphs before ever picking up their pencils and markers. When teaching area, another concept that can be hard for children to comprehend without the concrete, have your kids put together different-sized rectangles with Cheez-Its, then figure out the area of each one. Of course, when they're finished, let them eat their math. When beginning your fraction unit, give children long strips of construction paper and ask them to fold the strips to make halves, a second time to create fourths, once again to get eighths, and finally, though it takes a lot of muscle, one last time to make sixteenths. No matter how hard it is for little hands to fold a paper into sixteenths, all kids will press, push, pound, hammer, and wrestle that paper to the ground till they've made them.

I understand that you won't be able to use concrete objects all the time. Sometimes there's just not enough time, and some concepts lend themselves to the use of manipulatives better than others. But whenever possible, pull out those tubs. Move from C to A. It's good teaching and results in good learning too.

Textbooks

Sometimes I would tell my students jokes about school, and one of them went like this: "What did one math book say to the other?" Answer: "Don't bother me. I've got my own problems." Well, math books don't just have problems. They can also create them. In my first year of teaching, I was given a class set of old green math books, and my third graders would have to copy the problems out of them onto binder paper. Because of this, they were spending more time copying than doing math. Math time became copy time. I hated those texts, and it didn't take me long to stop using them. Fortunately, a lot of today's math programs don't ask children to do this anymore, but some still do. If your district requires you to use a math textbook in this way, do so sparingly. Limit the number of problems you assign. Eventually, I did find some uses for the math book. You can weigh it and measure its perimeter. It can also be used to teach science. Just drop it into the wastebasket to demonstrate gravitational pull.

Worksheets

What in the world would teachers do without all those 8½" × 11" pieces of paper full of numbers that we pull from idea books, get online, find in the piles of materials that come with the math program, or steal from our colleagues? Math worksheets provide children with practice, teachers with a little breather, and repairmen with steady work for the rest of their lives because after a copier's jam light comes on and a teacher opens the side door of the machine to try to pull out the worksheet stuck inside, the teacher is usually able to retrieve only a piece of it, which by this point is crinkled like an accordion and covered with toner.

There's nothing wrong with worksheets. Every teacher uses them. They can, however, be overused. Just as math time can become copy time, if you're not careful, it can become worksheet time too. And I'm including workbooks here. Math workbooks are basically just a bunch of math worksheets bound together. Also, worksheets frequently come loaded with problems. If there are thirty problems on a worksheet, and children demonstrate that they know how to solve the first five, should they really have to solve twenty-five more? If you do give your students a worksheet, consider having them complete just part of it. Ask them to solve only one row, or do just the even problems, or pick any five that they want to solve. Your kids will love you for not making them do the whole page.

Vocabulary

One day, when working with one of my ELL students to check his understanding of some math vocabulary, I pointed to a picture of a square and asked the child what it was. The boy said, "Square." Next, I pointed to a circle, and he answered, "Circle." When I pointed to a semicircle, he hesitated. I could see that he wasn't sure of the word. After a few seconds, he looked at me and said, "Taco?"

Sometimes it's not the math that a child doesn't understand, it's the words. To give an example, children might know how to subtract but not know what it means when you ask them to "find the difference." A student could understand multiplication but not know what a *product* is. Every year, I asked my English language learners which subjects they found the most difficult, and, every year, the kids' answers were the same: math and science. When I asked why, they'd always give the same answer: "the words." It made sense. At each grade level, children are introduced to a long list of new math vocabulary. In a typical fourth-grade geometry unit, for example, a student will learn: *congruent, equilateral, symmetrical, parallelogram, rhombus, intersection, perimeter, trapezoid, closed figures, polygon, segment,* and *three-dimensional.* And this is only a partial list. Learning new math words can be daunting for a native English speaker. Imagine what it's like for a child whose first language isn't English.

To help ELL students learn math vocabulary, I found a couple of strategies particularly beneficial. First off, have Google Translate open on a laptop during math time so that children can translate unknown words into their first languages. Also, before each new math unit, send home a list of the new words that your students will encounter, and ask the parents to review these terms with their children so that they understand them in both English and their native languages. This is called frontloading the information. Frontloading benefits not only English language learners but also children with learning disabilities. In June, consider giving your ELL students the vocabulary from the first two math units that they will be taught at the beginning of the next school year. Of course, you'll have to work this out with the other teachers. Every year, my colleagues and I would do this for our English language learners. It took some coordination, but it gave the children a big confidence boost because they started the new school year knowing all the words.

Review

"How do you kids not know this? Haven't I already taught you?" Most teachers have said this to their students or at least thought it. And we've all had that nerve-racking experience of preparing kids for the spring tests and discovering that they forgot what you taught them earlier in the year, so you give them a crash review while they wonder what just hit them.

When learning new skills, children need lots of repetition, but teachers don't always give students the review they need. With so much material to cover, we often plow through one math unit, then move on quickly to the next. Just because we've covered something doesn't mean kids have learned it. To ensure that students remember their math, make it a point to review skills throughout the year. Every year, no matter what grade I was teaching, the first thing I would have kids do when they entered the classroom in the morning was to solve five math problems that would be waiting for them on the board. I called it "Five a Day." This was a good time to review previously learned skills. When the children finished solving their five problems, we'd correct them together. Actually, I'd give my kids five problems plus a bonus. The bonus was usually something like $5 + 5$, which inevitably would bring out the ham in some students, who would take the opportunity to clutch their skulls and cry out that the bonus problem was too hard.

Another way to review math skills is to write one number large enough for the class to see, slide it into a pocket chart, then below it place index cards or sentence strips on which you ask kids to perform math skills that you have already taught. Let's say you're teaching grade three. It's late spring, and the day's number is 7,386. Your task cards could look like this: (1) *Add one more 100* [place value]; (2) *Round to the nearest 1,000* [rounding]; (3) *Subtract 192* [subtraction with regrouping]; (4) *Multiply by 2* [multiplication]; and (5) *Cut the number in half* [division]. You've just reviewed five previously learned skills using a single number.

Word Problems

One morning during our math unit about money, I gave my third graders a paper with the following question: "If Carter has four dimes and Amy has six nickels, who has more money?" I looked at Cindy's paper to check her work. She'd written "Carter," which was correct. The second part of the question said: "Show your thinking." When I saw Cindy's response, I held back a laugh. She had drawn a picture of herself and a thought bubble. Inside the bubble was "Carter."

Most children don't like word problems much. They slow kids down. It's way faster for a child to look at *5 x 7* and scribble down *35* than to have to read "There are 5 kids, and each has 7 lollipops. How many lollipops in all?," then draw five children, each holding seven lollipops, and finally circle the answer. But that's not the only reason kids aren't too keen on word problems. Have you ever noticed just where word problems are located in a math book or on a worksheet? They're almost always last. Your students will be feeling happy that they're just about finished with their work when all of a sudden, *Bam!* They're hit with a bunch of word problems. For kids, facing word problems at the end of a paper is like facing the vegetables on your dinner plate that your mom says you have to finish in order to be excused.

There are some word problems, however, that children *do* like. And these are ones that have their names in them. For kids, seeing your name and the names of your friends in a math problem automatically makes it fun. So write your own word problems every once in a while and include your students' names. Be silly. They'll giggle as they read 'em. Put in your name too. Save the problems on your computer for the next year, and just change the names. Of course, make sure to include all the children; you don't want to leave anyone out. And expect to get some goofy answers. One year I gave my kids the following problem about my student named Gary: "Mr. Done had 600 candy bars. He ate 167 of them and gave the rest to Gary. How many candy bars did Gary get?" Gary's answer: "Not enough." For a twist, let your kids come up with their own word problems—including the answer key. If you ask children to write them, you'll need to set some parameters, though, otherwise you will get problems like this: "Mr. Done has 600 candy bars. He gives all of them to Gary. How many candy bars does Mr. Done have left?"

Measurement

In terms of math skills, there was one that I always felt kids needed to practice more, and that was measurement. It didn't matter what grade I taught. I was always surprised at how many children had trouble measuring. Sometimes I'd get third graders who had barely ever used a ruler or a scale. I understood why. Nowadays, kids don't get a lot of opportunities to measure. If you teach math, I recommend giving your students more time with rulers and scales, yardsticks and measuring tapes. Don't have your kids measure for just two weeks during the measurement unit, then be done with it. Spread the weighing and measuring throughout the year.

For starters, put a pound of rice in a ziploc bag and label it "One Pound." Do the same with a kilogram. Let students hold the bags so they understand what a pound and a kilo actually feel like in their hands. A lot of children don't understand this. While you're at it, explain that a gram is approximately the weight of one paper clip. At the beginning of the school year, bring in a watermelon, and have all your kids hold it to guess the weight before putting it on a scale. (*Math fact*: Whenever children pass around a watermelon, one child will always pretend it's a baby.) Around Halloween, weigh and measure pumpkins. (*Math fact*: If you carve the pumpkins later, one student will always refuse to touch the goop.) In the fall, send your kids outside to measure leaves and the circumference of tree trunks. Before winter break, organize a Stuffed Animal Day, and ask your students to measure the body parts of their stuffed toys. Have the kids measure their own body parts at the same time to figure out the difference. (*Math fact*: When measuring children's heights, they will always raise their chins in hopes of making themselves a little bit taller.)

As a fun follow-up to Stuffed Animal Day, create a *Night at the Museum*–like experience by asking students to leave their stuffies at school overnight. After the kids go home, set the animals all around the classroom so that the next morning the children find them in the broom closet, on top of the projector, and head-down in the goody jar. Act like the toys must have come to life and made themselves at home.

One of the best ways to give children more measuring practice is through art. For kids, combining measurement with art always makes the learning enjoyable. Have your students cut buildings out of different-colored paper and mount them onto pieces of black construction paper to create skylines. After drawing on windows and doors (and the moon and stars), children measure the heights of the buildings. Or let kids construct pet shop aquariums, in just three steps: (1) Cover the sides of a shoebox with light-blue butcher paper; (2) Using a black Sharpie, make lines along all the edges to represent the edges of the tank; and (3) On all four sides, draw colorful fish and sea plants and little castles for the fish to hide in. When the aquariums are finished, students can measure the length and height of each side because, as I'd point out to my kids, people buying an aquarium want to know the dimensions. A third idea for practicing measurement is to let children draw their very own amusement parks. Just give each student a large piece of white construction paper. On it, the child draws several rides of different heights, including at least one giant roller coaster. When your students are finished drawing their parks, ask them to measure the height of the rides. Kids love this project, especially if they can add cars of screaming children with their hands in the air on the roller coasters. If your students create amusement parks, expect to say, "No, you may not draw me flying out of a car."

Measurement activities can be combined with other subjects as well. When teaching California history, as an example, I'd show my kids how to draw the Golden Gate Bridge. During our fairy-tale unit, I'd teach them how to draw castles. To give a directed drawing lesson to your class, hand out white drawing paper and put the sample you have made on the board. Then, demonstrating each step, walk the children through the lesson, saying things like this: "Okay, using your ruler, measure eight and a half inches from the bottom left corner of your paper and make a dot," or "Now draw a vertical line that is two and a quarter inches in length." By taking children step-by-step through a drawing lesson like this, they get lots of practice measuring, *and* they're hearing all those measurement words they've been learning used in an authentic way. Don't think you have to be a good artist to draw with your students. They don't care. More often than not, my castles ended up looking like haunted houses, and my Golden Gate Bridges looked like they were one earthquake away from toppling into the bay.

Mental Math

Mental math is fun for both kids and teachers. Kids enjoy it because there are no pencils. Teachers like it because there's little prep and zero mess. In school, we ask children to do a lot of math with paper and pencil but not enough without them. To have your students practice mental math, just give them a list of questions related to whatever it is they're currently learning. Then let them buddy up with a friend or two and ask each other the questions. Examples of mental math questions for third graders look like this: What is 12 - 7 + 9? What's (1/2 of 1/4) + 2/16? What is (50% of 60) + (25% of 100)? When creating pencil-less problems, make sure they're ones that most of your kids can solve. Add a couple of challenges too. I suggest creating the problems yourself, so that you can tailor them to your students. Homemade anything is always better than canned. After children practice in school, send the questions home to review with their moms and dads.

Edible Math

Math and treats are like ice cream and hot fudge: a good match. As a student of mine once said—"I just love when we eat what we're learning." During math time, apples can be weighed. Cheerios can be counted. Bananas can be measured. Oranges can be sliced into fractions. Froot Loops can be graphed. And schools of Pepperidge Farm Goldfish crackers can be grouped onto blue construction paper oceans to illustrate division problems like this: "There are 12 goldfish. They swim in 3 different schools. How many goldfish are in each school?" As far as math edibles go, nothing comes close to the M&M or Skittle. These two toothsome treats are in a class all their own. One handful of M&M's or Skittles can be sorted, counted, added, subtracted, grouped, multiplied, divided, graphed, weighed, and used to teach fractions. Heck, I wouldn't be surprised if you told me they could be used to teach calculus—or send a man to the moon. Of course, whenever children solve math problems with anything edible, there are rules: (1) When kids finish working with their treats, they get to eat them; (2) Any food item you hand a child should not be damaged. It is an unwritten law that children cannot measure broken candy canes as well as unbroken ones. They can't graph animal crackers that are missing their heads as well as those that have them either; and (3) Always have extras on hand. It takes a lot of willpower for a child to sort, count, or graph a cup full of goodies for an entire math period without trying at least one.

Movement

Movement and learning are powerfully connected. Researchers have discovered that when children are allowed to stand and move, their attention, memory, mood, and academic achievement all improve. When teachers incorporate movement into their instruction, they keep their kids' brains engaged and elevate the learning experience.

Math and movement go together. Teaching kids to read large numbers? Give them each a card with a single digit written on it (0 through 9). Call four students to the front of the room and have them hold their cards in front of them. Read the four-digit number as a class. Then call up six kids. Then eight. Then twenty! Build the human number so long that children have to start standing on the counter. Practicing decimals? Do the same activity, but let one student stand between two classmates while holding a red rubber ball (the decimal point). Then read the decimal.

Teaching kids how to make and read graphs? Make human ones: "If you are right-handed, line up here. If you're left-handed, line up next to them." Voila! Your class is now a bar graph. Then ask: "How many more children are right-handed?" "What's the difference between our right-handed and left-handed students?"

Reinforcing measurement? Take your kids outside and make a couple of lines on the blacktop with chalk. Starting with their toes behind the line, let the children leapfrog, then measure the distances. For fun, make the kids some paper headbands with frog faces for them to wear while they're jumping.

Reviewing geometry? Play Geometry Simon Says. Ask your students to stand up and face the front of the room. Call out: "Simon says turn ninety degrees!" "Simon says show me a point!" (a fist). "Simon says show me a ray!" (both arms extended, one hand in a fist). "Okay, now show me one hundred and eighty degrees!" Point to the children who flinch and say, "Gotcha! Simon didn't say. Take a seat."

Another fun way to review geometry is to have kids buddy up with a friend or two, lie on the floor, and use their bodies to show you various right, acute, and obtuse angles, as well as lines, line segments, and parallel lines. *Teacher tip*: Don't ask children to show you intersecting and perpendicular lines unless you're ready to see a pileup. I call this acting out math "Dramath." Kids love it. But don't confuse Dramath with "Dramarks." That's when you use your body to make exclamation marks, commas, apostrophes, and question marks on the floor with your friends.

Technology

When I was teaching, I had the chance to visit a lot of schools. Oftentimes, when I observed classrooms during math, I would witness entire classes of headphoned children playing math games on laptops or iPads. I'd wonder, *Just how much math is being learned here?* What also concerned me was what the students were *not* doing. When kids are playing games on their devices, they're not manipulating concrete objects with their hands or building anything. They're not interacting with their peers or moving their bodies. They're not jumping outside with frog masks. I'm not against on-screen math games. They're fun, and children enjoy them, but just like you wouldn't give your students Skittles Math every day, I believe that online games should also be limited and offered as a special treat.

Wiggle Room

These days, more and more teachers are asked to follow scripted math programs. I'm not a big fan. A lot of teachers aren't. One friend of mine calls scripted curriculums "paint-by-number teaching." When you're bound to one program, there's not a lot of extra room to implement ideas from other resources. It's a shame because there are so many wonderful ideas out there for teaching math. To compound the problem, there's a big push to have every teacher in a grade level teach the same unit at the same time. When you have to follow a canned curriculum, something valuable gets lost. You lose your autonomy. You can no longer try out an idea that you recently learned about or one that you just thought of and know your kids would enjoy. When all teachers have to be on the same page (literally), you also lose your flexibility. You limit the time you can delve into a topic, spend on review, supplement with enrichment, or follow a teachable moment. For teachers, this kind of lockstep teaching can be extremely frustrating.

It reminds me of one of my favorite *I Love Lucy* episodes, where Ricky puts Lucy on a strict schedule. One night, to get back at him, Lucy sets Ricky's dinner on the table only to whisk away his plate seconds later. She claims there's no time in the schedule for him to eat. Sometimes teaching math can feel this way. In order to keep the same schedule as our colleagues and keep in step with the program, we "serve" our students a skill, then whisk them to the next one before they've had a chance to taste it, let alone digest it.

If you are required to follow a program, the good news is that there are a couple of things you can do to free up your time so that you can do other things. To start, don't do every lesson in the teacher's manual. Pick and choose. Also, ditch those pretests that come with the program. Pretests take up valuable time. You don't need to give all of them. Posttests are enough. And don't be afraid to "close the door." If you want to deviate from the program, shut the door, tell your kids to keep their math books in their desks, and do something else. It's okay to take a little detour sometimes. We teach kids first. Then programs.

Real Math

All teachers of math know that it's important for children to have opportunities to apply what they've learned, and the best way to do this is what I call "Real Math." This is where you give kids real menus, catalogs, or advertisements to solve problems. I would try to provide a Real Math activity for my students at least once a month, usually on a Friday. Here's what it looked like:

In the beginning of the school year, I'd give my kids ads from Walmart and let them go on a "shopping trip" for back-to-school supplies. In October I handed out Target ads for children to "purchase" costumes and supplies for a pretend Halloween party. In November I'd distribute Scholastic book order forms to "shop" for books, and in December I would pass out catalogs from See's Candies to "buy" holiday gifts. Throughout the year, I also used menus from local restaurants for make-believe trips out to eat. After a few years, I'd pick up new menus and advertisements. *Teacher tip*: Do not collect your ads with a non-teacher. They won't get it. Non-teachers do not view the taking of a half dozen ads from the entrance at Michael's craft store the same as teachers do.

Using the prices in the printed material, write out a bunch of problems for your students. Include plenty of problems that pertain to what they are currently studying. As I pointed out earlier, use your kids' names. Real Math works best if you include them. On Real Math days, hand out the sheets of questions along with the catalogs, ads, or menus. Allow children to work individually or in groups of two or three. Most will choose to work with a friend. Math, like writing, is more pleasurable when shared with a buddy.

Hands down, Real Math days were always my favorite math times. They were the kids' favorite too. One day when my third graders had just finished going on a pretend shopping trip to Toys"R"Us, one of them called out, "Mr. Done—when's math?"

Talking to Learn

"And how old are you?" I asked Christine. I was going around the class-room asking my third graders their ages.

"Eight and three-fourths," she answered.

I smiled, then turned to Ethan. "And how old are you, Ethan?"

"Sixty-three," he replied. I pulled a face as his broke into a grin. "In dog years."

Next was Monica's turn. "And how old are you?"

"I'm eight," she responded, "but my birthday is in two months, so my mom says I can say I'm nine." She went on. "I'm a Scorpio. I wanted to be an Aquarius, but my sister got it."

When all the kids finished sharing, I said, "Can any of you guess *my* age?"

"Fifty," Finn jested. I was twenty-seven at the time.

I pretended to be insulted. "*Fifty?*"

Giggles.

"Fifty-five," Harper joshed with a grin.

Laughter.

"Seventy-five!" Brian burst out.

Hooting.

"A *hundred*!" Ethan whooped.

"Yeah, a *hundred*!" everyone echoed.

(*Cue: peals of laughter.*)

As it swirled around the room, I clutched my chest and pretended to have a heart attack.

* * *

THE CURRICULUM

Talking with children was one of the things I enjoyed most about teaching. I got a kick out of it. It was certainly never dull. Adults never fall out of their chairs in hysterics after guessing I'm a hundred.

Children love to talk. Every teacher knows what happens when you show a group of students a picture of a dog, cat, guinea pig, or hamster. Immediately all the children begin talking about their pets at the same time without being aware that anyone else is speaking. You get the same response when you bring up bee stings, allowance, getting stitches, or Santa Claus. All teachers have experienced being in the middle of a lesson when a child asks about something completely unrelated to what you are teaching. During a math lesson, no teacher would ever be surprised to be lobbed a question such as: "In the olden days, how did they churn butter?" Teachers try to keep kids' questions focused on the topic at hand by saying, "Is this a story or a question?" but it rarely works. Children know the difference. They just pretend not to. And all teachers know that when the police officer speaks at the school assembly and asks the kids if they have any questions (not stories), the child who is called on—after assuring her teacher that she really has a question—might very well proceed to tell the entire multipurpose room full of people about the time her dad got a speeding ticket.

During a science lesson, I once had the following exchange with a student:

TEACHER: (*seeing raised hand*) Is this a question or a story?
STUDENT: A question.
TEACHER: Is it about the topic we are discussing right now?
STUDENT: Yes.
TEACHER: Okay. What is it?
STUDENT: Yesterday I was outside and I saw a dog and then the dog disappeared and—
TEACHER: Hold it. Hold it. This sounds like a story.
STUDENT: No, I have a question.
TEACHER: (*looking skeptical*) What is it?
STUDENT: Can dogs be angels?

Children talk about everything, and I don't think parents realize just how much their kids talk about *them*. Over my career, I heard it all: "My mom hit the neighbor's car, but don't tell anyone. She didn't tell him." "My dad sleeps on the couch. He snores too much." "My mom has a tattoo on her (slaps fanny) right here." "My daddy steals copper pipes from old houses." "On the weekend, we went to Ikea to buy a new bed because my parents' bed broke." "My mom gives me candy right before she takes me to my dad's house so I can be crazy there." Kids freely share their parents' ages, favorite happy hour drinks, and where their moms hide the things they bought so their dads won't find them. Kids volunteer which parent they go to when they want something (usually Dad), who is less strict about bedtime (Dad wins here too), and who drives the fastest (always Dad).

Teachers have special names for their talkers: chatterboxes, Chatty Cathys. I called mine "Yacky Ducks." That's what my dad used to call me. One year I had a Yacky Duck whose real name was Ronny. He never stopped talking. It didn't matter where I moved him, he'd start chattering away. I tried putting an empty desk next to him. Didn't work. I tried seating him between two girls. It got worse. Ronny wasn't just a chatterbox in my classroom. He yacked everywhere. Mr. Miller, the science lab teacher, hung a sign on the human skeleton in his classroom that said "Mr. Miller waiting for Ronny to be quiet." One day when I needed a break, I challenged Ronny to not talk for sixty seconds. He accepted. I looked at the clock. "On your mark," I said. His classmates watched the clock with me. "Get set . . . Go!" As the second hand moved past the numbers, Ronny bit his lip. Then he started bouncing. He covered his mouth with one hand. Then another. Finally, after forty-eight seconds, he collapsed onto his desk and gave a defeated cry: "I can't do it!"

Of course, not all children's talk is the same. At school, there are actually four different kinds. The first is "normal talk," the pleasant childhood chatter that you hear when students are working in their classrooms, standing in line, or sitting on the reading rug waiting for the teacher to get settled in the chair and take one last sip of coffee before speaking. The second type of kid talk is "excited talk." Louder than normal talk, excited talk occurs when children are waiting for something to start like a class play, a school assembly, or a visit from a firefighter who might let one lucky child wear his helmet. Excited talk also takes place on bus rides to a field trip destination (never on the ride home), when the power goes out, or when the teacher looks at the clock at the end of the day and realizes that there isn't enough time to assign homework, so that night there won't be any. The third kind of talk is "loud talk." Similar to excited talk but not exactly the same, loud talk happens at three times in the day: recess, lunchtime, and during intense games of steal the bacon while out at PE. Loud talk occurs inside classrooms at rainy-day recess too. The fourth kind of kid talk, "secret talk," takes place at silent reading time when two children sit together in the corner of the classroom or under a table with books in their hands but aren't really reading. Secret talk happens when kids whisper in line during fire drills even though the rule is: No talking. Secret talk also occurs when the teacher needs to step out of the classroom for a minute but before doing so reminds the class to stay in their seats and keep working quietly. After the teacher leaves, a lookout will stand guard and announce when the teacher is returning. When the teacher walks back into the classroom, all the secret talkers will become perfectly quiet, pretending to work. Most children are quite adept at all four types of talking. A child like Ronny can switch from normal, to excited, to loud, to secret talk without any trouble at all.

As much as teachers would like a little quiet every now and then, we know that kids need to talk. We recognize that talk is central to learning, critical for children's language development, and foundational to literacy. We understand that it is through talk that children develop their ideas, polish their thoughts, sharpen their thinking, and solidify their learning. Talk enables kids to voice opinions, explore feelings, and work with others. It is in talking that children learn to understand how language works. In short, talk underpins everything we do. And so, teachers do a lot to get their kids talking. We host the morning meetings, run the literature circles, and set up the book clubs. We hold large and small group discussions and have kids turn to the children seated next to them to share. All day long, we ask children questions and listen to their answers. But despite teachers' best efforts to encourage talking in class, the reality is that schools could do more. Talk takes time, and teachers don't have a lot of it. In the classroom, talking often takes a backseat to subjects deemed more important. If the subjects in school were instruments in the orchestra, reading, writing, and math would be the first violins, violas, and cellos seated near the front. Talking would be a third fiddle way back under the exit sign.

Children aren't talking a lot out of school either. According to a study by the US Department of Education, the average American child talks with his mother fewer than thirty minutes a day. With fathers, it's even less. In today's plugged-in world, kids aren't talking to one another like they used to. We've all seen it: groups of students gathered together, but there's no conversation because everyone is looking at his or her phone. A longtime licensed family counselor I'm friends with named Bill told me that he sees more and more young people who don't know how to talk. Because they're on their screens all day, they're losing the ability to communicate face-to-face. "Today's kids are becoming conversationally incompetent," Bill said. "It's becoming a big problem."

Just like anything else, children need to be taught how to converse. We can't assume they know how to have a conversation. A conversation is like a partner dance. It involves give and take. There's a rhythm and a flow to it. You must be attentive to your partner. And just like it takes practice to learn to dance, learning to be conversant does too. The good news is that we *can* teach our students how. We can move talk out of the third-string section. Teachers understand the value of asking children open-ended and thought-provoking questions to stimulate conversation. What follows are a few additional ideas that not only encourage kids to speak but also help children to speak well.

Plan for Talking

One day when I was a student teacher, I sat down with my master teacher, Bob, to go over a lesson I'd just given to a class of fourth graders. Bob asked me how I thought the lesson went, and I told him that I felt it had gone pretty well. Then Bob said something that I will never forget. He gave his head a shake and said two words: "Too quiet." *Gulp.* Bob pointed out that during the lesson, *I* was the one who had done most of the talking. The kids had done very little, he noted, and several hadn't said anything at all. It was a valuable lesson, one that always stayed with me. "Children," he said, "learn with their mouths open." When creating your lessons, plan activities for kids to share and discuss, comment and converse. Embed speaking opportunities in subjects that don't normally have a talk focus, such as math and science. Be deliberate about it.

Model How to Converse

Before asking children to participate in a discussion with their peers, demonstrate how. Teach it explicitly. Sit down with a student or two in front of your class and model what a good conversation looks like. Show them what a bad one looks like too. One way to illustrate a good dialogue is to toss a tennis ball with a student. Explain that a conversation is like a friendly game of catch. In both, there is a back-and-forth: throw and catch, talk and listen. Of course, you can also use the tennis ball to illustrate a poor exchange. In this case, you might want to put on a catcher's mask.

Create Discussion Guidelines

To encourage respectful communication, create classroom discussion guidelines with your students early in the year. Mine would look like this:

- Keep your eyes on the speaker.
- Respect one another's ideas.
- Give everyone a chance to speak.
- Invite others into the conversation by asking a question.

After creating your guidelines, have students role-play what each one looks like. Post the guidelines on the wall and keep them up all year long. Refer to them often. As you observe children following the guidelines, compliment them on what you see.

I remember one particular group meeting where I was not only glad to see that the children were keeping to our discussion guidelines, I was pleased with what they'd come up with. It was our first student council meeting of the year. The third-, fourth-, and fifth-grade representatives from all the classrooms were gathered in my room at lunchtime, brainstorming rules for their upcoming campaigns for president, vice president, secretary, and treasurer (for the bake sales). When the students finished their list, I thought, *All politicians could learn a thing or two from these kids.* Here are the rules the children decided on: (1) Don't put up more than two posters. It should be the same for everyone; (2) No bribing others with candy to get votes. It's not fair; (3) You can't say anything bad about anyone else. That's not nice; (4) You're not allowed to make promises you can't keep, like "There will be pizza every day in the cafeteria!"; and (5) There's only one promise that you can make: to do your best.

Provide Speaking Starters

Just like we give kids tools to help them read and write, children also need tools to help them speak. Speaking starters not only provide students with the words they need while having a discussion but also build vocabularies and help children to express themselves in complete sentences. Lists of speaking starters can be found online. A few that I encouraged my students to use included: "I agree with _____ because . . ." "I disagree with _____ because . . ." "So what you're saying is . . ." "I'd like to add . . ." and "To piggyback on what _____ said . . ." After reviewing your starters with your kids, keep them posted in your classroom and give students hard copies to hold during small group discussions. It's impossible not to be charmed when you hear a third grader say, "I agree with what she just said, and I'd like to piggyback on that." Children can speak this way without any problem. You just have to teach them.

Hold Morning Meetings

The morning meeting is a popular feature in today's classroom. During this time, the teacher and students gather together to talk about the upcoming day and share their thoughts and feelings. There's often a message from the teacher and a short activity—maybe a warm-up game or a song. It's a nice way to start the day. Many teachers hold their morning meetings daily. I chose to hold mine two or three times a week, always on Mondays. On Monday morning, I'd go around the room and ask the children to share three highlights from their weekend. It was necessary to set a limit. Otherwise my chatterboxes would have gone on and on. It never fails that when you think a chatterbox is finished sharing, and so you call on the next student, the chatterbox will always protest, "Wait! I'm not done!"

For your Monday morning meetings, instead of having your students talk about what they did on the weekend, have some fun by asking them to share using only a single word. It'll be a hit, and you'll start the day with lots of smiles and chuckles. Here's how to play: Round (1) When it's your turn to talk, tell the class one noun associated with your weekend; Round (2) Say one adjective that describes the noun that you just shared; Round (3) Add a verb that has to do with your weekend; and Round (4) Tell everyone an adverb that describes your verb. Of course, you'll have to review the parts of speech ahead of time. For even more fun, ask all your kids to share one interjection that describes their weekend. If you do this, you'll hear "Eek!" "Yikes!" "Wow!" "Yuck!" "Hurray!" "Yippee!" "Ouch!" "Ugh!" "Yay!" "Uh-oh"—along with lots of hearty laughter.

Play Volleyball, Not Tennis

One Monday morning, as one of my students was talking about her weekend, it occurred to me that *I* was the only one responding. She and I were having a back-and-forth discussion while her classmates listened. It was as if the two of us were playing a game of tennis, and the other kids were spectators. *This can be better*, I thought. *I need to tweak this.* I decided to turn our morning sharing time into more of a volleyball match, where you pass the ball to several players. From then on, when a child finished sharing, I tried to refrain from making the first comment and would turn to the class and say, "Does anyone want to respond to this?" I'd also ask the children to direct their comments to each other and not to me. It took some practice for my students (and me) to converse this way. The kids were used to the teacher leading the conversation. But after a while, we all got better at playing volleyball.

Use Think-Pair-Share

One way to get students talking is to have them participate in a Think-Pair-Share, also known as a Turn & Talk. It's a popular strategy. For the Think-Pair-Share, the teacher asks children to consider something (think), turn to a partner (pair), and discuss their thoughts (share). Though simple, the Think-Pair-Share requires some guidelines in order for it to work:

1. Before asking kids to turn and talk with one another, check that they all have a partner. If you don't, some children may feel left out.
2. Make sure your students get equal time to talk. Establish who will be

the first one to share. Switch "talkers" about halfway through so that each child gets equal time.

3. Be mindful of your pairings. Don't just tell kids to turn to the child next to them. This can make some students feel anxious if they're not sitting by a friend. Most children don't need help finding someone to speak with, but some do. And:

4. Be involved. Even though the kids are talking with one another, be an active participant. Join a duo that needs you.

Read the Pictures

When children read, we often ask them to predict, evaluate, and infer. Well, rather than use a text to do these things, why not utilize a picture and give them a visual literary experience? I call this strategy "Reading the Picture," and it's a winner. To get started, choose about ten images that you'd like your children to look at. These can be illustrations, photos, or prints. I liked to use prints by Norman Rockwell because his works are often kid-friendly. Many of his paintings tell a story, are humorous, and have children and animals in them.

After selecting your images, write questions to go with them: "What's happening in the picture?" "What do you think will happen next?" "When looking at the print, where does your eye go first?" Set the images and their corresponding questions around the room. Divide your students into small groups of three or four, and send each team to an image, where they answer the questions orally. When they're finished, have the groups rotate. One of the reasons I enjoyed this activity so much was that it allowed children to just talk. As I've mentioned, so often we ask kids to respond in writing. A writing break once in a while is refreshing. Because the activity is done verbally, it also benefits students who do not read and write as well as other children. It levels the playing field.

Spice Up Your Sharing Time

Instead of having kids share random things from home, ask them to bring in things related to what they are learning in class. Teaching geography? Have your students bring in a map. Studying multiplication? Tell them to bring in something that "shows" multiplication, such as an egg carton (two rows of six), a pair of gloves (five fingers times two), or a six-pack. Of soda.

Once, I asked my fourth graders to share something that represented a family tradition. We'd been discussing them. Min-jun, a Korean student, showed us a ring. He said it was from his *Dol* party, which he explained is a celebration that Korean families have when a baby turns one. At some point during the party, the one-year-old sits on a table beside various items, like a book, food, and money. Whatever the little one picks up will show his or her future. If the children grab a book, they will be teachers. If they reach for money, they'll be wealthy. If they pick up a string, they will have long lives.

"What did you grab?" I asked Min-jun.

"I picked up an iPhone." He smiled. "And my dad was very happy."

"Why?"

"He thinks I will be the next Steve Jobs."

Ask "Would You Rather" Questions

Would You Rather questions are excellent conversation starters for kids. Not only do they get children talking. They encourage them to think. There are oodles of Would You Rather questions, and many can be found online. Some of my favorites to ask children were: "Would you rather sing or dance?" "Would you rather do your schoolwork alone or with a group?" "Would you rather be good with words or with numbers?" "Would you rather play on the beach or in the snow?" "Would you rather go back in time or into the future?" and "Would you rather eat a piece of cake or mashed potatoes?" To get kids moving, designate one side of the room for one answer and the opposite side for the other. Then ask the children to walk (they'll speed walk) to their answer. Of course, when asking your class these questions, you have to answer them too. For the record: I'd rather eat mashed potatoes than cake. Any day.

Talk for the Fun of It

When teachers ask students to talk with one another in class, it usually revolves around something they're learning about. It's academic. Because of this, some children can feel pressured to perform. From time to time, give your kids the opportunity to talk just for the fun of it. One way to do this is to ask students to get into groups of two or three. Write a question on the board, such as: "What's your favorite thing to do in your free time?" "What's your favorite holiday and why?" "What kind of funny things do your pets do at home?". "If you could make up a brand-new school subject, what would it be?" Then let your kids chatter away. No discussion guidelines. No sentence starters. No questions from the teacher. Just friendly sharing and listening. This casual and free kind of talk is nonthreatening. There are no right or wrong answers. It provides a safe and relaxed chance for your ELL students to speak, and your quieter ones too. Another way to talk for the sheer pleasure of it is to have a spontaneous whole-class discussion. Out of the blue, without any warning, tell your kids to put down their pencils or close their laptops. Then say, "Let's just talk." As a class, discuss what they're going to do on an upcoming break. Exchange views about something happening at school. Talk about a current event. Your Yacky Ducks will love you for it.

Grammar Lessons

Grammar matters. Good grammar is essential for succeeding in school, applying for college, interviewing for a job, and leading people. In survey after survey, employers report that they will not consider job candidates whose applications contain poor grammar or spelling errors. Their feeling is that if you make mistakes on a résumé or during an interview, you're more likely to do the same on the job. Good grammar represents you in the world. It's your calling card. It is also a trust signal. It shows your attention to detail. It says—I do good work. Conversely, poor grammar makes you look careless. Whether you agree with it or not, the truth is that we are judged based on how well we use the language.

One of our responsibilities as teachers is to help children use language correctly, both in writing and speaking. My focus here is on the spoken word. If children—and I'm talking about kids around nine years old and up—speak with incorrect grammar, gently bring it to their attention. Don't shy away from this. You will not squelch their willingness to talk or hurt their self-esteem. Kids want to learn the right way to do things.

At Back to School Night, I would tell my parents that one of my goals was to help their children speak properly. They were glad to hear it. All moms and dads understand the importance of speaking well. I'd share a couple of things we would be working on in class that they could reinforce at home. I will share some of the same things with you. If you are a teacher of grade three or higher, I recommend that you give a mini-lesson on each of them early in the year. Then expect to repeat the lessons fifty million times.

Lesson 1: Never Begin a Sentence with Me *(or* Him *or* Her*)*

This is hands-down *the* most common grammar mistake made by children when speaking. If you're talking about two people and you are one of them, name the other person first. Incorrect: "Me and my friend are eating pizza." Correct: "My friend and I are eating pizza." *Teacher's note*: Do not tell a student who continually makes this mistake that you are going to write this rule on a T-shirt and wear it to school to remind her. She will keep making the mistake in hopes that you wear the T-shirt.

Lesson 2: Can Is Ability and May Is Permission

When children ask to use the bathroom, they most always say, "Can I go to the bathroom?" Of course, the correct way to begin the question is "May I." Between the time that you first teach this to your students and the time they master it, there will be what I call the "oops" stage, during which kids will say, "Can I—oops—I mean, *may* I go to the bathroom?" Many children never get past the oops stage. *Teacher's note*: If a child says, "Can I go to the bathroom?" while bouncing up and down in front of you and looking like he is about to explode, this is not the time to teach this lesson. Let him go.

Lesson 3: Good Is Different From Well

For children, lesson three is easier to master than the previous two. As we know, *good* is an adjective, and *well* is an adverb. We say, for instance, "She sings well," not "She sings good." We also say, "The food is good," not "The food is well." A good rule of thumb is: *Good* modifies a noun, and *well* modifies a verb. But don't explain it this way to a third grader. If you do, she will say, "What's a verb?"

Lesson 4: He and Him, She and Her, I and Me

These six pronouns give children (and adults) a lot of trouble. The rule is that all prepositions (*with, in, on, for, between*, and so on) are always followed by the pronouns *him, her,* and *me*, never *he, she,* and *I*. For example, "Between you and me" is correct. "Between you and I" is not. After teaching this to children, some kids will avoid the word *me* altogether. When this happens, you'll have to reassure them that *me* is not a bad word and remind them when it is correct to use it.

Do not pull your hair out over this rule. Children do not master it. When it comes to teaching these six pronouns, you're planting seeds, not expecting mastery. When I was teaching, at the end of the summer, I'd email my students to wish them a good year in their new classrooms. Kids appreciate it if you have the time. One year I sent this email to my third grader named Emily, whose best friend was Abigail. I had put both girls into the same class on purpose. Emily liked to include Abigail in her stories, so in my message, I wrote: "Emily, remember to begin your sentences with 'Abigail and I,' not 'Me and Abigail.'" We'd worked on this a lot. Emily wrote back: "Hi Mr. Done! Thanks for putting Abigail and I in the same classroom!" I laughed when I read it because in this case, of course, she should have written "Abigail and *me*." I thought, *Oh, well. She tried.*

While we're on the subject of grammar, I'd like to say one more thing that bears mentioning. Teachers have to be particularly careful with their own grammar. If you use poor grammar at work, your colleagues will notice. School leaders do not like seeing mistakes in their teachers' communication to parents. I know more than one teacher who was reprimanded by a principal for a sloppy newsletter. And parents do not like when their kids' teachers make grammatical errors either—or punctuation or spelling mistakes, for that matter. You'll lose their trust, and they will question your effectiveness. I'm not talking about an occasional typo every now and then; most parents will forgive that. I had a colleague named Janet who sent home a newsletter containing a couple of mistakes. One of her parents went berserk. There were multiple meetings about it. The principal had to get involved. Janet said it was awful, but she learned three important lessons: The world holds teachers to a higher standard. Always double- and triple-check everything that goes home. And don't be sloppy.

A Word About Geography

We've all seen the headlines about Americans' lack of geographic literacy. It seems like every couple of years, there's some new report announcing that America's youth can't locate states, oceans, or even their own country on a map. In international surveys polling students on their geographic knowledge, US teens always rank poorly. A middle school teacher I know showed me some maps of Europe that he'd asked his seventh graders to label. One student labeled Portugal as "West Spain." Another couldn't remember the names of Finland or Sweden, so he wrote one word over both of them: "cold."

Whenever I see headlines that proclaim how little American children know about geography, my inner teacher cringes. Frankly, I'm embarrassed at our ignorance and discouraged that so many young Americans have such a limited understanding of the world. When I speak of geography, I'm not just talking about naming places on a map and knowing your capitals, though these are important. The study of geography is broader than that. It encompasses people and cultures, history, and economics. It's the study of the way the world works.

When I was teaching in Hungary and writing a blog about living overseas, I wanted to see for myself if Americans' lack of geographic literacy was as bleak as those surveys claim. I thought it would make an interesting blog post. So, one morning when I was back in California for my summer break, I grabbed a clipboard, drove to a nearby Starbucks, and stood out in front. As men and women approached the entrance, I stepped up to them, explained that I was conducting a survey, and asked them one question: "Do you know the capital of Hungary?" Some people knew right away. Others had no clue. One embarrassed mom turned to her grade schooler, hoping he'd know the answer. He didn't. Another guy kept looking around for a hidden camera. Out of a couple dozen people, fewer than half answered correctly. It was disappointing. Later that morning, I went to another Starbucks and asked the same question. The results were a little better but not much. I figured the improvement was due to the fact that at the second Starbucks, I asked people as they were walking *out* of the shop, which meant that they had already had their morning coffee and it had kicked in. I guess I should have expected these results. When my American colleague Michele told her family and friends that she would be moving to Budapest to teach, their responses were: "That's in Europe, right?" "Never heard of it," "Buda-*what*?" and "Why would you go live with Buddhists?" Of course, many Americans know and value geography. But the reality is that large numbers of the population don't, and that's alarming.

So why is it that Americans do not know their geography? Some think it's because we don't have much interest in the world outside of the United States. Others say that because Americans live so far from other continents, we just don't find geography relevant. We take an out-of-sight, out-of-mind view. Others blame it on the fact that most Americans haven't traveled outside of their country. A majority of Americans don't have passports. Some claim that children just find geography uninteresting, but I don't agree. Whoever says that doesn't know kids.

Children have a natural fascination for geography. If you give kids a poster with the flags of the world, they will pore over it, then ask you which flag is your favorite—and your second and third favorite too. If you distribute a world map to a group of students and tell them to locate a particular country, they will race to see who can find it first. When you hand children a map of the United States and explain that stars are often used to indicate capital cities, immediately they will stop listening to you and begin searching for all the stars. When you ask students to color in the oceans on a world map, they will not only color them. They will add tall ships, sea monsters, and surfers catching giant waves. One of your wise guys will draw you out in the middle of the ocean, sitting on a raft circled by sharks. Yes, children enjoy geography. We can't blame *them*.

The reason Americans don't know geography is that it's not a priority in schools. In fact, in our public schools, geography seems to be on life support these days. The problem, however, doesn't appear to exist at every grade level. From what I have seen, the teaching of geography gets off to a pretty good start in elementary schools. Look in any grade school classroom, and you'll see cities built from cereal boxes, landform maps made from clay, compass roses constructed out of paper plates, and globes created by dipping newspaper strips into liquid starch, laying them onto a balloon, then rubbing your hand over the wet sticky surface to smooth out the wrinkles. Elementary teachers' bookshelves are full of atlases and picture glossaries and read-alouds sporting covers of children flying around the globe and states with silly-looking faces. We ask our kids to mail out Flat Stanleys so that their friends and relatives can send back snapshots with him, while, back in the classroom, our students get to track Stan's whereabouts on a map. When I was living in Budapest, my cousin mailed me a Flat Stanley from his daughter's class in California. Well, they should have sent along a life jacket. As I was taking a photo with the paper doll beside the Danube, a gust of wind whipped him out of my hand. Stanley started flying, and I nearly had to jump into the river to save him.

The breakdown in geography instruction seems to come after kids leave the elementary grades. But it's not the fault of middle and high school teachers. The problem is that in most of the country, geography isn't compulsory in middle school, and few states require it for high school students to graduate. High school geography courses are taught under the umbrella of social studies and incorporated with history, civics, and economics. These teachers report that in the midst of all they have to teach, geography is not the priority. Furthermore, geography is not a tested subject like reading, math, and science. When forced to compete for precious class time with subjects measured by standardized tests, geography loses out.

It wasn't always this way in the United States. Geography used to matter. Up until the early part of the twentieth century, geography was specifically taught as a core subject along with reading, writing, and arithmetic. Geographic literacy was an expectation for all educated citizens. Our founding fathers believed it was necessary for Americans to understand how and where they fit into their new nation and the world. I'm sure many would agree that this need to understand our place in the world hasn't changed. If anything, in today's uber-connected world of FaceTime, Skype, Zoom, WhatsApp, and, of course, the World Wide Web, we need to understand geography now more than ever.

Teachers know that geographic literacy is profoundly important. An awareness of geography helps us make mental maps so that we can determine the "where" of places and events. We all use mental maps every time we memorize a route in the car or plot one through the subway. A knowledge of geography allows us to better understand current events: a hurricane off the coast of Florida, an earthquake in the Pacific Rim, or tensions in the Middle East. Geographic literacy is also essential in understanding history. How can you speak of the Pilgrims' journey to the New World, the World War II Battle of Dunkirk, or the tearing down of the Berlin Wall, if you don't know where those places are? A command of geography connects us to literature as well: to Jane Austen's England, John Steinbeck's California, Mark Twain's Mississippi River. Literature begins with geography. And look at all the maps in children's books: C. S. Lewis's Narnia, A. A. Milne's Hundred Acre Wood, J. R. R. Tolkien's Middle Earth, J. K. Rowling's Hogwarts, and Robert Louis Stevenson's Treasure Island. All these maps connect characters to land and readers to stories.

So what can teachers do to promote geographic literacy in a system that doesn't prioritize it? The answer: Become a geography champion. Wage your own personal campaign against geographic ignorance. If you're not required to teach it, slip it in anyway. Consider it enrichment. If you feel that you don't have time in your teaching day, squeeze it in whenever you have an extra minute here and there. At the end of the school day, I liked to stand at the classroom door and ask my students questions as they left. This was their exit ticket. Many times, I'd ask geography questions. The kids could choose an easy question or a hard one. If they got it right, they could leave. If not, I'd give them another one. Some students who answered correctly would sneak back to the end of the line so they could get another question. When you include geography in your instruction, you're doing so for the same reason that moms slip in avocado when making brownies or put cauliflower into the frosting—because it's good for children.

There are countless ideas and materials for teaching geography. This doesn't mean they're all good ones, though. I've seen plenty in books and online that didn't look like they were ever tested on children. One year I found an idea for making miniature globes out of oranges. It looked fun, so I decided to try it. Well, it turned out to be a complete bomb. Little hands cannot draw continents with black Sharpie onto the bumpy peels of oranges. To assist you in your geography crusade, following are a few activities that I used to do with my classes. Some you may already be familiar with. All are teacher tested. None involves oranges.

Maps Without Pencils

For children, most map work is just that—work. Rarely do we pass out maps to kids with the purpose of just letting them enjoy them. Oftentimes, when a teacher hands out maps or atlases to students, they're accompanied by a list of questions that they have to answer. Well, in this activity, no pencils are allowed. Simply pass out atlases or US or world maps (with the states or countries labeled) and use them as a springboard for a class discussion. Ask the kids questions like this: "Where on the map have you been?" "Where do your relatives live?" "Where would you like to visit?" "Is there any place you'd like to live one day?" Expect the conversation to become lively. Children like talking about maps. During your discussion, one child will ask where Disney World is located. At this point, the conversation will shift from geography to how much they want to go to the Magic Kingdom.

Map Books

One of my favorite books for teaching kids about maps is the charming *My Map Book* by Sara Fanelli. Illustrated from a child's perspective, it includes maps of Fanelli's bedroom, school, neighborhood, face, and even the inside of her tummy. Using Fanelli's illustrations as inspiration, I'd have my students create their own map books. These books included maps of their bedrooms, classroom, city, state, country, and the world. The children mounted their maps on 11" × 17" pieces of construction paper, and these became the pages in their books. The project was ongoing. The kids added new pages as the year went on. When the last maps were finished, my students made their book covers (titled *My Very Own Map Book*), then we put them all together. At the end of the year, the books lay on the kids' desks for Open House, where their parents flipped through the maps with their children and told them how beautiful the books were.

Like Fanelli's, my students' map books included maps of their hearts as well. If you'd like your kids to make them, which I recommend you do, here are the directions: (1) Draw a large heart on white construction paper; (2) With a pencil, divide your heart into puzzle piece–like sections. The larger the piece, the greater your love for it; (3) Label each section and draw a little picture to represent it. Children's heart maps always include their families, friends, pets, summer vacation, and (*smile*) their teacher. Sometimes a child will draw a question mark to represent a secret crush. One student will write the teacher's name as small as possible inside his heart so that he can race up to you and show you how tiny your name is, then start cracking up. Before your kids make their maps, share yours. Teachers' heart maps always include their families, friends, pets, and summer vacation too—and, of course, their students.

Geography in the Car

Remember that license plate game you played on road trips as a child, where you tried to see how many different states you could spot? I wouldn't be surprised if that one car game was responsible for teaching millions of Americans their states. It's amazing when you think about it, just how much geography can be learned on the road. So, to reinforce local geography, send home a note with a list of geography-related questions for parents to ask their kids in the car: "Do you know in what direction we are driving?" "We've just entered the city north of the one we live in. Where are we now?" "See that population sign. Can you read the big number on it?" In your note, recommend that children read aloud road signs, billboards, and street signs, so they can practice reading too.

Ancestor Graphs

I love this activity because it integrates geography, math, and language. Plus, it gets kids talking. To make ancestor graphs, have your students ask their parents about their family heritage, then share what they've learned with the class. As an illustration, a child might report, "My dad is Italian, and my mom is Irish," or "My parents are both Chinese." As the children share their backgrounds, keep a tally on the board. Every time a country is mentioned, point it out on a world map. This is a good time to review countries and their corresponding languages. Some young kids think Canadians speak Canadian. It's also a good time to review capitalization. When you're finished recording what your students have shared, let them pick a dozen or so of the countries on the board and turn the tally marks into a bar graph. When explaining this activity to children, be clear about what you mean by ancestors, though. For third graders, I'd explain that your ancestors are "your relatives from a long time ago, *before* they came to the United States." If you don't make this clear, one child who didn't quite understand the assignment will report that all of his ancestors are from Phoenix.

Signposts

You know those signposts that you sometimes see in city centers with arrows on them that tell you how many miles away you are from other cities? For example, a marker in San Francisco might display arrows that say "Los Angeles, 347 miles," "Chicago, 1,854 miles," "New York, 2,572 miles." Well, you can make one of these signposts in your classroom. It's not hard. Just get a plastic pipe or a broomstick. Choose the cities you want on your post and have the kids google the distances. Cut some arrows out of poster board and write the names of the cities and distances on them. Then put it all together. If you make a signpost with the little ones, one Santa-believing student will want to make an arrow for the North Pole.

Clocks

Whenever I check into a hotel, I always like seeing clocks on the wall that show the different time zones around the world. They remind me of the big, yellow clocks with the large, plastic hands that grade school teachers move into different positions to help kids learn to tell time. For children, a row of clocks set to other cities' local times helps them understand that there is a big world out there. These clocks give meaning to places. To set up some "hotel clocks," as I liked to call them, just hang a couple of inexpensive ones on the wall, label them with the names of major cities, and set the times accordingly. When I taught in California, I hung three clocks in my classroom. Under them were cards that read "San Francisco," "New York," and "London." One morning a child came up to me and said he was hungry. I pointed to the clock and said it was only nine o'clock. Without missing a beat, he said, "But it's lunchtime in New York."

Stacking Cups

This idea is a variation on the stackable Russian dolls. Primary teachers know that some children mix up the words *state*, *country*, and *continent*. They're not always sure which one is bigger. To start, give each of your kids nine plastic or Styrofoam cups to label: home, city, county, state, country, continent, planet, and solar system. For fun, let the children draw themselves and their pets on one of the cups too. Next, ask students to stack the cups from smallest to largest. Mix up the cups, then have a race to see who can stack them the fastest in the correct order. You can also use stacking cups to teach food chains by labeling them like this: grass, grasshopper, lizard, snake, and owl. Speaking of food chains, I once asked a student if he could give me an example of one. His response: "Burger King." *Smarty pants.*

Theme Park Maps

When I was six years old, I learned to read from a map of Disneyland. My parents had recently taken the family there for vacation and bought me a large map of the park, which I kept on the wall beside my bed. I'd stare at it every night, trying to figure out the words. Since I had visited the park, I knew the names of the rides and could match them with the words on the map. When learning to read, kids' first words are typically ones like *cat* and *bat*. Mine were *Jungle Cruise, Fantasyland,* and *Autopia.*

Kids love poring over theme park maps. The next time you're at a theme park or a zoo, pick up a stack of free maps at the entrance, then use them to write out a list of questions for your students. Hand them the questions and the maps, and let them work in teams to answer them. When teaching map skills, I'd give my students maps of Disneyland with questions like this: "When entering the park, will you find Tomorrowland on the east or west?"

"Looking at your map, is the castle north or south of King Arthur Carrousel?" "If you get off of Space Mountain, in what direction do you walk to reach the Matterhorn?" Sometimes I'd even bring in the map of Disneyland that I got as a kid—I still have it—and for old time's sake, I'd gather my kids around it, and we'd read the words.

Travel Brochures

In elementary school, a lot of teachers have their students write country reports. It's a teaching staple when you want kids to do research. The problem with country reports is that when gathering the information, oftentimes children end up just copying it. There isn't much room for original writing. Instead of asking my students to compose the standard country report, I preferred to have them create travel brochures. They're easy to make.

To start, have each child fold a piece of 11" × 17" white construction paper into three equal-sized sections. If you teach young kids, you'll need to help them fold. Young hands have trouble folding papers into thirds. The children will write and draw on each panel, front and back. On the cover, let kids write a greeting such as "Welcome to Florida!" and draw a picture. On one of the inside panels, ask them to write a paragraph trying to convince people to go there. On the remaining panels, have them draw a flag or symbol, describe the must-sees, or list some tips for tourists. One year, one of my students (a smart aleck) wrote the following in his "Tourist Tips": "Wear your water wings and don't pee in the pool."

Virtual Visits

Bring the world into your classroom with online outings. These "trips" inject life into geography, and children love them. With Google Earth and other sites, kids can explore countries and cities, buildings and landmarks, even their own neighborhoods. Talking about the wonders of the world? Take your students on a virtual tour of the Taj Mahal, the ancient Incan Peruvian city Machu Picchu, or Angkor Wat, a twelfth-century temple in Cambodia. Studying famous landmarks in the United States? Fly with your class over the Brooklyn Bridge, Mount Rushmore, and Niagara Falls. Teaching children about immigration?

Journey over to Ellis Island. Discussing the tallest mountains or buildings in the world? Take your kids to the tops of them.

Continent Boxes

The idea of continent boxes comes from Montessori schools and can be adapted for multiple age levels. They're simple but effective. To begin, get seven large boxes or tubs and label each one a different continent. Fill each box with all sorts of things related to that particular continent: postcards, currency, plastic animals, postage stamps, maps, flags, and so forth. Also include photographs of people, food, animals, clothing, and artwork. Putting all these things together in one place gives them a context. Over the years, keep building your collection. Invite your students to add to the boxes too. If you know anyone traveling to another continent, ask for a postcard or souvenir for a box. Continent boxes create excitement and spur conversation about the world. They also provide teachers with a place to store all the stuff we collect. If you have some extra foreign coins from a trip, drop them in a continent box. If someone gave you a kitschy fridge magnet of the Eiffel Tower, you know just where to put it.

To kids, continent boxes are like treasure chests, in a way. Mine were always stuffed. (Remember, I'm a magpie.) In my Asia box, I had spice packets from India. In my Africa box, I kept a sheet of papyrus from Egypt. My Europe box held a piece of the Berlin Wall that a student had brought me. In my North America box, I included a miniature White House, a tiny football, and a measuring tape in inches. The possibilities are endless. *Note*: An adorable stuffed koala will make your Australia box a class favorite.

Silly States

Most fifth graders have to learn their states or at least some of them. It can be daunting for some children to identify all fifty states on a map, especially if they haven't had much exposure to them. Kids never have a problem learning what I call the "corner states" (Washington, Maine, Florida, California) or the "big states" of Texas and Alaska. States that resemble various distinctively shaped objects are easy for students to learn too. There's Michigan (looks like a mitten), Kentucky (a drumstick), and Massachusetts (a mom's finger telling a child to "Come here"). It's the other states that are harder for children to learn.

When I taught fifth grade, I found that one of the best ways to teach the location of the states was to create silly sentences to go with them. To start, have all your kids look at a US map with the names of the states written on them. Begin on the West Coast. From north to south are Washington, Oregon, and California. Take the first part of each of these states' names and make a silly sentence like this: "I *wash*ed clothes, ate an *or*ange, then pet a *cali*co cat." Next, continue to the second column of states, also from north to south (Idaho, Nevada, and Arizona), and create another silly sentence such as: "*Ida nev*er *ar*gues." After that, go to the neighboring four states (Montana, Wyoming, Colorado, New Mexico), and tell the kids a third silly sentence, like: "*Mont*y's *wi*fe *call*ed for *new me*dicine." If children learn these three sentences—which they will in no time—they have just learned the location of ten states! Not bad. When using this strategy, the crazier the sentences, the easier they are to remember. My favorite silly sentence was actually for the next column of states, including North Dakota, South Dakota, Nebraska, Kansas, Oklahoma, and Texas: "*Never da*re *si*t *d*own *ne*ar *k*ooky *o*ld *te*achers."

Scavenger Hunts

During the pandemic, the at-home scavenger hunt was a go-to activity for many a teacher. When teaching remotely, teachers asked children to look around their homes and bring something back to their screens to share: "Find a picture of when you were a baby." "Share a food you like to eat." "Go find something that is in the shape of a cylinder." When Jill asked her kindergartners to find something blue, one of them came back with a box of tampons.

The scavenger hunt is a tried-and-true activity for teaching geography. To hold one, make a list of questions that you want your kids to find the answers to about the world, country, or their state: "Which states border ours?" "What's our state's capital?" "How many people live in our state?" Then have your students answer the questions using maps, atlases, or the internet. Let children work with their friends to find the answers. Before sending kids on the hunt, complete it yourself to make sure that they can find everything easily. To make your scavenger hunt more like a real one, don't list all of the questions on the paper that you give to the kids. Instead, write something like this: "You'll find your next question under the teacher's desk." Or better yet: "Look for it under the slide."

Be a Rick Steves

Without question, one of *the* best ways to get children excited about geography is to share your own travels. If you've journeyed out of the country, talk about it. If you've lived out of state, speak about that too. If you drove to an interesting place over the weekend, tell your kids a little about the outing. No trip is too small to talk about. Something special happens when teachers share their travels with their students. You ignite a fascination for these places just because *you* have been there.

The Case for Cursive

A couple of years ago, I was sitting with my great-niece sharing the letters that her great-great-grandparents had written to each other during World War II. My great-niece was in fifth grade and learning about the war, so I thought she'd enjoy them. There was, however, a problem. Though a strong reader, she could not read the letters. They were written in cursive.

In 2010, when the Common Core standards were adopted by most states across the country, the teaching of cursive (also referred to as handwriting, longhand, or script) was no longer required in our nation's schools. The argument was that students' fluency on keyboards was more important than learning cursive. In the years that followed, most states stopped requiring handwriting instruction. Combined with the proliferation of screens in classrooms and the emphasis on high-stakes testing, this led to a gradual disappearance of longhand across the nation. America had a cursive collapse.

A lot of parents were not happy about cursive's demise. School boards across the country heard from upset moms and dads that their kids in middle and high school couldn't read what their teachers wrote on the board. Parents complained that their children couldn't even write their signatures. In the backlash, many parents started teaching handwriting at home. Some even started cursive clubs after school.

There are essentially two cursive camps, and each has strong opinions about it. Some feel that this flowing form of writing is an antiquated, useless relic. Others contend that learning longhand is valuable and should continue to be taught in schools. I'm in the pro-cursive camp. Like many teachers, I feel that handwriting should not go the way of chalkboards, card catalogs, and hairnets on the cafeteria ladies.

When handwriting instruction was no longer required in my district, I still taught it to my third graders. We were permitted to, and the kids' parents were happy their children were learning it. At Back to School Night, I told them that one of the reasons I was teaching cursive was so that their kids could read *their* writing. "Then again," I'd say with a wink, "if I don't teach it, you could have your own secret code."

When I began teaching, I never dreamed that one day I would be arguing for loops, swirls, and slanted letters. But here I am. The benefits of cursive are well documented. Experts have determined that learning longhand provides similar value as learning to play an instrument. Researchers argue that cursive may be effective for children with neurological disorders such as dyslexia. Studies show that writing in script stimulates the brain in ways that typing doesn't. Without question, handwriting helps children develop eye-hand co-ordination and strengthen fine motor skills. Though today's kids may know how to swipe a screen, many need help holding a pencil.

The advantages of learning handwriting go beyond cognitive ones. Cursive is creative. Some would even call it an art. When children write in longhand, they can express their personal style. When practicing their cursive letters in the air, kids look like they're conducting an orchestra. Soon after students master the letters, they start embellishing them with flourishes. When writing in script, many kids move their pencils as though they're holding a paintbrush. I saw it all the time. For some children, cursive is like dancing on paper.

Learning handwriting also allows children to read it. Today many kids can't understand things in their own language because they are written in script. Children who cannot read longhand are cut off from being able to read historical documents, family letters, even recipes from Grandma. Sadly, these kids are cursive illiterate. We all know how it feels to receive a card written in someone's own hand. It's special. Writing in cursive involves the human touch, which in our increasingly automated world is important to hold on to.

One of the greatest pluses of learning cursive is how it affects children. In third grade, the year instruction in penmanship usually begins, kids are eager to learn it. Every third-grade teacher knows how delighted students become when making their first loopy letters an index finger apart. And all teachers of handwriting know that when you ask children to write three cursive *c*'s on

their paper, they will make a whole row because they just can't stop themselves. All kids get excited the first time they get to join *c*, *a*, and *t* to write
their first word—and smile happily at it when they are finished. Children
take their handwriting very seriously. A child who normally rushes through
his work will write *mom* over and over with the most intense focus and
concentration, until his *m*, *o*, and *m* are perfectly slanted and all exactly the
same height on his dotted-lined paper. In addition to this, cursive for kids is
a source of pride. Just like adults, children also take pleasure in writing with
a handsome hand. When kids learn their last cursive letter, which is usually
capital *Z*, they feel a great sense of accomplishment. They're big kids now.

Those who don't want cursive instruction in school claim that we don't
need it because everyone writes on a computer nowadays. I don't agree. Using
the same logic, does that mean we don't need to teach children how to add
or subtract because they have calculators, or that we don't need to instruct
students in spelling because autocorrect will do it for them? I understand that
education is constantly changing and that it needs to keep up with the times,
but we have mistakenly assumed that because we have keyboards, we don't
need handwriting. We need both.

Fortunately, I have some good news for those in the pro-cursive camp. After
years of being absent from classrooms, handwriting is beginning to make a
comeback. Some states are rediscovering its value and reinstating longhand.
I'm happy about this and hope the revival continues. I realize that some people
who view cursive as a dinosaur will also call me one. I anticipate that I'll even
get a few letters from these folks telling me how they feel. When I do, I'm sure
the letters will be typed and not handwritten. If I respond, I just might write
back in cursive—with lots of flourishes, swirls, and curlicues too.

Singing with Children

"Okay, everyone," I said, tapping my head with both hands. "What's this?"

I was standing with a small group of young English language learners, reviewing the song "Head, Shoulders, Knees and Toes." I had introduced it to them the day before.

"Head!" Eliana called out.

"Good," I praised. I pointed to my shoulders and looked at Joo-won. "Joo-won, what are these?"

"Shoulders!" he announced.

"Excellent." Then I leaned over, touched my knees, and looked at Kuba. "Kuba, do you remember what these are?"

He smiled proudly. "*Kneesand!*"

Singing is one of the most important teaching tools. Actually, it's a power tool. Singing offers enormous educational benefits. It promotes a positive classroom environment, creates a sense of togetherness, enriches the curriculum, and bolsters literacy. Full of rhymes, alliteration, and patterns, songs are celebrations of language. Singing enhances listening skills and strengthens memory. It energizes and uplifts, reduces stress, injects fun, and enlivens the classroom.

Songs are sticky. They stay in kids' heads long after you've taught them. Learning information attached to a tune embeds it in a child's mind. As children, we learn our alphabet attached to a song. How many of us memorized the preamble to the US Constitution because of *Schoolhouse Rock*? I can still sing it. All of us can remember TV jingles we heard as kids.

There's another reason that singing with children is so important. For many kids, music is a great source of joy and inspiration. If you've taught children for any length of time, you've witnessed this student: the child who lights up when it's time to sing; the kid who writes on her All About Me survey that one day she wants to be on *The Voice*; the student who stands up during sharing time to sing a song from *Frozen* (a cappella), then when she's finished, asks the class if they'd like to hear another one. I once had a young music lover named Victoria who liked to sing while she worked. Before giving a test, my instructions would be: "Try your best, keep your eyes on your own paper, and Victoria—no singing."

I understand this kind of child because I was one of them. When I was young, I lived for singing time at school. Whenever my teachers asked who would like to be the song leader, I'd be on my feet in an instant, stretching my arm as high as I could and looking like I was going to die if I wasn't chosen. It usually worked. My classmates didn't want to compete with that. After walking up to the front of the classroom, sometimes I'd make everyone wait as I pretended to be thinking about which song I wanted to choose, when the truth was that I really knew all along. Once in a while, my teachers would make me change my selection. Sometimes they just didn't want to sing "The Star-Spangled Banner" at eight thirty in the morning.

Of all my teachers, the one who sang the most was my fifth-grade teacher, Mrs. Murayama. She sang every day, and I loved her for it. Mrs. Murayama insisted that the class sing with enthusiasm. "No sleepy singing!" she would shout. Sometimes, if my classmates and I didn't sing with enough energy, she would stop us midsong, shake her head, and say, "Come on, you guys. Put some *life* into it. Give it some *gusto*!" And she'd make us start all over again.

Singing's rewards are well researched. Studies show that singing involves the brain at almost every level. Researchers at the University of Southern California's Brain and Creativity Institute found that musical experiences in childhood can actually accelerate brain development. But no teacher needs to read a scientific journal or look at neuroimaging photos to figure this out. They can tell just by observing their students during singing time. Kids' faces light up. There's joy in their voices. Humans are musical beings. We're hardwired to respond to it. Our auditory system is the first to fully function in the womb, which means that we are musically receptive before anything else. Infants sway, bounce, and move to music. Toddlers bang on everything. Turn on some music, and grade school kids will tap, drum, dance, clap, twirl, spin, sing along, and touch their "kneesand."

Once, I gave a workshop in my school district where I shared the benefits of singing and encouraged the attendees to sing with their students. A few weeks later, I ran into one of the teachers who had attended. Her name was Bonnie, and she taught special education. After taking the class, Bonnie decided to start singing with her kids every day. Up till then, she hadn't thought it would be beneficial, as several of her students had severe language delays. Bonnie thought, Why would she try to sing with them, when some couldn't even speak? To her surprise, those students who couldn't speak *could* sing. One morning Bonnie forgot about singing time, and a student who rarely spoke blurted out, "We didn't sing! When are we going to sing?" And then, without any prompting, her whole class launched into song. "I was on a high for the rest of the day," Bonnie told me. That day, she learned something else about singing with children: It touches teachers too.

Teachers, especially those who have young students, understand the value of singing in the classroom. We sing songs to get our kids' attention, to invigorate learning, and to remind children of everything. One teacher I used to work with turned "Uptown Funk" into a cleanup song. A high school math teacher I know breaks into "YMCA" (with hand gestures) when teaching his students about the y-axis. Of course, the teachers who know the most songs are those who teach kindergarten. They are walking songbooks. You name it, a kindergarten teacher has a song for it: songs for teaching the weather, colors, shapes, and numbers; songs for getting their lunches, putting on snow gear, and starting at "the top" when writing letters. Kindergarten teachers know welcome songs, listening songs, circle time songs, transition songs, and train songs. Train songs, in case you don't teach kindergarten, are the ones you teach the first week of school when trying to get a classroom full of five-year-olds who have never walked in a single file line before to follow the person in front of them while being led by their teacher. God bless those conductors.

When I was teaching, I'd sing just about every day with my students, just as Mrs. Murayama had. My kids and I sang songs about math and science and history. We'd sing in the morning and just before the last bell. Songs were the bookends of our day. I remember one time, after teaching a song about the times tables, I was giving the class a math quiz when a girl came up to me and tattled that the boy next to her was cheating. "Why do you say that?" I asked. She whispered, "He was singing the math song."

Nowadays, it's easier than ever to sing with your students. You don't even need a songbook or song sheets. You don't have to write the lyrics on an overhead transparency or on a large piece of lined poster paper in your best teacher printing, like we did in the "old days." If you're not as well versed in song ideas as those kindergarten teachers, just noodle around on YouTube. There you'll find songs and raps about so many of the things we teach kids: seasons and planets, continents and states, rounding numbers and telling time. You'll discover phonics songs, feeling songs, brain break songs, holiday songs, and songs to shake the sillies out. When you sing with your class, don't worry about how you sound. Children don't care. Also, allow your students to stand on their chairs once in a while when they sing. It adds to the joy. Want them to sing louder? Let them stand on their desks.

Only once did I ever have a problem during singing time at school. Oh, it all ended okay, but it could have fallen apart. It happened in December, when I was teaching third grade at the American School in the Netherlands. My students came from all over the world. I'd just introduced them to "Rudolph the Red-Nosed Reindeer." Only the American children knew the song. The rest of them weren't familiar with it. Everyone had a paper with the lyrics.

After singing the song all the way through, I said, "You know, boys and girls, there's another part to this called *the echo*. Listen." I began singing. "Rudolph the red-nosed reindeer." I paused and pointed at the children. "Now you say *reindeer*."

"Reindeer," they copied.

"That's right." I continued: "Had a very shiny nose." I stopped again. "Now you say, *like a lightbulb*."

"Like a lightbulb," they chanted in unison. The kids were smiling.

"Good." I sang on. "And if you ever saw it."

"Saw it," they mirrored.

"You got it."

The children and I continued back and forth until we reached the end of the song.

"You'll go down in history," we sang together.

And then I finished. "Like Columbus!"

Dead silence.

Lars, a student from Sweden, looked up from his paper. "*Huh?*"

"Like Columbus," I repeated.

"Who's *he?*" asked Amir.

"He discovered America," I answered.

A sea of blank faces looked back at me. None except the American kids had a clue who Columbus was. I might as well have said Dick Cheney. *Hmm*, I thought, *This isn't going to work.* (*Ding!*) I got an idea. "I know," I said. "Let's pick a famous person you *all* know."

I went around the room and asked the kids the names they wanted to call out. Their answers included: Michael Jordan, Dutch soccer players, an Israeli swimmer, Wayne Gretzky, a Korean ice-skater, and Obi-Wan Kenobi. The Americans still insisted on Columbus. After hearing everyone's request, I thought—*There is no way we are going to come to a consensus.* And then I got another idea.

"How about this," I offered. "When we reach the end, everyone just say the name of the famous person you want. Okay?"

They agreed and we started back at the beginning. I sang the verse, and the children sang the echo. As we neared the finish, their voices grew louder, their smiles bigger. Some kids stood up. Ariel was standing on his chair. They couldn't wait to get to the end.

Finally, I sang the last "Rudolph the red-nosed reindeer."

"Reindeer!" they echoed.

They looked ready to pop.

Here it comes.

And then I sang, "You'll go down in history!"

Before I could get the last word out, all the kids shouted their favorite famous person at the same time. The room shook with gusto. And when the merriment subsided, they begged me to do it again.

Mrs. Murayama would have been so proud.

Art Lessons

It was an exciting day. All my third graders lay on their backs underneath their desks. Taped to the bottom of each one was a large piece of white paper. The children held paintbrushes and cardboard painters' palettes that they'd made themselves. Beside the kids sat plastic cups filled with paint and water. It was Michelangelo Day, and my students were painting the way Michelangelo must have done when working on the Sistine Chapel. As the children painted, tempera paint dripped onto their faces and smocks made from their dads' old dress shirts. Some kids whined that their arms were getting tired. "You think *your* arms are tired," I said. "You've been painting for ten minutes. Imagine how poor old Michelangelo felt."

The arts, which include music, theater, dance, and visual arts, are vitally important in every child's education. Their merits are invaluable and well studied. Children's participation in the arts builds critical thinking, problem solving, and communication skills. Research indicates that students who take part in the arts are more likely to have good attendance at school and be recognized for academic achievement. They are also less likely to use drugs or drop out. When involved in the arts, children develop focus and perseverance, confidence and responsibility. The arts motivate, engage, and encourage. They can heal, unite, and create a sense of well-being. For some kids, the arts are a lifeline.

Teachers are aware that the arts are a necessity and not a frill. We know that the arts provide important foundations for a child's growth. That is why we project song lyrics onto screens, push desks aside so that children can act things out, and cover desktops with newspaper so our students can paint, then wipe up the paint that didn't land on the newspaper. That's the reason our cupboards are full of colored paper and watercolor trays, glue bottles and Popsicle sticks, tissue paper and glitter—which we secretly hate. That is why our smocks look like Jackson Pollack canvases covered with splattered layers of paint.

All children are natural artists. Music, drama, dance, and art flow freely through them. I once had a student named Marina, a darling little kid, who couldn't talk to me without practicing her barre routine, complete with grand pliés in first, second, and fifth position. Marina never just walked to the pencil sharpener. She chasséd, jetéd, and pirouetted to it. Her cursive was full of flourish too. Come to think of it, Marina moved around the classroom as if she were one of her own cursive letters. At my first parent-teacher conference with Marina's mom, I recall that she looked pretty anxious, as if she was bracing herself for bad news. When we started talking about her daughter's behavior, I said that she was an absolute delight. Marina's mom looked surprised. "She's not out of her seat all the time?" I laughed. "Well, yes," I said. "She *is* out of her seat a lot, but she needs to be." I smiled. "Your daughter is a dancer." Instantly Marina's mom covered her mouth. After a pause, she said, "Thank you for seeing it." Then she explained that more than one of Marina's previous teachers had suggested she be taken to a doctor and checked for ADD. To that, I said, "Nonsense. The only place she should be taken to is a ballet class."

Today the arts in schools are in a state of crisis. Funding for arts programs has been disappearing at an alarming rate. Whenever education budgets tighten, choir, band, theater, and visual arts classes are often the first to go. In the last decade, more than 80 percent of US school districts have wiped out funds for arts programs. Oklahoma alone eliminated more than a thousand arts classes. I'm always heartbroken when I read news like this. I'm sad that we're denying something so valuable to children. I'm sad for all the students who will miss out. I'm sad for all the kids who may not reach their artistic potential because it wasn't nurtured in school.

If you are already including the arts in your classroom, I applaud you. Actually, I give you a standing ovation. If you'd like to infuse more art, music, drama, and dance into your teaching—and create those lifelines—adopt or adapt the following ideas:

Teach One Artist a Month

If you haven't incorporated a lot of the arts, teaching children one artist a month is a nice place to start. It will provide you with some structure and ensure that you're integrating art into your instruction. To begin, select a famous painter and read a short picture book about the artist's life and works. Many wonderful books about artists are available: *The Noisy Paint Box*, *Henri's Scissors*, *My Name Is Georgia*, *Pocket Full of Colors*, and *Vincent Can't Sleep: Van Gogh Paints the Night Sky*. If you have any prints or postcards of the painter's work, share these too. (*Teacher tip*: On Michelangelo Day, it is best to show your kids all photos of Michelangelo's *David* from the waist up.) After reading the book to your students, have them create a piece of art in the style of the artist. Teaching one artist a month is a popular teaching strategy, so lesson plans and student samples can easily be found online.

Choose any artists you like. My artists of the month included van Gogh, Monet, O'Keeffe, Kandinsky, Mondrian, Picasso, Warhol, and, as you already know, Michelangelo. I also included the famous Disney artist Mary Blair, creator of the It's a Small World attraction at the Disney parks and whose work can be seen in the animated classics *Sleeping Beauty*, *Alice in Wonderland*, and *Cinderella*. The reason I selected these artists was because their works lend themselves well to art projects. When studying van Gogh, my students painted their own *Starry Night*s. When learning about Monet, they drew water lilies. After teaching the children about Georgia O'Keeffe, they made giant pastel flowers. For Picasso, they painted peace doves just like his. Have your kids work in a variety of mediums, including paint, oil pastel, and watercolor. If possible, connect the art project to other skills. Mondrian's geometric patterns, for example, can be used to teach angles, while Kandinsky's circles work well for measuring diameter. Of course, when your students are finished with their projects, have them sign their names. Some of your kids' signatures (Marina's!) will be filled with embellishments so that theirs look famous too.

Integrate the Arts

When planning a lesson, stretch your creative muscles by looking for ways that you can incorporate the arts into it. For instance, when teaching children how to tell time, have them make their own colorful construction paper cuckoo clocks with movable hour and minute hands that they can turn to practice. Add paper pinecone weights and a cuckoo bird on a spring. Integrate art and writing by asking students to draw before they write. When reading *Charlie and the Chocolate Factory*, let kids design a new candy room in Wonka's factory, then write a description about it. After reading Shel Silverstein's poem "Homework Machine," invite children to sketch out their own homework machines complete with conveyor belts, buttons, and switches before they describe how their inventions work. Drawing something before writing about it helps students develop their thoughts. If you're teaching kids how to write a persuasive paragraph, ask them to create their own new breakfast cereals and design cereal box covers to go with them. When they're done, have everyone bring in empty cereal boxes and mount their new covers onto them. Then let the children write advertisements encouraging people to buy their new products. It's a fun way to combine art with writing.

To integrate music and writing, lead your students in rewriting the lyrics to a song. One year my third graders and I rewrote the lyrics to "My Favorite Things" with *their* favorites. "Raindrops on roses and whiskers on kittens" became "Recess and *Fortnite* and red Jolly Ranchers." You can also rewrite the words to a familiar tune to help children remember something. Take a song like "Oh, My Darling Clementine" and turn it into a ditty about the water cycle: "Evaporation, condensation, precipitation on my mind. They are all part of the water cycle, and it happens all the time."

Incorporate drama into your reading of folk and fairy tales by taking the characters to court. Say you're reading "Jack and the Beanstalk." Assign your kids the parts. Set up a mock courtroom. Put Jack on trial for stealing. Call the giant's wife, the golden harp, and the goose that lays the golden eggs to the witness stand. Speaking of Jack's beanstalk, let your students create their own by covering paper towel or wrapping paper rolls with green paper and leaves, topping the beanstalks with paper plates, then setting paper castles into cotton ball clouds. Of course, when you do this, some kids will connect their beanstalks to see if they can make them touch the ceiling.

Hold Carpet Concerts

Carpet concerts are opportunities to shine the spotlight on children who study an instrument. This is not a talent show. It's more of a recital. To have a carpet concert, invite your students who play an instrument to perform for the class. If you need a piano, ask the custodian to roll one into your classroom from the multipurpose room, or take your class there. If your school doesn't have a piano, someone will know where you can borrow a keyboard. Carpet concerts can be set up any way you'd like. For mine, I would focus on the instrumentalists, but you can certainly invite children to sing and dance too. Before a concert, I'd ask my students to tell me the titles of their pieces. I wanted the children to perform something that they had been working on. This was not a time for kids to show me that they could play "Chopsticks." During our carpet concerts, I would also remind the class how to be a good audience. I called it "sitting practice."

Watch Online Art Classes Geared for Kids

You'll find lots of online tutorials for teaching art to children, but one of the best channels on YouTube is Art for Kids Hub. I'm a big supporter. There you'll discover hundreds of fun and kid-friendly lessons for students of all ages. At Art for Kids Hub, children can learn to draw animals, superheroes, holiday-themed figures, and characters from their favorite video games. Some of the most popular videos on the site include lessons on how to draw a unicorn, a mermaid, a shark, an emoji, and Spider-Man. Each of these lessons has millions of views. If you're unable to use the videos during class time, definitely recommend them to the budding artists in your room.

Visit a Museum

Every year, I'd try to take my class to a local art museum. If you want to take your kids to one, consider scouting the museum ahead of time. Once on a pre–field trip visit, I discovered a row of nude sculptures in one wing of the museum that I knew would cause a couple of eight- and nine-year-olds to absolutely lose it. On the day of the trip, I asked the docent if she would kindly skip that wing. She agreed. When planning your field trip, also make sure to double-check the museum's schedule. One year we arrived at that same museum to find that it was closed. The children were okay with it, though. We had lunch on the lawn, and there were a couple of ducks. So basically, I had sent out permission slips, organized parent drivers, arranged bag lunches from the cafeteria for those on free lunch, and resupplied the first aid box so that we could drive across town and picnic with some ducks.

If you can't go to an art museum with your class, take them on a virtual museum tour instead. Many of the world's great museums offer online tours of their collections. In the States, the Metropolitan Museum of Art, the Getty, the Guggenheim, the Frick, and the Seattle Art Museum have virtual programs geared specifically for students. Other world-class museums with excellent online educational resources include London's National Gallery, the Louvre and Musée d'Orsay in Paris, the Vatican Museums in Rome (including the Sistine Chapel), and two of my favorites: the Rijksmuseum and the Van Gogh Museum in Amsterdam. One of the nice things about virtual field trips is that they are free. When I taught in the Netherlands, parking at the Van Gogh Museum cost about as much as buying one of his paintings.

Teach the Language of Art

When you show children an image of a painting, most of the time they will not say much more than they like it or they don't. The reason for this is they don't have the words. So give the words to them. Point out that colors have hue and intensity. Show them that lines can be horizontal, vertical, and diagonal, as well as straight and curved. Explain that shapes are geometric or free and natural. Teach them to look at balance and pattern, proportion and movement. These terms are not beyond children, not even young ones. A nine-year-old can easily talk about the balance, proportion, and movement she sees in a painting. You just need to give kids the words.

Invite Your Students to the Dance

Among the arts, dance gets the shortest end of the stick in school. We hardly give it any attention. If you're lucky, the Parent-Teacher Association will ask the local dragon dancers to perform at the Chinese New Year assembly. The PE teacher might spend a few periods teaching a dance too. Otherwise that's about it. It's a shame that dance doesn't get more attention, because so many children are dancers.

At school, kids are dancing all the time. To know what I mean, all you have to do is watch a group of children standing in line. The longer kids wait in a line, the more likely they will start bouncing, spinning, twirling, and breaking out into a dance they learned from their favorite pop star in a video that went viral. If *you* attempt to copy any of these moves, your students will crack up because for children, one of the funniest things in the world is seeing their teacher trying to dance like a teenage pop star in a viral dance video. When the TikTok dance craze started, *everyone* was dancing. All of a sudden, boys and girls couldn't just walk anymore. They were all doing little dance sequences. Children couldn't stand and talk without jumping, stepping, slapping, and doing jazz squares. There were times my classroom felt like a rehearsal hall. Once, one of my kids raised her hand, so I called on her. "Oh," she said, "I was just dancing."

Thanks to YouTube, you can expose students to some of the greatest dances of all time. I used to show my kids classic dances by Fred Astaire and Ginger Rogers, the Nicholas Brothers, Eleanor Powell, Gregory Hines, Ann Miller, Mikhail Baryshnikov, and Michael Jackson. I would show them Dick Van Dyke's "Step in Time" from *Mary Poppins*, Gene Kelly's famous pas de deux with Jerry the Mouse from *Anchors Aweigh*, Michael Kidd's spectacular barn-raising dance in *Seven Brides for Seven Brothers*, Bill "Bojangles" Robinson's stair dance with Shirley Temple from *The Little Colonel*, and Donald O'Connor's "Make 'Em Laugh" from *Singin' in the Rain*, which is hands down *the* funniest routine in the history of film. The children always enjoyed watching the performances. Many had never seen them before. I would share these numbers not only to expose my students to great dancing but also to celebrate the kids who danced. It was a way to tell them: I see you, and what *you* love to do is important too. While watching the clips with my class, I'd speak out loud to the dancers in the room, to validate *them*: "Marina, do you like this routine?" "Marina, did you see that?" "Marina, can you do that step?" If you watch any of these performances with your students, make sure that they have plenty of room. Before the number is over, a couple of them will be trying to spin like Gene Kelly.

Sharing dances like this is important for another reason. You're teaching children that dancing is for men too. Sadly, even today, there's a stigma that it isn't. It's hard to believe that we're still there, but alas—we are. In exposing children to great male dancers, you're helping to change this. One day after showing my third graders a clip of Gregory Hines performing a tap routine, I excused the children back to their desks, but one of my boys stayed behind. His name was Austin. When we were alone, Austin cupped his hands over my ear and whispered, "I take tap too." I hadn't known. When he dropped his hands, he was smiling from ear to ear. We both were. *Mission accomplished.*

Have Your Kids Respond to Great Music

I'm very fond of this activity because it combines music and writing, and it exposes children to some of the greatest composers and musical compositions of all time. To start, have your students sit at their desks and close their eyes. Let them put their heads down if they wish. You might also want to turn out the lights. Each student should have a piece of paper and a pencil. Then play a piece of classical music or a selection from it. When it's over, ask the kids to jot down how the music made them feel and what it made them think about. ("Today we listened to _____. It made me think of _____.") Don't say the title of the piece until after they're finished writing, as this might sway their thinking. When everyone's done, ask who'd like to share.

There are so many famous works to choose from. Some of my favorites included: the "Hornpipe" movement from Handel's *Water Music*, Mozart's "Eine Kleine Nachtmusik," Vivaldi's "Spring" from *The Four Seasons*, Beethoven's "Moonlight Sonata," "Für Elise," and Fifth Symphony, as well as Tchaikovsky's "Waltz of the Flowers" and "Russian Dance" from *The Nutcracker*. Other popular pieces with children include Wagner's "The Ride of the Valkyries," Khachaturian's "Sabre Dance," Mussorgsky's *Night on Bald Mountain*, Strauss's "The Blue Danube," Bizet's overture to *Carmen*, and Gershwin's *Rhapsody in Blue*. As you play the pieces, expect to observe tapping feet, bouncing knees, and bodies swaying with the music. A couple of kids will be conducting.

Attend a Performance

If the opportunity is available to you, take your class to a live performance. For children, there is great value in it. For some of your students, it may be the first one they have ever seen.

It's a lot of work to take children to a live performance, that's for sure. The most difficult part is not the planning or getting there. The hardest part is that window of time between when kids sit down in the theater and when the show begins. This period of time (there should be a name for it) requires rapid problem solving skills and split-second thinking on the part of the teacher. As your students begin taking their seats, you have to quickly figure out which kids should be separated and who needs to sit as close to you as possible. After everyone is seated and until the lights come down, you will spend all your time telling children to not turn around, to get their feet off the seats in front of them, and to stop standing up so they can see their seats snap up when they get out of them.

If you can't go to a performance, bring them to your classroom. Just as the internet offers an abundance of virtual museum tours, art classes, and dance numbers, a myriad of theatrical performances are available online too. Take students behind the scenes of the making of Broadway shows such as Disney's *Aladdin*, *Beauty and the Beast*, or *The Lion King*. Show them clips from *The Nutcracker* and symphony concerts. While you're at it, teach the names of the instruments. Acquaint your kids with the performances of Marcel Marceau, then ask them to pantomime like him. Introduce your students to the laugh-out-loud antics of Lucille Ball and silent screen actors Buster Keaton and Harold Lloyd.

A lot of teachers like to give their students "brain breaks"—short pauses during the day to rest the brain cells. Children need them. Sometimes for my brain breaks, I would take my class on short virtual trips like the ones I just mentioned. I liked giving breaks like this. In doing so, my students were getting a little rest *and* a little culture at the same time.

Welcome an Artist to the Classroom

Children enjoy having guests visit. Classroom visitors liven things up. When guests speak to your class, you get an opportunity to see your students from a different perspective. If you have the opportunity, invite an artist into your classroom. Ask them to bring in their work and give a demonstration. The artists don't have to be professional. They can be parents or colleagues. When I lived in California, sometimes I invited my mom in. She painted landscapes. My mom would bring in a painting that she was working on and talk about the process. Although it was nice to have her visit, I wouldn't recommend inviting your mom. If you do, your students will ask her more questions about what kind of trouble you got into as a kid than about her painting. After one of my mom's visits, a student asked why she didn't bring in cupcakes on my birthday. The children knew she lived close by. Later, I told her what the child said, and we had a good laugh about it. The next day she brought in thirty-two cupcakes. *Smart kid*.

Encourage the Artists

Sometimes I wonder what it would have been like to teach some of the world's most famous artists. Take Meryl Streep, as an example. Imagine having had *her* in your class play! Or Mikhail Baryshnikov. How many times did his teacher have to tell him to stop jumping in line? Or what about Pablo Picasso? Can you imagine if you had saved all the doodles he scribbled in class? You'd be a gazillionaire!

Whenever I'm watching an award show like the Academy Awards, and an actor thanks his teacher, the corners of my mouth turn up into a big teacher smile. It makes me proud. I once heard an interview with actress Hilary Swank after she won her first Oscar, during which she thanked her fourth-grade teacher for casting her in *The Jungle Book*. It made me wonder just how many professional artists got their start because a teacher recognized a talent and said, "You should think about pursuing this."

As we all know, school isn't geared for artists. Just look at the amount of time we spend on math and science compared to the time we devote to the arts. But we all have students who may one day choose professions in the arts. In our classrooms sit the future performers, designers, filmmakers, photographers, and choreographers. We teach tomorrow's recording engineers, commercial artists, architects, illustrators, and *teachers* of the arts. These children deserve to be nurtured and celebrated too. So take every chance to elevate the artists in your room. Acknowledge and celebrate their talents. Talk about their dreams. Help these kids discover their gifts. Some might not even know what they are.

Effect Change

When Winston Churchill was asked to cut funding for the arts during World War II, he replied, "Then what are we fighting for?" In education, sometimes we have to fight for a student, a schedule, a program, something we believe in. Years ago, my school district decided to cancel all instrumental music in the elementary grades due to budget cuts. Up until that time, fourth and fifth graders could learn to play an instrument. It was a wonderful program—the same one that I'd participated in as a child. When I heard that it was on the chopping block, I was terribly disappointed. I went to the board meeting, where I explained on the open mike the positive impact that learning to play an instrument had made on my life. It didn't help. The program was eliminated. Actually, my own principal at the time seemed to be furious with me for speaking up. She'd supported the cuts and acted as though I was undermining her. My dad had always said to me, "Pick your battles." Well, this was a battle that I was willing to fight. And so, even though I had no idea what I was doing, I decided to start a band.

I sent a flyer to all the parents of the students in grades four and five at my school explaining my idea and asking if they'd be interested. The children would meet once a week after school for band practice. We would teach three instruments: flute, trumpet, and clarinet. The response from parents was overwhelmingly positive, so I decided to move ahead. I found a flute teacher who believed in instrumental music as much as I did. She was paid out of the fee we charged the parents. The dad of one of the kids volunteered to teach the trumpets. I taught the clarinets. The families rented instruments and bought their music at a local music store. Parents chipped in to a scholarship fund for those who couldn't afford it so that every child who wanted to participate could. To my surprise, it wasn't that hard to set it all up. On the first day of band practice, we had forty-seven students.

After rehearsing for several months, it was time for our debut concert. The kids wore red T-shirts donated by a local company. On each shirt was a circle of white letters that spelled out "Cumberland Band." (The name of the school was Cumberland.) One of the moms offered to accompany us on the piano, and I found a former student to play the drums. The multipurpose room was full of parents. A few board members even came. And there on the stage, I conducted forty-seven young musicians in "Hot Cross Buns," "Mary Had a Little Lamb," "Three Blind Mice," and "Jingle Bells" (in June). For thirty minutes, clarinets squawked, trumpets pointed toward the floor, and flutes bounced up and down to keep the beat. Music fell off the stands, and the band got out of sync with the drummer. It was one of the proudest moments of my life. When we finished our last piece, and the kids stood up for their bows to a standing ovation, the smiles on the children's faces showed how proud and happy they were too.

I share this story not to bring attention to myself or pat myself on the back. I tell it because oftentimes teachers feel powerless to effect change. But we *can*. If you want to start a chorus during lunch, why not? If you'd like to offer a little art class or drama club after school, just dive in. Heck, if you want to start a band, go for it.

There's a nice ending to this story. When I left that school, the band kept going. The parents took it over. I was pleased about that. It's been years since I taught there, but once in a while, a photo of a red T-shirt with the words "Cumberland Band" will pop up on my Facebook feed. It warms me up when I read the comments from the former band members, who are all adults now: "I still have that, too!" "Loved it!" "Great memories!" And the best comment of all—"Well, I've come full circle. I can't believe it. Now *I* teach band!"

Indent Your Teaching

A few years before I retired, I received an email from a former student named Caleb who had been in my fourth-grade class twenty years earlier. It was nice to hear from him. In the note, Caleb reminisced about fourth grade, recalled things he had learned, and asked if I remembered the time he had hidden my glasses. I did. I remembered the hour it took me to find them too.

Caleb wrote that his favorite memory of the class was when we pushed the desks together and pretended it was a covered wagon. I recollected the lesson. After the kids piled into the "wagon," I walked around spraying water on them for that authentic crossing-the-Missouri-River experience. I also recalled that as the children tossed back and forth, Caleb leapt off and pretended he was drowning.

It didn't surprise me that Caleb's fondest memory was when he'd acted something out. Very often, when children participate in dramatic play, it produces a lasting impact. Drama and children are a winning combination. When I speak about drama here, I'm referring to creative dramatics, which doesn't involve reading scripts, handing out parts, memorizing lines, or performing for an audience. Those activities, which are also valuable, fall under what is known as theater arts. Another way to think of it is this: In theater arts, the focus is the audience. Creative dramatics focuses on the participants.

All kids love pretend. They default to it. And schools are full of it. In grade schools, you don't just find students and teachers, principals and secretaries, custodians and crossing guards. You also come across kings and queens, soldiers and police officers, pilots and prisoners. One morning I spotted a group of boys digging a hole beside the bike racks. When I asked what they were doing, they proclaimed, "We're escaping from Alcatraz!" To witness pretending at school, just stick your head into any kindergarten classroom. There you'll see boys and girls role-playing in make-believe houses, grocery stores, bakeries, flower shops, pizza parlors, and hospitals. My friend Jill changes out the role-playing area in her kindergarten classroom every few months. One time she set up a veterinarian's office where her little ones could listen to their stuffed animals' heartbeats with stethoscopes. *Cute.* Another time she put together a mini coffee shop with real Starbucks cups. For fun, one day I ordered a coffee from a five-year-old barista. After scribbling my order on a pad of paper, she handed me a cup and asked me to write my name on it. Then she leaned over the counter and whispered, "I can't write yet. I'm really only in kindergarten."

The use of creative dramatics has long been recognized as a potent teaching strategy. When students engage in it, their learning is active. Drama creates excitement and nurtures creativity. When children participate in playacting, they're not just using their imagination. They're immersed in it. Einstein once said that the highest level of creativity unfolds through play. When teachers incorporate drama into their lessons, they tap into this. Creative dramatics is especially beneficial because it gets kids moving. Their bodies become the learning tool. Furthermore, this kind of imaginative play provides children with an emotional outlet. I always say that drama is the only subject in school that allows students to scream, whine, argue, throw a tantrum, and clown around, and it's totally okay. In other words, it gives kids permission to act out—in the good way. Of course, I can't leave out the fact that for children, playacting is just plain fun. When we learn with pleasure, we remember.

Creative dramatics is also powerful in enhancing the curriculum. Drama helps develop literacy skills by supporting speaking and listening. Incorporating dramatic play into history, math, or science can increase students' interest in these subjects. It can decrease kids' anxiety in these subjects as well. We all know the old proverb "Tell me, and I will forget. Show me, and I will remember. Involve me, and I will understand." Drama involves the learner completely. It deepens learning. In other words, it *indents* it. Years ago, I had a very good friend named Betty who used to talk to her house keys whenever she'd leave her home. "Okay, keys," she would say, "you're in my purse now."

Betty told me that saying the words out loud helped her remember where she put them. "It *indents* it," she said. Well, creative dramatics has the same effect on learning. When you incorporate it into your teaching, it helps kids remember. It indents it too.

Time and time again, I witnessed the power of drama in the classroom. I saw students who struggled in academics come alive when given a chance to play make-believe. I observed children who spoke little English become active participants when asked to act something out. I watched kids who had trouble getting along with their classmates suddenly able to collaborate. I saw shy children come out of their shells when allowed to play in an imaginary world. Every teacher witnesses these things when they invite children to pretend.

Many teachers recognize the value of drama as a teaching strategy but don't know where to start. A lot of them lack confidence. Many lack training. In the following pages, I will share some of my favorite drama activities for the classroom. Most of them can be modified for different grade levels. I won't include any games or warm-ups here (you'll find lots of those online), just activities that can be used to augment your teaching of the core subjects. Give them a try. Your smiling students will be glad you did. I guarantee that these strategies will make a valuable contribution to your instruction—and indent your kids' learning as well.

Showing Words

I have one hard-and-fast rule for teaching vocabulary: If a word can be acted out, do so. The best way to learn any new word is with your body. This is especially beneficial for ELL students. Like the Synonyms for *Said* activity I wrote about earlier, when discussing "feeling words" such as *exhausted* and *petrified, famished* and *disgusted, skeptical* and *astonished*, invite your kids to act them out. When you're reading to children, and a character in the book "pierces his lips," "furrows her brows," "sighs deeply," or "gives a mischievous grin," ask your students to do these things too. If you're discussing the different ways that characters move, let the kids creep, dash, hobble, limp, march, pace, saunter, shuffle, stagger, and trudge around the room. Your little thespians will love this. When teaching children what *sizzle* means, tell them to lie down with their backs on the floor and pretend they're eggs in a frying pan. Announce that you're turning up the heat. Then observe your little eggs shake, tremble, and shout, "It's getting hot in here!" *Warning*: When asking kids to act out words, stay clear of *crash*, *demolish*, *destroy*, *explode*, *smash*, and *wreck*. Children perform these words *too* well. And never, under any circumstances, ask third-grade boys to act out *predator* and *prey*. If you do, you'll end up shouting, "Okay, that's enough. Break it up!" as you pull them apart.

Hot Seating

Hot seating is when a student takes on the role of a character from history or a book and responds to questions posed by the class. Before sitting in the hot seat, the children need to have researched their characters and know them pretty well. Students don't have to be famous people. They can also be eyewitnesses to a historical event. In my classroom, many famous people sat in the hot seat. Among them were Thomas Edison, Jane Goodall, Walt Disney, Neil Armstrong, Sacajawea, Louis Armstrong, Brazilian soccer star Pelé, and Charlie Chaplin. Gold miners, pioneers, and witnesses to the San Francisco earthquake sat in it too. When hot seating, invite your kids to dress up. It adds to the fun. Some children will go all out. One year "Jacques Cousteau" wore flippers, swimming goggles, and two oxygen tanks on his back that he'd made out of empty liter-sized plastic Coke bottles painted silver. *Clever*. Before asking students to sit in the hot seat, it's best that you model it first. When I modeled it, I would usually show up as Johnny Appleseed and field questions with a pot on my head.

Once, after our hot seating, one of my boys named Simon asked if he could sit in the hot seat and be *me*! At first I said no, but the kids begged, so I gave in. Simon jumped into the chair and introduced himself in a low, stern voice. I cut through the chuckles. "Wait a minute," I said, pretending to be offended. "Do I sound like *that*?" All the kids answered, "Yes!" The children asked several questions of their "teacher," including: "What's your favorite song?" "What's your salary?" and "What's your favorite movie?" Here were "my" answers: Favorite song: "I'm a Little Teapot." Salary: Ten thousand dollars a week. To that, I let out a laugh. Favorite movie: *The Little Mermaid*. To that, the children let out louder ones.

Tableau

Tableau is a highly effective strategy for incorporating creative dramatics but is not widely used. To create a tableau, children make still images with their bodies to represent a scene. Start with all your students seated in their chairs or on the floor. In front of them, leave an open space. One by one, ask the kids to stand and enter the space in a freeze-frame, until the tableau is complete. The children must stand completely still. Take a photo when your kids are finished creating the scene.

Tableau can be used when teaching a variety of subjects, including literature, history, and art. One way to use this strategy is to have students re-create a scene from a book they are reading in class. For example, when reading *Charlie and the Chocolate Factory,* ask your kids to form a tableau showing how the five golden ticket winners must have looked when they first stepped into the Chocolate Room in Wonka's factory. When creating this scene, students will assume freezes with dropped jaws, wide eyes, and hands on their heads. Some will look like they're ready to sprint. Another way to use tableau is to project a historic photograph, illustration, or painting onto the screen, then have children stand in front of it to mirror the image. When I taught grade five, I'd project an image of the signing of the Constitution. While wearing wigs made out of construction paper and cotton balls, my students would assume the same positions as the figures in the painting. A nice photo op. An art teacher I know uses tableau to have her students re-create famous paintings. Before standing still in front of the projected images, the kids grab what they need from the teacher's prop box: wire-rimmed spectacles for the small-town farmer in *American Gothic*, a handkerchief for *Whistler's Mother*, a globe for Vermeer's *The Astronomer*, and a stuffed animal for da Vinci's *Lady with an Ermine.*

When your students are standing in a tableau, you can ask questions of either the audience or the frozen figures. Walk around the tableau, tap the children on the shoulder, and interview them like a reporter. One day, when my kids were standing still in front of the famous painting of George Washington crossing the Delaware, I asked the soldiers in the boat how they were feeling. Their responses: "Scared," "Nervous," and "Got any whisky? I'm freezing."

When teaching history to my fifth graders, I would show images of a more serious nature as well. These included civil rights heroine Rosa Parks sitting on the segregated bus in Montgomery, Alabama; Norman Rockwell's painting of a young Ruby Bridges escorted by US marshals on her way to desegregate an all-white elementary school in Louisiana; and US Marines raising the American flag after the Battle of Iwo Jima.

One year, after talking with my students about Japanese internment camps during World War II, I found a haunting photo from that period of a Japanese family, including children, waiting to board a bus bound for a camp. Each person was wearing a coat and holding one suitcase. That was all they were allowed to bring. I told the children that these families had lost everything: their homes, their businesses, their livelihoods. Before having the kids replicate this image in a tableau, I turned off the lights, asked the class to not talk and to think about how these people must have felt. Then, using some suitcases and coats I had brought from home, I invited a few students to echo the scene in front of the image. No one spoke. The children took it seriously. When the kids in the tableau sat back down, I saw one girl wiping away tears.

Wax Museums

This popular activity is highly effective for teaching biographies. In a Wax Museum, students pretend to be famous people in history. It's sort of like the Hall of Presidents attraction at Disney World, but the children are the animatronic robots. Wax Museums work with any grade, are nice to put on with multiple classes, and are accessible to English language learners of all levels. To prepare for a Wax Museum, first let your kids pick a famous person they'd like to research. It's okay if more than one child wants to study the same person. Next, have students find out why the people they chose are famous and learn some highlights about their lives. After the children have gathered their information, ask them to write it in a paragraph and commit it to memory. Select a date for the event and invite other classes and parents to attend. Additionally, encourage the kids to come dressed up like the famous people they'll be portraying and, if they'd like, to also bring props.

On the big day, your classroom will be full of little Amelia Earharts in goggles, Shirley Temples in tap shoes, and Harry Houdinis in shirts stuffed with newspapers to look like big muscles. Before opening the museum, have the children spread out so that there's plenty of room between them. The performers should have chairs in case they get tired. Tape paper "buttons" onto their shoulders. Allow students to keep their notes close by in case they need them. When the guests arrive, your kids should be frozen like statues. During the event, visitors go around the room and listen to the famous people speak. A figure comes to life when someone presses the "button." When the figures finish speaking, they resume their freezes. From the moment your Wax Museum begins, you will be busy listening to speeches, taking photos, watching parents record their kids, and telling your little Albert Einsteins that they may take off their fake mustaches that are too scratchy.

Teacher Reader

This strategy is one that teachers don't use much, but children really enjoy it. Select a passage from a book that lends itself to being performed and let your kids act it out as you read it aloud. To give an example, when reading an abridged version of *Strange Case of Dr. Jekyll and Mr. Hyde* to my students, I'd set up a fake laboratory on a desk with candles and beakers full of colored water. As I read the scene where Jekyll drinks the potion and turns into Hyde, a child would stand in the "laboratory" and act out what I was saying. If you do this kind of activity with kids, give everyone a chance to participate, of course. Also, allow for plenty of time. Once, when reading that scene from *Dr. Jekyll*, I ended up watching a child drink the "blood-red liquid" (Kool-Aid), convulse wildly, then collapse onto the floor—twenty-seven times.

Bringing Lessons to Life

When planning your lessons, ask yourself, Is there something here that my kids can act out? Imagine you're studying rain forests. Have your kids pretend to trudge through jungles and wade across alligator-infested rivers. Throw in some quicksand too. They'll pretend they're trapped in it. Learning about explorers? Take your students outside and let them climb onto the jungle gym and make believe it's a ship. Tell them that they've just spotted land and let them shout, "Land, ho!" Teaching children about the Boston Tea Party? Turn off the lights and ask them to creep silently to the "ship" made of desks in the center of the room. Once they reach the ship, allow them to throw crates of tea (banana boxes) off of it.

In teaching, we don't often think of combining creative dramatics and science, but if you put on your thinking cap, you'll find that drama can be used to represent all sorts of phenomena. Say, for instance, you're teaching kids about red and white blood cells and how the white blood cells attack germs. Have all your students stand up. Assign some kids as red blood cells and others as white ones (the favorite). Ask a few children to be germs. Then let 'em go at it.

If you're teaching kids about gravity, go outside and pair them up. Have one child in each twosome be the Earth and the other the moon. Give each pair a jump rope and tell them to hold on to it. The rope represents gravitational pull. When you say "Go," the moons orbit the Earths. After a while, have the moons and Earths switch. As the moons are orbiting, it won't take long till they start picking up speed, and one of them breaks off and flies off into space. When this happens, it is time to bring all your little moons and planets back inside.

The three states of matter can be acted out too. To start, divide children into groups of three or four. Ask them to stand close together and pretend they're water molecules in ice cubes. The water molecules can move a little but not a lot. Next, tell the kids that you're going to turn up the heat so that they will transform into liquid molecules. Now the children may move around more. Lastly, announce that a few days have passed and the liquid molecules have evaporated. They're all gas molecules now. Watch your gas molecules run around the room and bump into the walls. At this point, you will need to remind them that they are molecules, not bumper cars.

One year, when my third graders were acting out solids, liquids, and gases, one of my little gas molecules named Trevor flew out into the hallway. (I'd left the door open.) I followed him and shouted, "Trevor, *what* are you doing?" Beaming, he answered, "You said gases can escape, so I escaped!" I just laughed. To tell you the truth, I wouldn't be surprised if one day I receive a message from Trevor like the one I got from Caleb. And when I do, it will probably say something like this: "Mr. Done, remember when I was a gas molecule? It was my favorite thing we did all year!"

Putting On a Play

All children (and adults) remember their school play. It's one of the truly special moments in a child's education. And I believe that every student should participate in one. To me, being in a school play is part of being a kid—just like licking ice cream cones, playing in the mud, and building forts. There is enormous value in it. When children participate in a play, they develop responsibility and accountability. They learn to work with others toward a common goal. They experience a great sense of accomplishment. Putting on a play helps shy students become more confident and wiggly ones get the wiggles out. Preparing for and performing in a play engages and motivates kids like nothing else. If you've ever directed one with children, you know what I mean. The second you say, "Okay kids, time for play practice," they jump into action. The energy in the room instantly changes. If you could measure the room's voltage on a machine, the needle would swoop all the way to the right.

I understand that some teachers could be intimidated by the idea of mounting a play, but it's really not as difficult as you might think. One of the first things you will need to decide is where to perform it. You can present it to another group of kids in your classroom or to a larger audience in the multi. If you're new at this, I'd suggest keeping it simple. After you've chosen a script or written one yourself, it's time to cast the parts. Make sure everyone who wants a part has one. If you have more students than parts, just create a few more. One year, when getting ready to do *Snow White and the Seven Dwarfs*, I had to rename it *Snow White and the Seventeen Dwarfs*. (*Director's note 1*: If you put on *Snow White*, most of your students will want to be Dopey. And if you choose to do *The Wizard of Oz*, all your boys will ask to be flying monkeys.)

If your kids don't wish to perform, let them be in the stage crew. The stage crew is very important. They set up the scenes, call the actors to their places, and put everything back after the rehearsal. My stage crews also included lighting technicians. The lighting technicians were coveted positions because they got to stand on the chairs, hold lamps (without their shades), and point them at the performers during the show. (*Director's note 2*: During rehearsals, give each member of your stage crew a clipboard with a script and a pencil. Some will try to balance the pencils behind their ears. Most will give up on this after a while because their pencils keep falling.)

When preparing for your play, you'll need to practice a couple of times a week. I'd usually have my rehearsals in the second half of the day after teaching the core subjects. To cut down on taking too much class time, sometimes I would hold rehearsals at recess. In the weeks leading up to your performances, let your students paint the backdrops and some posters advertising the show. Hand the kids masking tape and send them out to hang the posters around the school. Have them make and deliver the invitations too. (*Director's note 3*: If you're doing *Hansel and Gretel*, tie your invitations to lollipops. If you're putting on *The Elves and the Shoemaker*, deliver some in shoes.) For costumes, send a note home asking parents for help. It's a good idea to get a mom or two to assist with coordinating the costumes so that you can focus on other things. As the costumes come into your classroom, hang them on a rack where the children can see them. This adds to the excitement.

On the day of the performance, after your audience is seated—and your stage managers have called "Places!" and your lighting technicians have turned on the lamps—welcome your guests. Then take a seat in the front row and hold the script so you can cue the performers who forget their lines or miss their entrances. Don't worry if your students make mistakes. It adds to the charm. When the performance is over, make sure you leave plenty of time for a curtain call. Kids like to bow. A lot.

After the final show, have a popcorn party in your classroom and watch a recording of the play with the whole class. As you watch it, your room parents will stand in the back of the classroom and smile and laugh while they pour juice. Your students will smile and laugh and cover their faces with both hands when they see themselves on the screen. And when they're covering their faces, a few kids will peek through their fingers so they can see.

Enrichment

I hesitated writing this chapter. In fact, I considered asking my publisher to make the font size on this page so small that you'd skip over it like people do when reading documents with too much fine print. You see, I'm sure some readers are going to disagree with what I say here. How do I know this? When I wrote my first book, I expressed a similar opinion to the one I'm about to share, and some people got pretty hot under the collar. One woman went so far as to hunt down my unlisted home address so she could send me a letter expressing her disagreement. In her letter, she also scolded me for using the word *damn*. Well, sometimes in life you just need to say what you believe in even at the risk of being unpopular. This is one of those times. Actually, right now I feel like Kathy Bates in the film *Fried Green Tomatoes* when she purposely smashes her car into a younger woman's vehicle in the parking lot of the Winn-Dixie supermarket. When the young car owner screams, "What are you doing?" Bates famously replies, "I'm older and have more insurance." Well, I'm old now, and my insurance is pretty good. So, here goes.

The issue I want to discuss is pullout enrichment programs, also known as gifted programs. I'll just say it: I'm not a big believer. Before you start looking for my home address, please understand me here. It's not enrichment that I'm against. I'm *all* for enrichment—when it is offered to everyone.

Let me explain how enrichment programs work in many schools. In grade school, when children are identified as "gifted," what often happens is that they leave their regular classrooms and go to the enrichment class. This isn't a problem for students who are pulled out. It's not good for the children left behind. In fact, it's detrimental. If kids see their classmates leave for enrichment, they feel bad. They don't understand why they do not get to go too.

They don't feel smart. To children, if they were smart, they'd also get to go. In my career, I witnessed this many times. It breaks your heart, and I think it's terrible that we do this to children. In education, we like to say that all students are gifted. It sounds nice. But our actions don't match our words. If we really believed this, then why do we only send a select group of children to the pullout class? Why wouldn't we send them all?

So why do we offer gifted education anyway? One reason is that there is a huge lobby behind it. It's extremely well funded. Another reason is that it inflates self-importance. Moms and dads can say, "My child is gifted." Throughout my career, I listened to many an upset parent when their children didn't get into the enrichment program. I knew parents who spent a lot of money getting their kids tested outside of school when told that they didn't qualify. I had parents beg me to put their children into the gifted classes after they didn't get in. One mom brought me food as a bribe.

Not all parents feel this way, of course. My friend Susan has three kids. A successful educational consultant, she was once a huge proponent of gifted education. In fact, she spoke all over the country about the need for it. Her two older children had been identified as gifted and benefitted from enrichment classes. But then something happened. Susan's third child did not qualify. Suddenly Susan saw everything differently. Her third child would not receive the same extras that her first two had. "It's discrimination," she told me. And after that, she started speaking out against it.

In schools, children typically qualify for enrichment by performing at a certain level on a test. Sometimes this is coupled with teacher recommendations. But we all know that tests are flawed and that some children don't test well. Everyone knows that tests can't measure giftedness in music, art, dance, and athletics. One year my principal asked me to make a list of the students in my class who I thought were gifted. Based on my recommendations, these children would be considered for the enrichment program the following year. I listed all thirty-two of my students. The principal called me in and said I couldn't do that. I told him how I felt. He made me change it, but I felt good about standing up for my kids.

One argument for pullout enrichment is that gifted children need to be challenged at their level and that a specialist teacher can offer this in a way that the homeroom teacher can't. This isn't true. Homeroom teachers know how to differentiate their instruction. They're trained in this. All teachers have access to the same resources. I once worked in a district where all the homeroom teachers were expected to offer enrichment in their own classrooms. No students were pulled out. Just as we were responsible for supporting the remedial students in our classrooms, we were expected to support the gifted children in class too. Sure, it was more work for the teacher and required more differentiation, but it was effective. It was also the right thing to do. No child got hurt.

By offering enrichment to only a select group of children, there is an assumption that the material is beyond the capabilities of the kids who aren't pulled out. This isn't true either. One year my fifth graders who went to the gifted class were challenged with a pre-algebra program. It was actually a good one. I liked it. So I got ahold of the program and offered it to all my students. No one said I couldn't. I let the children who were not pulled out work on it at the same time as the enrichment class. The results didn't surprise me. Several kids who were not identified as gifted did better than those who were.

If you're a teacher, I understand that you might be required to send children for enrichment, but this doesn't mean your hands are completely tied. There are things you can do to enhance all your students' learning. To begin with, if your district has an enrichment specialist, see if the teacher will come into your classroom and teach your whole class. Also, ask if you may have a look at some of the teacher's resources. Most specialist teachers are more than happy to help. When your kids leave for the gifted class, consider offering your own enrichment to the children who stay with you, as I did with the algebra. This way, everyone receives it at the same time. And educate your parents. Bring up the topic at parent-teacher conferences. Many parents don't realize that they can choose not to have their kids participate in the pullout program. At my conferences with parents, I would explain this to them, but rarely would a parent opt out. As I said, the "gifted" label can be awfully attractive.

When providing enrichment, it is common practice for teachers to assign students some challenging math, a more difficult book to read, or a special project. These extras are fine, and there's nothing wrong with them. I used to give them myself. But when I gave kids these types of tasks, I'd often feel like I was just loading them up with more work. Consider other possibilities when offering enrichment. Ask your kids to teach something to the class or explore a personal interest. Let your students have a say in what they'd like to do. Some of the best enrichment projects are those chosen by children.

When discussing enrichment possibilities with parents, I would always recommend these two things: (1) Have your child begin piano lessons, or any instrument for that matter; and (2) Start them on an additional language. These are some of the best forms of enrichment you can offer any child. Each allows children to explore worlds that are often unknown to them. In making these suggestions, I was also taking the full responsibility of providing enrichment off the teacher. I would further explain that enrichment doesn't just mean challenging oneself. It encompasses enhancing the lives of others as well. A child can help out at a soup kitchen, raise money for a cause, visit a nursing home, or work in an animal shelter. By giving to others, don't we better ourselves? When you think of enrichment this way, it becomes so much more than just giving a child some harder math.

So seek to enrich all your students. Challenge all their minds. Stand up for the giftedness of all your kids. Educate your parents and offer them alternatives that they may not have considered. And most importantly: Protect the hearts of those in your charge who have not yet discovered that they are gifted too.

The Craft

Teachers as Artists

I've always found it fascinating just how many famous artists were once teachers. Georgia O'Keeffe taught drawing and penmanship in the public-school system. J. K. Rowling, Stephen King, and Sting were once English teachers. Lin-Manuel Miranda was too. Billy Crystal was a substitute teacher when he was starting his stand-up comedy career. Hugh Jackman taught gym, Sheryl Crow taught elementary music, and John Hamm of *Mad Men* fame taught drama to eighth graders. Before they were famous, legendary Hollywood costume designer Edith Head was a French teacher, and Gene Kelly gave dance classes to little kids at camp. Dan Brown, author of *The Da Vinci Code*, used to teach math. Believe it or not, Gene Simmons, lead singer in the band Kiss, was once an elementary school teacher. And before becoming an actress, Margaret Hamilton, best known for her role as the Wicked Witch of the West, taught kindergarten. Can you imagine if she went back to teaching after making that film? If she used her scary witch voice, she would have frightened her newest Munchkins to death.

It makes sense that so many artists had once been teachers. Although teaching can be a science (teachers collect and analyze data) and also a craft (teachers can create anything out of a paper plate or an egg carton), it is mainly an art form. You can know all the data, but without artistry, your teaching can still fall flat. It's an art to know the right questions to ask, to know when to assist and when to stand back, and to be able to explain something in such a way that a child will understand. It's an art to create lessons about subjects that students might not care about but need to learn. It's an art to read a child's feelings, to be able to win over a student who has built up walls, and to bring out a shy child until she is comfortable participating in class. It's an art to get a crying kindergartner into the classroom on the first day of school, then ensure that he has a good day. It's an art to gauge the waning engagement in a room and know when to switch gears to restore it. It's an art to convince children that events that occurred before they were born are more important than what's happening on their phones. It's an art to make kids smile and laugh and to connect to the human heart. It's an art to be able to lead, model, motivate, differentiate, and help a child find his homework all at the same time. It's artistry that makes learning happen. It has been said that one who works with his hands is a laborer, one who works with his hands and his head is a craftsman, and that one who works with his hands, head, and heart is an artist. Teachers use all three.

If you think about it, teachers and artists *do* the same things. Both call upon creativity, sensitivity, and passion. Both surprise, inspire, and stimulate. Artists create paintings and sculpture, dances and songs. Teachers create lessons, seating charts, and construction paper flags for Presidents' Day. Artists paint on canvases. Teachers paint on butcher paper. Artists transform spaces. Teachers transform empty spaces into reading nooks. Artists play concertos. Teachers play hangman. Artists observe their surroundings. Teachers observe little people run up the slide when they're not supposed to. Artists raise questions. Teachers ask them. Artists commemorate events. Teachers commemorate birthdays. Artists use colors to express mood. Teachers use colors to name their table groups. Artists tell stories. Teachers tell bad jokes. Artists have the ability to see things that others don't. Teachers have the ability to see the bunny ears behind their heads on Picture Day without turning around. Artists people-watch. Teachers watch kids put their fingers over the spout on the drinking fountain to see how far the water will shoot. Artists see the beauty in things. Teachers see the beauty in children.

Just like painters, teachers also use the elements and principles of art: line, form, space, pattern, and symmetry. In our lines, children talk and bounce balls. On our forms, parents sign their names so that kids can go on the field trip. Our spaces are the empty ones that we ask students to make between words when practicing their penmanship and those that we request children leave between one another on the reading rug so they don't get too silly. Our patterns involve words and numbers: single paragraphs in September and multiple paragraphs in January, place value in the fall and geometry in the spring. Our patterns are also seasonal: Halloween parades in October, Thanksgiving feasts in November, hyper kids the week before winter break. There are symmetries in school as well: students and teachers, first period and last, school days and weekends, fall and spring conferences, a fresh teacher in August and a worn-out one in June.

And just like composers and musicians, teachers use the elements of music too. These include timbre (sound quality), pitch (high or low sounds), texture (sounds that overlap each other), tempo (fast or slow), and dynamics (soft to loud). In schools, these elements are always at play and constantly changing. Take a typical grade school PE class with thirty children playing capture the flag, for example: timbre (earplug worthy), pitch (high), texture (thirty overlapping sounds), tempo (fast), and dynamics (forte fortissimo).

Of all the art forms, I'd have to say that teaching is most like acting. We act happy when we teach three-digit by two-digit multiplication, though there is absolutely nothing fun about teaching it. We act interested while a Student of the Week shares his five binders of Pokémon trading cards. We act delighted to see a mom even when she walks into her six o'clock conference, your last one of the day, twenty minutes late. Yes, there's no question that teaching is a performing art. Day after day, we stand in front of our audiences, trying to hold their attention and keep them engaged. Actually, actors have it way easier than teachers. In the theater, the audience leaves after a couple of hours. Ours stay for nine months.

The art of teaching cannot be learned in Teacher School. The art of teaching is learned the first period on Monday morning when you're faced with a room full of sleepy children and the last period on Friday when you push through your final lesson. It is learned at Back to School Night and parent-teacher conferences and school carnivals and Open House. It's learned in hallways, on playgrounds, and inside cafeterias. It's learned on rainy days when you're holding down the fort. It is learned while standing at whiteboards, crouching beside desks, sitting with reading groups, and bending over little chairs.

Now that I'm retired, maybe I too will go on the stage. It would be an easy transition. Since I spent most of my life surrounded by children, it ought to be a cinch to play roles that share the stage with lots of kids, like Fagin in *Oliver!*, Captain von Trapp in *The Sound of Music*, or Daddy Warbucks in *Annie*. Retired female teachers could easily transition to the role of Miss Hannigan, who spends her days surrounded by youngsters while constantly on the verge of a nervous breakdown. I figure I'm a shoo-in for the part of Bob Cratchit in *A Christmas Carol*, seeing that his job as Scrooge's clerk resembles a teacher's: long hours, underpaid, looking forward to his day off. If I audition for these parts, my résumé would say: "Stage experience: thirty-three years. Special skills: singing 'Happy Birthday,' opening juice boxes, reading upside down, and cutting construction paper hearts for valentines so that both sides match. References: a thousand nine-year-olds."

Teachable Moments

All teachers have an inner teacher voice. It's that little sixth sense that tells you when your class is pooped and needs a five-minute break. It's that niggle that makes you aware that your students aren't really understanding what you're trying to teach, so you need to reteach it. It's that Jiminy Cricket on your shoulder that whispers in your ear to check the broom closet when Scotty is missing from his chair, and the rest of the class is staring at the closet looking like they're ready to burst out laughing.

One morning I was about to begin a math lesson on fractions, when my third grader named Eli walked in late. He was carrying a gigantic sunflower, taller than he was. All the children turned to him and shouted "Whoa!" at the same time. At that moment, I had a choice to make. I could continue with the math lesson, or I could let Eli teach us about his sunflower. Fortunately, I listened to my teacher voice.

I put down my marker and asked the kids to gather around Eli's desk. As he told us where he got his flower, I grabbed my set of magnifying glasses and handed them out so that the children could have a look at the seeds and their patterns. I got my tape measure, and together we measured Eli and the height of the sunflower to see which one was taller. We measured the diameter of the flower too. I pulled out my bathroom scale, and Eli stood on it with his sunflower, then again without it, to find out its weight. I asked the children to look closely at the petals and to tell me what colors they saw, then introduced words such as *mustard*, *golden*, and *amber* and wrote them on the board. For my ELL students, I went over words like *seeds*, *petal*, *stem*, and *leaf*. Finally, I gathered my students on the carpet, where I took out my big van Gogh book and showed them his paintings of sunflowers. We compared and contrasted Eli's to van Gogh's.

In one period, my class weighed, measured, reviewed math vocabulary, learned new science terms, and had an art lesson. The children applied previously learned skills and integrated different subjects. They analyzed, synthesized, and evaluated. They listened, shared, and supported a classmate. In all that time, each child was completely into it. My fraction lesson would not have come close.

The minute Eli walked into the classroom was a teachable moment. Teachable moments occur when unplanned questions, comments, or events can be used as learning opportunities. They address a sudden interest when listeners are open, fascinated, and receptive. The teacher's response is spontaneous. You don't plan for it. In order to catch these fleeting moments, you must listen to your inner teacher voice.

Teachable moments can pop up at any time. Sometimes the moments are brief; sometimes they can evolve into a whole lesson or a whole new interest. Once, when I was sorting through books in the classroom library, one of my fourth graders named Julia picked up a biography of Anne Frank and asked, "Who's she?" I could have said, "Oh, you'll read about her when you're older." We weren't studying biographies. But something inside of me said, *She might be interested in this.* I stopped sorting and told Julia a little about Anne Frank and World War II. Julia was hooked. She read the book and others like it, and became an Anne Frank expert. And when it came time for our Wax Museum, you guessed it. Julia chose to be her. If I had not seized that teachable moment, that spark of interest could have faded.

When I was teaching fifth grade, one day I brought in some menus from a local Italian restaurant, and my students used them to solve math problems. While they worked, I made spaghetti (noodles and jars of Ragú) on a single burner in the back of the room. We'd eat after math. During the activity, one of my kids announced, "We should have a restaurant day!" The rest of the children shouted, "Yeah!" Immediately I started shaking my head, but then I stopped and thought, *Why not?* I looked out at the kids and said, "You really want to have one?" Thirty-two children shot back, "Yes!" Their eyes stayed glued on me as I thought about it a little more. "*Well*," I said, stretching out the word. "I *guess* it would be okay." Happy cheering filled the room. "Wait a second," I said. "Wait a second. We'll have it on one condition. *You* have to do all the work." I grinned at them. "And one more thing—I'm not going to be the waiter. I get to eat."

The kids planned the whole event. They named the restaurant and designed the layout of the "kitchen" and "dining room." They discussed the food, made menus (including a child's plate), and mapped out how the day would go. They decided that half of them would work in the restaurant and half would be guests. In the middle of the event, they would switch. This way, everyone would get a chance to do everything. The children even planned the entertainment. When I asked if they wanted me to walk around and sing to the tables, they all said no.

Over the next few days, the kids toted in dishes, utensils, aprons, and tablecloths. They brought in flowers and vases for centerpieces and made a sign for the door. The day before our special lunch, they set the tables and hung the decorations. At the entrance, they placed a podium borrowed from the multi to serve as the check-in desk. On it they set a book labeled "Reservations" and a jar of toothpicks. One of the boys wanted a tip jar, but I vetoed that.

On the big day, they carried in trays, platters, and Tupperware full of food. Since the children had decided it was a five-star restaurant, they came dressed up—the girls in their best outfits, several of the boys wearing clip-on ties. Then, for an hour, with music playing in the background, they sat around candle-lit desks, read their school-made menus, ordered food, and ate lunch. They escorted guests, took orders, plated food, served their friends, and handed over pretend bills on small plates. With mints.

After Restaurant Day, some parents popped by to say they'd never seen their kids so excited about school. Ashley's mom said that a few days after the special day, she and her family were at a restaurant when Ashley, who was generally very shy, confidently ordered her own food, then ordered for everyone else at the table too. At the end of the school year, when the children reflected on all they had done, Restaurant Day was hands down one of their favorites. The following year, on the first day of school, my new students asked when we were having Restaurant Day.

Seize the teachable moments. Don't feel like you need to always cling to your original lesson plan. It's okay to change course now and then. I'm not saying you need to turn your classroom into a restaurant. And I'm not recommending that every time a child walks in with a flower or a potato bug that you have to stop what you're doing. But spot those authentic opportunities for learning. Tune into your teacher voice. Pay attention to your Jiminy Cricket. What you're doing is good.

Teacher Shoppers

"Do teachers make a lot of money?" Alexander, a third grader, asked me one day in class.

I shook my head, then tossed him a grin. "We do it because we love our kids."

"You have *kids*?" he asked, surprised. The children knew I didn't.

I chuckled. "Our *students*."

Sylvia piped up. "If you need money, just get a credit card. That's what my mom does."

"Mine too," Ella added.

Half grinning, I pretended to not understand. "Really? How do they work?"

"Easy," Ella said. "You just put the card in the machine, and it buys whatever you want."

When I started teaching, I knew I'd spend a lot of time at school, but I had no idea that I'd spend so much of it in a store. Teachers are always shopping. In the beginning of the school year, we're buying supplies on Amazon, checking out what's new in Target's Dollar Spot, and searching for things we can use in our classrooms on Facebook Marketplace. In the fall, we're in Goodwill hunting for Halloween costumes and standing in line before stores open for their Black Friday sales. In the winter, we're using the gift cards that our students gave us for Christmas and grabbing DayQuil and NyQuil to battle the bugs we picked up from our kids. We're also at Walgreens buying conversation hearts and pink Hershey's Kisses, then back into the store when all the Valentine's Day candy is 50 percent off. In the spring, we're getting the deals at

Michael's and Barnes & Noble for Teacher Appreciation Week. At the end of the school year, we're picking up wine for the school secretary, colleagues who are retiring—and ourselves, to get through the last week of school.

Sometimes when we're shopping, we run into our students. Whenever this happens, a child will do one or more of the following things: (A) She will stare at you because she hasn't considered that you shop for food; (B) She will not speak, which will surprise you because in class she does not stop talking; (C) She will follow you around the store, dodging behind endcaps and peeking from around corners like you are both in a Matt Damon spy movie. The next day at school, she will tell you that she saw you at the store, as if you do not remember. Once, I ran into one of my third graders at the grocery store, and, the following morning, she walked into the classroom and announced, "You wear jeans!" *Warning*: If you do meet your students in the supermarket, they will memorize everything in your shopping cart and report to the class that you drink Budweiser.

Stores love teachers. Contrary to what you might think, they do not put their back-to-school supplies out for children and parents. They put them out for teachers. Stores know our weaknesses. They're aware that teachers can't resist plastic tubs or colored file folders or see-through bins that we can put fancy labels on after we've run them through the laminator. They know that teachers lose their self-control when it comes to pens, bulletin board borders, and those cute miniature erasers in the shapes of apples, pencils, rainbows, letters, pizzas, globes, and jack-o'-lanterns that fit perfectly inside the squares of our Halloween bingo cards. Even if we try to be strong, we can't help ourselves. (*I am not spending any more money on my classroom! Wait! Are those jungle animal erasers?!?*) Stores are also wise to the fact that teachers love a good discount, so they lure us in with special deals just for educators. Once these stores get us inside, they know that we will fill up our shopping carts with all sorts of goodies. They've figured out that a teacher who steps into a store to pick up one pack of markers will leave having spent hundreds of dollars. All the stores are in on this: Target, Walmart, Staples, Rite Aid, Costco, Office Depot, the Container Store. They're *all* in cahoots.

But these stores aren't the worst. For teachers, the worst store of all is Dollar Tree, otherwise known as "Teacher Heaven." Teachers go absolutely crazy in this place. Who cares if you don't need swimming pool noodles or glow sticks? So what if you don't need any more tissues or sandwich bags or boxes of elbow macaroni for kids to glue onto their papers to represent apostrophes, commas, and quotation marks? Everything is only a *dollar*! And what does it matter that you don't know what you would do with five hundred clothespins, a dozen rolls of crepe paper streamers, and ten bags of colored pompoms? You'll figure it out later.

Teachers also lose their minds in the children's sections of bookstores. We love these places because they're everything we want our own classroom libraries to be: shelf after shelf of crisp and shiny kids' books, all with that delicious new-book smell and wrapped in wrinkle-free, smudge-free, and tear-free dust jackets that haven't had to undergo surgery yet with the tape dispenser. Teachers delight in opening up a brand-new book and hearing the faint crackling sounds that let you know you're the first to open it. To me, opening up a new book is like stretching out your arms in the morning right after you wake up—a little stiff and crackly. Some people have a weakness for clothes, purses, or shoes. For teachers, it's children's books. They're our kryptonite.

And I'll let you in on a secret: Many teachers are closet children's book hoarders. The books you see on classroom shelves are just part of our collections. These books are there to throw you off the new-book scent coming from the cupboards. Our book hoarding is the real reason teachers have locks on the cabinets. We're hiding our habit. A friend of mine buys so many picture books for her classroom that her husband told her she needed an intervention. During the pandemic, he also suggested that she "social distance" from Amazon. Didn't happen.

Teachers get weak-kneed at garage sales too. Life doesn't get much better than leaving a Saturday morning garage sale with a big stack of children's books that you got for next to nothing. Once, Jill and I held a sale together. We were both getting rid of things we'd bought for our classrooms that we didn't need anymore. Well, I learned that was a bad idea. Jill and I ended up buying each other's stuff! (*Tip*: When you're at a garage sale and find things that you can use in your classroom, say that you're a teacher. There's a good chance you'll get a deal.)

One day I stopped at an estate sale where I came across five or six boxes in the back of a garage. Someone had passed away. As soon as I opened the boxes, I knew immediately that they had belonged to a teacher. They were full of old flash cards, bingo games, and well-worn lesson planners. There were grade books, seasonal decorations, and faded construction paper crafts that the teacher had obviously made to show her kids before they started making their own. It was a lifetime's worth of work.

In one of the folders, I found dozens of old class photos, several black and white, on which the teacher had written the name of each student so that she wouldn't forget. In each photo, I saw the owner of the boxes. For several years, she sported a high bouffant hairdo. As I looked through the images of the kids, I tried to figure out who her pistols were. When I finished going through the boxes, I picked up a few items and walked over to a woman taking money. I asked her what was going to happen to the things that didn't sell, and she said that most likely it would get dumped. My heart sank. It killed me to think of a teacher's life being thrown away like that. It felt so dishonoring. *These things need to be saved!* I bought all the boxes.

Every year, teachers spend hundreds if not thousands of dollars out of their own pockets to purchase all kinds of things for their classrooms. Oftentimes, they are not reimbursed. Once, I found a shopping list in a cart at Walmart. It read: *disinfectant wipes, address labels, highlighters, folders, index cards, jumbo crayons, sidewalk chalk, pretzels, Advil,* and *3 boxes of Apple Jacks.* I knew instantly that the list had to have been written by a teacher. The dead giveaway was the cereal. It's a staple classroom treat. Someday we're going to find out that there are more boxes of cereal in classroom cupboards across the country than in cupboards at home. The fact that teachers spend their own money is almost expected. Heck, it's even in the tax code. Educators get a deduction. Most teachers just accept it as part of the job, but that doesn't make it okay. It shouldn't be this way. Imagine if you worked in an office, and your boss told you to bring in your own pencils and Post-it Notes! Why is it that teachers spend so much of their own money like this? Why do we buy books and manipulatives, posters and pocket charts, ant farms and butterfly kits with our own money? We do it because we know that classrooms full of these things are good for children, and we'd rather spend the money than deprive our kids.

When it comes to classroom supplies, the teachers who have it the worst are the new ones. Besides getting some wobbly desks and chairs and maybe an old, gray file cabinet, new teachers usually inherit a basket full of dried-up markers, a can of stiff paintbrushes, some rainy-day games that are missing pieces, and desk drawers full of rubber bands, paper clips, thumbtacks, a whistle, and a box of those brass fasteners with the pointed prongs that no teacher knows what to do with. Except for some money they might get from the PTA, the reality is that they will end up purchasing much of what they need on their own dime. To help out the newbies, I think we should start throwing them teacher showers. Why not? Mothers-to-be get showers when expecting a child. It only makes sense to throw one for a teacher-to-be who is expecting *thirty*. Come to think of it, teacher showers could be pretty fun. The games could be played using multicolored sticky notes. The favors could be boxes of No. 2 pencils. The prizes could be Mr. Sketch scented markers. And teachers could register at Dollar Tree! Actually, one of my third graders came up with a good solution for helping out teachers. One day Lauren looked around the classroom and asked, "Where do you get all this stuff? Do you buy it, or does the school give it to you?" I thought, That's *an insightful child. Most kids wouldn't think about that.* "Well, actually," I replied, "I bought most of it myself. Most teachers do." Then, matter-of-factly, Lauren said, "You need to start a GoFundMe page."

When shopping, teachers can be pretty choosy. We like a certain kind of dry erase marker (Expo Low Odor Chisel Tip) and have strong opinions about the best pen for correcting (Paper Mate Flair, Pilot G2 Retractable Gel). We prefer a particular brand of hand sanitizing wipes (Clorox) and are even partial to certain fragrances of air freshener (Glade Clean Linen). In terms of things that teachers buy, there is one that we are extremely finicky about. And that is our Halloween pumpkin.

One October day when I was teaching in Budapest, I went to the store with my Hungarian friend Gábor to pick out a couple of pumpkins for my class. We would be carving them into jack-o'-lanterns. Gábor had never bought a pumpkin for Halloween before. At that time, Hungarians were just starting to celebrate it.

At the store, we found the pumpkins in a large cardboard crate that looked like a giant playpen. Gábor grabbed one of the pumpkins and started to set it into the shopping basket.

"Stop!" I said, putting my hands up. He froze. "You can't just take the first pumpkin you see!"

"Why not?"

"Well, for one thing it needs to have a good color." I surveyed the pumpkins and pulled out another one. "Like this." I ran my hand over it. "See how nice and orange it is."

Gábor looked back into the crate. "They're all orange."

"But this is a *deeper* orange. Yours is too light."

Gábor raised his eyebrows, put back his pumpkin, and grabbed another one. "Is this one okay?"

Cringing, I shook my head.

"What's wrong with this one?"

"It doesn't have a stem."

"So what?"

"It *has* to have a stem," I declared. "Otherwise it looks like it lost its hat. And try to find a stem that curls. They're cuter."

Gábor rolled his eyes and put it back. Then he took out a pumpkin with a stem and set it into the basket.

I made a face.

"*Now* what?"

"It's lopsided. Plus, it's bumpy. A pumpkin must be nice and smooth. And it has to be round."

He handed me the pumpkin and said, "Why don't *you* pick them?"

As I started going through the crate, I realized that it was pretty slim pickings. Most of the pumpkins were bumpy or lopsided or stemless. I figured another American teacher from my school had already been here and grabbed the good ones. Eventually, I found three that fit all the requirements.

Just as Gábor and I were about to leave, a man and a woman stepped up to the crate with a shopping cart. In it were two young boys dressed in matching striped shirts. They each had a buzz cut. The man asked me how much the pumpkins were, and I told him. His accent told me he was Hungarian.

"Are you going to carve them?" I asked. He didn't seem to understand *carve*, so I picked a different word. "Cut," I added.

"Ah yes," he answered. He smiled at his boys. "It's our first time. We have never cut a pumpkin for Halloween before." Then he reached into the bin and pulled one out. It looked like a Cyclops.

I cringed and glanced at Gábor. He knew what was coming. I turned to the dad. "Uh . . . pardon me, but that one isn't good for cutting."

"Why not?" he asked.

"Well . . ." I looked at the boys. *They can't carve* that *for their very first jack-o'-lantern. It will look terrible!* I quickly scanned the crate. I knew they wouldn't find a good pumpkin in there. Then I eyed my three round, smooth, bright-orange pumpkins with cute, curly stems. Gábor was grinning. I reached into the cart and handed the largest pumpkin to the man. "Here," I said. "Take this. For the boys. And Happy Halloween."

Personal Teaching

I've never met a child who didn't like making paper chains. For kids, there is something special about taking a strip of construction paper, forming a loop, gluing the end, holding it for a few seconds until it's dry, slipping another strip of paper through it, then repeating this over and over again. Every December I let my students make paper chains to decorate the classroom, and every year the same thing would always happen. After handing out the green and red strips, the children would start putting together their chains individually. Soon one child would connect his to a friend's, and, before long, all the kids in the room would be attaching theirs to make one giant chain that they'd excitedly stretch from one corner of the room to the other and sometimes even out the door.

Teaching, like those paper chains, is all about connection. Teachers help children connect to the material. We connect lessons to previous ones. We help our kids connect to one another. We make connections with parents and colleagues. And, of course, all day long we foster connections with our students. As I discussed in the chapter "The Fourth *R*," education is powered by connection. For children to meet their greatest learning potential, they must connect with their teachers.

Teaching is an intensely personal profession. So it makes sense that one of the best ways to spark connections with kids is to practice what I call "personal teaching." Personal teaching is when you let children in on your life. All students want to know their teachers. They crave it. Just witness what happens when kids discover their teacher's middle name, for example. They act like they've just learned the greatest secret—then tell everyone else in the class. Sharing your life with children makes you more human, welcoming, and real. Students like the teachers they know, and if they like you, they are more apt to trust you, work for you, and believe in what you wish to accomplish.

There are many ways to teach personally. If you ask kids to fill out All About Me questionnaires in the beginning of the year, fill out one yourself and share your answers with your students. They will remember everything you say better than their times tables. When children discover that they like or dislike the same things as their teacher, they feel an instant connection. If you're taking any kind of course outside of school, tell your kids about it, and explain that you also have to write papers, study for tests, and do homework. It's good for children to see their teacher as a student. They not only connect with you as a learner, but they also see that learning never ends. They will like that you have homework too. Years ago, I used to study French with a tutor. I wasn't very good, but I enjoyed it. Every so often, I'd teach my kids some French words, and they'd repeat them back to me with cute French accents.

Also, if you saved any of your schoolwork from when you were a child, definitely share it with your students. Growing up, I saved quite a bit of mine (for playing school), and from time to time, I would show my kids. I shared my old artwork and stories, even the first "book" I wrote after a visit to the fire station when I was in kindergarten. One paper was from second grade. My mom sent it to me when I began teaching. It started like this: "Someday I want a golden retriever. Someday I want my own bedroom. Someday I want to become a teacher." I always kept that paper on my classroom wall. Whenever you show students any of your schoolwork from grade school, they will crack up at your sloppy penmanship, bad drawings, misspelled words, and your punctuation errors. Children take great delight in seeing that their teachers didn't put their periods in either.

Another way to let kids in on your life is to share your hobbies and passions. It personalizes you. If you love books, bring in one you're reading and show your class. It doesn't matter that the book is beyond them. You're showing them something that brings you pleasure. If you studied an instrument, play it for your kids. If you knit or crochet, give a demonstration. If you like to go fishing, share some snapshots of a trip. I remember when I was in fourth grade, my teacher grew bonsai trees and brought them into class. To this day,

whenever I see one, it takes me right back to grade four—seated in the back
of the room near the movie projector, sporting that David Cassidy haircut.

One of my passions is classic movie musicals, and every year my students
learned that I am crazy about them. When it rained, I'd croon, "I'm singin' in
the rain . . ." and my kids would beg me to stop. I wouldn't. When teaching
cursive, I taught my kids my own call-and-response. I'd call out, "Give it flair!"
and my kids would chorus back, "Like Fred Astaire!" It made me happy. Once,
when I mentioned the name of the famous film star and singer Judy Garland,
a student asked, "Who's she?" I grabbed my chest, staggered a few steps, and
fell onto my desk. After I "recovered," I called the class over to my computer
and showed them some clips of her films. It became our inside joke. From
then on, whenever this group wanted to tease me, they'd say (while smirking),
"Mr. Done, *who's* Judy Garland?" and I'd pretend to get upset. Sometimes I'd
play "Name That Tune" with my kids as they were leaving at the end of the
day. For their exit ticket, I would sing the beginning of a song, and they'd have
to tell me the name of the show that it came from: "Doe, a deer, a—" "*The
Sound of Music*!" "You may go."

One year I saw a movie poster on eBay that I really wanted, but the auction
started during school hours. Rather than sneak to my computer during class
time to make my bids, I decided to bring my students in on it. I showed them
the poster and let them know when I put in my bids. Well, these kids really got
into it! All day long, they'd ask if I was still the highest bidder. The auction
was scheduled to finish about ten minutes before the end of the school day.
By that time, none of us could get any work done, so we all stood around
the computer and watched the clock on the screen. In the final seconds, we
counted down together. The kids hooted and whooped and jumped off their
chairs when I won the poster. Soon the bell rang, and they ran out shouting,
"He won! He won!" When I saw some of them telling their moms what just
happened, I slinked back inside. I decided that if any parent questioned why
I was bidding on eBay during school hours, I would tell them that we were
studying e-commerce.

One of the best ways to let children in on your life is to tell them a personal
story. Nothing builds connection faster between teachers and their students. If
the story takes place when you were a kid, so much the better. If it lends itself

to being acted out, all the better still. Every teacher knows what happens when you start to tell children a story. They become captivated and hang on every word. And that evening, they will tell every one of them to their parents. Kids are not inspired by textbooks or devices, but they *are* inspired by the stories we tell. It has been said that a story is the shortest distance between two people and that stories are the bridges from one mind to another. And so, to make bridges with my students, I would tell them mine.

I'd tell them about the water balloon fights and squirt gun fights and rolled-up sock fights that I used to have with my brothers. I recounted the time I got my tie stuck in the laminator at school. (I have never lived that one down.) I demonstrated how Roxie my dog would come to me and whine as I was sitting in a chair, so I'd get up because I thought she needed to go out. Then she'd jump onto my chair because she wanted to steal it. I would act out how when I was their age, my brothers and I used to sneak downstairs with flashlights on Christmas Eve and search for our presents while my grandma snored loudly on the couch. Whenever I told these stories, I'd ask my kids not to tell their parents, which I knew would make the children want to share them even more. Personal stories build bridges between teachers and parents too.

A couple of years ago, I was at a bank in my hometown, and the teller happened to be a former student of mine. His name was Craig. We got to talking and figured out that he had been in my class about fifteen years earlier. As we were chatting, Craig said something that absolutely floored me. He told me the story about my sneaking downstairs on Christmas Eve! He still remembered it. And he remembered that my grandma snored too! It just goes to show you: Our stories are powerful. Don't underestimate them.

We are all storytellers. We all carry stories about our families and friends, our childhoods and our classrooms. Through your stories, you not only reveal your passions and humor, your successes and mistakes, your hardships and joys. You also share your vulnerability. And vulnerability is an important part of teaching and learning. When you are vulnerable, you give children the freedom to be vulnerable. You let them know that their classroom is a safe place. You give them permission to struggle with a subject or even not to like it. Say, for instance, you tell your students that reading didn't come easily to you at their age. What a relief this is for a child who finds reading difficult. When you are willing to be imperfect in front of children, they feel that they also can be imperfect. Nothing gives children the freedom to make mistakes more than when teachers share theirs. So keep building those bridges. Share your passions and interests. Teach personally. In doing so, your heart will touch your kids' hearts, and your humanity will touch their humanity too.

Laughter and Learning

It was hot in the classroom, and I could see that my fourth graders were wilting. "Okay, everyone, pencils down," I announced. The kids stopped working and looked at me. "Have I shown you my disappearing leg trick?" I asked. Immediately the children groaned and rolled their eyes, even though they were smiling. They had seen my disappearing leg trick before. I grabbed my sport coat and held it in front of my legs like a matador. Singing a silly fanfare, I slowly lifted the coat while raising one leg behind it at the same time. "Ta-da!" I cried. My leg disappeared. The kids shook their heads and rolled their eyes some more at their wacky teacher, then got back to work. A humor break.

Laughter and learning go hand in hand. Using humor in the classroom reduces tension, magnetizes children, and creates a positive learning environment. When classrooms are injected with amusement and mirth, subjects that kids find stressful can be less so. As teachers, we all want to motivate our students and create an atmosphere of openness and respect. We want our kids to feel comfortable, to take risks, and to be active learners. Humor helps facilitate all of this. All kids enjoy a good laugh. They're built for it. Research tells us that in a single day, most adults laugh fifteen to a hundred times. A six-year-old, on the other hand, averages three hundred laughs a day.

So, when you can, infuse your teaching with humor once in a while. I'm not suggesting that teachers become comedians who toss out one-liners. You don't need to dress up like Patch Adams. Do what works for you. When trying any of the following ideas, if your kids are smiling, giggling, laughing, or even falling out of their chairs now and then, you can be sure that you are on the right track.

Play Dumb

Pretend you've never heard of Beyoncé, Lady Gaga, or Rihanna, and ask your students who they are. Watch heads shake and palms hit foreheads. Do the same for Xbox, Game Boy, and *Minecraft*. All this is good practice for April Fool's Day, when you have to play like you don't notice the whoopee cushion on your seat, the plastic snake on your desk, or the sticky note on your back that says "Kick Me."

Make Mistakes

When writing on the board, misspell a word or do a math problem incorrectly—on purpose. If you tell your class that in the next few minutes you are going to make a mistake, they will watch you like a hawk to catch it.

Be Wacky

When your kids do well on a test, start dancing. After you solve a difficult math problem in front of your students, strike a bodybuilder pose like Arnold Schwarzenegger. Ditch the pointer sometimes and use a Darth Vader light saber instead. When passing out stickers, take one for yourself and slap it on your forehead. When teaching contractions or possessives, put on a cape and say you're Apostrophe Man. Wear it when Captain Capitalization visits as well. When teaching kids about strong verbs, bring in a plastic dumbbell. On each end, tape an index card with a strong verb. Then (because the verbs are so strong), pretend that it's really hard to lift the weight. Of course, when you do this, all your little Popeyes will beg you to let them lift the verbs too.

Act Shocked

When your last student finally brings in his permission slip for the field trip, grab your heart, fall to the floor, and pretend to faint. If you do, be ready. A dozen small paramedics will rush over to help you.

Be Out of Touch

Pretend that you think the TV series *Hannah Montana* is still really popular and ask your kids if they still watch it. They'll all shout, "No!"

Wear Funny

Put on a tie with the Superman logo. Slip on *Stranger Things* socks. The day after Halloween, pin on a button that says "Official Halloween Candy Taste Tester." Wear a funny T-shirt that says "A, B, C, D, E, F, G, H, I, J, K, elemeno P."

Pretend You're Lost

Imagine you're teaching grade three. When all your students are on task and working quietly, walk outside and check the room number with the door open. The children will stop to see what you're doing. Then look back at them with a confused expression and say, "This can't be the third-grade classroom. You all are too well behaved. Third graders don't act this well. You kids are acting like fourth graders. I must be in the wrong room." Then in your best are-you-pulling-my-leg voice, ask, "Are you *fourth* graders?" Beaming, they will all shout, "Yes!"

Play Sad

When all your students are working quietly and no one is at your desk, act like the lonely repairman in the old Maytag ads. Sigh deeply, fake pout, and whine, "I'm sad. Nobody needs my help." When you do this, one wise guy will sprint up to your desk for help even though he doesn't need any.

Dress Up

Put on an eye patch, and you're Long John Silver. Don a black top hat when reading *Frosty the Snowman*. Wear a chef's hat if you're making applesauce. Stick a couple of paintbrushes in your pocket and a few Band-Aids over your left ear, and you're Vincent van Gogh. Other handy costume pieces include: funny glasses, a fake mustache, a silly wig, and *the* most versatile costume piece of all—the cape. Put it on, and you're a king, queen, prince, princess, nobleman, wizard, vampire, the headless horseman, a founding father, Puss in Boots, or Zero the Hero on 100th Day. Speaking of which, my friend Lucy dresses up as Cruella de Vil on day 101, and all her first graders paint their faces to look like Dalmatians.

Predict the Future

Turn a rounded glass lamp globe into a crystal ball and pretend to see into the future. If some of your students are fooling around, stand over it and say, "I see three boys who are going to get into trouble very soon if they don't get to work." For greatest effect, tie a scarf around your head like a turban and draw on a swirly mustache with an eyebrow pencil. Don't forget about the mustache, though. Once, when I was at the supermarket, I was wondering why everyone was smiling at me. I'd forgotten to wipe off my mustache.

Share Your Masterpiece

Draw one thing on the board really badly. Claim that it's a "masterpiece" and that the Metropolitan Museum of Art has offered you five million dollars for it. When your kids shout, "That's not true!" cross your fingers behind your back and fake argue with them. One child will run up to you and turn you around to reveal your crossed fingers.

Supersize It

When writing punctuation marks on the board, make them huge. Suppose you're teaching kids how to put commas in a sequence, and you write a sentence on the board like this: "I like to eat hamburgers, hot dogs, and spaghetti." When writing the sentence, don't just make nice, little, sweet, demure commas. Make them bold and humongous! The bigger the punctuation marks—the bigger the laughter.

Check for Fevers

When walking around the classroom with a box of cereal to hand out as snacks, put your hand on a child's forehead and say it feels like he has a fever. Then in a serious doctor voice, ask if he needs any "medicine" (the cereal). The child will begin to act like he's very sick. In between sneezes and coughs, he will moan, "Yes." Immediately the rest of your class will start coughing, sneezing, and holding their tummies too.

Break into Song

Out of the blue, grab a ruler, put it up to your mouth like a microphone, and start singing. Or sing with no mike at all. Dealing with recess drama? Start performing "Let It Go." None of your students are answering you? Launch into "All by Myself." Waiting a long time for kids to line up? Begin imitating the jingle from *Jeopardy!* Everyone completed the homework? Sing the first few bars of "Hallelujah Chorus." When someone doesn't put his name on his paper, hold it up, and start marching slowly toward the wastebasket while intoning "The Funeral March": "*daaa da-da-daaa da da-da da-da da-daaa.*" Want to drive your class nuts? Belt out Barney the dinosaur's cleanup song when they're tidying up. I know one teacher who threatens to sing to her middle schoolers if they don't work. She says it helps not to have a good voice. Her kids' response: "No! Don't! We'll work!"

Dance

When your students need to burn off some energy, put on a video of "Macarena," "Cha-Cha Slide," "The Chicken Dance," or "The Twist," depending on their age level. Obviously, you have to dance too. Then your kids will be moving *and* chuckling. Even better.

Post a Meme of the Week

Hang a sign on your classroom wall titled "Meme of the Week." Under it, place a funny photo and a caption to look like a meme. For example, put up a photo of a sleeping dog, and write: "He just corrected your papers." Pin up a picture of a baby with a surprised expression, and add: "What do you mean we have to write in complete sentences?" Post a photo of students concentrating seriously over their schoolwork and write: "When your teacher walks by, so you pretend that you're working." For a twist, hang a funny photo and ask your kids to provide the captions.

Pretend Something Is Really Hard

When writing math problems on the board for children to solve in their notebooks, finish with a bonus problem. Before you write it, tell the kids that the bonus problem will be the hardest problem of all. You don't expect them to know how to do it. In fact, it's so difficult that they shouldn't even try. Then on the board write *1 + 1*.

Add Hair and Ears

When drawing smiley faces on kids' papers, don't just make a circle with two eyes and a mouth. Give the smiley some funny hair and big ears. The second you do this for one child, you will get a line of children wanting funny hair and big ears on their smiley faces too.

Have One Joke—and Repeat It

Much like my disappearing leg trick, every time you tell the joke to your students, act like you don't remember bringing it up. Begin by saying, "Did I ever tell you guys about . . . ?" Your kids will roll their eyes and shake their heads and groan, "Yes." Tell them anyway. They want you to. When you're finished, laugh at the joke because you think it's so funny. The dumber the joke, the better. One of my go-to jokes was this: "What did the zero say to the eight?" Answer: "Nice belt."

Teacher Says

One of my all-time favorite movies is the holiday classic *It's a Wonderful Life*. And one of its best scenes comes at the end, when goodhearted banker George Bailey stands with his family beside the Christmas tree—his youngest daughter Zuzu in his arms—as all the townspeople in Bedford Falls pour into his home bearing cash to save him from financial ruin. As George and his family look on, a bell on the tree rings. Zuzu points to it and says, "Look, Daddy! Teacher says every time a bell rings, an angel gets his wings." It's one of my favorite lines in the movie—not just because I'm charmed by the thought of an angel receiving his wings at the sound of a bell. It moves me for another reason. I'm touched by the beginning of the line when Zuzu speaks the words "Teacher says."

For children, there is something truly special about the words spoken by the teacher. If the teacher says it, don't try to tell kids anything different. Every teacher knows what I'm talking about. I've had parents come to me and say they'd tried to help their children with the math homework, but they wouldn't listen because I had shown them a different way to solve the problems. One day a dad wanted to know if I'd make a video of myself reading aloud and send it to him. I asked why, and he replied, "When I read to my daughter, she wants me to read it like you do." When a mom requested that I tell her son to take piano lessons, I said, "Why don't *you* tell him?" Her answer: "Because he doesn't listen to me. He'll listen to you, though."

A teacher's words are immensely powerful. What we say to children and how we say it can inspire and invigorate, energize and uplift. I have a friend named Leslie who is an editor at a large publishing house in New York. She told me that she would always be grateful to her high school English teacher

Mrs. Stewart for telling her that she had a gift for words. Leslie was shocked when Mrs. Stewart suggested that she might want to consider pursuing journalism when she went to college. Up till then, she hadn't even planned to go. "Mrs. Stewart knew I was going to college before *I* did!" she marveled. Another friend of mine, Ron, is a professional novelist. He told me that one of the reasons he became one was because of the day in second grade when his teacher, Mr. Phillips, read his poem about the color blue and said, "You should be a writer someday." It stayed with Ron forever.

Teachers are encouragers. It's in our DNA. Every day, all day long, we sing encouragement to our children: "Good work." "*Now* you have it!" "What a clever idea." "This sentence is so well written." "I love to watch you learn." It has been said that 90 percent of teaching is encouragement. I don't doubt it. I read an article once that listed different ways to encourage a child. The premise of the piece was that not all children want to hear the same kinds of encouragement and praise. I was interested to see if it was true, so I copied off the list, gave it to my fourth graders, and asked them to highlight the words that they wanted to hear. Well, the article was right. The kids all highlighted different words. I had the children keep the lists on their desktops so that I'd know how they wanted to be encouraged. One day as I was working with Ariya (he could be a little monkey), I said, "Good job, Ariya." Immediately he tapped his paper and said, "That's not on my list. Choose another one."

Children remember their teacher's encouragement. All kids deposit the uplifting words from the teacher into their memory banks. Unfortunately, words of discouragement remain with children too. A good friend of mine named Mark has a beautiful singing voice. Mark began taking vocal lessons when he was in his thirties. I asked him why he hadn't started when he was younger, and he said that his choir teacher in middle school told him that he had a bad voice. It destroyed Mark's confidence and took him twenty years to start getting it back. Children don't forget when their teachers withhold encouragement either. In my last week of middle school, the PE teacher called all the eighth-grade boys in for short conferences. In mine, he told me that I would have been a good wrestler. I was shocked. It was the first time he'd ever said anything like that. *Why hadn't he told me this before?* I thought. *I would have tried out for the team!* I still remember it.

When giving encouragement or praise to children, it is best to keep a couple of things in mind. First of all, focus on the child's accomplishment, not his or her character. As an example, instead of saying "You're smart," say "I see you worked really hard on this." And be sure to speak with sincerity. Though well intended, some teachers throw out "Good job!" and "Way to go!" so much that the words don't mean anything anymore. Too much praise loses its effectiveness. You don't need to praise kids for something they are expected to do, such as walk in line, hang up their backpacks, or push in their chairs. A thank-you is sufficient. Praise children when they do something beyond what is normally expected: for instance, when a young learner who has difficulty staying focused reads all the way through silent reading time; when a student helps a friend without being asked; when a young learner who struggles in writing finishes a paragraph. I remember one day I was helping a third grader named Claudia at her desk when a lightbulb went on, and she figured out how to round numbers. It had been a challenge for her.

"You got it!" I said. "Good work!"

Claudia looked up at me and smiled. "You too."

I gave her a confused look. "For what?"

"For teaching," she replied. "You did a good job too."

Precious.

One way to encourage students is to give them a group compliment. Tell your whole class how much you appreciate them: "Boys and girls, I've noticed how hard you've all been working this week, and I just wanted you to know how much I appreciate it. Thank you." Then add, "Teaching all of you is why I love my job." Watch their faces brighten and their backs straighten up.

Another way to encourage children is to send them to the principal's office—for *good* things. Let's say one of your students writes a nice story. Send the child to the principal to read it. It's one thing to read your writing to the teacher. It's something completely different to get to read it to the principal. Make the arrangements ahead of time, so you know when to send the student. If possible, send a couple of kids at a time. When they return to the classroom, they might be holding certificates or new pencils. I guarantee that it will be the first thing they talk about when they get home.

One of the best ways to encourage a child is to write a note. Write it in your own hand on a piece of paper (sticky notes are too clunky) and set it on the student's desk after school so that the child sees it first thing in the morning. For children, finding a handwritten note from the teacher is like discovering a note from Mom or Dad in your lunchbox. It's unexpected, secret, and special because it is just for you. A note from the teacher starts a child's day on a positive one. Notes help build rapport, defrost defenses, and strengthen trust. They can bring big dividends. And they can soften hearts too.

When I was teaching fifth grade, I got a new student named Travis mid-year. He had been transferred into my room out of another teacher's class. She claimed that she couldn't handle him. Travis had experienced problems all through school. Sadly, he'd been labeled a "difficult" kid. But even worse, he had labeled himself as one. By the time Travis reached my classroom, he had been subjected to a lifetime of trips to the principal's office, email and phone calls home, time-outs, detentions, missed recesses, flat-out bribes, and reflection forms on which he had to write what he did, why he did it, and what he could have done differently. His previous teacher had put him on a behavior contract that his mom had to sign daily. The librarian and the PE teacher had to sign it when he went to their classes too. Needless to say, Travis didn't trust teachers. Who'd blame him? When he entered my class, no doubt he expected me to treat him the same way. But I knew I couldn't. None of those things would have worked.

I needed to handle Travis carefully. In order for him to start feeling good about himself and as part of the class, I spoke to him in the same way I did to the other children. Kids like Travis want to be treated like everyone else. I refrained from praising him too much—no thank-you for keeping his hands to himself in line or for sitting quietly during the read-aloud. When I did praise him, I did so privately. Some children are embarrassed by public praise. I made a conscious effort not to hover over him, micromanage, or overdo the reminders, as teachers tend to do with children who can be challenging. When Travis had a good day, I didn't give him a certificate or let him pick something from my prize box. I acted like his good behavior was to be expected. I wanted him to experience that proud-of-yourself feeling that comes from behaving well. Once in a while, I gave Travis responsibilities that he had never been entrusted with, such as delivering messages and helping run copies in the staff room. The first time I took Travis into the staff room, he looked around, taking in everything as if he'd just entered King Tut's tomb. He'd never been in the teachers' lounge. I remember him saying, "You have a refrigerator in here— and a couch!" I threw him a smirk and said, "Didn't you know? We live here." Additionally, I gave Travis an important part in our school play. He told me that he'd never had a speaking part before. He was our narrator, and though he had only a couple of lines, he sold those lines as if he were the master of ceremonies at the Emmy Awards.

And—I decided to love Travis with notes. Every now and then, I would write him one and tape it onto his desk after school. I wanted him to see it as soon as he walked in. Whenever Travis spotted it, a smile would spread across his face—and get bigger as he read it. On these mornings, I'd watch Travis out of the corner of my eye, but I never made eye contact with him. Notes unacknowledged are even more special. When Travis finished reading, he'd tuck it into his desk. He and I never spoke of them.

I would like to point out that Travis did not misbehave in my classroom. Oh, he got into conflicts outside of class, but not in mine. I'm not saying this to puff myself up. There were several reasons for this. My expectations of him were clear, and Travis knew I would follow through. I purposely put his desk far from mine so he'd see that I trusted him. Oftentimes, children who exhibit discipline problems sit under the teacher's nose. What's more, I allowed him to move. Movement helps children regulate their energy. In school, sometimes children are in trouble for nothing other than they need to move around. On top of that, Travis knew that I cared for him. Kids try harder for teachers who do. But most importantly, Travis wanted to succeed. All children do. I also believe that one of the reasons he behaved was because of those notes. At my final conference with Travis's mom, she actually brought them up. She told me that before coming to my classroom, she didn't think Travis had ever received a positive note from a teacher. Only behavior contracts.

Several years later, when Travis and his classmates graduated from high school, I went to their graduation. I hadn't seen him since he left elementary school. Travis had grown into a strapping young man who towered over me. He had a mustache now and was built like a linebacker. I joked that if I ever needed a bodyguard, I'd give him a call. He cracked a smile when I said it. After the ceremony, I stood with Travis and some of his classmates, chatting, laughing, and taking photos together. I could tell they were glad I'd come. I hadn't spoken with most of them since they left my class, but they acted just as sweet as when they were in fifth grade. Child love is like that.

After the celebration, I was walking back to my car when I heard a voice call out, "Mr. Done!" I turned around, and there was Travis running toward me. When he caught up to me, he said, "I forgot." Then he reached into his back pocket and grabbed his wallet. He opened it, pulled out a folded piece of paper, and handed it to me. He smiled at me as I unfolded it. I smiled at him when I saw the words. Of course, I recognized the handwriting. The note was short. It said: "Dear Travis, I'm glad you're in my class. I believe in you. Warmly, Mr. Done." Next to the words was a happy face.

"I saved it!" Travis said, beaming. "I saved them *all*."

As I handed back the note, I could feel my teacher heart begin to swell. Then, without any warning, this great big linebacker of a guy threw his arms around me and squeezed me tight. "Thank you," he said. "Thank you for believing in me." And then, just like that, he was off, back to his friends. About a hundred yards away, he turned and gave me a giant smile and a wave.

When I got into my car, I sat for a few minutes in silence. I leaned my head on the steering wheel and squeezed my eyelids to keep too many tears from falling out. If the school bell had rung at that moment, I wouldn't have been surprised—for I felt like an angel who had just been given his wings.

Teacher Mode

"What are you doing?" my friend Marion asked me as we were sitting on an airplane waiting to disembark. I'd just taken a white barf bag out of the seat pocket in front of me.

I shot her a grin. "I can use them at school."

Marion looked horrified. "You are kidding me!" As I started to reach for hers, she slapped my hand. "No way!" I grabbed it anyway.

A few minutes later, as I walked toward the exit, I nabbed more bags on my way out. Marion pretended not to know me.

On that airplane, I was in teacher mode. Teacher mode hits teachers when they see something they can use at school. If you've ever saved a brochure, a program, a map, or a postcard to show your students, you were in teacher mode. If you have ever held on to an old hat, shirt, or tie because you thought it might make a good costume piece one day, you were in teacher mode then too. And if you've ever kept a jar, pie tin, shoebox, or doodad for an art project that you weren't sure what to do with at the moment but might find a use for in twenty-five years—you experienced it.

Teacher mode is what motivates us to dress up like Pippi Longstocking or Viola Swamp or Pinkalicious on Book Character Day and to not give a darn if we have to stop at the store after school while still in costume. It's what tempts us to take the free pens and pads of paper from the receptionist's desk at the doctor's office. It's what causes us to stop at a tree when we discover an abandoned bird's nest and wonder how we can get it down so we can show our kids. Once, I was pulling into our school parking lot when I spotted a colleague kneeling on the sidewalk. I rolled down the window and asked if she was okay. She lifted her head and smiled. "Oh yes," she said. "I'm just picking up pinecones for a craft." Teacher mode to a T.

As you'd expect, teacher mode kicks in whenever children are around. Kid radar. It's instinctive. It switches on when children are on playgrounds, in swimming pools, and near conveyor belts at baggage claim. It always turns on when a child gets hurt, starts to cry, or needs help. Some liken this mode to Mom mode, but it's not the same. Mom mode kicks in with your own kids. Teacher mode starts up no matter whose kids they are.

When I was teaching, my teacher mode was always on. If I stood beside children at a traffic light, I'd fight the urge to remind them to look both ways before crossing the street. If I spotted kids riding their bicycles, I'd watch to see that they were riding safely. If I saw students walking along the sidewalk on their way home from school, I'd check that their backpacks were zipped up all the way. If I drove by a group of children walking on a field trip, I would look to the end of the line to see how far back the stragglers were. If I got some late trick-or-treaters on Halloween, I'd ask them why they were out so late on a school night. Once, as I was standing in line at the post office, a young child around five or six years old pulled a greeting card off the rack and tried to read it. His mom was busy at the counter. I couldn't help myself. I crouched down and helped him sound out the words.

Teachers aren't the only ones who go into teacher mode. Non-teachers can too. If a relative, friend, or significant other saves cottage cheese containers for your class, buys you Jolly Ranchers because that's what you keep in your treat jar at school, helps you cut anything out, or makes a late-night run to the store for Cheerios because you need them for the next day's math, they are also in teacher mode.

After I retired, I wondered if my teacher mode would still be as strong. It didn't take long for me to get my answer. I was in an airport, putting my belt back on after going through security, when I noticed a woman and her two young sons waiting to walk through the metal detector. The boys, each around six or seven years old, sported crew cuts.

The security officer, a big man whose bald head was as shiny as his badge, waved the first boy to walk through the metal detector, and his mom gave him a nudge. When the boy stepped through, a beep sounded and a light turned red. The officer asked the child to stand on the X marked with yellow tape and put out his arms. Then he swept his black sensor around the child. The boy's smile went from ear to ear. For him, that sensor may as well have been a magic wand.

Next, the officer waved the second boy for his turn. Smiling in anticipation of also setting off beeps and lights, the child walked through the detector. But this time nothing happened. The officer waved the boy on, and he looked back at his mother with a sad expression. His lip began to quiver. He would not get to stand on the X and be checked by the man with the shiny badge. With his head down, the child joined his brother.

Instantly my teacher mode zoomed straight into high gear. It was still there. I stepped over to the officer and said, "Excuse me, sir." I pointed to the second boy. "I think that little guy needs a swipe of your sensor too." My voice had a wink in it. "You see, his brother got one, but he didn't." The officer gave me an understanding smile, then called the child back, asked him to hold his arms out to the side, and moved his big black magic wand all around him. It was a thorough search. When the officer was finished, he patted the youngster on his head and sent him off. The boy looked back at his mom. This time his face was one giant smile.

Thank You

One afternoon my neighbor Laurie was telling me how happy she was with her son's second-grade teacher. Laurie raved about her.

"That's wonderful," I said, "Have you thanked her?"

Laurie's eyes grew wide. Then she cringed. "I hate to say this," she confessed, "but it hadn't even occurred to me."

"Don't feel bad," I replied. "A lot of parents don't think of it. But the best thing you can ever do for a teacher is to say thanks. And don't send an email. Take the time to write a handwritten note. It will mean a lot to her." I smiled. "And she'll probably save it."

The following week, Laurie said, "You were right about that note. I wrote it. And the teacher wrote back that it made her day."

Thank you. All day long, teachers remind children to say these two most important words. Teachers understand that they don't just teach children to read and write and solve math problems. They are teaching children to become good human beings. This is why we remind our students to say thank you when we pass out birthday cupcakes. This is the reason we ask our kids to write thank-you cards to the police officer who came to school with her dog.

When you ask a teacher what he's most thankful for about teaching, his first response might be "three-day weekends" or "snow days," but those are just the silly answers. Teachers are really very thankful. We are thankful for the parents who drive on field trips, perform the lice checks, and run the fund-raisers so that we can have markers in the supply room. We are thankful for the custodians who empty the overflowing wastebaskets after our class parties. We are thankful for the principals who understand that we are the ones on the front line and for the secretaries who run the school. We are thankful for the nurses who pass out the ice packs, the librarians who read the books, the music teachers who put up with the squeaky clarinets, and the art teachers who are constantly cleaning up. We are thankful for the substitute teachers who have to listen to children say "That's not how the teacher does it!" and for the noon supervisors who have to watch the second-grade boys see how loud they can make farting sounds under their armpits while waiting to be excused from the cafeteria. And we are thankful for our colleagues who completely understand if they find us lying comatose on the couch in the staff room during recess. Yes, it takes a village to teach children, and in my career, I'd been thankful for mine. But one day I learned that I had some more thanking to do.

I was speaking at a university to a large group of teacher candidates after the publication of my first book. The title of my presentation was "What Makes Teachers Excellent." During the talk, I spoke about the teachers in my life who had made the greatest impact on me. After the presentation, I opened it up for questions and answers. One young man raised his hand and said, "You talked about the important teachers in your life. I'm wondering: Have you thanked them?" I looked at him, surprised. Just like Laurie, I hadn't thought about it either. "Actually, I haven't," I answered, a little embarrassed. "But I should. Thank you for reminding me."

The man was right. Here I was talking about the teachers who made a difference in my life, but I hadn't told them. And so I decided to look for them. I found my high school music teacher, Mr. Stretch, and thanked him for being an inspiration. I contacted my German teacher, Mr. Kirschner, and told him how much I'd enjoyed his class too. Both men said they were grateful for the call. I reached out to a couple of excellent professors I'd had in college. I tracked down my fifth-grade teacher, Mrs. Murayama. She was in her eighties by then. I told her that I'd be giving a book talk in her area and invited her to come. She wished me well but said she wouldn't be able to make it. That was the same weekend as her annual trip to Las Vegas to play blackjack, and she couldn't miss it. I was even able to find my first-grade teacher, Mrs. Ranada. She was in a senior home now. When we spoke on the phone, her voice was soft and frail. At the end of our call, she whispered, "Thank you for the call, my dear. It's nice to be remembered."

I was happy I had found these teachers. It felt good to be able to thank them. My only regret was that I hadn't reached out sooner. I'd learned that some of the teachers I wanted to thank had passed away—like my second-grade teacher, Miss Greco, whom I adored; my fourth-grade teacher, Mr. Jacobs, who read to us every day after lunch and taught us how to make marionettes because, as he said, "Making a marionette is as important as math"; and my middle school art teacher, Mrs. Roben, who drove me home after school one day because it was raining. I'll never forget it. She was pregnant, and her stomach touched the steering wheel. I remember thinking, *What the heck do I do if she has her baby when I'm in the car?* I did reach Mrs. Roben's husband, though. He said Mrs. Roben would have been tickled to hear that I'd become a teacher. I told Mr. Roben the story about my being afraid I was going to have to deliver a baby, and we both had a good laugh.

All these teachers were my "balcony" people. In *Balcony People* by Joyce Landorf Heatherley, the author writes about those special men and women in our lives who have believed in us and rooted us on—our personal cheering sections. As I look into my own balcony, I see family members and friends, but the largest section is made up of teachers. Most of us have teachers in our balconies—men and women who have encouraged and inspired us, perhaps so much so that they are the reason you chose to teach. Find these teachers and thank them. Now is your opportunity to touch *their* lives. They will be happy you remembered. And never forget: If you are a teacher, you sit in balconies too. Many of them. So listen to your children and lift them up. Praise their efforts, point out their progress, and encourage their dreams. And when they look up into their balconies, be honored that they look for you.

Creativity

Caroline, who was nine, walked into the classroom holding an old yellow rotary phone, the cord hanging over her shoulder. I watched from the front of the room as she set it on her desk, took off the top part, and pulled out a pencil and some lip gloss.

"Where'd you get *that*?" I asked, pointing to the phone.

"I made it," Caroline answered with a smile. "It's my phone purse."

I walked over and picked it up. The insides had been removed. All that was left was the casing. "This is really clever," I said. "You could sell these." I leaned down. "I'll be your manager."

"You can't."

"Why not?"

"My dad already asked."

Children have incredible imaginations. To know what I mean, all you have to do is walk into a second-grade classroom in March and look at the kids' enormously clever leprechaun traps decked out with Irish flags, rainbow colors, and green marshmallow Lucky Charms clovers. Kids enter school motivated and inquisitive, eager and creative. And yet, in today's test-dominated, data-driven, and curriculum-packed schools, creativity gets pushed aside in favor of its two big brothers, literacy and numeracy. In school, creativity is often treated like footnotes in a book—important, but easily skipped over. It's not the teachers' fault; it's the system's. Few teachers would disagree with the importance of fostering creativity in children.

Creativity is much more complicated than the right-brain, left-brain explanation it is often given. There are many definitions for it. I like Albert

Einstein's: "Creativity is seeing what everyone else has seen and thinking what no one else has thought." Creativity doesn't belong exclusively to painters and writers, sculptors and musicians. It sweeps across all fields. It's not some mystical talent that you either have or you don't. Creatives need to create—and that includes creative children. It's not something they just enjoy doing. Forgive the double negative here, but creative people can't *not* create. They have to.

So, just how can teachers nurture and nourish the creativity in our students? How do we awaken and develop children's innate ingenuity? Giving kids choice and time are two ways to foster it. But there are other strategies, ones that may not be as obvious. And these can be found by examining just what it is that creative people do.

Creative People Go Outside

Throughout history, creatives have always been drawn to nature. We've all seen images of painters standing with their easels in the great outdoors and writers pounding on keyboards in front of open windows. Nature nurtures creativity. The French painter Claude Monet credited the richness of his work to the outdoors. Architect Frank Lloyd Wright said he went outside every day for inspiration. British writer Virginia Woolf claimed the desk that overlooked her garden was an ideal spot for writing.

So, do as creatives like to do, and allow your students to work outside from time to time. When the weather is nice, take your class outdoors for a lesson, or send kids outside occasionally to read and write. In the fall, I'd send my students outside with clipboards and paper (and sometimes warm apple juice) and let them spread out all over the field and blacktop, where they would write poems about the season. The kids wrote about the autumn things they saw and smelled, heard and touched. I'd do the same activity again in the spring. The children's poems were always better than what they would have produced had they written them inside.

One fall day, I took a group of beginning English language learners outside to search for verbs. They'd been learning them. The kids' task was to make a list of all the things that one can do with an autumn leaf. The school grounds were covered with them. I was the recorder. In order for a word to count on our list, the children had to act out the verb. As we walked around the campus, the kids came up with quite the list. They showed me that leaves can be twirled, waved, stacked, folded, held, carried, examined, and jumped on. Leaves can be dropped, torn, tossed, caught, rubbed, hidden, danced in, and kissed too.

On our verb hunt, one of my students named Zach ran up to me with a leaf in his hand. "I know one!" he cried. "You can *wear* them!"

I shook my head. "Zach, you *cannot* wear a leaf."

"Yes, you can!" he insisted. "Watch!" Then Zach struck a pose like an ancient Greek statue and slammed the leaf over the zipper on his jeans. "See!"

Creative People Observe

Years ago, I had a dear friend named Ann, who had once been an actress for MGM Studios back in the 1940s. Ann told me that when she began working there, she would take the bus to work and sit with another older actress named Marjorie. One day Marjorie gave Ann some advice. She told Ann to watch the people on the bus—to pay attention to their mannerisms, their expressions, and their movements. It is only by observing people, Marjorie said, that one can learn to be an actress.

Creatives are master observers. They catch details by using all their senses. They see things that others don't and incorporate them in their work. When discussing a writer's craft, novelist Henry James once wrote: "Nothing is lost." Screenwriter Nora Ephron used to say, "It's all copy." So, teach your students to notice. Bring their attention to detail: the colors in a cloud, the veins in a leaf, the grain in a piece of wood, the smoothness of a stone. Engage their senses.

Once, I had a fourth grader named Amber who was a very good writer. Her mother asked me what she could do to encourage her daughter's talent.

"Teach her to notice," I advised. Amber's mom looked surprised. She was probably expecting me to suggest she buy Amber a dictionary or have her start a diary.

"How do I do *that*?" she asked.

"Well," I said, "start with a walk. Notice sunlight and shadows, flowers and trees. Notice together. Notice everything: expressions on faces, patterns in fabric, smells in shops, pitches of laughter. Point these things out. In doing so, you're teaching Amber how to view the world with a writer's eye."

Creative People Need Time to Think

Creative types enjoy just thinking. They understand that creative thought requires time to blossom. In school, we claim that "think time" is important, but the reality is that we don't give kids enough of it. Children are conditioned to begin producing as soon as the teacher finishes giving directions. How many of us have given our students a writing assignment, then hurried them along to get started? It's no wonder that some kids say "I don't know what to write." One of the best things we can do for students is to let them spend time with their ideas before tackling an assignment. Rather than expecting children to move their pencils or tap on keyboards right away, allow them to sit still for a couple of minutes and contemplate the task before them. Give the thinking break. If your students aren't accustomed to this, they will be happily surprised at the luxury just to think.

Creative People Record Their Ideas

It's amazing to me just how many creatives kept notebooks: Isaac Newton, Benjamin Franklin, Pablo Picasso, Frida Kahlo, Paul Cézanne, William Turner, Jack London, J. K. Rowling, and Joan Didion. These artists all recorded their thoughts and ideas. Mark Twain filled notebooks over four decades of his life. Beethoven was apparently rarely seen without one. Leonardo da Vinci wrote in his notebooks backward. Some claim he did this so that others couldn't read them and steal his ideas. I once read that George Lucas carried a notebook too. When filming *American Graffiti*, someone asked Lucas for an "R2, D2" (reel two, dialogue two). Lucas liked the sound of it and jotted it down.

Notebooks are storage units for ideas. They help focus thoughts and strengthen imagination. Over the years, I've also kept notebooks. Whenever I'm working on a book, I always keep one with me. Ideas can visit at any time, and I don't want to lose one. I've written in my notebook while driving. I've excused myself from the dinner table to record a thought. I've woken up in the middle of the night to scribble something down. The following morning, it usually takes me a second to figure out what I wrote because I can't read my middle-of-the-night handwriting.

After teaching my students about da Vinci, sometimes I'd have them keep their own notebooks. Some children wrote poetry or stories in them. Others drew. And always, a couple of kids would write backward like Leonardo, then giggle when I said I couldn't read it.

Creative People Need Solitude

Solitude feeds the creative mind, and many creatives crave it. Thomas Edison said he did his best thinking when by himself. Mozart wrote that his ideas flowed best when he was entirely alone. Franz Kafka said he needed solitude in order to write, but not the "hermit kind" of solitude. That, he wrote, wouldn't have been enough. Kafka needed the solitude "of a dead man." The creative person's need for solitude has important implications for our students. In today's schools, there is a huge emphasis on group work. Walk into any classroom, and more often than not, you will see desks and tables clustered together. I'm not saying that children can't be creative in a group. Of course they can. But I am suggesting that teachers be mindful that many of our kids need time by themselves.

Creative People Seek Inspiration

Creatives exhibit a high sensitivity to beauty. They seek inspiration in music, travel, art, nature, photography, and the list goes on. Anytime you expose children to a painting, a symphony, a fine piece of writing—you feed their creativity. So, surround your students with loveliness. Put postcards of magnificent works of art and architecture on your classroom walls. Hang inspiring quotes. Play beautiful music. Flood your kids with these things. A fourth-grade teacher I used to work with would plaster one entire wall of her classroom with copies of great art, photographs, and famous quotes. She called it her "beauty board." When her students were getting too noisy, she'd tap on the image of *Mona Lisa* and say, "Okay, class, I want *Mona Lisa* quiet now."

One way to promote creativity is to show kids how things are created. Children are fascinated by how things are made. Thanks to YouTube, you and your students can visit the factories where all sorts of things are produced:

marbles, money, silk, fireworks, glass, bubble gum, balloons, Legos (a kid favorite), and even Oreos. Children can also discover how many of the things they use regularly at school are made, including crayons, pencils, highlighters, erasers, and books. I always found it surprising that most kids don't have any idea how the books they hold every day are made. So show them. These how-to videos are excellent for kicking off a lesson, when your class needs a break, or when you need five minutes of peace during rainy-day recess.

Certainly creatives are also inspired by people: other artists whose work they admire, not to mention their own teachers. Children get creative inspiration from their teachers too. One of the best ways to inspire creativity in kids is actually something that many teachers don't consider: creating in front of your students. Teachers do a lot of creating. We design bulletin boards, set up displays, draw anchor charts, create slideshows, paint sets for school plays, plan art projects, and decorate classrooms with strands of construction paper Christmas lights and tabletops wrapped with butcher paper to look like giant presents in December. We look at Q-tips and see that they can be laid out on black construction paper to make the bones of skeletons. We eye a Tootsie Pop and see that all you have to do is cover the top with a Kleenex, add two Sharpie eyes, and voilà—you've made a ghost. Teachers are masters at cutting, taping, stapling, and glue-sticking. (I know *glue-sticking* is not a word, but considering how much we use them, it should be.)

In the interest of time, most teachers do their creating when their students aren't around, but I'm suggesting that whenever possible, you let your kids see you create. Teachers model so many things in school for the benefit of their students, it only makes sense that they would model what creativity looks like too. We all know what happens when you create something in front of children. They watch you closely. They study you. Oftentimes, they will comment on what you are doing. You trigger their curiosity. And though you might not be aware of it, your creativity inspires theirs. Creativity is infectious, and when you share yours with kids—they catch it.

Fun

*D*o *I tell them?* I thought . . . *Oh, why not?* I'd been reading with a small group of third graders in the back of the classroom while the rest of the class worked independently. In our text, we had come across the word *tomato.* "Did you kids know that in England people don't say *tomato* like we do in America? They say *tomahto.*" I said it in my best Lord Grantham from *Downton Abbey.* The children giggled. Marshall raised his chin and repeated the word as if he lived in Buckingham Palace.

I smiled. "That's very good, Marshall."

Immediately Casey jumped up and slapped his bottom. "And they say *bum* there too."

"Thank you, Casey. You may sit back down on yours now." I continued. "Believe it or not, there's actually an old song about tomatoes and *tomahtoes.*" I started singing: "You say tomato, and I say *tomahto.* You say potato, and I say *potahto.* Tomato, *tomahto.* Potato, *potahto.* Let's call the whole thing off."

The children looked delighted to learn that there's a song about these things. I thought of more British words to share.

"Do you know the word *cheerio?*"

"Cheerio!" they echoed.

"What does that mean?" Renee asked.

"It means good-bye," I answered. Another word came to mind: "Oh, here's one for you. Have you heard of *spit spot?*"

"Spit spot!" they repeated in their cute English accents.

"It's in *Mary Poppins!*" Alina called out.

"That's right," I said. "It means hurry up." I tried to think of another word. "Oh yes. Do you know what *cheeky* means?" No one answered. "Well, when someone is cheeky, it means they're being a little rude, but in a funny and cute sort of way." I looked right at Casey, who definitely fit the description. He grinned.

I glanced at the clock. It was almost time for PE. Since we had only a couple of minutes, I decided to have some fun. I leaned into my little group and said, "Do you know we have a teacher here at school who says *tomahto*." The kids looked at me as if I'd just said an alien teaches down the hall. "You all know Mr. Thompson, of course." Mr. Thompson was the computer teacher. He was British. "*He* says it."

A few kids gasped. I grabbed a sticky note and wrote "tomato" on it. Then I handed it to Alina and said, "Okay, all of you go down to Mr. Thompson right now and ask him to read this."

Delighted with their assignment, the children shot out of their chairs and out the door. As they dashed out, I reminded them to walk, though I knew they wouldn't. No child walks when on a special assignment. A few minutes later, they came charging back into the classroom, out of breath and falling over the chairs.

I flat-eyed them. "I can see you all walked back slowly."

They tittered.

"Well," I said, "what happened?" The rest of the class listened on.

"He said it! He *said* it!" they bubbled. "He said *tomahto*!"

"And he said *bum*!" Casey panted out.

My eyes got big. "You *asked* him?"

"Yes!" they shouted.

I threw back my head and laughed.

Just then the bell rang, and I clapped my hands. "Okay, everyone, time for PE. You're excused." After the kids put away their things and pushed in their chairs, I stood at the door as they left the room. I clapped again for the stragglers. "Okay, hurry along now."

Martin, who was at the doorway, stopped dead in his tracks, held up an index finger, and proclaimed with a smile, "You mean *spit spot*!"

"Spit spot!" the remaining children echoed with glee.

Casey was the last to leave. Just as he stepped out of the room, he whipped back around and sang, "Cheerio!"

"Cheerio!" I sang back, nudging him out.

* * *

I share this happy interaction with you to illustrate an important point. The things you just read about—my sharing the British words and pronunciations, singing the song, and sending the children to Mr. Thompson—I did intentionally. My goal was to create some fun.

Fun plays an important role in the classroom. I'm not talking about playing games, though they also have their value. The fun I'm speaking of is more of a mood. It's a spirit of cheer and jollity. This spirit sparks kids' interest and captures their attention. It enthuses and energizes. Sometimes it brings laughter, sometimes not. But it always builds togetherness. Fun relaxes children and sweeps away hurt feelings. It creates warmth, builds camaraderie, and stirs up joy. Happy kids just learn better. They're also more apt to behave. But fun isn't beneficial only for students. It profits teachers too. A small dose of fun can help teachers recharge their energy, lower their stress levels, and stay positive. Having fun is a key ingredient to any teacher's longevity. It definitely was for mine.

Children live in a world of fun and play. They delight in climbing trees, building sand castles, and speeding through sprinklers. They enjoy roasting marshmallows, cannonballing into pools, and running away from waves on the beach. *These* are the same little people who sit in our classrooms. So join their world once in a while. They'll appreciate the effort, and you'll endear yourself to them. I'm not proposing that you play with your students, but I am recommending that from time to time you act play*fully*. Periodically, loosen the reins, so to speak, and have a good time together. What follows are some surefire ways to bring a spirit of merriment and delight to your teaching:

Mispronounce Words

Children like when their teachers mispronounce words on purpose. Instead of saying *scissors* correctly, say "skissors." Pronounce *science* as "skience" and *muscles* as "muskles" too. Just know that once you start doing this, your kids will never say these words the correct way again.

Slip In a Silly Step

When giving directions to children, try adding a silly step. For example, if you want your students to pick up their materials for an art lesson from the back table, rather than saying "Go to the table, grab a piece of paper and a paintbrush, then return to your seat," say, "Go to the table, grab a piece of paper and a paintbrush, *do three jumping jacks*, then return to your seat." If you tell kids that one of the directions you are about to give will be a silly one, they will listen sharply so they don't miss it.

Ask for Drum Rolls

Suppose you ask your students a question, and they toss out a few different answers. Before writing the correct answer on the board, say, "May I have a drumroll, please?" Immediately your kids will beat their hands on their desks. Every child knows how to do a drumroll. It's instinctive, just like when children pick staples out of the rug and bring them to the teacher. If you want more than a drumroll, let them add a cymbal crash.

Talk to Your Mascot

Bring in a stuffed animal and have it be your class mascot. Keep it where everyone can see it. From time to time, slip notes into its hands saying things such as: "After recess, we will have an assembly," or "Thank you for working so hard today!" or "Cory, I'm watching you" (with a smiley). Cory will like that. Pretend the mascot speaks to you and tell your kids what it says. My class mascot was a stuffed Snoopy. I'd keep him on my teacher chair on the reading rug or on a shelf where he could keep an eye on things. Every so often, I would lean into Snoopy, pretend that I was listening to him, then report to the class: "Snoopy would like a little less noise, please." "Snoopy says you're all being very good listeners." Or (while staring at Ryan) "Snoopy just told me that he would like Ryan to turn around now and look at the teacher." While we're on the subject, one time Ryan picked up Snoopy, acted like he was listening to him, then announced with a grin, "Hey, everyone, Snoopy says there's no homework tonight!"

Some primary teachers like to send their class mascots home with their students along with a journal in which they write about their time together. It's a clever way to get kids to write. A former colleague of mine named Emmie would send her mascot and journal home with her second graders once a week. Emmie's mascot was a real bunny named Whitey. One day as Emmie was reading a student's journal entry, she had a good chuckle. The child had written: "Whitey bit my dad and he said a lot of bad words."

Let Them Say No
Say you give each of your students a few Cheerios for a snack. Tell them in a serious voice that the Cheerios are donut seeds and that if they plant them, the seeds will grow into donuts. In unison, your kids will shout, "No!" Insist that it is true so they can shout it again. All children love to say no to the teacher. It's always fun for kids to do something they're not normally allowed to do.

Read the Punctuation
This strategy is a fun way to review punctuation. Write a few sentences on the board and read them out loud. But don't just *read* the words. Also read the punctuation. By way of illustration, say one of your sentences is: "Hello, Liam. How are you today?" Read the sentence like this: "Hello comma Liam period how are you today question mark." As you're reading, Liam will beam because you used his name. Have your kids read the sentences aloud in the same way. As they read, they will smile and giggle because they never "read" periods, commas, and question marks before.

A variation on this activity is to assign each punctuation mark a corresponding sound *and* a gesture. Give a comma a slicing sound plus a karate chop. Act out a period with a cluck of the tongue and a poking motion. Have a question mark sound like a kazoo while you make an *S* in the air with your finger. Then finish it off with a cluck and a poke. After teaching the punctuation marks' funny sounds and gestures, write a couple of sentences on the board with plenty of punctuation and let the kids read them with the sound effects and movements. They will beg you to write more.

Share Your Numbers
In the beginning of the year, when you tell your students about yourself, share the important numbers in your life too. For instance, you could write: "I've been to fifteen states." "I have three brothers." "I have taught for twenty years." *Warning*: If you tell children the year you were born, be ready for them to drop their jaws and stare at you in disbelief. If your students are old

enough, ask them to "figure *you* out" by solving math problems like this: My shoe size is *40 ÷ 4*. My birth month is *(5 x 4) - 9*. My age is *13 x 3*. Let your kids write math problems about their important numbers as well. Also, whenever you're the same age as a multiplication fact, tell your students. They'll remember it better. When I started teaching, I was eight times three. Whenever *8 x 3* showed up, the kids remembered what it equals immediately because they associated the problem with my age. If your age isn't exactly the same as a multiplication fact, you can fudge a little. When I became five times ten, I told the kids that I was still seven times seven.

Add This to Your Bag of Tricks

Sean walked up to me at my desk one morning and said, "Mom, can you—" Realizing what he had just called me, he slapped his palm over his face and shook his head.

I turned to him and said, "Yes, sonny?"

It happens every year: A child calls the teacher "Mom." Male teachers get it just as much. And it's not just little kids who say this. High school teachers hear it too. When a child accidentally refers to you as Mom, don't say, "I'm not your mother." Just respond like you are. It will get a giggle. Or, do as a friend of mine does and say, "You can call me 'Mom' by accident, but if you call me 'Grandma,' I'll triple your homework." Of course, when you say this, one of your weasels will immediately dub you "Grandma."

Use Different Voices

Children love when their teachers use a variety of voices. We all know to use them when reading aloud. Change your voice when you're not holding a book too. Out of the blue, talk like a robot. Phone home like E.T. Cry like the Cowardly Lion. Sing like Pavarotti. Speak like a Texan with a twang.

To add some merriment to reading time—and to develop your kids' reading fluency—invite *them* to use different voices as well. Give your students a short text and ask them to read it as if they were a baby, a robot, a pirate, a dinosaur, a cheerleader, a vampire, an old lady, and a very poky turtle. Also, let them read it as if they're scared, sick, exhausted, mad, and excited. The children will laugh as they read. Clearly, *you* have to have a go at it too. And when you do, your kids will laugh even more. After a child reads a text five different ways, she will have practiced reading it five times without even knowing it.

Play Television Tunes

All teachers have their strategies for getting students to clean up. When my classroom floor was messy, I'd usually say, "Okay, I need vacuums. Everyone pick up at least five things." Immediately my kids would drop down on their knees and clean the floor—with vacuum noises. When asking children to tidy up, or any task for that matter, consider playing television tunes. One of the best resources for these is the website TelevisionTunes.com. There you will find a huge archive of free theme songs from TV land. If you play one while your kids are "vacuuming," your little Hoovers will sing along.

Tell Fill-in-the-Blank Stories

This activity is like the *Mad Libs* we used to play as children, but instead of filling in the blanks on paper, kids fill them in orally. To begin, gather your students around you and start telling a story. Each time you come to the end of a sentence, stop, point to a student, and let the child "fill in the blank." Here's an example: "Once up a time, there was a _____." Ask a student for a word. Let's assume the child says "Penguin." When your kids are finished giggling (because any story about a penguin is bound to be funny), continue using the word *penguin*. "The penguin's name was _____." Call on another child. Suppose this one says "Albert." Again, when the laughter subsides (because Albert is a funny name for a penguin), carry on with the story. "One day Albert the penguin was walking through the snow, when he found a _____." Point to a third student to fill in the missing word. Say this child calls out "Skateboard!" After the next surge of laughter (because for children, a penguin that skateboards is quite hilarious), continue your yarn about Albert the skateboarding penguin, or start another story.

Tell Sound Stories

Children love these. To share a sound story, simply tell students a story, and let them make the sound effects. Scary sound stories work the best, so a good time to tell them is around Halloween. When weaving your story, point at your students when it's time for them to add their sound effects. Following is the beginning of a sound story that I'd tell my kids in October (in my spooky voice):

> On Halloween night, I stood in front of a haunted house and pushed the rusty gate. It squeaked as it opened (*point to students to make squeaking noises*). Slowly, I walked up the front steps. My footsteps were heavy (*footsteps*). As I stood on the front porch, I could hear my teeth chattering (*chattering teeth*). I knocked on the door (*knocking*). But no one answered. I rang the doorbell (*ding-dong*). Still no one answered. I reached for the doorknob and turned it. It was unlocked. The door creaked loudly as I pushed it open (*creaking*). I stepped inside, and the door slammed behind me (*slam!*). I screamed ("*Ahhh!*") and cried for my mom ("*Mommy!*").

I'd continue the story so that my students could sound like chiming clocks, meowing cats, moaning ghosts, cackling witches, and howling werewolves. Eventually, I'd get so scared in that haunted house that I'd run out, race home, and jump into bed, where I'd fall fast asleep (*snore*). When telling a scary sound story like this, use lots of expression. Add any sounds you'd like. For fun, throw in an unexpected one like an oink. It'll get a laugh. Put yourself into the story too. Kids like to hear stories about their teacher being a scaredy-cat.

Play Footprints

Every teacher knows that when you draw a noose on the board to play hangman or say "Put your heads down and your thumbs up" on a rainy day, children get excited. Kids especially love games that involve the teacher. A lively game to play when reviewing something is one I call "Footprints." It's sort of like red light, green light—for the teacher. To start, put a line of paper footprints on the floor. Stand in front of the class with a list of review questions and call on your students to answer them. If a child gets a question right, take one step on the footprint path toward the door. If a student gets it wrong, take a step back. If the kids get you out the door (which they always do), they win.

Grab the Wastebasket

Another fun (and spirited!) way to review material is to play Crumple &
Shoot, or as my kids liked to call it—"Wastebasket Ball." Children absolutely
love this activity. I learned it from a high school teacher, but it works just as
well for kids in upper elementary. Your students will need to know how to
write. Before you begin, divide the children into teams of four or five, and
spread the groups out around the room. Place a wastebasket in the center of
the room, and put down a piece of masking tape on the floor a couple of feet
away. This is the 1-point line. Lay down a second piece of tape (the 2-point
line) farther away than the first. To play, ask the class a question. Each team
discusses it (quietly), agrees on an answer, then writes it down on a piece of
paper. When you give your signal, the teams hold up their answers at the same
time. Those groups with the correct answer send one teammate up to the front
of the room to shoot the paper into the wastebasket. Each team decides who
gets to shoot. One child can be the designated shooter, or kids can rotate. The
shooter crumples up the paper, stands behind one of the two lines of tape,
and tosses it. If it goes in, the team gets a point (or two). You keep score on
the board. The team with the most points wins.

Leave Messages

If you're going to be out, write the following message on the board: "Dear
Mice, be good while I'm gone today. I'm sick. Love, the Cat." Once, when I returned to school after being out for the day, the substitute had written this note
on my lesson plan: "Dear Cat, I caught three mice not being very good today."

Create an Imaginary Character

"What are you kids doing?" I asked a group of fourth graders huddled outside
of the classroom one morning.

"Making Walter his coffee," Jeffrey said matter-of-factly. In his hands, he
held an imaginary mug.

"Who's Walter?"

"The *dinosaur*," he answered impatiently, as though I should have known.

"*Oh*," I said, nodding. "Of course. How does Walter like his coffee? With
milk and sugar?"

Jeffrey made a face. "Dinosaurs don't drink milk, and sugar's bad for them," he answered, again as though this were common knowledge. "Just black."

Imaginary characters appeal to kids, and this strategy capitalizes on that. Actually, I got the idea from the late, great movie star Jimmy Stewart. In the classic movie *Harvey*, Stewart talks to his tall rabbit friend (Harvey), whom only he can see. To amuse your students, try talking to an imaginary character from time to time too. In my classroom, I'd also speak with Harvey. Our conversations would go like this:

Me: (*turning to Harvey and speaking loudly enough for all the kids to hear*) What did you say, Harv? (*Pause to listen.*) The classroom library is a mess, and you don't think that the children should go to recess until it's tidy?" (*Watch kids scurry to straighten up the library.*)

Or:

Me: (*looking up at Harvey on a child's birthday*) What's that, Harv? (*Pause.*) You want me to wish her a happy birthday? (*Turn to birthday girl.*) Harvey says, "Happy birthday."

Sometimes in the middle of class, one of my students would call out, "Is Harvey here?" When this happened, I'd scan the room, smile when I "spotted" him, then turn back to the child and answer, "Yes." Every now and then I'd "discover" a half-eaten carrot on my desk, hold it up, and announce to the class, "Well, it looks like Harvey didn't finish his lunch."

Find the Fun

In the film *Mary Poppins*, the beloved nanny famously says, "In every job that must be done, there is an element of fun." This applies to teaching too. When teaching positive and negative numbers, tell your students that the positive numbers are happy and the negative numbers are sad. Make up a story about why the numbers feel this way. If you ask your kids, they'll tell you it's because the negative numbers got homework. When explaining the difference between main ideas and supporting details, call the main idea "Batman" and the supporting details "Robins." They'll understand. When going over spelling words, point out anything funny "inside" the words: *Hear* has an *ear* in it; *swimming* has an M&M in the center; the *t* in *witch* is her broomstick; the *principal* is your *pal*; in the word *eye*, the two *e*'s look like eyeballs, and the *y* is a nose; and if you draw two squiggly lines under the *o*'s in *balloon*, plus two circles above the *l*'s, you just made four balloons. When reviewing geometry, let kids write their names in capital block letters, then find the lines and angles in them. In the name TIM, for example, the T has two line segments, two right angles, and two perpendicular lines. In the M, there are four line segments, three acute angles, and two parallel lines. And, by all means, when teaching the order of the planets (Mercury, Venus, Earth, Mars, Jupiter, Saturn, Uranus, Neptune, and dwarf planet Pluto), use the following mnemonic: My Very Elegant Mother Just Sat Upon Nine Pillows (or Potatoes). Actually, teachers owe that very elegant mom a big thank-you. It's because of her that millions of children have learned their planets.

Fake Pray

When one of your firecrackers (let's call him Oliver) is driving you nuts, look up to heaven and announce, "God bless Oliver." Firecrackers like this.

Make a Call

If Oliver continues to drive you bonkers, walk over to your phone, pick it up, and say (loudly), "Hello. Is this Oliver's mom? This is his teacher. Oliver is driving me crazy today." Then hang up. But don't do this often. When you do, the rest of the class will want you to "call" their moms too.

Name Your Hair

If Oliver is *still* driving you bananas, point to the gray hairs on the side of your head and say to him, "See these gray hairs? I named them after you." *Note*: To children, naming your gray hairs after them is considered a high compliment.

Frosting

My mom is an excellent cook. When I was a kid, she kept her cans of McCormick and Schilling spices in a drawer beside the oven. Once, when I was running around the kitchen with my younger brother, and my mom had had enough, she opened that spice drawer and told us to set all the cans on the floor and put them in alphabetical order. We loved it. And my mom had a few minutes of peace. *Smart mom.* Years later, when I was teaching ABC order to my third graders, I remembered my mother's clever spice drawer trick and asked my students to do the same for homework. The next morning, a mom said, "Nice homework last night." She added that her son got so into it that he also alphabetized the fruit bowl.

Being a good teacher is like being a good cook. You carefully plan what you're going to serve. You gather all the necessary ingredients. You spend hours preparing. Finally, your guests arrive and take their seats, and you share all that you have worked so hard on. You hope they enjoy it. And when they leave, you get to clean up the mess. Like cooks, teachers have their spices too. Ours include delight and energy, enjoyment and excitement, liveliness and vigor. (Notice I put those in alphabetical order.) We use *our* spices to turn our classrooms into flavorful ones. Of all the spices in a teacher's "spice cabinet," one of the most important is enthusiasm.

Enthusiasm is charisma, fervor, and putting your whole heart into something. For teachers, enthusiasm is what conveys the zest you feel for teaching and learning. Children recognize it. In fact, if you ask students to name the teachers they feel are the most enthusiastic, and then ask them to name their favorite teachers, the lists are often the same. Kids are drawn to teachers who are passionate about their work. When teachers exhibit enthusiasm, children become more alert, interested, and eager to learn. They require less prodding and coaxing to pay attention. They are motivated to behave and want to be with you. All teachers want to instill a love of school in their students. Teaching enthusiastically increases the odds that you will accomplish this.

Enthusiasm does for teaching what piano accompaniment does for a song, lights do for a Christmas tree, and gravy does for mashed potatoes. It makes them better. I like to think of enthusiasm as frosting on a cake. Frosting holds the cake's layers together. It adds sweetness and makes a cake more appealing. Enthusiasm sweetens up your teaching and helps create its appeal too. You could eat just a plain piece of cake, of course, but it wouldn't be nearly as enjoyable as one slathered with frosting. Without enthusiasm, your lessons won't be as enjoyable either. A teacher can be weak in several areas and still be effective. But you can't be weak in enthusiasm. A lack of it can cause children to become bored and uninterested. And when this happens, they will start to tune you out and look to create their own fun.

One year a first-year teacher at my school named Tracy asked if I'd observe her give a lesson. She told me that her fourth graders weren't listening to her, and she wanted some pointers. I agreed. The following week, I walked into Tracy's classroom and took a seat at her desk. Spread out on top of it was a collection of Winnie-the-Pooh figurines. Soon Tracy began her lesson, and I took notes. Well, she was right. Most of her kids were not paying attention. They were fidgeting and side talking. One boy looked like he'd fallen asleep. To be honest, I had trouble paying attention myself. One of the reasons was that Tracy spoke in a monotone voice. There was zero energy behind her words. It felt like I was listening to a boring sermon in church. It was bad.

After the lesson, the children left for the library, and Tracy and I sat at her desk to talk. Gently, I told her where I thought she could improve. (I left out the boring sermon comparison.) At first, she was defensive, blaming her students and insisting that they should listen to her. I told her that it would be nice if all children listened with rapt attention on their own, but that's not the real world. I also explained that a big part of our job is to keep kids interested, and that one of the best ways to accomplish this is by being enthusiastic. Tracy got it. At the end of our chat, she looked at her Pooh figurines and said, "So what you're saying is I need to be less like Eeyore and more like Tigger." I laughed. "Yes."

Being enthusiastic doesn't mean you have to dart around your classroom all the time like a ball in a pinball machine. Nor does it mean that your lessons have to be circus acts. Enthusiasm is making direct eye contact with your kids as you teach, using your voice and face and body to hold their attention, and giving a smile and a thumbs-up when they understand. It's getting excited right along with children when the baking soda and vinegar you poured into the papier-mâché volcano starts spilling out of it or the stalk of celery that you let sit in food dye overnight turns red. The great Roald Dahl believed in the importance of being an enthusiast in life. "If you are interested in something," he wrote, "no matter what it is, go at it full speed ahead. Embrace it with both arms, hug it, love it, and above all become passionate about it. Lukewarm is no good." I couldn't agree more. I understand that there are days when you just don't want to act excited about teaching times tables, topic sentences, or tadpoles. But as much as you are able, teach full speed ahead. Pour your soul into it. Let enthusiasm be your engine. Embrace it, hug it, and slather it all over your teaching.

The Superpower

To most children, teachers are superheroes. Our X-ray vision enables us to see phones hidden in kids' laps. Our mind-reading capabilities tell us when a child doesn't really need to go to the bathroom but just wants to go with her friend. Our power to transform propels us to turn macaroni into necklaces and handprints into turkeys. Our bionic lie-detecting sense empowers us to know that there is gum hidden in the mouth that just said "No, there isn't." Our ability to move at lightning speed is evidenced when we eat lunch. Our telepathic powers can lock eyes with a coworker during a staff meeting that has gone overtime and know exactly what the colleague is thinking. We have bladders of steel. But one of our superpowers eclipses all the others. It spreads happiness and positivity and elevates the mood of those around you. This superpower is our smile. Superman and Wonder Woman have their capes. Teachers have their smiles. Nothing we wear is more important.

Every child wants to feel comfortable in school. They all need to feel safe and secure. A teacher's smile gives them this. When working with children, teachers think about their words a lot, but we don't always give much thought to the muscles in our faces. When you smile at your students, you send the message that they are welcome and accepted. Smiles build trust and respect. Your smile tells children that you are kindhearted and easy to get along with. Like a magnet, it draws kids to you. In the eyes of children (and their parents), a teacher who smiles appears more courteous, competent, and likeable. A teacher's smile is a key ingredient in creating a warm and safe classroom.

Smiling and its effects have been thoroughly researched. Smiling relieves stress, boosts the immune system, lowers blood pressure, and helps to keep you positive. Studies show that smiling reduces the level of stress-enhancing hormones such as cortisol and adrenaline, and the neurotransmitter dopamine, while increasing mood-enhancing brain chemicals like endorphins. In other words, smiling is free therapy. British researchers found that one smile is as stimulating to our brains as eating two thousand bars of chocolate. When I read that, I thought, *Did some guy actually get to eat all that? If so, sign me up for the next study.* Another study looked at the baseball cards of major-league players and concluded that those with the bigger smiles lived longer. At the University of California at Berkeley, psychologists discovered that students who wore wider smiles in their yearbook photos scored higher on tests of well-being and also ended up living longer. I was glad they hadn't looked at the yearbooks from when I was teaching. A couple of schools where I worked made yearbooks with everyone's photo. Mine never looked too relaxed. Usually I was pretending to smile. A lot of teachers do. The reason for this is that while we are sitting on the photographer's stool with our backs straight, chins raised, and feet planted on the line of masking tape, we are telling our kids through gritted teeth not to fool around.

Teachers have a variety of smiles. There's the fake smile that I just mentioned. Teachers also flash fake smiles when sitting in dunking booths at school carnivals and when a parent known to be a chronic complainer drops by your classroom unexpectedly after school. Fake smiles are formed by drawing back the lips and holding them there. They can be close mouthed or open. Think Cheshire cat. Sometimes teachers crack the embarrassed smile. It appears when the principal walks into your classroom to set something on your desk but can't find a clear spot. The embarrassed smile is usually asymmetrical and accompanied by a twisted expression. The most common teacher smile is the I-work-with-kids smile, which comes from the genuine enjoyment teachers feel being around children. You'll see this smile on a teacher's face when a child who couldn't read *fur* at the beginning of the year just read *furniture,* or a student who was struggling with a math problem announces, "I get it!" The I-work-with-kids smile causes cheeks to rise and laugh lines to deepen. Another, less common smile that teachers make is the ecstatic one. This smile shows up when you find out that the staff meeting has been canceled. The ecstatic smile is often accompanied by a little dance. And teachers also have their tender smile. Tender smiles emerge when a child holds your hand while you're on yard duty, sneaks a drawing of you onto your desk, or tells you at the end of the day on Friday that she will miss you. The tender smile involves the simultaneous movement of several parts of the face: the lips curve upward, the chin tilts down, the head cocks to one side, and the corners of the eyes crinkle because they are smiling too.

It seems obvious that teachers would smile at their students, but they don't always do so. Sometimes they miss the opportunity. In the rush to get things done, it's easy to go about your day without stretching those lips. So make a conscious effort to raise the corners of your mouth when with children. Ask yourself, When a child walks into my classroom, does my face light up? Does it say, I'm glad you're here? When taking attendance, smile at your kids as you say their names. When passing out papers, toss out smiles too. When you're standing in front of the line waiting for your students to face forward and stop talking, smile down at the child in front of you. She'll smile back.

Children are keen at reading their teachers' smiles. They know when a smile is genuine and when it is not. I can prove it. At the end of each school year, I used to give my students a report card—not for them but for me. A "report card for the teacher," I'd call it. I wanted to find out what the kids had enjoyed about the year, what they didn't, and how they thought I could improve. I told them that their answers would help me become a better teacher. One June day early in my career, I handed out these report cards to my fifth graders, including to a boy named Gabriel. He had been one of my challenges that year. Before entering my classroom, he'd been expelled from another school for throwing a music stand at his teacher. That year, I gave Gabriel lots of TLC. I doubted he'd gotten much in school. I remember once when Gabriel was seated at his desk and I stood beside him to help, I put my hand lightly on his shoulder and felt his body melt. When the children finished filling out my report card, they handed them in, and I began to look over them. When I read Gabriel's, I was struck by one of his responses. The question: "What did you appreciate most about your teacher?" Gabriel's answer: "You smiled at me." To that, all the muscles in my face made a teacher smile—the tender one.

Whoa!

The big day had finally arrived. Jill led her excited kindergartners outside to the field. In her hands, she held a netted house with new butterflies. For weeks, her students had observed hungry caterpillars fatten up, then hide inside their chrysalides, until one day they emerged transformed. Back in the classroom, the whiteboard tray was lined with butterfly books. On the wall flew butterflies made out of tissue paper, pipe cleaners, and googly eyes. When Jill and her little ones reached the field, she helped them form a circle, then walked to the center of it. A few parents had stopped by to record the big event. "Okay, boys and girls," Jill announced over the excitement, "here we go." And then she started counting. "One . . . two . . ." On "three!" she lifted the lid, and out fluttered the butterflies. Faces lit up. Mouths opened. Voices cried "Whoa!" And all the children's eyes followed their winged friends as if they were witnessing a flurry of fairies suddenly take flight. A couple of kids waved good-bye.

At that very moment, Jill's students encountered wonderment. We've all felt it. Wonderment is the sense of rapt awe you experience as you're hiking up a long trail and suddenly come upon an unexpected view that takes your breath away. It's that spine-tingling feeling of amazement when you're outside on an overcast day, and all of a sudden the sun breaks through, and all is golden. It's the astonishment that hits you when witnessing the magnificent scope of the Grand Canyon, the view from atop the Eiffel Tower, or the magic of the Northern Lights. It is that feeling of mystery and reverence that overwhelms you while sitting on a beach and looking out at the vastness of the water and sky. Wonderment grips us when encountering sweeping vistas, intense sunsets, and starry nights. It grabs us when we see fireflies, spiderwebs, and hummingbirds too.

A child's world brims with wonderment. It's this world of aliveness and fascination and excitement that makes young ones stop everything if a ladybug lands on a desk. It's what causes kids to gape and gawk with dazzled eyes at fireworks. It's what pulls a group of children to huddle around a single worm during recess. It's what compels students to check on the tadpoles by the classroom sink every day and what causes youngsters to squeal when they spot the top of a seedling that just pushed its way up through the dirt in a plastic cup. It's what draws boys and girls to check the classroom butterfly net every chance they get in hopes of witnessing the last stage of the butterfly cycle before they walk outside with the teacher to watch them get released.

Wonderment moves and inspires. It ignites curiosity. When children are wowed, they are fully engaged and completely present. Their brains are lit, and their minds and hearts open—a place ripe for learning. A sense of wonderment enhances their well-being as well. Researchers at a number of universities have shown that awe-inspiring experiences can elevate our mood, help relax us, motivate us to care for others, and even strengthen our immune systems.

How can teachers cultivate wonderment in their students? Nurture it with nature. Connect your kids to the natural world. This, more than anything, promotes a sense of wonder in children. Kids have an affinity for nature. They are instinctively attuned to it. Children don't need to be told about the joys of digging in the dirt, gazing at stars, throwing snowballs, or somersaulting down a hill. One of the best ways to connect kids with nature is to take them outside for a nature walk. Arm your students with clipboards, paper, pencils—and maybe some binoculars made out of toilet paper rolls—and let nature be the teacher. Have your kids search for things they see, touch, hear, and smell. Look for rocks and bugs and animal tracks. Sniff soil and leaves, pine needles and flowers. Listen for birds. Make a scavenger hunt out of it. On your walk, challenge children with questions that they haven't thought about before: "Can you smell morning?" "Does nature smile?" "Do you think the wind likes to play with your hair?" And while you're outside, be a codiscoverer. Comment out loud about the astonishing things you witness around you. Model a sense of amazement for even the smallest wonders: an ant carrying a leaf, new spring buds, the silvery path of a snail. In our high-tech world of computers and smartphones, kids still need trees and sticks, rocks and dirt, puddles and mud. More than ever.

Bring the natural world into your classroom as well. When possible, turn off the lights and open up the blinds. Keep potted plants by a window. Place a bird feeder outside your classroom window. Set up a Curiosity Corner brimming with seashells and snakeskins, honeycombs and bird nests, antlers and fossils. Allow your students to observe dirt and bark and leaves through magnifying glasses and microscopes. Collect leaves from around the school. Then use field guides and books to identify which trees they come from. Order some owl pellets and let kids dig to see what's inside. My friend Lambert's classroom has a Curiosity Corner, where he keeps dozens of jars of sand that he has collected from all over the world: "Sand from the Great Dunes in Colorado," "Black Volcanic Sand from Hawaii," and "Sand from the Sahara." Sometimes Lambert's students bring in jars from their travels to add to the collection. Once, for fun, one of his boys brought in a jar on which he'd written: "Sand from the Kindergarten Playground." It stayed in the collection.

Also, take your kids on some amazing virtual trips. Today there are so many incredible videos online. The site The Kids Should See This (thekidsshouldseethis.com) houses a collection of thousands of fascinating videos for teachers and parents. Children can watch time lapses of volcanic eruptions, see how bees make honey, experience rainbows in waterfalls, listen to the sound of millions of monarch butterflies, observe whales swimming with humans, and watch bears taking a bath in Yellowstone.

Be sure to allow for moments of wonderment in your classroom too. When your students run to the window to see rainbows, hail, or snow, don't send them back to their desks right away. Let them enjoy it. Allow yourself to enjoy it too. And when you find one of your kids staring dreamily out the window at the sky, an icicle, or a squirrel on a telephone wire, perhaps don't be too quick to tell the child to get back to work.

One December day when I was working in the Netherlands, I was reading the classic *The Snowy Day* with a group of students for whom English was not their first language. Winter hadn't brought any snow to the area yet. I went around the group and asked the children if they liked to play in the snow.

"I've never seen it," Laila revealed.

"You've never seen *snow*?" I asked, surprised.

She shook her head. It was Laila's first year in the Netherlands. She'd lived her whole life in India. "My mom and brothers have never seen it either."

Recognizing the teachable moment, I set down my book and said, "Boys and girls, what words can we use to describe snow to Laila?"

"It's cold," one child contributed.

"And wet," added another.

"It's fluffy," offered a third.

"Good," I said. "But how else can we describe it? Let's try to use some similes." The children had already learned about them.

Cherim shared first. "Snow is like icing on a birthday cake."

"That's a nice simile," I praised.

"It's like crystals," Gwen volunteered.

I nodded. "Excellent."

Arthur demonstrated his simile. "It's like God dumped a big giant bowl of sugar on everything," he told us as he pretended to hold something in his hand and then turn it over. With sound effects.

Everyone chuckled.

I turned to Jocelyn, whose face was scrunched in thought. She'd been thinking hard about hers. "Jocelyn, how would *you* describe snow for Laila?"

After thinking about it a few more seconds, Jocelyn turned to Laila and said, "It's like white magic."

A broad smile stretched between my cheeks. "That's lovely, Jocelyn. Thank you."

As the days went by, the weather grew colder and the skies grayer. The weather reports said we'd be getting snow any day. Then one afternoon near the end of the school day, I heard a shout.

"It's snowing!" Arthur cried, pointing outside.

Immediately all heads snapped toward the window. Soft snowflakes filled the sky. Then the kids looked at Laila, who sat motionless, her transfixed eyes staring out the window.

"Okay, everyone," I announced, clapping my hands, "put down your pencils. We're going outside."

"*Now?*" someone shouted.

I smiled at Laila. "Of course."

As chairs shuffled and kids hurried to their cubbies, Laila's friends pulled her out of her seat. Quickly we put on our jackets, mittens, and scarves. I helped Laila with her new, shiny red snow boots that had been waiting expectantly for this moment. When all the children were ready, we lined up and walked through the hall to the front of the school. I unleashed them at the door.

Laila ran and laughed and twirled and stomped in the snow. Giggling with delight, she watched snowflakes sift through her gloved fingers and tried catching them on her tongue. A blissful smile never left her face.

After a short while, the kids and I started back inside. The school day was almost over. It was then that I witnessed something I will always remember. There in the parking lot, I spotted Laila's mom, waiting to pick up her daughter. But Laila's mom wasn't huddled in the car with the heater on like the other parents. She stood in front of her car with her head back and her arms outstretched, gazing at the sky with the same smile as her daughter's, gleefully catching cold, wet, fluffy white magic on her cheeks too.

Engineer the Unexpected

"Kyle, what's wrong?" I asked from the front of the classroom. He was sitting at his desk with a finger up one nostril.

"My nose," he whined.

"What's wrong with it?"

He didn't answer.

I walked over to him. "What's the problem?"

"My eraser's in it."

As his classmates snickered, I spotted an eraser-less pencil on his desk. I sighed and looked heavenward. Then I crouched down, leaned Kyle's head back, and stared up his nose. Sure enough, there was an eraser up there. I stood up and looked down at him with my hands on my hips. I certainly wasn't going to dig that out. Shaking my head, I walked to the phone and rang Shirley, the school secretary. The room was dead quiet. No child talks when the teacher calls the secretary. They might miss something.

I tried to speak softly. "Hi. It's Phil. I'm sending Kyle to the office."

"What's the problem?" Shirley asked.

I turned away from the class, cupped my hand over the receiver, and whispered, "He has an eraser up his nose."

The room exploded with laughter. Cupping, whispering, and turning your back on kids never works. Shirley was unfazed. School secretaries are like moms and nurses. They're never shocked by anything. I sent Kyle to the office, and Shirley called his mom. She took him to the emergency room, where they dislodged the eraser. The next day, he brought it in for sharing.

* * *

Teaching is full of unanticipated moments. Bees fly into classrooms. Spiders crawl on the walls. Little ones pull out their baby teeth. Kids barf. Whenever these things happen, teachers end up shooing the bees, trapping the spiders, giving kids envelopes that they will hide under their pillows for the Tooth Fairy, and herding students out of the classroom so the custodian can clean the carpet. For teachers, these moments can be frustrating. Your lessons come to a grinding halt, then you have to settle down your kids and get them back on track. But children don't look at these moments in the same way. They *like* them. Let's consider Kyle's eraser episode. Why did the class enjoy it so much? First, it *was* funny. Second, the children got a short break from their work. But there was another reason: The moment was completely unexpected.

Surprise is powerful. Game designers use it to keep players interested. Mystery novels and plays rely on plot twists. Some of the best ad campaigns include an element of the unforeseen. We all have favorite movies with endings that we never saw coming. When considering teaching strategies, we don't usually have surprise in mind, but it's an important one. In the classroom, surprise brings vitality, kills boredom, and ignites engagement. It alerts children to pay attention, which in turn activates curiosity. What teacher wouldn't want that?

According to experts, surprise has brain-boosting benefits too. It actually builds new neural pathways in our brains, leading us to think more flexibly and creatively. During an unexpected event, an extra dose of dopamine is released in our brain, promoting long-term memory. This dopamine boost is what makes experiences more enjoyable. It feels good to get a surprise text, email, or phone call—or better yet, to receive an unexpected delivery of flowers, be treated to breakfast in bed, or discover that your significant other unloaded the dishes. It makes us happy when we open our desks at school and find snacks that we totally forgot about.

How can teachers engineer the unexpected in their classrooms? One way is to simply change your position. Instead of teaching in the front of the room, teach from the back, the side, or the center. Roam the room. Just changing where you stand can cause children to perk up. Let your students wonder where you'll be standing next. If you want to have some fun, circle the room while you're teaching, and tell your kids to keep their eyes on you the whole time. They'll giggle as they turn in their chairs trying to keep up with you. Or plop yourself in a missing student's desk and teach from there. That'll surprise 'em. In addition, be spontaneous every once in a while. Without warning, announce, "Okay, everyone, pencils down. Let's have a brain break," or "Okay, class. Grab your books. We're reading outside today." Another way to create surprise is to interrupt your routine. In school, routine is important, and children need it, but it's also good to shake things up every so often. No matter how smoothly things are running, if you do the same thing at the same time, day in and day out, it can get stale. And change the scenery now and then too. Take your class to the multipurpose room and let them spread out on the floor. Allow kids to work in the hallway. Teach on the blacktop.

One sure way to create surprise is to do something that a teacher isn't supposed to do. In the middle of a lesson, suddenly stand on a chair. The unconventionality of it (and mischievousness) will get your students' attention. Or kneel on the floor so that you're at eye level with your kids. They'll wonder, *What the heck is he doing down there?* When passing out papers, don't just hand them to students. Out of the blue, toss them into the air on occasion for them to catch. Sometimes, if I was standing at the whiteboard with a dry erase marker that wasn't writing well anymore, I'd just pop the cap back on and (for shock value) fling it over my shoulder. After the children turned to see where the pen landed, they'd look back at me like—Has he gone nuts? Teachers aren't supposed to toss markers.

One of my favorite surprise inducers was my mystery box. Every teacher should have one. Get a good-sized lidded box and wrap it up. Wrap the lid separately. From time to time, place something special inside the box that your students will enjoy: a fossil, a shark's tooth, a bag of treats. While the kids are working, pull out the box and place it on a table in front of them. Make sure someone notices that you've set it there. In no time at all, every child in the room will know that you have taken out your mystery box. When it's time to open it, delay the surprise. Lift the lid a tiny bit, peek inside, then grin broadly. Do this a couple of times until your kids hound you to open it. Mystery boxes work at any grade level. I once had a biology professor set a box with a giant question mark on it in front of hundreds of university students. We were hooked.

My favorite mystery box moment took place when I was teaching in Hungary. It was springtime, and I wanted my fourth graders to dye eggs. Several never had. But I ran into a big problem. At that time in Hungary, you could not buy white eggs. All the eggs in the stores were brown. Now, I *could* have dyed brown eggs, but they would have ended up looking like mud.

One evening, I was on the phone with my sister, Carol, who lived in California. She would be visiting me over spring break. As we were talking, I told her about my egg dilemma. I explained that in Hungary there were no jellybeans or marshmallow Peeps either.

The next week, Carol arrived in Budapest. After we got to my place, she opened her suitcase and handed me a bag. "Here," she said. "They're for your students. Happy Easter." The bag was full of jellybeans and pink Peep chicks.

"Thank you!"

"Wait," Carol said. "I brought you one more thing." She cringed. "I hope they made it."

I watched as my sister pulled a cosmetic bag out of her carry-on and unzipped it. Then, carefully, she took out a half carton of eggs.

"You didn't."

"I did!" she said with a playful grin. "I hope they didn't break." Carol removed the tape and opened the carton. And there they were: six white, unbroken, extra-large Grade A eggs. "Now you can dye eggs, and they won't be ugly brown."

"I'm assuming they're hard-boiled."

She shook her head.

"They're *not*?"

"Nope."

"Wait! Isn't it illegal to bring livestock into the country?"

Carol just shrugged. "It's not a chicken."

A few days later, I hid Carol's gifts in my mystery box at school. During math time, I reached under my desk and pulled it out. A few kids noticed right away. Quickly the children started tapping one another and pointing to the box. In seconds, every student knew that the mystery box was out. I pretended it wasn't there. Occasionally, the kids would look up from their work and smile at it. Eventually, I asked them to stop working and—with the appropriate delays and anticipation-inducing tactics—opened the box and pulled out the treats. But I did not take out the eggs. Not yet. I told the children that my sister had brought the goodies for them all the way from California, which I pointed to on a map. Since most of my students were not from the States, I explained that the treats were popular in America around Eastertime. Only the American children had eaten Peeps before. I handed each child a few jelly-beans and one Peep and said they could eat them.

"I'm famous!" Bence announced after taking a bite of his Peep.

"Why's that?" I asked.

"I'm the first Hungarian to eat a Pip."

"It's a *Peep*," I corrected.

"No, *I'm* famous," Erik jumped in. "I bit it first."

They began to argue about it.

I pointed to each of them. "You're both famous."

Then I smiled at the children and half sang, "I have another surprise for you!" The kids bolted up straight. "My sister brought you something else." I picked up the box, lifted the lid, and looked inside. Then I grinned at the children. "Would you like me to show you now or later?"

"Now!" everyone hollered.

"Are you *sure*?" I asked, stretching out the question.

"*Yes!*"

I invited the children up to my desk, and they hurried out of their chairs. After I was circled and made sure everyone could see, I pulled out the carton of eggs.

"*Eggs?*" someone called out.

"Why did she bring eggs?" asked another.

"Wait a second," I said. "*Wait* a second. These aren't just regular eggs. These eggs are *special*." I felt like the man in "Jack and the Beanstalk" who gives Jack the magic beans. "You Americans won't be surprised when I show you what's inside, but you Hungarians will be." Then I lifted the lid.

A flurry of "Whoa!"s wreathed the table.

"They're *white*!" someone stated.

"Are they real?" a child asked.

"Yes."

"How did they get white?" Bence inquired.

"Mmm . . ." I thought out loud. "I think it has to do with the breed of chicken."

After a few more questions, I took the eggs out of the carton and passed them around. The Hungarians were in awe. You'd have thought they were holding golden eggs, not white ones. As the day went along, news spread that Mr. Done's class had white eggs, and students came by to see them. One second-grade teacher brought her whole class. At the end of the day, a couple of kids, including Bence, pulled their moms into the room to show them the six white eggs that flew all the way from America. As Bence and his mother were leaving, I overheard Bence tell his mom that he was famous.

Hands

Several years ago, I was watching the Academy Awards when an animator at Pixar Studios named Peter Docter stood at the podium accepting his Oscar. Docter said, "Anyone out there who's in junior high, high school, working it out, suffering—there are days you're going to feel sad. You're going to feel angry. You're going to feel scared. That's nothing you can choose. *But* you can make stuff . . . It will make a world of difference." While the audience applauded, I called out, "Amen!"

Humans have a basic impulse to create. Teachers witness this daily. Set some markers and paper in front of children, and they will be drawing in no time. Put a pile of Legos before your students, and they'll immediately start building. Let kids loose with a bunch of large moving boxes, and pretty soon you'll see a fort. It doesn't surprise me when I read that the number one search on Pinterest is for "Do It Yourself" and that Etsy has more than a million artisan sellers. When I hear about schools, museums, and libraries across the country establishing maker programs and that the global attendance of Maker Faires around the world has surged, I get it. We are wired to make things.

We've all experienced that wonderfully satisfying feeling of having created something. Whether you work with wood, knit, sculpt, garden, cook, or sew, whenever we make things with our hands, we feel vital and productive. We experience a sense of accomplishment and fulfillment. Making fosters a spirit of inventiveness, industriousness, and creativity. It exercises the imagination. Working with our hands benefits our health too. It eases stress, decreases anxiety, and quiets the mind. The mind slows down when it matches the rhythm of our hands. But perhaps most importantly, making begets joy. It feeds the soul.

Teachers have long understood that a child's hands are two of his greatest

learning tools. In life, hands are what paint the paintings, sculpt the sculptures, and build the buildings. Hands write the books and pen the music. The
bones, muscles, and nerves in our hands create these things. Teachers understand that making activates a classroom like nothing else. That's why we ask
students to create cross sections of the Earth with Play-Doh, solar-powered
ovens to melt s'mores, and tissue box catapults for launching marshmallows.
That's the reason our counters at school are covered with plastic liter bottle
terrariums, shoebox dioramas, and science fair projects made out of trifold
boards that some parents had to run out and get at Family Dollar the night
before the projects were due.

Making is central to children's learning. Not only does working with their
hands help develop kids' fine motor skills, but it also gives them the chance to explore and discover, think and problem solve. Making helps children develop re-
silience. When creating, kids get to argue with materials and wrestle with ideas.
Making builds children's confidence. It requires listening to your own thoughts
and trusting your ideas. Making bolsters kids' concentration and increases their
attention spans. Your most wiggly student can become highly focused when
given something to do with his hands. Making also empowers children by giving
them freedom and choice. A child can choose his materials and mediums, as well
as follow his own lead. And making fosters a sense of competence. Children feel
gratified when seeing something they've made with their own hands.

There is something about the act of making that connects the heart, hands,
eyes, and brain in a special way. I don't remember my paper and pencil assignments from grade school, but I do remember everything I made. I remember
the city I built out of milk cartons in second grade and the kimono I tie-dyed
in third. I can recall the diorama of a general store I constructed in fourth
grade and the Spanish mission I built out of sugar cubes too. I remember the
plant hanger I macraméd in fifth and the purse I crocheted out of red school
yarn for my mom in sixth. Thinking back, I'm sure that purse was pretty dang
ugly, but my mom was a good sport. One night, when she was on her way out
the door for a dinner party, she held that purse as if it were made by Louis
Vuitton. Though I'm sure she switched it out in the car, I still remember how
proud I felt when she kissed me good-bye.

At school, making things doesn't require fancy equipment, and it needn't take a lot of class time. One project I liked to have my students participate in was an Invention Convention. To have one, provide each child with a motor, alligator clips, and a battery, and let the children construct whatever they want. Have the kids work on their projects at home and give them about two weeks to complete the assignment. Before they start, ask the children to submit designs showing what they plan to make. Occasionally, a child will assign his invention a patent number.

On the day of the convention, the kids bring in their creations and share them with the class. You'll see cars, carousels, boats, airplanes, Ferris wheels, and fans. One year one of my boys made a handheld fan and explained that it was for his mom's hot flashes. Not all the inventions will work, and that's okay. Tell your kids that it's the process that is important. After your convention, let the children create advertising campaigns for their projects, including posters, radio spots, and videos. When they're finished putting together their ad campaigns, invite the parents and a few other classes to a second convention. The key to a project like this is to give students the resources and adequate time. Then get out of the way.

When introducing the Invention Convention, I'd send a note home explaining the guidelines: (1) As much as possible, kids should build the inventions themselves; and (2) Children can get help from parents, but not a lot. The parents appreciated the guidelines. Generally, moms and dads don't mind helping, but they do not want to do their kids' work for them. As one mom told me: "I've already been to third grade." Of course, you will always get some parents who help too much. It's clear when Mom or Dad did the bulk of the work. Eight-year-olds cannot write in a straight line on foam core. When they mount their writing on trifold boards, it's crooked. I always preferred the inventions obviously put together by young hands.

There's no question that today's children spend too much time on their devices. Hands were meant to do much more than just press keys and swipe screens. They were meant to feel and sense, mold and shape, build and create. We've all heard the saying "Busy hands are happy hands." I am convinced that the more kids are forming and manipulating, building and tinkering, the happier they will be. So, when possible, have your students make stuff. Make a lot of stuff. It *will* make a world of difference. Do I hear an "Amen" to that?

The Steinway of Strategies

When riding the bus back to school after a field trip, I was sitting next to nine-year-old Kenny and his mom.

"What are you going to do this weekend?" I asked Kenny. "Play on your phone?" He had just gotten a new one. In class, I had already reminded him a couple of times to put it away.

"I can't," Kenny mumbled. I sensed that he didn't want to talk about it.

Then Kenny's mom opened her purse and pulled out a ziploc bag. In it was a phone and a charger. Written on the ziploc in big, black Sharpie letters were the words: "Phone Jail."

I laughed.

"It's a mom trick," she said.

"Good idea." I looked at Kenny. "I might have to make it a teacher trick too."

Kenny turned to me with a surprised expression. "You have *teacher* tricks?"

I winked at his mom. "Lots of them."

Teacher tricks are little maneuvers, practices, and strategies that make classrooms run smoother, get children more focused, and help to improve learning—our tricks of the trade. All teachers have sleeves full of them: (1) If a child is fooling around, stand close by. He'll stop; (2) Give students directions *before* handing out papers; (3) When the room becomes noisy, start talking in a soft voice. Your students will quiet down to hear you; (4) Celebrate birthdays at the end of the day so that the parents have to deal with the sugar high, and not you; (5) When introducing measurement, teach kids that an inch is approximately the distance from the tip of your thumb to the knuckle, and a centimeter is about the length from one side of your pinky to the other; (6) When teaching children North, East, South, and West, tell them to "Never eat soggy waffles"; (7) Save the caps of used-up glue sticks and dried-out markers. You can use them again when other caps go missing; (8) Commas are on the ground and apostrophes fly; (9) To help kids remember that a period always goes inside the quotation mark, say: "The period is too little to play outside"; and—for the man teacher (10) When your shirt needs ironing, wear a sweater; (11) If the cuff on your sleeve is missing a button, roll it up; (12) When you have a spot on your tie, tuck it into your shirt. If your kids ask why your tie is tucked in, say it's the new style.

Of all the tricks of the teacher trade, there's one that tops the list. It's the Steinway, the Waterford, the Mercedes of strategies. It is especially effective when kicking off a unit. Teachers begin units in many ways, of course. We pose questions, read picture books, and brainstorm what the children already know. We give previews and pretests. All these work, but the strategy I'm going to share with you right now is even more effective. And it is this: Tell your students a story related to the subject that you are about to teach. The use of story is one of *the* best ways to teach history, but it can be used to introduce science and math, art and music, biography and geography just as well.

Here's how it works: Imagine you are about to begin a unit on the California Gold Rush. Once you have your kids' attention, don't announce what you're about to do. Surprise them. Without any buildup, say, "Today, boys and girls, I am going to tell you a story. One day in 1848, a man named James Marshall was walking along the American River in California when something shiny in the water caught his eye."

An amazing thing happens when you start telling a story like this. Children become instantly and completely immersed in it. Words told through story penetrate like no other. There's something almost magical about it. We know how kids become riveted when teachers share stories from their own lives. The same is true when using story to teach the curriculum. We are all story listeners. In a way, we're all like Peter Pan. As you may recall, James Barrie's famous character from Neverland went to the nursery window every night for one reason only: to hear the stories.

You might wonder, Couldn't I just read a story instead? Though reading aloud has great benefits, telling a story without a book casts a deeper spell on children. When reading from a book, a teacher is focused on the text, and usually the story isn't memorized. But when telling a story without a book, you can look directly into your kids' eyes. And *this* is the key. The meeting of eyes is what pulls in students. The more you look into children's eyes when telling a story, the more captivated they become.

The stories you tell do not have to be true. You can make them up. When I was teaching, I created stories about a magical, wacky teacher named Mr. McDoogle. In a sense, Mr. McDoogle helped me teach. For example, when introducing multiplication, I told my kids about Mr. McDoogle's magical multiplying mini-marshmallows. When teaching children how to tell time, I introduced them to Mr. McDoogle's magic classroom clock. (When the teacher wasn't looking, the clock would move its hands to give kids the answers during math.) When reviewing geography, I acquainted my students with Mr. McDoogle's magic pull-down map that would suck children into it when you rolled it up. And every year, I always told my kids about the magic pencils that Mr. McDoogle would hand out to his students, especially those who didn't like to write. When a child wrote with one of Mr. McDoogle's magic pencils, he could not stop writing.

If you'd like to incorporate storytelling into your teaching, think of a unit you teach and create a story related to it. Make it as long or as short as you'd like. Write it down and practice it aloud until you've committed it to memory. On the day that you share it with your students, gather them on the reading rug. Keep an outline of the story on your lap in case you need to refer to it. After you've gotten your kids' attention, don't tell them what's coming. Just begin: "Today, boys and girls, I'd like to tell you a story . . ." I guarantee that once you spin a yarn like this, you will want to tell another, and all of *your* little Peter Pans will want to hear more. Each year, add one or two stories to your repertoire, until you have a cache of them.

It takes time and energy to prepare a story, two things that teachers don't have a lot of to spare. So to help you get started, I've included the story of Mr. McDoogle and his magical multiplying mini-marshmallows for you. I'm sure Mr. McDoogle would be happy to help you as well. If you teach elementary, share the story with your kids the next time you tackle multiplication. Modify it to your liking. Insert your students' names in place of mine. After telling the story, be sure to give your kids some marshmallows. And, of course, tell them that their marshmallows are magic too.

Mr. McDoogle's Magical Multiplying Mini-Marshmallows

Mr. McDoogle's third-grade classroom looked like any other. The globe sat on the teacher's desk. The backpacks hung in the cubbies. The class bunny slept in her cage. But sometimes things happened inside Mr. McDoogle's classroom that could *not* be explained—like the morning Connie saw the water in the bunny's bottle rise all by itself, or the day Lindsay witnessed the piano continue to play after Mr. McDoogle took his hands off the keys, or the time Troy stuck his crayon into the pencil sharpener, and after that it would sharpen everyone's pencil *except* Troy's. Whenever his students asked about these incidents, Mr. McDoogle would just laugh them off and act like he didn't know what they were talking about.

One of Mr. McDoogle's favorite subjects to teach was math. Sometimes during math time, he would sing silly songs, and sometimes he would wear silly ties with numbers on them. Mr. McDoogle wanted all of his students to love math too. But they didn't.

One day Mr. McDoogle stood in front of the class in his times table tie and started teaching the math lesson. "Today, boys and girls," he said, "we are going to learn about multiplication." Melody threw herself onto her desk. Hudson put his hands around his neck and screamed.

But Mr. McDoogle continued. "Multiplication," he explained, "is just groups of things. Like this . . ." He wrote a problem on the board and read it aloud. "There are two dogs. Each has three spots. How many spots in all?" Under the problem, Mr. McDoogle drew two funny-looking dogs. On each one, he added three big spots. "Now, does anyone know the answer?" No one did. Instead, Chelsea chewed on her pigtail, Timmy doodled on his name tag, and William tried to see how far back he could lean in his chair. "Well," Mr. McDoogle said, "there are six spots in all. See?" And he counted the spots by himself.

Then Mr. McDoogle wrote a second problem on the board and read it out loud. "Okay, let's say that there are five beach balls, and each one has five stripes. How many stripes altogether?" Mr. McDoogle turned to the class. Still no one was listening. Carl was launching erasers from his ruler. Jacquie was studying her fingernails. Valerie was trying to touch her nose with her tongue. Mr. McDoogle sighed. Then, once again, he solved the problem himself.

Soon the bell rang, and the class ran out to recess. Mr. McDoogle sat at his desk and rubbed his chin. *This isn't good,* he thought. *My students are not listening, and no one is interested in multiplication. Something has to be done.*

Mr. McDoogle looked down at his desk. No child had ever seen the inside of it before. The drawers were always locked. Mr. McDoogle grabbed his keys, unlocked the bottom drawer, and opened it. Then he pulled out a glass goody jar and set it on the desk. Inside the jar were mini-marshmallows. But they weren't ordinary marshmallows. They were magical multiplying mini-marshmallows. Mr. McDoogle grinned. *Now they'll learn about multiplication.*

When the school day was over, Mr. McDoogle counted out five marshmallows into each child's hand, and the children gobbled them up. As the kids raced out the door, suddenly Troy pointed to the bike racks and shouted, "Look! I see three bike racks, and there are six bicycles in each rack. That's eighteen bicycles in all!" As Lindsay walked home with her friends, she announced, "Hey! I've seen eight cars, and each one has four wheels. That makes thirty-two wheels!" While Connie was doing her homework at the kitchen table, she jumped onto the floor and started counting the legs of the furniture. "Mom!" she cried. "There are four chairs. Each one has four legs. That's sixteen legs!" Connie's mom replied, "Uh . . . that's nice dear."

Before long, all the students in Mr. McDoogle's class were running around their homes seeing multiplication in everything! Sally noticed multiplication in the dishwasher—two rows of dishes, five plates in each row. Hudson spotted multiplication on his dresser—seven drawers, two handles on each. And Chelsea discovered multiplication on her kittens! Three kitties. Each has four paws. Twelve paws in all.

That night, when Jacquie went to bed, she lined up all her stuffed animals and said, "I have eight stuffed animals, and each has two ears. That's a total of sixteen ears." When Valerie's mom and dad kissed her good night, she looked at them and smiled. "Two parents. Each gave me one kiss. That's two times one." When William got into bed, he shouted for his parents, and they came rushing into the room. "Look!" he exclaimed, staring at his pajamas. "I counted ten trees on my PJs. There are five monkeys in each tree. Each monkey has two bananas. I have one hundred bananas on me!" William's parents looked at him like *he'd* gone bananas.

The following morning, when it was time for math, Mr. McDoogle stood in front of the class and began the lesson. "Okay, boys and girls, let's review our multiplication, shall we? Hopefully today will go better than yesterday. Now, can anyone give me an example of multiplication?" Immediately every hand shot up, and all the children started talking at once. Mr. McDoogle tried not to smile too noticeably. "My goodness," he said, pretending to be surprised. "Yesterday you couldn't give me any multiplication problems. I can't imagine what made the difference." No one suspected it was his magical multiplying mini-marshmallows.

Teaching Truths

In teaching, there are certain things that are always true, no matter what grade level you teach, no matter where you work, no matter how long you've been teaching. Teaching truths, I call them—those laws of the classroom that never change. If you've been teaching for any length of time, most likely you'll soon be nodding and saying "Hear! Hear!" as you read the truths that follow:

Teachers refer to their students as their "kids." Moving students around on a seating chart is like playing a game of Sudoku. No matter how you set up the chart, you still end up with children who should be separated. You have a desk but rarely sit at it. Rainy days usually begin when kids arrive at school and end when they leave. Looking at your class list for the first time is like pulling your first set of tiles in a game of Scrabble. You don't know what you're going to get. You hope it's a good mix. When you wait in line for ten minutes to make copies, the machine will jam once it's your turn. Every classroom has a Bermuda Triangle: that mysterious place where pencils and papers are never seen again. No two teaching days are ever the same: One day you're changing the world, and the next you're hunched over your desk eating all the candy left over from the math lesson. If the teacher points out a lowercase letter on a child's paper that should be capitalized, it is faster for the child to write the capital letter over the lowercase one than to turn the pencil and use the eraser. When you begin teaching, you think that you teach a certain grade level or subject, but eventually you realize that what you really teach is children. Over your career, there will be hard years and harder ones, but none of them lasts forever.

The most important things you teach children won't come from a textbook. Teachers' classrooms are their castles. For primary teachers, the first day of school is a success if no one cries. Teachers count going to the bathroom as taking a break. Field trips are like giant games of duck-duck goose. You are constantly counting heads. At times, teaching kids can feel like living in a frat house: It's loud, and things break. The second year is easier than the first. When you're going to be out for the day, you "sticky note" everything. Teaching is like an iceberg: Those who don't teach see only a small part of what teachers do. When working with children, sometimes you'll see the results in minutes; other times you won't see them for years. Teaching is a dance. You change your style and movements depending on your partner. When you ask kids to weigh one object on a balance scale, they will stack as many things as they can onto it to make the arrow go all the way to the right. Sometimes the biggest learner in the room is the teacher. On days when you have a fire drill, a birthday party, and an assembly, you will wonder if your students learned anything at all.

On the first day of school, you figure out who your pistols are by the first recess. If it is windy outside, children are more wound up. If you whistle in class, half your kids will show you that they can also whistle. One will say he can't do it. When a child learns how to draw a star, he will practice it five hundred times on his papers and his name tag. Writing sub plans can be more work than just coming in yourself. If a student gets injured at recess and needs to go to the nurse's office, the child's friends will ask to help so they can go to the nurse's office too. The child who got hurt will limp to the office even if she just hurt her finger. When you tell your students about life in the '90s, you might as well be talking about the sixteenth century. Being away from school causes a teacher the same anxiety as if you'd left a bunch of puppies home alone all day. Teaching in May is like waiting for the ice cream truck. You can hear the music, but you're not sure when it's coming down the street. If you ask children to open to page thirty-eight in their books, and one child opens up the book to page thirty-eight on the first try, the student will announce it excitedly, then run up to you with the book to prove it. If recess is near, a child's handwriting gets sloppier. When looking inside some kids' desks, you understand why hurricanes are named after people. To most children, teachers are larger than life. To all children, what teachers are is more important than what they teach.

* * *

There is one teaching truth that stands above all the others. It is true every minute of our teaching day. It's the heart of what we do. What is this truth? You teach *you*—your personality, values, and character. When you smile at your students, they feel your warmth. If you crouch down to speak with them, they sense your respect. When you tell kids that they may hand in their homework tomorrow because they forgot it, they see your flexibility. When you sort through donations with children at the food drive, they witness your values. When you work at recess with students who need extra help, they'll remember your dedication. When you allow a child to put his head down on his desk because his dog died last night, he encounters your compassion.

Children notice everything about their teachers. They are always watching and taking everything in. If you get a haircut, they will tell you that your hair is shorter. If your car needs cleaning, they will point it out. If the teacher changes her toenail polish, they will announce the new color. If you get frustrated, they will watch to see how you handle it. If you have a Band-Aid on your finger, every child in the room will ask what happened, in very concerned voices. Teachers are not supposed to wear Band-Aids.

When children watch you, they are learning how to be people, and one of the most important things we can do for our students is to model the kind of people we would like them to be. Don't forget this. Write it on a sticky note and tack it onto your bulletin board just like kindergarten teachers pin important notes onto their little ones' shirts. And when you do have one of those crazy days at school with a fire drill and a birthday party and an assembly that causes you to wonder if your kids learned anything at all, remember that they did. They learned *you*.

Polish

After reading my third graders Judith Viorst's famous poem "If I Were in Charge of the World," I asked them to write what they would do if *they* were in charge. One child said she'd make homework illegal. Another wanted to make soccer a subject in school. One of the kids wrote: "If I were in charge of the world, I would give teachers more money and let kids bring their pets to school for show-and-tell." I smiled. It sounded good to me.

We'd all agree that much could be improved in our education system. Too many children fall through the cracks. Too many kids aren't successful in school. Too many students drop out. And the list goes on. Every few years, there seems to be another new initiative or program that teachers are asked to implement, but these won't solve the problems in education. Teachers know that. The reforms always come from people who aren't in the classroom. I'm always skeptical of being told what to do by someone who hasn't worked with children since George Bush Sr. was president.

A lot of teachers feel powerless to change the system. Many feel there's nothing they can do. It is what it is. But I believe there *is* something teachers can do to improve education: Make your lessons the best they can possibly be. In our profession, you don't hear much talk about lessons, really. We talk about a lot of other things—testing and technology and the latest trends— but not about the actual lessons we give to children. It feels like the teaching part of teaching has become secondary and taken for granted. In all the staff meetings I ever attended, I never once had a principal ask the teachers to turn to the person next to them and share a lesson they gave that week or one they were planning to give. But imagine if we started to.

Imagine if every teacher in your school decided to give one great lesson on the same day. What if they committed to giving a day full of them—or a week? Think of how motivated your students would be. Think of how motivated *you* would become because of this. Suppose the next staff meeting was devoted to talking about these lessons. Think how uplifted you would feel from all the positive feedback and helpful suggestions, and how inspired you would be to do it again.

Teachers know how to plan excellent lessons. We learn this in our training. During student teaching, teacher candidates spend hours making sure their lessons are just right. But once they begin their careers, reality sets in. Teachers can get so overwhelmed with all there is to do that they stop taking the time to make their lessons great anymore. Sometimes we wing it. We've all done this, me included. It's not because teachers don't want to give fine lessons. They do. But it takes a lot of time, energy, and creativity to prepare a first-rate lesson, and lots of teachers these days just don't have the bandwidth.

Great lessons begin with the right questions: What is it that I want my class to be able to accomplish? What's my end goal, and how can I get there? How can I present the skill or concept in an interesting way? How can I teach to all types of learners? Can I integrate music, art, or drama into this lesson? How can I incorporate technology? How do I make the lesson accessible to my English language learners and to kids with special needs? How can I have my students practice what they've learned in a way that is engaging? Is there something I can have the children make? Could I take them outside? How can I get my kids out of their seats?

Great lessons start strong. They grab their audience. Good books, stories, and songs have strong beginnings. Excellent lessons do too. We've all heard that teachers have their tool kits. I prefer to think of them as tackle boxes full of hooks and lures. Hooks create excitement and interest. They reel in children's attention and stimulate them to think *I want to listen to this*. Like appetizers, they increase your hunger for more. When beginning a lesson, aim to hook your kids. Pique their interest by having a question waiting for them on the board when they walk into the classroom. Try starting a lesson by pretending that you have laryngitis, then continue without speaking. Begin with a game of hangman that spells out what your students are about to learn. Create suspense by "discovering" a mysterious envelope on your desk that directs you and your class to go outside, where you find more clues. Visit your costume box. If you're going to perform a science experiment, put on an Einstein wig. When it's time to start teaching long division, wear a yellow hard hat. (Long division is hard.)

When starting lessons, sometimes teachers skip the introductions completely and go right into stating their objectives: "Today we're going to learn how to . . ." The problem with this is that there's absolutely nothing catchy about it. It's boring. And boredom is a sure way to lose learners. I'm not proposing that you entertain your students. I am saying, though, that in order for kids to listen, you have to first capture their attention. Then you have to keep it.

Great lessons engage children. In fact, if given the choice between having students who are focused and on task, a canceled faculty meeting, or your yard duty covered by the principal for a week, teachers would pick engaged kids. No question. Engaged is our favorite place for students to be. When children are engrossed in their learning, it sticks better, and in my experience, they rarely misbehave. So teach engagingly.

Reviewing measurement? Give kids a piece of a watermelon and ask them to save the seeds on a paper plate. Take your class outside, lay out a piece of butcher paper, then have a watermelon seed-spitting contest and measure the distances.

Planning to read a folk tale with your class? Turn it into a script and type it out. Give all your students a part, push aside the furniture, and let them act it out.

Studying biographies? Have older kids make Facebook profiles for famous people, including pictures, personal information, posts, comments, and even ads.

Introducing persuasive writing? Have students design a brochure for a haunted house attraction and convince people to visit.

Want your kids to write autobiographies? Put them in the form of a recipe in which they list "their" ingredients like this: 35 tablespoons of comic books, 50 cups of movies, and 2,000 pounds of Legos. One of my boys wrote, "100 cups of math problems." Under it, he added: "100 cups of answers."

Teaching children how to write descriptive paragraphs? Hand them all Tootsie Pops, tell them that they are aliens who have never seen one before, and ask them to describe this foreign object. Paragraph one: Describe the Tootsie Pop's waxy wrapper. What do you see, feel, and smell? How does it taste? Can you hear anything when you shake it? Paragraph two: After removing the wrapper, describe the hard candy sphere in the same way. Paragraph three: Describe the chewy chocolate center—after you've licked away all the hard candy, of course.

One simple but valuable strategy for engaging children is the use of real objects, also known as realia. Real objects create immediate interest and energize lessons. Reading *The Mitten* during story time? Wear one while you read it. Teaching kids about Native Americans? Show them some arrowheads and pass them around. Asking your students to write about their wishes on Saint Patrick's Day? Bring in a real four-leaf clover and tell them where you found it. Talking about rocks and minerals? Pull out your collection. Discussing the westward movement? Share items that a family would have brought with them on their journey, like a special dish or a handmade quilt. Teaching a unit on ancient Egypt? Show your kids some broken pieces of pottery on which you drew some hieroglyphics and tell them that the pieces were discovered in an archeological dig in the Valley of the Kings. Then ask what conclusions they can draw about the ancient Egyptians just from the shards. It's amazing how one little prop can turn an otherwise ordinary lesson into one that is special. This is the power of real.

In a small, unscientific way, I can actually prove this power. Over the years, I would conduct the following "experiment" on my students, and every time, the results were the same. To begin, I'd say the word *apple* and ask my kids to describe one. The children would toss out words you'd expect them to say: *red* and *green*, *round* and *shiny*. After that, I'd hold up a picture of an apple and ask if they could give me any additional words. The picture would always generate more. Now, I'd start to hear words such as *speckled* and *streaked*, *multicolored* and *waxy*. Next, I'd pull out a real apple, pass it around, and ask the kids to describe *it*. They would call out words they hadn't thought of before: *heavy, hard, smooth, lopsided, bruised, wormy*. Finally, I gave each child a piece to eat, which added even more words to their list: *crunchy, tart, sweet, sour, healthy, wet, rotten, juicy, yummy, ripe*, and *delicious*. Every time I conducted this little test with my kids, the real apple always elicited the most words. Real is richer. Use it.

One day I was standing in front of my third graders, ready to begin a lesson, and on the table in front of me sat a brown grocery bag (my hook). As the children looked on, I reached into the bag and pulled out a heavily tarnished silver bowl that I had brought from home, a container of silver polish, and a rag. (Note the use of real.) The kids were immediately interested in what I had to show them.

"See this?" I said, holding up the bowl. "It looks pretty dirty, doesn't it?" The children nodded. "Well, it's not dirty. It's what we call *tarnished*. Silver does this if it sits out." After writing *tarnish* on the board, I opened the jar of polish and dipped in the rag. "Now," I said, "watch closely." Then I began wiping the bowl. After a few rubs, I held it up. Surprised sounds filled the room. I continued polishing, and my students sat enthralled as they watched the dingy bowl become transformed into a shiny one. Most, I figured, hadn't seen this before. After a while, I set down the bowl and asked, "So, why do you think I am showing you this?"

No one answered.

I picked up a stack of the kids' stories they had written earlier in the week. We'd just started editing them together. "Well," I continued, "these stories that we've been editing are like this bowl. When we fix the spelling mistakes or add details or look for better words, we're doing the same thing as I'm doing with the bowl. We're polishing them up. We're making *them* shine too." I paused a second to let it sink in. "Understand?"

Heads nodded and mouths said "Ah." Someone from the back of the room announced, "I get it!"

Next, I pulled out two more tarnished bowls from the bag (more real) and asked the children who would like to have a turn at polishing. All hands went up. Then, one at a time, each child came up to my desk and had a go at it. I chuckled to myself as I watched the kids polish my silver. It reminded me of Tom Sawyer when he gets his friends to paint his fence for him.

Abbie was one of the last to come up. Abbie was a special child, always excited about whatever we were studying. You never knew what was going to come out of her mouth. As she worked on the bowl beside me, Abbie said, "Mr. Done, I know something else you polish."

"What's that?" I asked.

"Us," she answered.

"What do you mean?"

"Well, when you teach us things, you're polishing *us*."

I gave a little laugh. Abbie was right. Teachers *are* polishers. We shine up kids' knowledge and skills. We shine up their manners and behavior too. I looked at her and said, "I've never thought about it that way before—but if I'm a polisher, then what does that make you?"

Abbie stopped rubbing and smiled at me. "Your silver."

I smiled back. "That you are," I said, nodding. "*That* you are."

Teachers may not be able to change many of the issues they face today, but they can better their teaching. And if they improve that, there's a good chance they will improve their students' learning. *That* sounds like effective reform to me. So fill those tackle boxes with the right questions, strong hooks, and activities that engage your students. Shine up your own teaching by buffing up those lessons. If I were in charge of the world, that's what I would ask teachers to do.

Colleagues, Parents, and Mentors

Parents

When I was working in Budapest, my fellow fourth-grade teacher Margaret and I decided to make apple pies for our upcoming Thanksgiving feast. Margaret purchased the ingredients, and I collected the supplies. We both sent notes home asking for parent helpers. We would bake the pies in the school kitchen.

On pie-making day, our classes gathered together in the cafeteria, where Margaret and I had covered the tables with butcher paper and set out all the materials. We divided the children into groups. Each group would make one pie. Six moms came to help: one from China, a second from Israel, a third from Hungary, two from Korea, and one from the United States. We assigned one mom to each group. The kids washed their hands, and Margaret walked everyone through the directions that she'd written on a piece of chart paper and taped to the wall. Then we turned it over to the moms.

After a couple of minutes, Margaret and I were faced with something that we hadn't expected. To our surprise, we discovered that among all the helpers, only one of them, the mom from the States, knew how to make a pie. The others had never made one before. Margaret asked me why I thought they volunteered to make pies when they didn't know how. I shrugged and said, "Who knows? Maybe they thought it would be fun."

Margaret and I took it in stride, and together we taught the moms right along with the children. We showed them how to cover the rolling pins with flour, how to cut the apples, and how to pinch around the edge of the crusts. The whole time, the moms were laughing and chattering and taking photos. They were having as much fun as the kids. When the pies were ready to go into the oven, we took a group photo of the parents and the pies. You'd have thought they had just won the Pillsbury Bake-Off.

Most parents are great. They volunteer at school, help with homework, send in birthday treats, drive on field trips, and serve goodies at classroom parties, then help clean up. They show up for important events but don't show up every day in your email box. They know that there are two sides to every story. They understand that we're on the same team. If you contact them about their child's misbehavior, they respond with "Taken care of." Right before winter break, one might even slip a bottle of wine onto your desk.

Just as teachers work with all types of kids, we work with all kinds of parents too. Some we never see, and others we see every day. Some correct their child's homework, and others don't look at it. Some push their children too hard, and others are too permissive. ("What do you mean you go to bed at midnight? You're nine!") We work with parents who won't let their kids fail, ones who make excuses for their children, and those who have way too much time on their hands. Some parents are bulldozers, and others are "skippers" (skip the teacher; go straight to the principal). Some are mosquitoes (always around), and some are hovercrafts. One year I had a hovercraft who stopped by school every day at lunchtime to cut her third grader's meat. My friend who taught grade one could top that. One of her hovercrafts came to blow on her child's soup.

When the coronavirus shut down schools, and teachers moved to online learning, they had a whole new kind of mom and dad to deal with: the pandemic parent. Some of these mothers and fathers didn't know how to behave when their kids were in online school. They vacuumed in the background, talked loudly on their phones, interrupted lessons, gave their children the answers when they thought they couldn't be heard, and walked around in nothing but boxers. Some parents thought their kids' teachers were on call for twenty-four-hour tech support. One teacher friend of mine had a parent who repeatedly sent her messages after midnight—and then emailed the principal complaining that the teacher wasn't answering right away. At another friend's virtual Back to School Night, a dad joined the meeting, introduced himself to the group, then cracked open a beer.

As all teachers know, some parents can be pretty high maintenance. I call these parents "doozies." Over the years, I had my share. One year, on the drive back to school after a field trip, one of my doozies decided to take her car full of children out for ice cream but neglected to tell anyone. This was before cell phones. We had no idea where they were, so we called the police. Another year, I had a doozy who had a little crush on her daughter's teacher (me!) and would find reasons to stop by after school. The school secretary used to call me on the intercom and say, "She just pulled into the parking lot," and I'd go hide.

I remember the doozy of a mom who implied that I was racist because I had one more Asian child on the right side of the room than on the left. She'd counted. I also remember the night I opened the front door of my home to find a mom standing on the front step. She'd found out where I lived and wanted to talk with me about why her daughter didn't get onto the student council. There was the doozy who insisted that her child always sit in the same chair in the classroom. She'd taped some kind of new age star under his seat so that his energy field would be protected. Not to be outdone was the doozy who stormed into my classroom one morning, demanding to stay there all day and watch the boys because her daughter told her they were picking on her. As my students looked on, I politely said that this wouldn't be happening and escorted her out. This same parent was known to flip off teachers when they held up the stop sign at morning drop-off. And I'll never forget the doozy who showed up at my classroom door in the middle of the school day, waving me over. When I asked what I could do for her, she whispered that she needed to talk with her son because he had just sent her a telepathic envelope.

No matter what type of parent you work with, all of them want their children to thrive at school and to have the most wonderful year ever. All parents hope their kids are safe from bullies. Every parent wants their children to learn the academics but, just as much, to be honest and kind and to treat others with respect. They want teachers to value these things too. All parents wish to be notified if there are any issues at school and to be informed if their child is struggling so that they can help at home. They also wish to be told about the good things. Parents desire teachers who will love and encourage their children, even on days when they don't act very lovable. They want teachers who are creative, passionate, and willing to go the extra mile. They do not want teachers to take away recess as punishment, pile on too much homework, or surprise them with lists of missing assignments at the parent-teacher conference. Every parent hopes for teachers who will "get" their kids and understand what makes them unique. And they all want teachers to remember that when they drop off their children at school, they are dropping off their whole world.

When teachers begin their first teaching positions, they've usually had little experience dealing with parents. There is no class on parents in Teacher School, but there should be. If you think about it, teachers actually interact with a greater number of parents than they do children. So, if you're a new teacher, or a veteran with a doozy, here's a little survival guide to help you work with Mom and Dad.

The First Weeks of School
In the beginning of the school year, it's necessary to create positive relationships not only with your students but also with their parents. If children come home from school happy, their parents are happy. They relax. They are less likely to judge and find fault and are more likely to support you. It's that simple. And always make sure that your first communication with every parent is a positive one.

Email Expectations
One year I worked with a young teacher named Allison who would cry in the workroom. The reason: One of her moms was abusing email. By midyear, Allison had received literally hundreds of negative messages from this parent and, unfortunately, had gotten into lengthy exchanges with her over email. It's a common new-teacher mistake. At the start of the school year, it's important to explain your email expectations to your parents. Be very clear, so that you don't end up crying in the workroom too. In your first newsletter and again at Back to School Night, tell your parents that email is for reporting things such as a child will be late for school or should take the bus home. That's it. Email is not the place to address concerns. Let your parents know that if they do have an issue to discuss, they are welcome to set up an appointment.

Phone Numbers and Texts

Nowadays, some teachers feel that they need to give parents their personal phone numbers. You don't. Just as with email, there's a risk that a parent might misuse it and text too much. Providing parents with your school email address is enough. If you want to send texts to parents, use an app that allows you to send them but not receive replies. Personally, I would not text with parents. To communicate with them, I'd send email from my school account. That was sufficient. No parent ever said it wasn't. Also, do not give parents access to your social media. Your professional and private lives should be separate. Parents do not need to know what you did on the weekend.

Parent-Teacher Conferences

Parent-teacher conferences are extremely important, especially the first one. At these meetings, you are doing much more than informing parents about their children's progress. You are building your working relationship with them. To ensure that your conferences are a success, here are a few tips:

- Before the meeting, prepare folders for each student with the work you want to share. (The first set of conferences can sneak up on you, so make sure you save plenty of student work.)
- If you teach grade school, show work in multiple subject areas.
- In each folder, also keep notes of the points that you wish to cover.
- When the parents arrive, greet them with a smile and thank them for coming. Have their chairs already pulled out for them.
- Sit side by side, not across from one another. It's more collegial.
- On the table, have the child's work already set out.
- Of course, always start with the positive.
- As you are talking, be careful not to use too much teacher jargon.
- If you do have to bring up a concern or report that a student is having difficulty, choose your words carefully. No parents want to hear that their child is struggling. Always have work to back up what you say.
- During the meeting, make sure to ask the parents if they have any questions. Keep a paper and pen handy to take notes.

- When the conference is over, thank them for their support and for helping out at home.
- Follow up with an email thanking them for coming.

Ask Your Colleagues

At the end of the school year, grade school teachers fill out what is known as a transition card for each student. These cards are used for class placements and sent on to the next year's teachers. One year, as I was going through my new stack of transition cards, I had to laugh. One card said "Severe behavior issues." Another read "Severe allergies." A third said "Severe mom!"

Before the school year begins, ask your students' previous teachers about the parents. Find out who's supportive and who can be difficult. It is helpful to know this ahead of time. Then you can be proactive. Anytime I found out that a mom had a history of being problematic, I'd try to win her over. I wasn't phony about it. I would just make a little more effort than usual to chat with her after school or send positive email messages home about her child. Remember, you catch more flies with honey than with vinegar. Parents too. Once parents trust you, more often than not, they don't give you a hard time.

If you anticipate having a difficult conference with a parent and think you'll need support, invite your principal to attend. Or you can do what a colleague of mine did and arrange for backup. If a conference wasn't going well, she'd pretend to take notes on her laptop when in reality she was instant messaging another teacher to call her and interrupt the meeting.

Other Children

You may have parents who will want to talk with you about kids other than their own. Make it a rule not to. If a parent starts to speak with you about another person's child, just smile politely and say, "Oh, I make it a point to never talk about other people's kids with anyone." Parents will respect you for saying this because they wouldn't want you to speak about their children with someone else either.

On the Fly

Sometimes when parents run into you on campus, they will ask you how their kids are doing. It's natural. Some ask you this at Back to School Night, even after you've announced that it's not the time for individual conferences. Though it's tempting to respond, it is best not to. You are not prepared. If this happens, say something positive, such as how much you enjoy having the child in your class. But don't get into a discussion about academics or behavior. Tell the parent that you'd be happy to talk, but best to set up a conference.

Be Honest

This sounds like a no-brainer, but some teachers avoid difficult conversations with parents. When I taught fifth grade, one of the fourth-grade teachers wasn't always truthful with parents if their child was having difficulty, so when I informed them of this the following year, it would come as a shock. Needless to say, the parents were not happy. After a couple of years of this, I finally went to the fourth-grade teacher and told her what was happening. She didn't deny it. In fact, she admitted that it was easier to say nothing. No matter how difficult it might be, always be completely honest with parents.

Handle with Care Messages

This idea I learned from my friend Dana, who said it has been a great help. In the beginning of the school year, Dana sends a note to her kids' parents saying: "If your child had a difficult night or morning, please send me a quick email with the subject line: 'Handle with Care.' No other words are necessary. Nothing will be asked or said. Your note will let me know that your child might need some extra attention, help, or TLC during the day." The first week that Dana sent this note, she received three email messages titled "Handle with Care."

Being Friends

Though having a good relationship with parents is very important, I do not recommend that teachers become friends with them, at least not while their children are in your class. It's enough to be friendly. Being friends with parents can inhibit your communication with them if you need to bring up any academic or behavioral issues that their kids are having at school. It can cause a child to expect to be treated differently because you are friends with Mom or Dad. It can also upset other parents who might think that you're playing favorites. Keep the relationship professional.

The End of the Day

In every school day, the time that always goes the fastest is that stretch right after your kids leave. One minute it's three thirty, and the next minute it's five o'clock. It's important to guard this time. When you excuse your students at the end of the day, step outside with them and say hello to the parents who are waiting, but don't stay more than a couple of minutes. If a parent has a question, address it quickly. Then walk back inside and shut the door. A closed door sends a message that you're getting back to work. Most parents will respect this. If parents do step inside, speak to them while standing at the door. This also sends a message that the conversation won't be long. If a parent stops by just to chat, don't be afraid to say you're busy. Some parents are Yacky Ducks too.

Active Listening

It happens. Parents become disgruntled, displeased, or dissatisfied. They don't like how you handled something at school. They have a problem with the homework. They challenge a grade. Once, I had a mom beg me to change her son's C to a B. She said if I didn't, it would affect his chances to get into a good college. The child was in *third grade*. It's never easy when a parent is unhappy about something. And it doesn't get easier. It can eat you up. You might have sixty parents, and if one is giving you trouble, you will focus on him or her and not on the other fifty-nine who are happy. It's how we're wired. Teachers are pleasers. If parents are unhappy about something and come to speak with you about it, I found that the best thing to do is to let them get it off their chest. Be an active listener and don't interrupt. When they are finished, assure them that they have been heard and validate their feelings. Once they have gotten it out, then you can start working on a solution.

The 90 Percent Rule

It was my first week of my first year of teaching. A mom (a bulldozer) stopped by my classroom and told me that her third grader wasn't being challenged. I tried to explain that the children and I were still getting to know each other and that we hadn't jumped into the curriculum yet, but it didn't help. Naturally, I was rattled. So I went to see my principal, Frank, and explained what had happened. Frank knew the mom well and explained that she said the same thing every year to all her kids' teachers. She had three children at the school. Then Frank told me something very important, something that always stayed with me. He said, "Phil, if you're pleasing ninety percent of your parents, you're doing great." It was the best advice about parents I ever got. Throughout my career, whenever I was faced with a difficult one, I'd remind myself of Frank's 90 Percent Rule. If you're dealing with a challenging mom or dad, I suggest that you do too. It helps. A word of caution: Refrain from telling a difficult parent that she is in the 10 percent group. Keep that to yourself. A colleague of mine said this to a mom once. Didn't go well.

By the way, that bulldozer mom eventually pulled all three of her kids out of the school and put them into a local private school. I knew a young teacher who worked there. When I asked her if she knew this mom, she clutched her heart and let out a scream. I decided that this was a good moment to teach her the word *doozy*.

Principals and Principles

It was the morning of my formal observation, and John, my principal—Mr. Williams to the children—would be coming into my classroom soon. I had tidied up and cleaned my desk. I'd typed out my lesson plan and made an extra copy for John. I had double-checked my materials and walked through what I was going to say. I was nervous. Many teachers are before their principals come in for an observation.

"Boys and girls," I said to my third graders on the reading rug, "this morning, we are going to have a special visitor. Mr. Williams will be coming in."

"Why?" Leo called out.

"Well," I said, smiling—I didn't want to tell them I was being evaluated—"I've told him how wonderful you are, and he would like to see for himself." The children brightened. "Now, when he comes in, I want you all to be on your best behavior. Will you do that for me?" They agreed. Then I leaned toward them and said, "And if you're *really* good, I'll give you some extra Friday free-time minutes." The children hurrayed. I didn't feel too bad about my little bribe. It was nothing compared to what a friend of mine said to her second graders before her observation. She told the kids that when the principal came in with his laptop, he would be emailing all their parents to let them know if they were behaving.

A few minutes later, John walked in, took a seat in the back of the room, and opened his computer. The children looked at him, then turned to me and sat up straight. A couple of them even folded their hands in their laps. As I proceeded with the lesson, the kids listened and participated and followed directions. A few times, I glanced at John. He was smiling as he took notes. It was going well. When it was time for the children to begin their independent work, I sent them back to their seats. On the way to his desk, Leo walked up to John and asked, "Did we get a good report?"

I winced when I heard it.

"What's that?" John replied, unsure of what Leo meant.

"Mr. Done said that if we're good when you're here, we get extra free-time minutes." John laughed. "Did we get a good report?" Leo repeated.

John looked my way and saw me shaking my head. Then he smiled at Leo and said, "Yes."

There is no question that a principal's job is enormous. From the morning when they greet children in the hallway, to the afternoon when they stand on bus duty, principals are constantly solving problems and putting out administrative fires. All day long, people are streaming into their offices with questions, concerns, complaints, ideas, suggestions, and red alerts that the boys' bathroom is flooded again because some little troublemakers thought it would be fun to clog the urinals with paper towels. Every day, principals' mailboxes are flooded with email too. When people pop their heads into the principal's office and say, "Do you have a minute?" they never just stay that long.

In the evenings, principals attend band concerts and sporting events, board meetings and school plays. To raise money for school fund-raisers or as incentives for student achievement, principals have been known to dye their hair and allow kids to throw pies in their faces. A principal friend of mine let his grade school students turn him into a human sundae when they met their reading targets. As the entire school looked on, a few lucky children got to pour chocolate syrup onto his head, then douse him with sprinkles. Unless you're a principal, you can obviously never know all that they do. Once, a colleague asked her first graders to dictate what they thought the principal did all day in his office. Their answers: "Does a lot of paperwork," "Talks on the phone," "Takes a nap," "Plays chess," and "FaceTimes with his wife."

I never aspired to be a principal. To me, a principal's life always seemed kind of lonely. On bad days, teachers have other teachers to talk with. Principals are on their own. Also, principals are continually dealing with unhappy people: irked parents, tired teachers, naughty children. No one ever goes to the principal's office to say, "Hey, I just wanted to stop by and tell you that everything is great!" I never wanted to make all the phone calls that principals have to make either. A principal friend says she is constantly calling parents, and sometimes it's hard to keep from laughing—like the time one of her kindergarten teachers was transitioning her little ones from art time to math when a child shouted, "Are you *f—ing* kidding me?" or the time a first grader took a selfie with his iPad—of his rear. One day at recess, I spotted Leo—the same Leo who gave away my Friday free-time bribe—sitting in front of John's office. I poked my head in and asked what happened. John told me that the boys had spent recess mooning the second-grade girls. He was just starting to call the kids' parents. As I stepped out, I sang, "Glad you're the boss and not me." He fake-grinned back.

All teachers want the same things from their principals. Sure, teachers appreciate the donuts that their bosses put in the staff room the morning after Back to School Night and are grateful for the "Thanks for all you do" email that comes after Open House, but these aren't the things that really matter. Teachers want their principals to create positive work environments for their staffs, just as teachers work hard to do for their students. Teachers would like principals to come into their classrooms for more than just observations and to talk with the kids when they visit and be completely present. Teachers wish that principals would protect their time, not hold meetings when the content could be covered in an email, and not add new programs to their plates without taking anything off of them. Teachers want their leaders to have their backs too. If a parent brings a concern about a teacher to the principal, teachers hope that their boss will stand up for them. And teachers want their principal's trust: to have confidence that on professional development days, their time will be spent wisely, or their lessons will be well planned so that they don't have to submit them every week. Most principals were once teachers. Teachers want principals to never forget what it was like to be one.

In school, things often come in threes. There are three different classes (the normal class, the dream class, and the class that the kindergarten teachers warn everyone about in the staff room); three kinds of students (quiet, chatty, and in-between); three types of days (good, not good, and terrific—these are snow days); three types of colleagues (novices, midcareer, and those counting the days until retirement); and three kinds of principals (great, mediocre, and bad). Over my career, I worked with all three types. Fortunately, I had only a few in the latter group.

One of them just didn't get it. When he was transferred to my school, he had never worked in elementary before. At my first observation, he watched my third graders clapping out multisyllable words (a common strategy to help kids read longer words). After the lesson, he came up to me and asked with a confused expression, "Uh . . . why were they clapping?" Thought to self: *This isn't good.* During another observation, he witnessed my students making their own "fraction kits" by cutting multiple fractions out of construction paper and labeling them, a tactile activity that teachers commonly give to children to help them understand. In our post-observation meeting, he told me that all the cutting was a waste of time and that I should have just given the kids the kits. Thought to self: *Yikes!* He completely missed the point. His only comment on the evaluation form was: "At the end of the lesson, the kids didn't clean up fast enough." Thought to self: *God help me.*

I had another principal who rarely ventured out of his office, and if he did, it was to get his lunch. In the two years that I worked with him, he never came into my classroom. The teachers rarely saw him. Come evaluation time, he made them up. We called him "the phantom." The worst principal I worked for was a former military officer. He had a my-way-or-the-highway approach and treated his teachers like subordinates, not coworkers. He didn't believe in offering praise and told the staff so. When evaluating teachers, he would give low marks without any evidence. If the teachers questioned him about this, he claimed that he didn't have to give examples; it was a "feeling" he had. We called him "the sergeant." We called him other things too. Luckily, after just one year, the sergeant was moved to another school. Most likely, enough people complained. When the teachers found out that he'd been transferred, a couple of us gathered in the library and did the Snoopy dance. Unfortunately, a bad principal can cause more distress than all of your most difficult students put together. I always say that in teaching, it's not the kids that give you the most problems. It's the grown-ups.

Principals are like the characters in Dickens's *A Christmas Carol.* The bad ones are like the Ghost of Christmas Yet to Come. These principals create a sense of gloom. They can be fearsome. The less time spent with them, the better. Good principals are like Fezziwig, the jovial merchant for whom young Scrooge was an apprentice. Fezziwigs are warm and caring. They make going to work a pleasure. The best principal I ever had was my first one, Frank. He was a Fezziwig.

Frank knew the name of every child in his school and engaged with them in the halls, in the cafeteria, at the bus stop. He was everywhere. He knew the kids who had behavior challenges and those who struggled. Frank looked out for his teachers. If parents went to him with a concern, he wouldn't give them an ear until they had met with the teacher first. When a teacher walked into Frank's office, he'd drop whatever he was doing and say, "What can I do for you today?" He was there to serve his teachers. They were not interruptions. His motto: How can I remove obstacles so you can teach? Frank was constantly popping into classrooms too. In fact, his way of testing your classroom management was to walk through your room, get your students all riled up, then leave.

And Frank was an encourager. If he liked your bulletin board, he told you so. Before Back to School Night, he'd leave a note on your desk wishing you a good evening. If he came into your room when no one was there, he'd write a message on the board saying, "Sorry I missed you. Have a nice day." Frank checked on teachers, not lesson plans. He believed that if principals take care of their teachers, they take care of their students. And Frank trusted you to be a professional. He didn't look over your shoulder or micromanage. He let you teach. Now, Frank wasn't perfect, not by any means. He'd get behind in his paperwork and didn't make all the right calls, but he loved teaching, learning, and most importantly, children.

I learned a lot from Frank. He taught me that if a student is misbehaving, look at what *you* can do differently before pointing the finger at the child. He felt that teachers should exhibit the same energy that they expect from their kids. He taught me that children who seek attention often just want connection, and that what a child did yesterday doesn't exist today. He taught me that learning is messy, not linear. He told me that, as a principal, he'd learned that sometimes children are more like adults, and adults are more like children. He taught me that on those days when a child isn't responsive to your teaching, you can still love them. If Frank walked into your classroom and saw that your desk was tidy, he didn't like it. He believed that the time you take to straighten it up should be spent working with kids. Frank and I got along well. My desk was always a mess.

One of the main reasons I loved working with Frank was that he believed in me. I felt it. Knowing this gave me confidence and security and enabled me to flourish. Just as children feel empowered when they sense a teacher's belief in them, teachers feel empowered when their principal believes in them too. When teachers sense this from their principal, it's like someone put gasoline in our tanks. We run better.

Unfortunately, many teachers don't have a Frank. I speak with a lot of educators who feel unsupported by their principals. Online teacher forums are full of stories about difficult bosses. This lack of support takes a heavy toll on teachers and causes some to want to leave the profession. Some actually do.

Not long ago, I was talking with a young teacher named Greg. He was passionate and creative and excellent with children—a born teacher. But he was working for a Ghost of Christmas Yet to Come. Greg said he loved teaching and the kids, but his boss was making him miserable. He dreaded going to work. It broke my heart to hear it. One day when Greg was sharing all this, I said, "Greg, this isn't about your shortcomings. It's about his." And then I offered him some advice: "This principal is stealing your joy. He's keeping you from being the teacher you want to be. If you feel like you've done everything you can to make it work and it's not getting better, go somewhere else. Life's too short." A few months later, Greg called and said he'd transferred to another school in his district. He was much happier and so glad he had made the change.

Too many teachers stay in schools where they are unhappy. The system does not encourage teachers to move around. In fact, it discourages it. In some states, after ten years of service, you can't move to another district without taking a salary cut. If you aren't happy in your workplace and you're unable to improve the situation, consider looking for another position. You're not stuck. There are lots of teaching jobs out there and plenty of good schools and excellent principals. Yes, it takes time and energy to look for another position, especially if you leave your district. But a change in schools can make the difference between staying in the profession and leaving it. I should know. Once I left my school too.

I'd been teaching for about ten years. The district where I worked had shuffled around some principals, and my school got a new one. From the moment he arrived, this principal decided that there was a group of teachers he didn't like. He would talk behind our backs and play favorites. Instead of building his teachers up, he'd tear them down. He was a bully. I tried winning him over with kindness. I tried staying out of his way. Nothing worked. It got to the point where I didn't like going to school. I, like Greg, was becoming miserable. Finally, after much thought, I made the decision to leave and go to a different school. I didn't want to start all over. I would miss my colleagues and the families I worked with, but I knew that if I stayed, I'd just continue to feel this way. It was the right decision, and I never regretted it. Sometimes the grass actually is greener on the other side.

New Teacher

Since the release of my first book, I have heard from many novice and veteran teachers alike asking for all sorts of advice: "Do you have any classroom management tips?" "How do you teach math?" "Parent-teacher conferences are coming up soon. Any suggestions? I'm petrified!" I answer the best I can. Sometimes I feel like a second Dr. Phil.

One first-year teacher named Jeremy used to phone me every month, usually on a Friday evening. He called our chats "Fridays with Phil." Actually, Jeremy had once been a student of mine. I'd taught him when he was in third grade and hadn't seen him since grade school. When he and I spoke on the phone, I still pictured him with freckles and braces. During our chats, Jeremy would pick the topic that he wanted to discuss. Once he said, "Okay, Phil"—it took him a while to call me by my first name—"tell me everything you know about teaching reading." I laughed. "Well, this might be a very long phone call." "Okay," he said. "Not everything. Just *most* everything."

Every year, tens of thousands of new teachers enter the workforce in America. That means every year tens of thousands of teachers just like Jeremy will need encouragement, help, and support. So, in the next few pages, I'd like to offer some advice specifically for those teachers just starting out. If you are one, pretend you've just called me for a Friday with Phil.

Give Your Students a Fresh Start
Every student has a cumulative folder. These contain report cards, assessments, and other important information. Cumulative folders follow children from their first day of kindergarten through their last day of high school. They are usually kept in a metal file cabinet near the secretary so that she can

keep an eye on them. Generally, you aren't allowed to take them out of the office. These folders always reminded me of the ones you see on the back wall of the dentist's office, minus the X-rays. If a child receives extra support in school, sometimes these folders can be pretty thick. At the beginning of the year, some teachers read through them. My advice is not to. You don't want to be swayed by something that another teacher says about a child. I witnessed many a student with a thick cumulative folder have a positive year after an unsuccessful one. On that note, don't listen to others if they tell you that so-and-so is a difficult student. Form your own opinion. Every child deserves a clean slate.

Don't Reinvent the Wheel

They say that being a new teacher is like trying to fly an airplane while building it. Beginning teachers have so much on their plates that they need to grab extra time wherever they can. One place to do this is in your lesson planning. If you're a new teacher, do not create your lessons from scratch. Beg, borrow, and steal from the others on your team. Teachers like to help. We all remember what it was like to be new. I've read that good artists steal and that great artists steal a lot. This also applies to teachers.

Visit Last Year's Teachers

At the beginning of the school year, before the first day, visit your new students' previous teachers to learn about the children. Bring your class list and take notes. These conversations can be extremely helpful. In addition to finding out about the kids' academic levels and behavior, inquire about their home lives and friends. Ask if there's anything special you should know: additional support services they receive, a good place to seat them, what they like to be called, and so on. Also, find out about the children's interests. Want to make an immediate connection with your new students the first week of school? Say to a child, "Hey, _____ (student's name), I heard from _____ (previous teacher) that you like _____ (swimming, horses, Legos, gymnastics . . .)." When the corners of that child's mouth rise, which they definitely will, that smile is proof that you've just connected.

Aim for Terrific Classroom Management

Remember when you were a kid, and you'd fall on the trampoline but couldn't get up because all the other children around you were still bouncing? Sometimes that's exactly what teaching feels like. To avoid that out-of-control feeling, teachers need to have excellent classroom management skills. It doesn't matter how well you know your subject or how dynamic your lessons are. If your classroom management isn't strong, your school year will not be as successful as it could be.

In the first few weeks of school, focus on management. Make it a priority. Establish procedures for everything: how students line up, how they get materials, how they hand in their work, and so on. Have these all thought through before the first day of school. You can always change them if they're not working. As I discussed earlier in the book, practice these routines with your kids until they master them. It may feel like overkill, but it will make for smooth sailing later on. A classroom is like an ocean. The waters can be tranquil or rough, and the more solid your procedures, the calmer your ocean will be. Ships and children make the most progress on smooth waters.

Default to Compassion

When a child continually shows up late, instead of saying, "Why are you late again?" respond with, "Is everything okay?" If students repeatedly don't bring in their homework, ask if there's something going on that's making it difficult to get it done. If a child doesn't understand something, refrain from saying, "I already explained this to you." Instead, say: "Maybe I can show you another way." Compassion won't solve all your management problems, but it will go a long way. If you treat kids like decent people, more often than not they will act like them.

Be Kind, Firm, and Not Their Friend

To children, there are only two types of teachers: nice and mean. Ask any child who the nice and mean teachers are, and they'll give you the list. Once, I was explaining to my third graders what it meant to be *firm*. Kids don't use this word. I asked my students if they thought I was a firm teacher, and they said yes. I was glad they thought so. "But," one child clarified, "you're nice firm." It made me laugh.

When working with children, it's important to be both kind *and* firm. Kids need and want boundaries and will honor them if they sense that you care. If you are kind but lack firmness, you will not gain your students' respect. If you're firm without being kind, children won't see you as approachable. And do *not* be your students' friend. Too many times, I've seen new teachers make this mistake. It never works. Doing so diminishes your effectiveness and is an invitation for disrespect and misbehavior. It's very important to build relationships with kids, but never try to connect with them on a peer-to-peer level. There will come a point where they lose respect. Never forget—you are there to lead and guide your charges, not be their buddy.

Meet Children Where They Are

Every year, your students will display a wide range of ability levels. Depending on the subject, some will be "on grade level," some will be advanced, and some will struggle. Accept this. Refrain from getting frustrated because kids are not where you think they should be. At the beginning of the school year, find out where your students are in reading, writing, and math, and move them on from there. What's important is not getting children to a particular level, but that they continue to improve.

Accept That You Won't Reach All Your Students

It's a hard pill to swallow. I remember the child who taught me this. His name was Hironori. It was my second year of teaching. He was one of thirty-four third graders I had that year. Hironori spoke little English and struggled in school. Every night, I would worry about this kid. I wasn't meeting all of his needs, and I felt badly about it. I call this kind of child a "pillow student"— the child you go to bed worrying about. One night as I lay in bed thinking about Hironori, I suddenly realized, *Of course I can't meet all his needs! I have a classroom full of kids who need me. As much as I'd love to be there for Hironori all the time, it's impossible.* Coming to this realization took a giant load off my shoulders. You are only one person. So give it your all. Do the best you can. Do it again tomorrow.

Remember That Children Are Not Adults

I hate to say it, but some teachers get exasperated with their students for being kids. Children need help organizing their binders and cleaning their backpacks. They need assistance with time management and prioritizing tasks. Don't make the mistake of thinking of kids as irresponsible or immature. Think this instead: *They need my help.*

Follow These Correcting Tips

Once, for fun, I went with a friend to see a fortune-teller. After studying the lines on my hand, she looked up and asked, "Are you a lawyer?"

I shook my head. "No. Why?"

"I see lots of papers."

I chuckled. "I'm a teacher. What you're seeing is probably my correcting basket."

Correcting papers is the bane of most teachers. Frequently, my correcting would just go for a ride. After work, I'd put it into my car and drive it home. The next day, I'd drive the papers back to school, uncorrected. Now that I'm retired, I have a confession to make. For years, my correcting basket and I didn't have a good relationship. I admit it wasn't the basket's fault. I could have been nicer to it. I'd spend time with it only when I had to. During conference week, Open House, and formal observations by the principal, I'd hide it in the closet. Sometimes I'd call it bad words. Over the years, though, our relationship improved. I worked on it.

If you and your correcting basket are not getting along, here are a few pointers to get your relationship back on track: First, don't grade everything. Not all practice needs to be corrected. If you've got a week's work of math homework to correct, not grading one batch isn't going to hurt anyone. I understand that your students worked hard on it, but sometimes your sanity is more important. Second, get yourself a stamp that says "Spelling Not Corrected" or "Reviewed by Teacher." It'll save you a lot of time. Also, have a marking session with another teacher. It can turn an otherwise dreaded time into one that's fun. Tricking yourself helps too. When you have stacks to correct, go through the easiest ones first. It will feel like you're getting a lot done quickly. If you've been grading for hours, and you're starting to not see straight, stop, and come back to it another time. You never want to get to that place where you summon your best Oprah voice and start shouting, "*You* get an A! And *you* get an A! *Everyone* gets an A!" As a bonus, try correcting during happy hour. Wine (at home) helps. But keep the glass off your students' papers. Otherwise, when you hand them back, you will have to explain the mystery rings to your kids.

Ask for Help

Grayson. Janessa. Sam. These students are indelibly printed on my memory bank. I had them my first year of teaching. Grayson was reading at a kindergarten level in third grade. Janessa bullied other children. Sam vandalized school property and stole things from the classroom. All three kids' cumulative folders were thick with reports. For months, I tried to help these children on my own. I believed that I should be able to because I was their teacher. But then one day I came to the realization that I just couldn't do it alone. I needed help. Finally, I asked for it.

Many new teachers don't ask for help. It's understandable. You want to appear as if you know what you're doing. But the truth is that when you ask for help, no one thinks you're incompetent. On the contrary, asking for help reveals that you care. It shows that you will do anything to help a child, including put aside your pride. If you're having trouble with a student, seek the advice and support of your colleagues. We've all been in your shoes. Do not go it alone.

If you are a veteran teacher, check in with the new teachers once in a while. Ask how they're doing and if they need anything. They'll appreciate it. It's a nice way to give back to the profession. One year I was asked to support a group of new hires in my district. At our first meeting together, after the introductions, I began talking when immediately they all threw open their notebooks and started taking notes. I started to laugh. "I'm sorry," I said, chuckling. "As you know, I teach third grade—and third graders do *not* take notes."

Avoid This Teacher Trap

Once, I worked with a teacher who would arrive late to meetings and wouldn't follow through with the things she had promised to do. She'd leave school right when the kids left. A few days before report cards were due, I walked into her classroom to find her writing them while her students were doing seat work. The same thing happened the following day. I thought she was slacking off. And then one morning at our grade-level meeting, she told the team that she had recently been diagnosed with multiple sclerosis. She apologized for dropping the ball. I felt bad. I had judged her.

We all judge. It's human nature. At school, we hear criticisms like that teacher's classroom is "always out of control," or so-and-so "isn't good with technology," and we end up believing it. It's easy to do. All of us know it's not good to judge others. It separates people and puts you in a negative frame of mind. It can sour a work environment. If you find yourself judging a colleague, here are some ways to get yourself back on track:

The first step is to acknowledge that you're being judgmental and call yourself out on it. Remind yourself to cut others the same slack you'd want them to give you. No teacher has it easy. Your colleagues are dealing with the same things that you are. The truth is that we really don't know what people are going through. We don't know what it might have taken a coworker to just get out of bed that morning. Likewise, aim to accept others where they are. We're all in a different place in our learning. Just as children grow at different rates, so do teachers. We have different styles, and none is better than the other. Don't forget that there are many paths in teaching, and just because someone is traveling a different road than you, it doesn't mean they're on the wrong one. When you start to feel that others are lacking or failing, move your spotlight. Shine it on the areas where *you* can improve. Look at your own attitude and professionalism. Spend your energies on your teaching, not someone else's.

Be Kind to the Custodian

One day when Keith, the custodian, stepped into my classroom after school, I felt bad. We'd done an art project. The floor was littered with paper, and the sink was splattered with paint. It had been a busy day.

"Sorry about the mess," I said.

"That's all right," Keith replied.

"Please tell me my room isn't the messiest one in the school."

He laughed. "It's not."

"Yay."

"It's the second messiest."

I cringed. "Yikes!"

Then Keith proceeded to list all of the classrooms in order from cleanest to messiest.

"You keep *track*?"

"Oh yes," he said. "All custodians do."

In teaching, there are days you need a ceiling bulb replaced, a ball pumped up, or your classroom cleaned early for parent-teacher conferences. There will be times when you need a desk for a new student, paper towels for the dispenser, or your door unlocked because you can't find your keys. Always be kind to the custodian. Always say thank you. And this goes for the school secretary, the clerk, and the librarian too.

Realize That Not Every Lesson Will Be Legendary

Lessons are like meals. Some are better than others. Some aren't that exciting. Occasionally, you'll knock one out of the park. Every year, you'll give some wonderfully creative and compelling lessons, but they all won't be this way. Sometimes kids just need to practice their times tables.

Observe Master Teachers

All new teachers aspire to be excellent, and one of the best ways to get there is to observe excellent teaching. Teachers don't get the opportunity to watch other teachers in their classrooms much. They're too busy in their own. Ask your principal if you may observe some master teachers in your district. Chances are you'll get a yes. When you visit, notice how they interact with their students and manage their classrooms. If possible, meet with the teachers afterward to debrief what you've seen. Ask a lot of questions. Observing other teachers is *the* best PD. And make sure you snap some photos of their rooms while you're there so you can steal . . . I mean *copy* their bulletin board ideas too.

Remember That Skillful Teachers Are Made, Not Born

Whenever you observe a master teacher who makes it all look so easy or read the blog of a teacher whose classroom and lessons always look better than yours, bear in mind that they did not just step into their schools completely capable, delivering captivating lessons to fully engaged students. It took them years to get there. Don't compare your first chapter to someone else's twentieth.

Understand Learning Windows

Have you ever noticed that elementary school windows look pretty much the same? In the fall, the windowpanes are covered with jack-o'-lanterns painted with tempera paint. In winter, they are filled with paper snowflakes that were opened up after being folded and snipped. In spring, the snowflakes have been replaced with ziploc bags holding lima bean seeds wrapped in wet paper towels. But these aren't the only windows in school. There are others—ones you cannot see. These are the windows of learning.

Windows of learning are the times children learn something best. When children grasp something with ease, their learning windows are open. We've all known kids who picked up something quickly, be it a language, a sport, or an instrument. Their windows were wide open. The opposite is also true. If a child is having difficulty understanding something, it could be that his window isn't open. Now, this is not to say that children can't learn things when their windows are closed. Of course they can. The learning just won't come as easily. If a student can't grasp a skill or concept, don't immediately assume something is wrong. Be patient. A mind has to be ready to learn. You can't force it.

Be Mindful of How You Refer to Caregivers

Our students come to us from diverse living situations. Some children are raised by Mom and Dad and others by their grandparents. Some are in foster care. Others have two moms or two dads. When speaking with your students, instead of always saying "parents" or "Mom and Dad," consider saying "families." It's more inclusive. One teacher I know refers to her students' caregivers as "the big people" in their lives. In her notes home, rather than writing "your child," she writes, "your young person." I am not suggesting that you stop using the words *mom*, *dad*, and *parent*, but I urge you to be sensitive to those who don't have one. In the beginning of the year, find out who takes care of your students. Ask them what they call their caregivers. When my friend's daughter was six, her teacher would refer to her students' caregivers as their "grown-ups." The term stuck, and the six-year-old started calling her own parents "my grown-ups" too.

Help Children Listen

We've all experienced it. You're in the midst of giving directions to your kids, and they start grabbing their materials and moving around because they think they know what you want them to do. They stop listening. Your voice gets louder as you talk over the noise. "Hold it. Wait till I'm finished. Stop moving!" Fortunately, there's an easy and effective way to fix this: Before giving your instructions, tell your students not to begin until you say "Go." By saying this, your kids will listen as they wait for your signal.

Every teacher wants a classroom full of good listeners. Here are a couple of additional strategies to add to your arsenal: First, lower your voice in class. A lot of teachers use louder voices to keep their kids' attention, but, although it may seem counterintuitive, speaking softer can be highly effective. When you speak softly, children make a greater effort to listen. It has a calming effect on a class too. Along with that, consider cutting down on your talking time. Too much talk can cause kids to check out, daydream, and become more interested in the ceiling tiles than in you. Be careful about repeating yourself as well. If children know that you're going to repeat the directions, they won't feel that they need to tune in the first time. If you tell kids that you'll be giving your instructions only once, they'll also listen better. Another way to improve your students' listening is to make eye contact with them while you teach. It's easy for teachers to get so focused on the material that they see the class as one large group, not as individuals. When you make brief eye contact with children during a lesson—just a second or two with each student—they are more inclined to look at you and listen. It's also an excellent rapport builder.

In addition to this, let your students move. A little movement at the top of a lesson—or whenever children need a break—always clears heads for listening. Movement reboots. Ask your kids to stand up and stretch. Let them shake and wiggle. Lead them in some neck rolls, arm circles, jumping jacks, or air swimming where they can do the breast stroke, backstroke, and butterfly. Throw on a pair of swimming goggles to get giggles.

Treat Your Students as If They Are Your Own Children

There are times when you will have important decisions to make about a child: Do I seek extra help because this student is struggling? Is it time to call a conference with the parents? Do I involve the principal or the counselor? Whenever I was faced with questions like these, I would ask myself how I'd respond if the child were my own. This always helped. Sometimes when speaking with parents, I would even say it aloud: "I'm thinking about how to handle this as though your child were mine." Parents like to hear that you think of their children this way.

Reflect on Your Lessons

One afternoon when my fourth graders were finished making treasure maps on large pieces of construction paper, I took the kids outside one at a time. To give their maps the appropriate buccaneer appearance, I lit the edges, let them burn a few seconds, then allowed the children to blow out the flames. When Jay handed me his map, I lit one corner of it as I'd done with the others, but suddenly the flame got out of hand. I tried blowing on it but couldn't put it out. Shouting at Jay to stand back, I threw the map onto the ground and stomped on it. By the time the fire was out, several kids had gathered in the doorway to see what was going on. "Jay, I'm so sorry," I said, sure that he'd be upset because his map was ruined. But he wasn't upset at all. As I picked up the map, he cried, "That was cool!" All the onlookers shouted, "Do mine! Do mine!"

Sometimes lessons don't go as planned. PowerPoints won't load. Seeds don't sprout. The idea that you pulled off the internet ends up looking nothing like the photo. You forget the batch of gingerbread men baking in the oven. (*Note*: Never bring burned gingerbread men back to a kindergarten classroom. Jill did this once, and her kids were horrified. One of them cried, "You killed them!") If a lesson goes south, cut yourself slack. Give yourself permission to make mistakes. No teacher bats 1,000. Chalk it up as a learning experience. The reason many lessons go haywire is because teachers are trying something new. The fact that you tried something you'd never done before shows that you're willing to take a risk and stretch yourself. Also, look for the positive in the flop. Most likely there was *something* that went right. And most importantly, take the time to reflect. Bad lessons make good teachers—if you learn from them.

One simple way to reflect on a lesson is to jot down some notes about it in your plan book. It takes little time, and the following year, when you look back in your planner, you'll have the comments right there. Try to write your reflection as soon as you can so that you don't forget. And be sure to pat yourself on the back after a lesson goes well too. I would often make quick notes in my planner about what worked, what didn't, and what I wanted to do differently the following year. Good lessons got a happy face. Jay's map-burning incident did *not* get a smiley.

Learn from Everyone

Teaching is like a roller-coaster ride. Both have twists and turns. After getting over one hump, you're climbing another. At the end of both a roller-coaster ride and a school year, you feel dazed but happy to still be alive. And just as roller coasters have their steep curves, new teachers face steep learning curves too.

If you're just starting out, make it a goal to learn from everyone. Be a sponge. Ask a lot of questions and pick your colleagues' brains. You can learn from the teachers you don't wish to emulate as well. From them, you'll see what you do not want to do. And don't dismiss veteran teachers because they might do things differently than you or because they may not be as up on the latest practices. Keep in mind that they have stayed in the profession. Find out how they accomplished that. As you learn from your colleagues, don't do something simply because someone else is doing it. Just because other teachers hand out treats at the end of the week or give their kids a pizza party when the quarter ends doesn't mean that you have to. Follow your instinct. Do what aligns with your style and values, and choose what works for you.

Write a Letter to Yourself
Before you begin your first school year, write yourself a letter in which you put into words why you went into teaching. Slip the letter into an envelope and ask a trusted friend to hold on to it for you until January. By then, you'll need the reminder of why you chose to go into the profession. If it's a really bad year, ask your friend to deliver it to you in November. Hopefully you won't need it in September.

Ask Yourself This Question
This one question will help you in your planning. It will help you stay focused. It will help you create the learning environment you wish to have and guide you in becoming the teacher you aspire to be. Write it in your lesson planner. Put it on a sticky note and keep it in your desk so that you see it every time you open it. The question is this: Would I want to be a student in *my* class?

1,001 Back to School Nights

Only a few of us were eating lunch in the staff room that day. The other teachers were in their classrooms scrambling to get ready for that evening's Back to School Night. As I sat there, I announced, "Is it wrong to call a sub for tonight?"

For most teachers, Back to School Night is without question the most nerve-racking event of the year. The stakes are high. Teachers dread it. Talking to children is one thing. That's what we're trained to do. Talking to their parents is entirely different. On this most important night, we stand in front of a room full of moms and dads who hang on our every word. Some will even take notes. After your presentation, you know that every one of them will talk about you on the car ride home.

All teachers have their way of getting through Back to School Night. One friend of mine turns off the lights and shows a PowerPoint the whole time so she won't have to look at the audience. Another bribes the parents with cookies. Her thought is that if she feeds them, they'll be nicer. Jill talks until the very last minute so that there's no time for questions. She doesn't want to be thrown a curveball. I had a strategy too. I'd pick the mom in the audience who was smiling the biggest and direct most of my talk to her. *Poor woman.*

No matter how many years I taught, I always got the Back to School Night butterflies. To get through my talk, I'd write down my key points on large pieces of paper so I could see them easily—like cue cards that soap opera actors use so they don't forget their lines. It made me less nervous. I realize this will sound silly, but for my first few Back to School Nights, I even wrote down my jokes. Once I got a laugh or two, I could relax. Beside each joke, I'd write

"Joke," with a smiley face. But I stopped doing that after a mom walked by my desk and started reading my cue cards. She must have seen the word *joke* because she turned to me with a grin and said, "Did we laugh enough?" I felt the blood rush to my face. "Yes," I answered. Then I asked her if my face was red. She nodded.

To prepare for the big night, there are a couple of things you should do. To start, it's important to have lots of children's work on the walls. Parents will look for it. Besides that, make sure your students clean their desks inside and out. Parents always check. If the name tags on your kids' desks already look like they've gone through a war, replace them. Also, have students set out welcome letters on the desks for their moms and dads. It's a nice touch. One year a child wrote: "Dear Mom, listen to the teacher. He likes that." In his PS, he added, "Enter desk at your own risk." To show what your kids are studying, set out books and materials around the classroom. But don't lie. Once, I was in Audrey's classroom as she was getting ready for Back to School Night and watched her put out a globe and some atlases. "You're teaching geography?" I asked. "No," Audrey said. "But if I put these out, the parents will think I am." As you get ready, it is also time to play hide-and-seek with your piles. Stash them in your cupboards, then retrieve them in the morning.

Before giving your presentation, it's a good idea to practice what you're going to say, especially if you're a new teacher. I always did, even after years of teaching. I wouldn't practice in my classroom, though. If a parent saw that the lights were on, they might knock and want in early. So I'd rehearse in the large supply closet next to the office. It was quiet there. One year, about a half hour before Back to School Night started, I walked into the supply closet as usual, closed the door, and started practicing my speech. Suddenly I heard a noise from behind the bookcase. "Is someone there?" I called out. Around the corner stepped my friend Dana. "What are *you* doing here?" I asked. She made a sheepish face. "The same as you. I hate this night."

As the parents enter your room, and you point out where their children sit and apologize to big dads when they have to squeeze into pint-sized chairs, I recommend that you give everyone a few minutes to fill out a questionnaire titled "What Do You Know About Your Child's Teacher?" It's a nice way for parents to get to know you. My questions included: "What is Mr. Done's favorite food?" "Where did he go to college?" and "When did he begin teaching?" Answers: lasagna, San Jose State University, and 1986, which, in my later years of teaching, was before some of the parents were born.

During your talk, you will introduce parents to the new grade, walk them through the different subject areas, talk about your expectations, go over the field trips, and share how they can help at home. All these things are important, and parents want to hear them, but that's not the main reason they come that night. The main reason moms and dads make the effort to leave work early that evening, change their dinner schedules, and get a sitter for the kids is so that they can get to know *you*. Do you seem kind? Are you enthusiastic? Will you care for their baby? *This* is what parents want to learn that evening. Each day, their children become yours, and all parents want assurance that their kids will be precious in your eyes too.

At the end of the evening, ask your parents to write notes to their children, seal them into envelopes, and slide them into the desks. If a child's parents can't make it, write the note yourself. My students always knew the notes were coming. The morning after Back to School Night, the first thing the kids would do was look inside their desks, tear open the envelopes, and read the messages. It was like watching children open up their valentines. I always enjoyed seeing the kids' faces light up as they read the notes. Oftentimes, the children read them aloud. It warmed me up to hear them. I got a kick out of discovering the special nicknames the parents had for their kids: Lizard, Scooter, Pickle, Monkey, Noodle, and My Little Egg (David was born bald).

After reading the notes, some of the children would tape them into their desks and keep them there the whole year. The parents' messages were always the same: "Looking good!" "Well done!" "Keep up the good work!" "We're proud of you!" Every year one child would bring his note up to me and say, "I can't read my dad's writing." And every year I'd read it, then ask if I should send home some handwriting practice for Daddy.

Influence

When President Eisenhower invited the renowned author James Michener to the White House, he declined. Michener had already accepted an invitation to speak at a dinner honoring his high school English teacher who had taught him to write. Michener wrote to the president, "I know you will not miss me at your dinner, but she might at hers." Not long afterward, Michener received a handwritten letter from the president, who wrote: "In his lifetime, a man lives under fifteen or sixteen presidents, but a really fine teacher comes into his life but rarely. Go and speak at your teacher's dinner."

We all can remember a special teacher—one who inspired us, one who made an invaluable contribution toward making us who we are today. For me, one of these people was my second-grade teacher, Miss Greco, whom I've mentioned earlier. Miss Greco would tease her hair really high and use lots of hairspray. She wore lots of perfume too, and I used to inhale it when she stood close by. Once I told her that she "smelled happy." It made her laugh. I remember how incredibly creative Miss Greco was. She could turn a paper towel roll into a rocket, a sock into a snowman, and a couple of cereal boxes into a castle. I also remember that she would share her travels with us. On the classroom walls, she hung airline posters of the places she had visited. One day she passed around a piece of real sugarcane that she'd brought back from Hawaii. On it were the teeth marks from kids who had tried to taste it after being told not to.

Mrs. Murayama, whom I've also written about, was also one of those special teachers. But not right away. When I discovered that I was going to be in her fifth-grade class, I got nervous. Mrs. Murayama had a reputation for giving lots of homework and making kids learn all the states. But it didn't take long for me to fall in love with her too. Every couple of weeks, especially after PE when her students needed a rest, Mrs. Murayama would play albums on the big gray record player that every teacher seemed to have when I was in grade school. It was from that record player that I first heard some of the most famous pieces by Mozart, Beethoven, and Tchaikovsky. When the class complained about the "old-fashioned" music, she'd say it was good for us. Then, to emphasize her point, she'd turn up the volume. While listening to those records, I had no idea that they were igniting my own love of music. Years later, when I went to college, I majored in it.

My high school English teacher, Mr. Duncanson, also inspired me. Mr. Duncanson loved art and would often weave it into his teaching. In his class, I learned about many of the great artists and their works. Some years later, when I visited the museums of Europe, it delighted me to stand in front of the artwork I'd first seen on Mr. Duncanson's slides. He believed that each of us has a mental studio: a world of artists and art that inhabits the imaginary chambers of our mind. Aesthetic ghosts of inspiration. By exposing his students to great art, Mr. Duncanson was building *our* mental studios.

One of the teachers who had the greatest impact on my life was my high school choir teacher Bill Stretch. A fine musician, Mr. Stretch didn't just teach music. He gave his students something special to belong to. He boosted our confidence, taught us discipline, and challenged us to strive for excellence—lessons we carried into our lives. I remember after singing through a piece, sometimes he'd shrug and say to us, "Well, that was fine, I guess—if you want to sound like an ordinary high school choir." Then we'd sing it again, better.

While writing this book, I received news that Mr. Stretch had become ill. His heart was failing. He was at home on morphine and oxygen and had been given only a few weeks to live. Someone started an email thread where his former students could thank him. The outpouring of love and appreciation was enormous. So many attributed their life paths back to him: "Because of you, I went on to study music." "It's on account of you that I became a professional performer." "Thanks to you, I now teach music and hope to instill in my students the same passion you instilled in me." I learned that Mr. Stretch's caretaker read all the email messages to him and was grateful that he heard them. After his passing, the thread continued for a while. It was clear to all of us that his students had been the true music of his life. We had been his symphony.

I have often wondered: Out of all the teachers I've ever had, from grade school through university, what was it about these four that made them so exemplary? Why is it that my answer to the security question "Who is your favorite teacher?" on every website is always one of them? After reflecting on this, I understand why. All four were passionate about their work. You could hear it in their voices. Their love for teaching showed on their faces. And their excitement rubbed off. You felt it. In the same way, these four teachers were committed. They knew their work mattered. They understood that they were building more than knowledge. They were building people.

And these teachers were warm. They were kind and caring, friendly and patient. They recognized that sometimes the thing that students need most is not in the lesson plan. They understood that students are like seedlings that need to be tended to and cared for, and that just as warmth is key for the growth of a seedling, kids need it too. Of course, I didn't realize it at the time, but these four were also showing me how to teach. Through their words and actions, they were modeling what good teaching looked like. So, I guess you could say that I started my teacher training when I was seven.

As teachers, you never know how you are going to impact a student. One day I received a letter from a former fifth grader named Deborah. She'd recently become a mom. In the letter, Deborah reminisced about our year together and recalled several things I'd forgotten. As I read her note, something Deborah wrote completely surprised me. She said that the subject she enjoyed most about the class was science. *Science?* I did not view myself as a very good science teacher. Sure, I had rubbed balloons on my head to illustrate static electricity, made "rock candy" crystals on sticks, and traced my kids' shadows on the blacktop with chalk. Like a lot of grade school teachers, I'd held marble races on pool noodles and had my kids dunk Chips Ahoy! cookies into milk to demonstrate the scientific process: Question: Do cookies sink or float in milk? Hypothesis: Cookies will float in milk. Prediction: The cookie will float. Conclusion: It sank. All teachers have their strengths, and science was not one of mine. And yet here was a former student thanking me for teaching it. Who would have thought?

It is said that a teacher's influence goes on and on, that we touch the future—affect eternity, even. This isn't just *Chicken Soup for the Teacher's Soul* talk. These aren't just fluffy words on teacher planners, coffee mugs, and memes to help teachers get through the school year. We really *do* make an impact. Think about this: Children who enter kindergarten in 2025 will graduate from high school in 2038. These young men and women will use the skills and values they learned in school throughout their careers. Many of them will work until 2088. If you ever doubt your power to influence lives, think of those numbers.

For teachers, once a child is part of your life, he or she stays forever. But more importantly, once *you* are part of a child's life, you stay forever too. The longer you teach, the more you understand how true this is. One afternoon I was in the supermarket standing in line at the checkout when I heard, "Mr. Done!" I turned around and saw a brawny, bearded, tattooed man walking swiftly toward me. He flashed a giant grin and said, "It's Michael! Remember me?" (Whenever you meet former students, no matter how old they are, they assume you will remember them and forget that the last time you saw them, they were small.) Quickly my mind shuffled through the Rolodex of past students in my head. "Ah yes," I said. (He'd been one of my third graders.) "But . . . well . . . you've changed a little."

Another day I was sitting in my classroom after school when I heard a tap on the door. I turned around to see a tall man in uniform. I thought it was a parent. I stood up and walked toward him. "May I help you?" I said. "It's me," the man said, patting his chest. "Tom. Tom Robinson." Now *this* student I remembered immediately: Tom Robinson. Fifth grade. Never sat still. Liked to eat pencils. As we got caught up, Tom said, "I wanted to apologize for all the trouble I gave you." I chuckled. "I also wanted to tell you that if it weren't for your pushing me to take school seriously like you did, I probably wouldn't have gotten into the navy. So thank you." His words filled my teacher tank. Before he left, I asked if he still ate pencils. He liked that I remembered. Teaching is one of the only professions where someone comes back years later to thank you.

Some time ago, I used to volunteer as a "visitor" at a local hospital. Once a week, I'd walk around the rooms and touch base briefly with patients. My father had been treated in this hospital before he passed away. They'd been good to him, and I wanted to give back. If the patients were awake, I'd say hello, introduce myself, and ask if they needed anything. Some patients would want to talk. A few asked me to read to them. Sometimes they wanted to be left alone.

One night as I was making my rounds, I poked my head into a room where a woman lay awake in bed. She was the only one in the room, which was unlit save for the light coming in from the hallway. When I introduced myself from the doorway, the woman looked afraid. I thought perhaps I had startled her. I asked if there was anything she needed, but she didn't answer. I asked again, and this time she made a sound. At that moment, I realized—the woman was deaf.

And then the most surprising thing happened. Suddenly, without thinking, my right hand rose and started to sign, "Hello. My name is Phil." The woman smiled softly. Her whole countenance changed. With my fingers, I asked if there was anything I could do for her. She turned toward an empty glass on the bedside table. I pointed to it and signed, "Water?" She nodded. I left the room and fetched some from the nurses' station. I returned and handed her the glass. Her eyes thanked me. When she finished drinking, I set the glass on the table. Then I signed good-bye and left.

In the hallway, I leaned against the wall and puzzled over what had just happened. My hands had not formed those letters in over thirty years! I had learned them in fifth grade when Mrs. Murayama taught the class how to sign the alphabet when we were learning about Helen Keller. Now, after all these years, I was able to use these letters to help a stranger in need. *Amazing*. Mrs. Murayama *had* touched the future. Decades later, she'd touched the life of a woman she never met. And unless I told her, she would never know.

Teachers rarely get to see the fruits of their labors. We usually have little contact with children after they leave our nests. It's impossible to know our influence. That's one of the mysteries of our work. But once in a while—if you're lucky—you find out.

I was sitting at home in California when my landline rang.

"Hello," I said into the phone.

A voice on the other end of the line piped, "Mr. Done, is that you?"

"Who's this?"

"It's András!"

András was ten. I had taught him the year before in Budapest. He was calling from Hungary.

"*András?* How did you get my number?"

"My mom had it."

"Does she know you're calling me?"

Pause. "Well . . . not really."

I laughed. "Then we better keep this short." This was before the time when calling international could be free. Surely it was costing a pretty penny. "Why are you calling?"

"I just wanted to say hi."

"Well . . . *hi!*"

Now, let me tell you a little about András. As much as I loved this kid, András was one of the most challenging students I'd ever had. He sat right in front of me in class, stood close to me in line, and was seated two inches away from me at all of the assemblies. It seemed like every week we were out in the hallway working out a conflict. Once, when András was absent, it felt like half the class was gone. And yet, after all we had gone through together—look who was calling.

If you are a teacher, remember this: You are all Miss Greco and Mrs. Murayama. You are all Mr. Duncanson and Mr. Stretch. Behind each one of you are countless children whose minds you have broadened, whose character you helped shape, and whose lives, like András's, you have touched. Ahead of you are many more. The passion, commitment, and warmth that you share with your students really do follow them for the rest of their lives. Be the teacher children remember fondly when they look back on their education. Be the teacher who comes into a child's life but rarely.

The Challenges

The Back-to-School Blues

The beginning of summer break is always a happy time. You made it. By the end of June, you're sleeping in, taking naps, and wearing flip-flops. Your bladder has settled into a new routine. But as summer progresses, things begin to shift. In July anxiety starts to edge its way in when you spot store clerks clearing aisles for back-to-school supplies and hanging banners of dancing rulers and smiling glue sticks. Too early. Actually, have you noticed that these banners never have teachers in them? There's a reason for this: The teachers wouldn't be smiling. Come August, your anxiety kicks into full gear. Everywhere you look—on TV, in store windows, online—you are reminded that school is just around the corner. By now, every other post on Facebook seems to be a meme with a crying teacher guzzling wine or a sexy shot of Jake Gyllenhaal or Leonardo DiCaprio purring, "Hey, girl, put your feet up. I'll set your classroom up for you." Come to think of it, a teacher's summer fun resembles the bell-shaped story arc with the rising and falling action that we teach our students. A teacher's fun rises in June, peaks in July, and tumbles in August. When I shared this thought with a friend, he said it followed the same trajectory as his General Electric stock.

By mid-August, every teacher gets the back-to-school blues. These blues hit because you realize that your leisurely summer life is about to be turned upside down. You know that before long you'll have to reset your alarm clock, break your seventy-five-plus-day streak of wearing shorts, brave rush-hour traffic, remember what day of the week it is, and put on real shoes again. You understand that soon you will be waking up to stacks of papers around your bed and drinking mugs of half-slurped cold coffee at work because you were too busy to drink it when it was hot. Male teachers' necks start to swell up because they realize that shortly they will have to put on dress shirts and ties again. Female teachers lament that they have to go back to wearing a bra all day. The back-to-school blues kick in because you know that in a little while, you'll be lugging fans into your classroom that you took from home because the only room in the school with AC is the office. (Usually people steal supplies from the office. In teaching, you steal things from home.) You are aware that in a short time, you'll have to open your computer and see all the school email that you didn't look at over the break, including the reminders to read the summer professional development book that you have yet to crack open. And you know that pretty soon you'll need to try recalling all the school usernames and passwords that the guys in the tech department recommended, and they look like this: #3@156&%4!

One reason teachers get the back-to-school blues is because they know that during that first week before the kids arrive, they won't be able to do what they want to do. Teachers want to be in their classrooms the first week back, but they can't. That week is always packed with meetings and professional development and first aid courses where you have to watch videos with bad actors performing CPR, then get down on the floor to give mouth-to-mouth resuscitation to a plastic dummy. During all the meetings, you pretend to type notes on your laptop, but, really, you are making your to-do lists. If you could read the thought bubbles above your colleagues' heads, they would be full of exclamation marks, question marks, and swear words.

For many teachers, the worst part of that teacher workweek is the icebreakers. I'm not a party pooper, and I like to have fun, but that first week back, I did not want to walk around the room with a sticky note on my back while I asked other people questions so that I could guess what my sticky note said. I didn't want to make a long line with my colleagues in the order of our birthdays—without talking. I did not want to form two speed-dating circles where I had one minute to talk about my summer before moving on to my next "date." Teachers have other things to do! Jill felt the same as I did, but she had an exit strategy. As soon as anyone began an icebreaker, she'd start fake coughing, leave the room, and hide out in the bathroom till it was over. *Smart*.

Around the time that teachers start coming down with the back-to-school blues, they also begin experiencing back-to-school nightmares. These bad dreams are the brain's way of reminding you that the new school year is approaching. They typically fall into five categories: (1) Being unprepared; (2) Losing your students; (3) Running late; (4) Losing control of your class; and (5) Arriving at school in your PJs when it's not Pajama Day. I once had a student teacher tell me that she had the pajama dream. "Congratulations!" I said. "You're a teacher now."

Every August, like clockwork, I would get teacher nightmares. One morning I woke up in a fright after dreaming that it was the first day of school, and I hadn't unpacked a thing. Another time I bolted up in bed after having a dream that my third graders were going through my desk and found bottles of whisky. In one recurring dream, I was transferred to a new school with no notice to teach Italian to an auditorium full of eight-year-olds. I don't speak Italian. And, once, I flew out of my bed panicked that I was late for school and raced to get dressed—until it dawned on me that it was Saturday. In July.

Teachers deal with the back-to-school blues differently. Lucy says she tries not to think about it. Audrey shops for new clothes. Dana hides anything that has to do with school in her garage, so that she doesn't have to look at it. Once, my friend Mike put a plastic Halloween tombstone on his front porch at the end of August. Under the *RIP*, he wrote: "Summer Vacation." Jill always gets a really bad case of them. One year I had a couple of teachers over a few days before it was time to report back. When I asked Jill what kind of wine she wanted, she gave a heavy sigh, flopped her head onto the counter, and cried, "What goes best with *back to school*?"

Teacher Heart

Doesn't he have a coat? I wondered as I watched Devin, one of my third graders, on the playground. The weather had turned cold. All the other children were wearing coats and jackets now, but not Devin. He wore only a hoodie to school, and it wasn't enough. Huddled in my own coat and scarf, I called him over.

"Aren't you cold in just that hoodie?" I asked.

"Nope," he answered.

"Do you have a coat?" I said casually. I didn't want to make a big deal of it.

"I don't need one."

But I didn't believe him. I knew Devin's family was struggling financially. I spoke with the school counselor about it, and together we went to the PTA closet, where they kept donated clothes. We found a coat for Devin: navy blue with a removable plaid liner. It looked like it hadn't been worn much. The counselor called Devin's mom and asked if we could give it to him. She was grateful.

The next day, I called Devin into the classroom during recess and said I had a present for him. When I pulled the coat out from under my desk, his face lit up. "For *me*?" he asked. "Yes." Devin put on the coat and rubbed his hand over it as I rolled up the cuffs. The coat was too big for him, but he didn't mind. After he was buttoned up, he ran back out to recess. Seconds after he left, the door swung open, and Devin's head poked around the corner. "Thanks!" he said, and he was off.

When the class came back in, and the children hung their coats and jackets in their cubbies, Devin kept his on. I called the kids to the carpet for a story, and Devin sat down beside me like he usually did. With his hands in both pockets, he hugged himself and said, "It's so *warm*."

Teachers are witnesses to society. In our classrooms, we see poverty and neglect, depression and anxiety, sadness and pain. We work with students who are exposed to domestic and neighborhood violence, whose parents have lost their jobs or been incarcerated, and whose families have lost their homes. We teach kids who come to school dirty, hungry, or sick because no one is at home to take care of them. According to the US Centers for Disease Control and Prevention, more than half of US children have experienced some kind of trauma in the form of abuse, neglect, violence, or challenging household circumstances. That means that out of the approximately seventy-five million kids in the United States, more than thirty-seven million of them have experienced trauma. And they bring it with them to the classroom. Heavy backpacks aren't the only loads children carry to school.

Teachers learn about some of the trauma, but most we don't. We don't hear about the drug busts or fights or drunken rants witnessed by our students at home. Most of the time, kids don't tell their teachers that they saw their dad in handcuffs, that a grandparent has cancer, or that they're not eating lunch at school because their mom owes the cafeteria money. A child doesn't bring up that his older brother got kicked out of the house and got caught living in a storage unit, or that her family is living in a run-down motel now because the apartment was too expensive. A student doesn't volunteer that he had to sell his bicycle. The truth is that most children don't reveal their hurt and fear and sadness. Most put on brave faces. Sometimes kids who have been traumatized will misbehave or act defiant. More often than not, there is a story behind the misbehavior. And that story will oftentimes break your heart.

The trauma our students carry takes an emotional toll on teachers as well. Some call it the cost of caring. A friend of mine had a fifth grader who started crying when she found out it was a three-day weekend. She didn't want to be home that long. It was then that my friend realized that school is a safe place for those children who have a difficult life outside of it. I remember when a first grader named Savannah ran up to me at recess to show me her dress.

She'd just gotten it for the winter concert. I knew the school had bought it for her. Savannah said it was her first new dress. "And," she said proudly, "we got one of those triangle things for it." For a second, I didn't know what she was talking about. When I realized what she meant, my heart clenched. She had gotten a hanger.

Teachers are first responders. When we learn that children have endured trauma or we suspect it, we do all we can to help. We keep our eyes on these kids and check in. We let them know that we are there for them if they want to talk. If necessary, we cut these students some slack because we understand that brains in pain have difficulty learning. Teachers build support teams and provide extra TLC. We keep granola bars, crackers, and juice boxes in our classroom cupboards for kids who are hungry and set up spaces that are warm and peaceful so that children can feel safe. We maintain consistent schedules and routines because these things give children a sense of security, and we create room environments that are orderly because we know that they bring comfort to children whose lives are not. We are calm, gentle, and refrain from raising our voices. In a world that is not always kind to our students, we show them that we will be. We do this because our teacher hearts won't let us do anything else.

When hundreds of thousands of children were displaced from their schools during the Hurricane Katrina disaster that struck the Gulf Coast, teachers from California to Florida welcomed these students with open arms. All across the country, we added desks and chairs to our already full class-rooms to take in Katrina's kids. As they entered their new schools, we hung signs saying "Welcome!" and handed out school T-shirts and stuffed mascots because we knew that getting these children back to school was a vital step in supporting their emotional recovery. At recess time, we turned jump ropes, pushed swings, and sat with our new students because we recognized that *we* played an important role in creating stability. During class, we encouraged these kids to tell their stories because we understood that sharing them brings healing and builds bridges to those who listen. We gathered these children close to us on the carpet and read *The Very Hungry Caterpillar* and *Harold and the Purple Crayon* and *Cloudy with a Chance of Meatballs* because these stories are familiar, and familiarity brings comfort. Long after the special reports about the hurricane ended on the news, we continued to fill backpacks after school for the Red Cross and make change at bake sales for Katrina relief. In doing so, we were teaching our students what compassion looks like.

Years later, when the Covid-19 pandemic threw schools everywhere into a crisis, those teacher hearts kicked into high gear once again. All across the country—all over the world—teachers scrambled, oftentimes with little notice, to switch to distance learning. Harnessing new technologies, they shouldered the impossible task of replicating school from their homes. Suddenly millions of teachers transformed their kitchens and dining rooms and home offices into classrooms, where they put up bulletin boards, hung student art, and set up whiteboards on which they wrote messages that said "Your teacher misses you so much!" From these new classrooms, teachers Zoomed, emailed, chatted, and got dizzy when virtual first graders ran around carrying their Chromebooks with their cameras on. Teaching changed overnight.

During the pandemic, many teachers went the extra mile. Some of those miles became marathons. When schools closed, teachers dropped off packets of materials on doorsteps, read virtual bedtime stories (pets and stuffed animals encouraged), held online sing-alongs, and handed out tablets from school parking lots with the usernames and passwords already set up to make everything easier. They delivered Citizen of the Month and birthday certificates so they wouldn't be missed. When giving lessons from home, teachers wore silly hairdos and hats on virtual dress-up days because the ones at school had been canceled. They didn't skip wearing costumes for Halloween either, teaching in front of screens dressed as book characters and school supplies and Teenage Mutant Ninja Teachers. A couple of teachers I know sent out Flat Stanley–like drawings of themselves so that their students would have their teacher with them as they worked at home. One teacher friend told her second graders that she was going to take a day off on Friday and that a surprise guest would be teaching the class. Come Friday, the online class started, and there she was disguised as her grandma, complete with a gray wig, thick glasses, and pearls. The kids loved it, and "Grandma" returned the following week. If children didn't understand something in their virtual classrooms, some teachers jumped into their cars, drove to their students' homes, and taught lessons from sidewalks, driveways, front lawns, and porches. When the school day was over, many teachers stayed online to assist children needing extra help. A friend of mine who teaches grade four did just that with one of her boys. When she finished teaching, the child asked her if she would stay with him while he worked. He just wanted someone to be with. She stayed.

During the lockdowns, millions of those teacher hearts were heavy. Teachers missed being with their students. They missed their kids' laughter and silly answers and quirkiness. They missed their thousands of questions. Teachers missed the loud hallways before school and at the end of the day. They missed watching their kids learn and grow. They missed turning the pages of a book together. Heck, one teacher I know said she even missed cafeteria duty. Teachers wished they could reach through the computer and help their kids. Distance learning just wasn't the same. Teachers longed to get back.

One of those teachers was my friend Sabrina. When her school closed because of the pandemic, Sabrina was teaching fifth grade to thirty-two children, whom she called her "babies." She always referred to her students this way. It was Sabrina's thirty-seventh year in the classroom. She liked to tell her kids that she would be there till they buried her in the soccer field. Most of Sabrina's students were from low-income families, and 90 percent of them qualified for free breakfast and lunch. Many had challenging home lives. During the shutdown, Sabrina spent her mornings with other volunteers at her school putting together breakfast boxes to make sure the children ate. Then she'd stand at the grab-and-go in the school parking lot and pass them out as cars drove through. When she got home around ten, she'd take care of her elderly mother. Finally, she'd turn on her computer, connect to her class, and begin her real job.

Sabrina told me that the first month of distance learning was difficult for her. Having never taught remotely before, she felt like she was flying by the seat of her pants. "There were plenty of tears," Sabrina admitted to me one day. Then she laughed. "And a lot of stress eating to boot." But she forged on. Sabrina said the bigger challenge at this time was rallying her students. In the beginning, most of them didn't log on, but Sabrina persisted in tracking them down. Some of the families didn't know how to access the online classrooms. Some homes didn't have internet. While she and her principal sorted this out, Sabrina kept in touch with her students over the phone. She knew that some of them wouldn't be able to participate because they were watching younger siblings. "Poor darlings," she'd say. "They just have too much going on in their lives right now." But Sabrina didn't give up on these kids. She didn't give up on any of them. She gathered their addresses, mapped out routes, and drove to their homes, where she rolled down her car window and held up signs she'd made at her kitchen table that said "Be strong!" and "I'm here for you!" More than once during this time, Sabrina said to me, "Schools might be canceled—but *I'm* not."

The November Wall

November is a rough month for teachers. The new-school-year adrenaline rush is long over. By now, all the tips of your Expo markers are smushed, the ends of your highlighters are discolored, and your once pert and shiny pencils are now chewed, stubby, or lying in pieces on the bottom of your pencil basket. The piles on your desk are starting to resemble a New York skyline, and your correcting basket looks like a dam at full capacity and ready to collapse. Your kids are eating Halloween candy for lunch. In November you work longer hours to input data, set up conferences, write reports, and meet with parents before and after school. You've already attended about a dozen staff meetings and realize there are three million more to go. The days are colder, darker, and wetter, which means more indoor recesses. It feels like the weeks are 875 percent longer than normal and that the end of the school year won't come for decades. By now, someone has taped a sign on the inside of the bathroom door in the teachers' room that says "Keep Calm—It's Almost Thanksgiving."

Thank goodness for Thanksgiving. In November all teachers are counting the days till that three-day week. There is nothing better than a Wednesday that turns into a Friday. Teachers owe Franklin Delano Roosevelt a huge debt of gratitude. When Abraham Lincoln declared Thanksgiving a holiday, it was celebrated on the last Thursday of the month. In the 1930s, to boost retail sales during the Great Depression, FDR moved it a week earlier. If he hadn't changed it, some of us would never make it.

So what can you do to conquer the November wall? If you are buried in work, plan a day or an evening to get caught up. Make it a giant catch-up day. My friend Mike calls it "hell day." On this day, Mike barrels through his marking. He usually has a couple of hell days a year. Every year, I would have a big catch-up day too, usually the week before report cards were due. I'd bring my correcting baskets home, turn on some music, and start chipping away. When the baskets were empty, I'd feel much better. You know that sense of satisfaction you experience when you finish folding all the clean clothes in your laundry basket and put them away? It feels like that. (Well, I've *heard* it feels like that. I'm not good at folding laundry.)

Come November, if you are starting to have thoughts like: *I need a different job*, or *I should have been a* _____ (fill in the blank with your fantasy occupation), or *I don't want to see anyone shorter than four feet tall*, it is probably time to take a mental health day. Take one of your sick days and give yourself a break. We all need a day off once in a while. School will still be there when you get back. I understand it's no fun to write sub plans, and it's never enjoyable to deal with a bad report from the substitute, but sometimes you need a day off to keep your sanity. When my friend Diane needed to take a day off from school, she'd say that she had an appointment with "Dr. Green." That was code for the golfing green.

When I was teaching in Hungary, a teacher I knew named Joe desperately needed to visit Dr. Green. There was one problem, though. In Hungary, in order to take a day off from work, you have to show your employer a note from the doctor. Joe didn't know how he was going to get a doctor's note when he wasn't really sick, but then he got an idea. And it worked. The doctor took one look at Joe's throat and said, "Yes, it's red. You probably have a virus." Joe certainly didn't tell the doctor that just before his appointment, he'd brushed the back of his throat with a toothbrush.

Another way to push through the dreary days of November is to talk with some teachers you trust and let them know how you're feeling. Go see someone on your staff who will tell you that you're not alone. Find a teacher who has lived through lots of Novembers. To me, seasoned teachers are like the Skin Horse in *The Velveteen Rabbit*. In the story, the Skin Horse, who has lived in the nursery for many years, offers the new, young bunny the wisdom that comes with age and experience. When I was a young teacher, I was lucky. I had three Skin Horses at my school. I went to one for a pep talk, another when I wanted a sounding board, and a third when I needed candy.

When facing the November wall, it also helps to think back on all that you've done since the school year began. If you do this, you will see that you have accomplished a great deal. By November, you will have set up a classroom and kicked off another new school year. You will be well on your way to establishing relationships with your students. You will have assessed all your kids in multiple subjects, determined their strengths and areas of need, and gotten to the point where you feel that you really know them. You will also have changed your seating chart a dozen times and practiced lining up more times than you can count. By the end of the month, you will have survived Back to School Night, Picture Day, Halloween madness, a few birthday celebrations, your first set of parent-teacher conferences, and maybe even a field trip. All of this didn't just happen. *You* made it happen.

Beating the Bullies

As I read Hayden's journal entry, I began to tear up. Once a week the children wrote in their response journals, the type in which kids write and the teacher writes back. Children have the choice to keep their entries private. Hayden would always let me read his. The previous week, he had written a list of what he wanted for Christmas: a PlayStation, an Xbox, Nintendo, a MacBook Pro. In his latest entry, he wrote: "I don't want those things anymore. I just want kids to stop picking on my sister."

Bullying in schools is a huge and serious problem. Child and teen bullying is at an all-time high. According to a Unicef study, more than one in three kids ages thirteen to fifteen has experienced bullying. In the United States, the National Center for Educational Statistics reports that over 30 percent of students ages twelve to eighteen have been bullied at school. Bullying is perhaps the most underreported safety problem on American campuses today. Every day millions of students stay home from school because they're afraid.

Bullying comes in many different forms: physical, verbal, damage to property, and relational, where bullies seek to harm the relationships or reputation of someone. Today bullying is no longer confined to campus hallways, cafeterias, or walks home from school. The newest form is cyberbullying, which occurs through text, email, online chat rooms, and social media.

Students who have been bullied are more likely to have low self-esteem, difficulty trusting others, feelings of isolation and anger, and suicidal thoughts. They are more inclined to experience health problems, depression and anxiety, increased sadness and loneliness, changes in sleep and eating patterns, decreased academic achievement, and a loss of interest in activities they used to enjoy. Some bullied children retaliate through violence. When investigating school shootings, law enforcement has discovered that, more often than not, the shooters have a history of being bullied. Often overlooked is the fact that bullying others has a detrimental effect on the bully too. He or she is more prone to abusing alcohol and other drugs, getting into fights, stealing, vandalizing property, dropping out of school, engaging in early sexual activity, and racking up criminal convictions as an adult.

According to various surveys, most victims of bullying do not report it. Some of the reasons include: fear of retaliation, not wanting to worry parents, concern that they would not be believed, thinking that it's wrong to tell, and feeling that nothing will change as a result. Studies show that many bullied children do not trust their teachers to intervene appropriately. In one survey of American middle and high school students who had been bullied, more than half said that school professionals responded poorly to bullying that they observed.

The truth is that many teachers feel ill-equipped to deal with bullying. Teachers receive little if any training in how to handle it. Because most bullying goes unreported, teachers may not even be aware of its extent on their campuses. All children have the right to learn and to feel safe at school. It is our responsibility as teachers and administrators to ensure that this happens. To help beat bullying, teachers know to teach kindness, involve parents, and to share books about the issue. Here are some additional steps that served me well. I'm confident they will help you too.

Take Bullying Seriously

Acknowledge that it exists and that it happens in every school. Don't turn a blind eye to it or put your head in the sand. Commit to taking it seriously. This is the first step to dealing with bullying effectively.

Educate Yourself

Take some time to learn about the issue. Several websites are devoted strictly to bullying and its prevention. Two especially helpful sites are StopBullying .gov and StompingBullying.org. On these sites, you will see testimonials by students who have been and still are being bullied. I'll warn you. These testimonials won't be easy to read. Here are a few: "I was bullied for not being strong and athletic." "I was called ugly for my cleft palate." "I don't know how to live without being in constant fear." "I was bullied almost every day because I'm in foster care." "It isn't fair that if adults bully, it's called illegal harassment, but if kids do it, it's just bullying."

Know Your School's Anti-Bullying Policy

Teachers receive a lot of information from their school districts that they don't always have the time to read, but this is one you should. A solid understanding of your school's anti-bullying policy will allow you to communicate it to students and parents, as well as help you know what to do when you encounter it.

Develop a Classroom Plan

If your school does not have an anti-bullying policy, I recommend developing your own classroom action plan, so that your students know what to do if they are victims of bullying or observe it. Share the plan with your kids. By having a classroom plan, you open the door for them to speak to you about it.

Talk About It with Your Students

This strategy is key. No matter what grade level you teach, have an open and honest discussion about bullying with your class. Don't talk about it just once and never visit the subject again. A one-off discussion isn't enough. Speak with your kids about it in the beginning of the school year and also a couple of times throughout the year. During your discussions, talk about what bullying is, what it looks like, and role-play different scenarios. Inform students of your school's anti-bullying policy, and make them aware of the consequences. Encourage kids to come to you if they are victims of any type of bullying or have witnessed it. Let them know that you will be confidential and assure them that you will take action. When I spoke about bullying with my students, I would always tell them that part of my job was to protect them. Children want to hear this from their teacher. It helps them feel safe.

Watch Your Class Closely

Good teachers are observers. Listen to what your kids say and watch their body language. Look for behaviors that can lead to more intentional types of bullying, such as making jokes about a person, laughing at others, or excluding classmates. If you notice these behaviors, nip it. Also, keep a close eye on those children who might be potential bullying targets: kids who are smaller, larger, or who don't have a lot of friends. If you suspect that certain students in your classroom might be targeting others, keep these kids separated during group work. Most of the time, you can't control what children do outside of the classroom, but you can affect what's happening in it.

Respond Quickly and Appropriately to Every Bullying Incident

If you observe bullying or a student comes to you and reports it, take an active role in stopping it and ensuring that it doesn't continue. Listen to the child and assure him or her that you will help. If the victim is your student, contact the parents. If the victim is not your student, inform the child's teacher. Do the same for the bully. Inform the principal and the school counselor, if you have one. When speaking with the children who are involved, always talk to them privately. Do not speak to the victim and bully together. And do not encourage victims to simply "stand up" to bullies or ask a victim and a bully to talk through the problem.

Use a Bully Box

For students who do not want to come to you directly, create a box where they can drop a note to alert you about problems. The notes can be anonymous or not. When introducing the bully box to children, let them know that anything in it will be kept confidential. Also, take this opportunity to reassure your kids that you will do all you can to fix the problem so that they feel safe to learn.

Enlist the Principal

A principal's commitment to and involvement in addressing school bullying is crucial. Research suggests that a principal's investment in preventing and controlling bullying contributes to fewer incidents. Veteran principals will have had plenty of experience dealing with it. Invite them in to speak with your class. Elicit their support.

Share Your Own Story

The following strategy is highly effective but one that teachers don't often employ. If you were ever bullied as a child, consider sharing your personal story with your students. Talk about how it made you feel and how you handled it. Doing so is powerful. Teachers don't usually open up to children in this way. In telling your own story, you show the kids in your room who are or have been victims of bullying that you understand. When discussing bullying with my students, sometimes—especially if I was aware that one of my students was being bullied—I would tell my class about when I'd been bullied as a child. My aim was to offer support to the victim and, hopefully, to curb the bullying. Once, after sharing an incident where I was bullied in grade school, one of my third graders came over to me and just started rubbing my arm. It was her way of saying, I'm sorry that happened to you.

Check In

This step is very important. After dealing with a bullying incident, check in now and then with those involved. Ask how things are going. This brings comfort to a child who has been bullied. It also assures both the victim and the bully that you are still keeping an eye on things.

Beating the bullies requires a concerted effort by the teacher. It necessitates taking a stand and following through. You can't just hope for it. In order to be successful, you have to be vigilant. If I may, you have to be willing to "take the bullying by the horns." The good news is that it can be stopped. A bully can be turned around, as the following story proves. It happened to the son of a friend of mine. She had tears in her eyes when she told me.

Maurice was a sweet and happy child, wise for his young age. He had type 1 diabetes and wore a diabetes sensor on his upper arm to monitor his body's level of glucose. The sensor was round and white, about the size of a quarter. When he wore a short-sleeved shirt, you could see it. Not long after Maurice started using the sensor, the school principal, who also had diabetes, went into the boy's second-grade classroom and talked to the children about the disease. He invited Maurice to join him at the front of the room and show his sensor to the class. With Maurice's approval, he let the students come up and touch it. During the talk, the principal reminded the children not to make fun of those who are different. He understood the importance of being proactive like this. He explained that he had diabetes too.

Soon afterward, Maurice's teacher followed up with her own class discussion about the disease. She kept a watchful eye on her students to make sure that no one picked on Maurice. Once, after getting permission from Maurice's parents, the teacher surprised Maurice by drawing two eyes and a mouth with black Sharpie on his sensor. He was delighted. After that, every few weeks when Maurice changed his sensor, he would ask his teacher to add a smiley face. Only she was allowed to draw one. Well, as you would guess, the rest of the children also wanted smileys like Maurice's, so pretty soon most of his classmates had quarter-sized Magic Marker happy faces on their arms too. So did the teacher.

The following year, Maurice and his family moved, and he began attending a new school. His experience there was completely different. Maurice was bullied. Every day, kids pushed and hit him. They said that Maurice was sick and told the other children to stay away from him because they might "catch" it. Maurice was not invited to any birthday parties. At the new school, the principal never came into the classroom to talk about diabetes. Nobody reminded the children to be thoughtful to those who are different. Meanwhile, the teacher seemed to ignore what was happening. There was never any discussion about it.

One day Maurice's younger sister told his parents what was going on. They hadn't known, as Maurice had never mentioned it. After speaking with him, Maurice's mom contacted the parents of the boy who was bullying her son the most. His name was Harrison.

Around this same time, without any prompting from his parents, Maurice decided to take the matter into his own hands. One morning, without asking his teacher, Maurice walked to the front of the classroom and announced, "Listen up, please." Surprised, everyone stopped working. The teacher let him speak. "I have diabetes," Maurice continued. He raised his elbow and pointed to the plastic circle on his arm. "And this is my sensor. I know it looks funny, but I need it for my disease."

For the next couple of minutes, Maurice talked about diabetes and explained how his sensor worked. He invited his classmates to come up and touch it, just like his previous principal had done. After that, he opened it up for questions. As he took the questions, there was one he didn't know the answer to. All of a sudden, a hand went up in the back of the classroom. Maurice was surprised to see whose it was. "I can answer that," Harrison said. "My parents told me all about your disease. Can I answer it?"

Maurice nodded and waved Harrison to join him. Harrison walked to the front of the room and answered the question. When he started back to his seat, Maurice said, "No, wait. Stay with me." And there the two boys stood side by side talking about Maurice's diabetes. From then on, neither Harrison—nor anyone else in the class—ever bullied Maurice again.

'Twas the Week Before Winter Break

The week before winter break is one of the hardest of the year. Teachers everywhere are hanging on for dear life because it's packed with holiday craziness. On top of your regular teaching, the week is chock-full of class parties, chorus rehearsals, holiday assemblies, staff potlucks, food drives, evening concerts, sing-alongs, extra band practices, get-togethers with buddy classes, visits to the senior center, ugly sweater contests, holly jolly cookie swaps, and covert trips to your colleague's classroom because you're their Secret Santa. By the end of the week, you will have gained ten pounds because for days the tables in the teachers' lounge have been covered with boxes of donuts, bowls of candy, trays of fudge, and leftovers from the staff potluck and twenty-four class parties. By Friday, you will feel like a burned-out Christmas light, a broken candy cane, and an Elf on the Shelf that has toppled headfirst from his perch.

We're all familiar with the famous countdown in Manhattan's Times Square on New Year's Eve. Typically, around a million people gather there that night. Well, there's a much bigger December countdown, and that's the one held by millions of teachers across the globe the week before winter break. During this week, every teacher in the world is counting down till Friday. We keep countdowns in our plan books, on our classroom whiteboards, and on the boards in the staff room too. All week long, the first thing teachers do when entering their classrooms is change the countdown. It makes us happy to cross out a 5 on the corner of a whiteboard and make it a 4, and so on throughout the week.

When emailing or texting our friends, especially another teacher, we will often include the countdown: "Three more days to go." "Only two more sleeps." "We're almost free!" When we pass another teacher in the school hallways, we like to call out the number of days left till the first day of the break. We do this even if students are around. The children don't get it, but our colleagues understand. Sometimes our messages to one another are coded. If a fellow teacher passes you in the hallway singing "It's the Most Wonderful Time of the Year," you can bet she's not referring to the holiday season. By the way, you will not hear a teacher sing "White Christmas" at this time of the year. The lyrics aren't true. Treetops might glisten, but children don't listen. And we don't sing "Silent Night" either. All is *not* calm.

The week before winter break can feel like five days of full moons and Friday the Thirteenths. Your best-behaved students will start fooling around, and your quietest girls will become Chatty Cathys. Children who always hand in their homework will forget to do it. Between their sugar highs, the antic- ipation of vacation, and waiting for Santa, some of your students will start bouncing off the walls. A few days before the break, a colleague of mine sent one of his fourth graders to my classroom with a note that said "I'm sending Nathan over to bounce off *your* walls for a while." *Warning*: If, in the begin- ning of this week, your kids are behaving, don't buy it. It's a ploy. They are luring you into a false sense of security and waiting to let loose by the middle of the week. Also, if you tell children that the light on the smoke detector or Wi-Fi box is really a camera with a direct link to the North Pole and that Santa is watching them, it doesn't work. They won't believe you. If you sing "All I want for Christmas is a *quiet class*," this won't work either. Kids just giggle.

To be honest, this crazy week isn't all our students' fault. Teachers contrib- ute to the excitement. During this week, we give our kids holiday crosswords and word searches. We make snow globes out of baby food jars, dreidels out of craft paper, and reindeer out of candy canes and googly eyes. We wear Santy Claus hats and antler headbands while reading holiday books and sing- ing songs about bells that jingle and snowmen who come to life. We sing songs about lighting the menorah too. We bake sugar cookies, build graham cracker houses, and take our kids on scavenger hunts for gingerbread men that we've hidden around the school. We invite parents in to talk about Hanukkah and, if we're lucky, eat the latkes that they demonstrate how to make. We practice math with gumdrops and peppermints and reindeer noses (malted milk balls). We pull down the shades and let kids read by flashlight as a projected fireplace crackles on the screen. We perform edible science experiments with steaming cups of hot chocolate that we made in a crockpot to illustrate the three states of matter: solids, liquids, and gases. (The solid is the marshmallow that floats on top.) We decorate our classroom doors to look like giant packages and nutcrackers and winter scenes with slogans such as: "This class is only silent at night!" We ask children to write about what they would do if Santa got stuck in a chimney. The most common answers: "Tickle him," "Pinch his rear," and "Call 911." Why do we do this during an already wild week? Because most kids love the season, and there is something truly magical about being with children at Christmastime.

When the last day before break finally comes, you will try your best to hold down the fort. You know not to teach anything new on this day. It's pointless. You won't win. Teachers can't compete with Santa. On this final school day in December, your students clean out their desks and cubbies. You play Holiday Bingo, serve treats that the room moms sent in, and listen to your classroom get louder and louder as the kids empty their goody bags. You are grateful that they will go to PE or art so those teachers have to deal with them. When the children are away at these classes, you take down the December calendar, pass out holiday art to go home, and push down garbage cans full of paper plates, Styrofoam cups, and cupcake wrappers that were licked clean during the class party. In the afternoon, you turn out the lights and show your kids a movie. While they lie on the popcorn-covered floor watching *A Charlie Brown Christmas*, *Home Alone*, or *The Polar Express* in their jammies—because why not throw a Pajama Day in there too?—you sit zonked in the back of your classroom thanking God for Christmas movies. As the DVD nears its end, you look up at the clock. Your mouth stretches into a smile. In a short while, you will happily erase the large "1" written in red Expo marker on the corner of the whiteboard. Your countdown is almost over. Winter break is almost here.

Teacher Tired

Every year, I would teach my students that certain words have different intensities. Take *rainy*, for example. When it rains, it can sprinkle, drizzle, or pour. The same is true for *happy*. When you're happy, you can be pleased or joyful or ecstatic. To be *ecstatic*, I'd explain, is much happier than to feel pleased. *Tired* is another example. *Drowsy* means a little tired, *sleepy* is more tired than drowsy, and *exhausted* is super tired. If you ask kids to show you pouring rain, they will pound on their desks. When they demonstrate how it looks to be ecstatic, they will jump on their chairs and cheer. If you say, "Show me *exhausted*," they will collapse onto the floor and start snoring. Loudly.

I have come to the conclusion that there is one form of tiredness even greater than being exhausted—and that is teacher tired. Teacher tired is the state of absolute and utter run-over-by-a-Mack-truck exhaustion that only teachers can understand. There's no tired like it. How does it feel? When you are teacher tired, you know that your alarm clock will not be enough to get you out of bed in the morning. You'll need an air horn. You feel like a laptop when the tiny battery on the upper corner of the screen turns red, alerting you that it has only 1 percent charge left.

There are different types of teacher tired: first-week-of-school tired and report card tired, conference week tired, field trip tired, and end-of-the-year tired too. Come May, you'd swear the month has sixty-seven days. I remember one student teacher I had named Ted. He had left the corporate world because he wanted to be a teacher. At the end of his first day of student teaching, Ted fell into a chair, shook his head, and cried, "I've never worked so hard in my entire life! I'm beat! How the heck can you do this every day?" I started to chuckle. The funny thing? Ted hadn't even taught anything yet.

You can easily spot a teacher who is teacher tired. There are signs: when you notice a teacher sitting inside her car in the staff parking lot waiting till the very last minute before school is about to start to get out; when you eye a colleague trying to click open his classroom door with a remote car door opener; when you receive an all-school email from a teacher asking if anyone has seen a lesson planner, ID badge, coffee mug, or a stack of spelling tests; when a teacher posts a photo on Facebook of the two mismatched shoes she wore to work that day. If you are unable to see what's wrong in the photo, you are teacher tired too.

There are other telltale signs: You look everywhere for your phone while having a conversation on it. You turn to your students and ask what year it is. You laugh yourself to tears at something that's not even funny. When reading *Charlotte's Web* to your kids, you use the exact same voice for Charlotte, Wilbur, Fern, Templeton, and the goose. You can't remember your students' names. You plan to get ahead over Thanksgiving break but end up binge-watching Netflix instead. You know the kids have seen *The Chronicles of Narnia* fifty times, but you show it anyway. You're jealous of teachers whose school years end before yours. You brew a pot of morning coffee but forget to put the coffee in it. You put "WOW" stickers on your students' papers upside down, so they all say "MOM." When getting off the phone with a parent, you say, "Bye. Love you." You stop at a McDonald's drive-through and try to order breakfast from the garbage can. You play Teacher Tired Bingo at the staff meeting and win. The winning squares on your bingo card say: "Forgot how old you were," "Lost your car keys," "Misspelled a basic vocabulary word," and "Still had snowflakes on your bulletin board in May."

Teachers don't get teacher tired just because of our crazy workload and long hours. There are other reasons. One is that teachers work at a high intensity level and expend an enormous amount of physical, mental, and emotional energy. We go two thousand miles per hour. This can wipe you out. And we are always multitasking. A teacher can answer the phone, tell a child how to spell a word, poke a hole in a glue bottle, and look into a student's open mouth so he can show you where he lost his tooth—all at the same time.

Teachers tend to be big worriers too. We worry about parents, bosses, colleagues, and, of course, our students. We stew about observations, finishing report cards on time, and our kids' spring testing results. All this worrying can keep us up at night. In fact, it's hard for teachers to turn off their brains when they go to bed. If you could look into teachers' brains when they're trying to fall asleep, you'd see thoughts like this: *I need to call Henry's mom . . . Remember to cut more paper . . . I should make Stephanie a new name tag . . . Don't forget to send the field trip notes home . . . I have to listen to Martina read . . .* and *What the heck am I teaching tomorrow?* It makes sense that a lot of teachers have dark circles under their eyes. Jill says that a cosmetic company needs to come out with a concealer for dark under-eye circles and call it Teacher Tired. It'd be a hit.

When schools moved to distance learning during the pandemic, teacher tired took on a whole new level. As teachers faced the daunting task of figuring out how to teach their students from home, countless new challenges were thrust upon them: How do I use the new technology? How do I ensure that my students are learning? How do I teach my own children who are at home while I'm working? How do I get a classroom full of first graders to find a page in their practice books during a Zoom meeting? Organizing a space shuttle launch would be easier.

Those who taught during this time claim there's normal teacher tired, and there is 2020 teacher tired. 2020 felt like ten years in one. During the shutdowns, a friend of mine arrived late to her virtual staff meeting on Zoom. She told her colleagues that she'd fallen asleep. Everyone just nodded and smiled. They understood. When teachers finally returned to their regular classrooms, many of them had to teach both in-class and remote learners simultaneously. Double the work. Just take the simple act of taking attendance. Suddenly teachers had to keep track of those who were fully face-to-face, students who were fully remote, those who were being quarantined, kids who were waiting on Covid test results, and those who were just absent. All day long, as teachers worked in masks that fogged up their glasses and slid down their noses as they spoke, they wiped down classrooms, disinfected devices, tried to keep students six feet apart, reminded kids to wash their hands, and gave lessons on mask wearing: (1) "Do not eat them"; (2) "Masks go over mouths, noses, and chins—not mouths, noses, and eyes"; and (3) "Your mask is not a feedbag. You are not a horse."

Being teacher tired is one of the reasons that so many teachers drink crazy amounts of coffee, or as Jill likes to call it, "lesson planning juice." Teachers need it to survive. One morning before work, I was in Starbucks ordering a coffee when I looked out the drive-through window and noticed a long line of cars. I commented on it to the clerk, and he said, "Ninety percent of the people in that line are teachers." I let out a laugh. "And," he added, "you will never hear any of them ask for decaf."

I experienced my worst case of teacher tired my first year of teaching. I was twenty-three and still living at home with my parents, who lived close to the school. As many new teachers do, I was spending every night at school burning the midnight oil to get ready for the next day. One afternoon I drove home for lunch and decided to grab a quick nap on the sofa. It was 12:10, I had to pick up my third graders at 12:45, and it took less than five minutes to drive to work, so I could grab a few minutes of shut-eye and get back to school in time. Well, it didn't take long till I was out like a light. When I opened my eyes, I turned to look at the clock, then bolted off the couch. It was 1:05! Panicked, I jumped into the car and raced to school. I dashed to the blacktop, but my students weren't there. I ran into my classroom. Empty. Then I poked my head into Mrs. Smith's room next door. *Thank goodness!* She'd brought my kids into her classroom and was showing them a movie.

I went back to my room and tried to calm down, when suddenly my principal (Frank) walked in and shouted, "Where were you?" *Here it comes,* I thought. *I'm going to get fired.* I'd left the children unattended for who knows how long. "I'm sorry," I said, almost crying. "I'm so sorry. I went home and took a nap and fell asleep and—"

Frank put his hand up. "Never mind that. We were worried that something happened to you. Thank God you're okay." At the end of the day when I was excusing my kids, Frank was back in my classroom. As soon as the last child was out the door, he told me to go home and forbade me to come back till the next morning.

I know the dictionary says that a teacher is a noun, but I definitely felt more like a verb. Verbs are action words, and teachers are always in a state of action. All day long, we give lessons, correct papers, read stories, kick copiers, clean messes, love children. Our jobs are a thousand verbs put together. What we do is *do*. To define myself as a noun—as just a person, place, or thing—put me in the same category as a glue stick. And that just didn't feel right.

Being a verb is tiring. It's tiring to give lessons in multiple subjects every day. It's tiring to remind children all the time to say "please" and "thank you" and to not interrupt. It's tiring to monitor playgrounds and cafeterias and bus stops. It's tiring to manage squabbles when kids come in from recess and to follow through if children break the rules. It's tiring to email and call parents, to lean over small furniture all day long, and to mark hundreds of papers every week. It's tiring to be creative, motivating, firm, challenging, enthusiastic, and engaging all day long too.

But—when a student reads a sentence fluently that she previously couldn't, understands a math concept that he hadn't before, or stands in front of the class and gives a presentation in English when only months before she could barely speak the language; or when a child checks out the same book you've been reading to the class, helps out a classmate without being asked, or comes up to your desk three times in the same period, asking for more paper so he can make his story longer because now, as he says, he "loves to write!"—then being teacher tired is worth it.

Popsicle Tulips

One day as I was cleaning out a closet at home, I pulled out a large box full of children's papers. For years, I'd saved pieces that my students had written—ones that touched me or made me laugh or were written so beautifully that you'd never guess they were penned by a child. Kids see things differently than grown-ups do. From time to time, I would pull out the box, go through the papers, and smile and laugh just as I did the first time I read them. Reading old papers with grade-school penmanship gives me the same warm feeling as looking at old pictures in a photo album.

As I thumbed through the box, I let out an audible sigh. I had just accepted an overseas teaching position in the Netherlands and needed to whittle things down for the move. My shipping allowance was limited. My flat wouldn't have much storage. And so I decided it was time to let the papers go. It pained me to do it, but I just couldn't keep them any longer. Some I'd had for thirty years. But before I tossed them out, I sat down and looked through them one last time.

The box had a little of everything. In it were poems the kids had written about colors and happiness and the seasons. There were autobiographies, paragraphs, lists, and pirate journals deliberately written in a shaky hand to show that the pirates were sailing on rough waters. Some of them had been doused with water to look more authentic. I found stories, cliffhangers, descriptions, and "What I Did This Summer" papers with a twist. (I'd let the children make the whole thing up.) I discovered "History of Anything" reports in which students could write about any subject that they were interested in and "Point of View" papers where they wrote about a famous person or event from a different perspective. One child described Ben Franklin's famous nighttime kite flight from the key's point of view. Another wrote about Elvis from the perspective of his guitar. "Without me," her paper began, "there would be no King."

As I read through the papers, I came across a folder with the name Mischa on the cover. Mischa had been one of my fourth graders many years earlier. Even at a young age, he was gifted with words. I opened the folder and started reading. When writing about happiness, Mischa wrote: "Happiness is poking chocolate chip cookies to see if they are ready for eating." When writing about his favorite color, he described silver as "the gleam of my dad's hair gel." The poem he composed about spring took my breath away: "Spring is glittery shamrocks taped onto classroom windows, drooping cherry blossoms that look like they just lost their best friends, Iceland poppies as wrinkly and delicate as my grandma, and tulips closing up at night like small hands grasping for a Popsicle." Mischa was nine.

When I finished reading his papers, I put them into a bin along with the others but immediately had an uneasy feeling. Something inside of me said, *Hold on to these.* I looked down at the folder. *One set of papers isn't going to take up too much room.* I pulled out the folder and kept it.

As happens with most students, Mischa and I had little contact after he left my class. The following year, I'd see him occasionally on the blacktop or in the cafeteria. After he went to middle school, I never saw him again. When Mischa was in sixth grade, I ran into his mom at the store. There she told me a cute story. One day Mischa came home disappointed with a grade he'd received on a paper. It wasn't a bad grade. He actually got an A. When his mom asked why he was upset with an A, he told her that the paper wasn't very good and that he could have done better. He also said, "Mr. Done would never have let me get away with that." When Mischa was in high school, I would get updates from his mom on Facebook. She let me know that he got into Stanford. It didn't surprise me.

Then one day when I was teaching in the Netherlands, out of the blue I got a message from him. Mischa was traveling around Europe on holiday and wanted to see me. I was touched. Unfortunately, it didn't work out to meet, but we had a nice exchange over text. He was delighted to hear that I'd saved some of his papers. When I asked if he'd like me to send them to him, he wrote, "Yes! I'd love to read about the fourth-grade me."

But Mischa never saw the papers. A few days after he contacted me, I received an email that no teacher ever wants to get. It came from one of Mischa's classmates. When I read it, I shook my head in disbelief, then sobbed into a pillow. Mischa was dead. He'd been hiking in Spain, slipped off a trail, and fell off the side of a mountain. He was twenty.

The following week, Mischa's mom contacted me. She wanted to make sure I knew. She wrote to me from Spain, where she and Mischa's father were trying to sort things out. She said she was experiencing every parent's worst nightmare.

Tragedy. When your work is people, you are bound to experience it: a family breaks apart, a child becomes ill, someone has a terrible accident, a parent gets sick, a relative passes away, a former student overdoses or commits suicide. It can be forgotten that teachers deal with all of this. Over the years, I had lost a couple of students, one to cancer and the second to homicide. Mischa was now the third—that I knew of.

Nothing prepares you for the death of a student. Nothing can. When a student dies, it feels like you've lost one of your own children—because, in a way, you have. And you never forget. You never forget holding a very sick child during recess after his chemo appointment. You don't forget the moment his mom tells you that he won't be coming to school now because he's too ill. You never forget your visits to the hospital where you keep up a happy face, then break down after returning to your car. Your brain never erases the sight of a small coffin being lowered into a grave. You never forget the gut-wrenching day when you face his empty desk at school. These memories stay with you forever.

That evening, I found Mischa's papers and reread them. I was thankful that I'd held on to them. A couple of times, I had to stop reading to remove my glasses and press my fingers against my eyes. Though filled with tears, they were also smiling. The combination of Mischa's words and his handwriting took me back to when he was still in my class. I could picture him looking out the window while working on an assignment, his forehead furrowed and his hand bouncing up and down as he tried to think of just the right word. I remembered a time when, amazed at something he had written, I asked him how he came up with his ideas. He shrugged and said, "They just pop into my head." I recalled the time I was reviewing one of his papers and noticed that certain words were not written in his usual handwriting. They were slanted. I asked him why, and he said he wanted to make them "heavier," like real writers do. (I'd recently shown the kids that authors italicize words when they want to emphasize them.) And I remembered when I burst out laughing after reading one of his stories. At the end of it, he had added fake reviews. One of them said: "This story is better than any of mine!—J. K. Rowling."

The next day, I made copies of Mischa's papers and put them into an envelope along with a letter for his parents. I wanted to do something for his family, and this was all I could think of. Weeks later, I received an email from Mischa's mom. Here is what it said:

Dear Phil,

Words cannot express how moved we were to receive Mischa's papers. We'd forgotten about them. I'm amazed that you kept them all these years. His father and I cried over them together. But at the same time, we were comforted. When your child dies, one huge thing you lose is a future in which you slowly discover more about him as the years go on. Getting something like this—that shows a piece of Mischa that was new to us—fills in that hole a little bit. Thank you for sending these. I will never look at tulips the same way again.

The Testing Speech

Have you ever noticed how teachers never refer to standardized tests by their full names? When we speak about them, it's always in code. We say ITBS or MAP or CST. Why is this? In doing so, we try to trick our minds into thinking that we're talking about cute little robots like R2-D2 and not about those dreaded tests.

The word *testing* makes most teachers want to cuss. I hated those tests like a ten-year-old hates homework. You can't put a number on creativity or a score on communication. You can't measure kindness on a Scantron form. Teachers do not need pages of charts and graphs to tell if a child struggles in reading. When taking standardized tests, the only thing children learn is how to get stressed out. Those tests make teachers anxious too. In the weeks leading up to them, we scramble to review skills that our students have forgotten and cram in ones that we haven't covered yet. When the testing begins, we tape signs onto our classroom doors that say "Test in Progress. Do Not Disturb," but the sign we'd like to put up is "SOS!"

Administering the tests isn't what raises our blood pressure. You just read, "Open your test booklets," "Follow along as I read the directions," and "You may begin" over and over again for two weeks. The stressful part is when you monitor the room. I always felt bad when a student asked me what a word meant, and, of course, I couldn't tell him. I'd cringe if I saw a child fill in a wrong answer. I wished I could help when a student insisted that there were two correct answers to the multiple-choice question. I'd shake my head if a child said she was all finished, and I saw that she had an unmarked bubble on the bottom of her answer sheet, which meant that I needed to help her figure out where she started filling in the wrong bubbles.

To make the tests a little less stressful for my kids, every spring just before starting them, I would give the Testing Speech. All teachers have their speeches, and this was one of mine. When I gave it, I'd summon my inner Grinch.

"Boys and girls," I would say, holding up a copy of one of the tests that they were about to take. "Do you know what I think of these?" I answered my own question. "I think they're poo-poo." Yes, I would say the word. In *How the Grinch Stole Christmas!*, the Grinch exclaims, "Pooh-pooh to the *Whos*!" Well, I figured if the Grinch could say this to the cute little people in *Who*-ville, I could say it to my little people too. Of course, whenever I said this, my kids would absolutely lose it. Teachers don't say *poo-poo*.

Once my kids settled down, I would continue. "The scores you will get on these tests do not matter to me one bit," I'd declare. "You know what does? The fact that you work hard, you try your best, and that you're nice to one another. *That's* what matters. I mean it. I care more about the people you become than any scores on some tests!" Then I'd lean into the children and lower my voice as though I were letting them in on a secret. "And do you know *why* I give these tests?" I'd pause. "I give them because I *have* to—not because I want to." I knew what would happen when I made the next statement. "If I had my way, *none* of you would have to take these!" Immediately the room would erupt with cheering and hooting. Several kids would be out of their seats, and papers would be flying like tasseled caps at the end of graduation.

But I wasn't finished yet. At this moment, I would walk to the corner of the room, grab the wastebasket, and set it on my desk. The children's eyes would get big. *He wouldn't.* I'd pick up a stack of tests and hold them over the can. *He won't.* Then, with a Grinch-like grin, I'd raise the tests high above the basket and drop them. *HE DID!*

"There!" I'd proclaim over the whooping. "*Now* you see what I think of these tests." But I still had one final thing to say. The best part was yet to come. Leaning into my students one more time and raising my voice with each word, I would say, "I . . . THINK . . . THEY'RE . . ." I'd let the children finish.

"POO-POO!"

You never heard such relief.

* * *

I knew my kids would tell their parents about the Testing Speech, but I was okay with that. I wanted them to know how I felt too. Every year, I'd get a little nervous that a parent might disapprove, but in my entire career, *never* did a parent question it. Most feel the same as I do. If you're a teacher or a parent, I grant you full permission to use the Testing Speech with your kids. All you need is a good snarl and a garbage can.

Screening the Screens

"Why are you so tired?" I asked Robbie, one of my third graders, who was slumped over his desk with bed head. "Were you up late last night?"

He nodded.

"What were you doing?"

(*Pause.*) "Playing *Fortnite*."

I shook my head. This wasn't the first time I'd had this conversation with one of my students. In fact, I was having it more frequently. "How late were you up?"

He hesitated. "Three."

"On a *school* night?"

I hate that game.

In today's digital world, screen saturation is an increasing concern for parents and teachers. The American Heart Association urges parents to limit screen time for children to a maximum of two hours per day. And yet, studies show that kids and teens ages eight to eighteen spend an average of seven-plus hours a day looking at a screen. It's a mind-boggling statistic. When the coronavirus swept the country, and kids were parked in front of their computers at home, these numbers soared. Screen time went on steroids.

Too much time with digital devices has been linked to a host of problems, including sleep disorders, obesity, mental health issues, low self-esteem, depression, aggressive behavior, and poorer academic performance. The more time kids spend in front of screens, the less time they are outdoors, being physically active, and developing social skills. It has been suggested that too much screen time can also impact children's imaginative play by stunting their senses with a constant stream of entertainment.

It's no secret that tech products are designed to be hyperarousing. The use of technology increases dopamine levels, the neurotransmitter most involved in addiction. Some digital health experts call screens "electronic cocaine." And our kids are overdosing. If you work with children, you've surely seen it. A friend of mine told me that her seven-year-old has a meltdown when asked to stop watching his favorite shows on the phone. It's pretty much a daily occurrence. Another friend got a call from her daughter's school saying that they had reason to believe she had stolen an iPad from the tech cart. Sure enough, they found it. In his clinical work with teenagers, Dr. Andrew Doan, the head of addiction research for the Pentagon and the US Navy, has reported that in some cases it was easier for him to treat crystal meth addicts than video gamers or social media addicts.

We'd all agree that technology in the classroom has its advantages. The internet allows students and teachers to access endless resources and materials. Using technology helps children develop their digital literacy and adds interest to lessons. For many kids, it is highly engaging. But teachers see the problems with devices firsthand. We see the students who resist pen and paper but can't resist the YouTube videos that are only one click away. We observe the trancelike expressions on our kids' faces when using educational programs that resemble video games. We witness the children who can't focus, have wandering attention spans, aren't able to finish a book, and don't want to write about anything else but *Minecraft*. We see the students who are apathetic and uninterested unless they are plugged in.

Many teachers, especially those in middle and high school, also see how distracted students get by their phones. A high school teacher I know teaches six classes a day with an average of thirty kids in each one. One day she asked her students in each class to tell her how many notifications they got on their phones during the period—not at lunch, not in another class, just hers. Here are the totals from these six classes: Facebook, 21; Twitter, 29; Instagram, 58; YouTube, 74; Snapchat, 352; text, 996. To control the distractions, many teachers collect their students' phones before class time, and some are pretty clever about it. I've seen phones placed in vintage Coke crates, old cassette racks, plastic shoe organizers that usually hang on the back of a door, and locked inside cabinets covered with mug shots and labeled "Cell Block." One teacher friend got so tired of competing with her high schoolers' phones that she made a giant one out of cardboard, cut out a hole where the screen should be, and sat behind it to teach. When another friend told her parents at a meeting that the school would no longer be allowing kids to use their phones at school, they applauded.

In today's classrooms—and I'm speaking about brick and mortar classrooms here—students spend a huge amount of time in front of screens. In a typical third-grade class, for example, it's not uncommon to see children practicing math with a program such as Freckle, pecking away on iPads during writing time, reviewing spelling words with SpellingCity, reading e-books on Raz-Kids during silent reading, and conducting research on the internet for social studies. Then they go home and complete their homework online. As children get older, the amount of screen time only increases. And, of course, kids are on their devices for recreation too. They get no break from it.

Parents are pushing back. Across the nation, moms and dads are asking school boards for less screen time, not more. They are urging districts to offer low-tech classrooms or those that are screen free. Some parents are taking their children out of tech-heavy schools and putting them into those that offer less. Others are pulling their kids out of school altogether to homeschool them. But how can teachers tackle this problem that is (literally) right in front of our eyes? With the ever-increasing dependence on technology in our schools, it's not easy, but there are things we can do to stem the tide. Following are a few guardrails that help:

To start, have an honest conversation with your students about screen time—just like you would about bullying, smoking, or drugs. You can even have this talk with the little ones. The average age of children who have smartphones is now nine. In your discussion, ask the kids to share any rules they have about using technology at home and brainstorm ways to limit it. Also, explain the negative effects of too much time spent in front of a screen. Talk about how children who spend an excessive amount of time on their devices may not want to play with their friends as much, make things, read books, or spend time outdoors. Your students will get it. They witness this happening with their siblings and classmates.

Talk with your kids' parents about screen time too. In a class newsletter or at Back to School Night, raise the issue and let parents know that you'll be implementing measures to address it. They'll be happy to hear it. At your parent-teacher conferences, if parents have concerns about their children, don't be afraid to bring it up. When I did, I'd get a range of responses. Some parents were oblivious. Others thought they had a handle on it but didn't. Some admitted that they didn't know what to do. If a parent asked me for suggestions, I'd share the following tips:

- Know what your child is playing and watching. Many don't.
- Set no-tech zones at home, including the bedroom, the dinner table, the car, and so on.
- Have children complete their homework in a central location—say, the kitchen table—so you can keep an eye on them.
- Control the internet at home by giving kids a password with a time limit. (Some children figure out how to override this.)
- Be a stickler about the rules. If kids break them, have a consequence such as they're offline for twenty-four hours. I'd also leave the parents with this: books instead of tablets, sports instead of TV, Legos instead of Xbox.

One effective way to get students thinking about screen time is to have them track their classroom screen minutes for a week, or, as I used to say, the time they spent "staring at glass." Do it again the following week and challenge your class to see if they can lower the total. Screen minutes are like calories. It's always a surprise when you start adding them up. One week, while my students were tracking their classroom time with devices, I asked them to get out their laptops. One child piped up, "Mr. Done, could we possibly do it without them?" The whole class agreed. They were determined to beat the previous week's number. For older kids, have them keep track of their time on social media. Children are often surprised at how many hours they spend in the black hole of cyberspace.

When planning lessons, offer students a balanced digital diet. Create some lessons that require tech and others that do not. A teacher I used to work with had the following goal: For every lesson that required students to use devices, she gave two that didn't. Also, think about offering tech-free days every now and then. This means, of course, that *you* would have to stay clear of the screens too. Once, on a screen-free Friday, one of my third graders walked into the classroom at recess and caught me on my phone. She shook her head, wagged her finger at me, then tattled to the rest of the class.

Many teachers let children grab a tablet or laptop when they finish their work. It keeps kids busy and quiet. When your students finish early, give them other alternatives: read a magazine, write a letter, make a book jacket, play chess, organize your backpack, help a friend. When my friend Audrey's first graders complete their work, they can refer to a chart titled "Pickle and Ketchup": Pick an activity or "ketchup" on your work. Sometimes teachers let their students use devices during free time or as a reward. If you want to reward your kids, open the door, not the laptops. Then take them outside.

Also, consider holding a screen-free contest by challenging your students to stay away from all screens (outside of school) for a couple of days or an entire week. In my screen-free contests, I used to include screens at school, but this became impossible. If my kids met the challenge, their reward was a week without homework. I'd hold the contest toward the end of the school year when we were wrapping things up, so I was okay if they didn't have homework for a few days. Participation was optional. Before you begin, send home a note explaining the contest, and give your parents a paper to sign each night verifying that their kids stayed away from all screens. Most of your students will begin the challenge, excited at the prospect of no homework. But as the week goes on, more and more of them will drop out. When you ask why, their reasons will be: YouTube, the Disney Channel, video games, and Netflix. Once, a child told me that she was doing great until *Dancing with the Stars* came on TV. That did her in.

During your no-screen week, have your students make a list of all the things that kids can do instead of using a device. It's a nice way to remind them that there is life beyond the screen. One day when I was reading Robbie's list—the same Robbie who was going to bed at three in the morning—I laughed when I saw what he had written: "ride a bicycle, chase pigeons, slide down the stairs," and "stand in another room while your brother is playing *Fortnite*, but don't look just listen."

To conclude, don't let tech blind you. In schools, there is an unquestioned bias that anything incorporating technology is simply better. We're told that children will be unable to compete in the modern world if they're not on their screens. Educational technology companies want us to believe that technology improves student learning, but the truth is that there is little rigorous evidence to support this. The use of tech in schools is industry driven, not pedagogically driven. In my own teaching, I didn't see kids retain more when reading from screens than from books. I never found an app that taught math better than a teacher could.

Perhaps tellingly, it is well known that Silicon Valley titans put their children in low-tech schools. The Waldorf School of the Peninsula, one of the most sought-after private schools in the area, bans the use of electronic devices for students under eleven. The school teaches the children of Facebook, Apple, and Google giants how to cook, knit, and build go-karts instead. Educators at the Waldorf Schools don't seem to be worried that their students won't be prepared for the future. The parents aren't either. They understand that twenty-first-century employers are looking for graduates who are curious, intrinsically motivated, can think out of the box, and solve problems—not if they can make a PowerPoint. There's a lesson to be learned here. Remember that a screen is only a tool, just like books and pencils, props and markers, thermometers and microscopes. Teaching and learning are human experiences. Connect your kids to the people in their classroom, not the pixels.

Teacher Tears

E very year, I would tell my students about the crying spoon. When I was a child and would start to cry, my mom would get a soupspoon, put it up to my cheek, and hold it there to catch the tears. I'd get so distracted by what she was doing that I would stop crying. One year, as I was reading a sentimental story to my third graders in the reading corner, I started to get choked up. As I wiped my eyes, Mackenzie got up and walked to her cubby. When she returned, I asked her why she'd left. Mackenzie held out a plastic spoon from her lunch bag. "For your tears," she said, "so you can catch them."

Teachers cry. It's what happens when you work with your heart all day. We give way to tears when we're alone in our classrooms and in the bathroom at school. We shed them at home and in our cars. I once worked with a first-year teacher who told me that she'd already had three "car cries" in the last month. I smiled and said, "You're doing well. I've known new teachers who cried every morning, afternoon, and night for weeks."

Teacher tears come if we're feeling overwhelmed, when we're running ourselves ragged, or after a difficult conversation with a parent. They appear as we watch former students perform in school plays and cross stages at graduations. They show up after all the children are gone on the last day of school. They arrive when we watch teacher movies like *Mr. Holland's Opus* and while we read *The Giving Tree*, *Old Yeller*, or *Where the Red Fern Grows* to our kids. They emerge when reading heartfelt cards from parents and children too. One year I was out of school for a couple of days because my father had passed away. When I returned, waiting for me on my desk were thirty-two construction paper cards. Inside one was a daisy-chain necklace. In another, a child offered to share her daddy with me. I lost it.

Sometimes our teacher tears surface when we are moved by a student's kindness. I recall the day I was working with a child named Skyler, who struggled with reading. As Skyler read aloud, another boy, Andy, was standing nearby. Andy wasn't always the kindest child. He'd been through some pretty rough times. Out of the blue, Andy looked at Skyler and said, "You sound good, Skyler. I remember how you read at the beginning of the year. You've really improved." My eyes welled up as Skyler beamed. Sometimes it is the sweetness of children that brings about those tears. During the pandemic, when kids started going back to their schools, one of Dana's second graders asked her to please take off her mask because she missed her smile. Dana removed it for a moment. Then she cried.

And sometimes we need those crying spoons when we witness a student's bravery. A friend of mine who teaches high school did her best to hold it together during a virtual lesson with her class but fell apart when it was over. One of her high schoolers who had tested positive for Covid-19 showed up to her Google Meet. From his hospital room. With IVs.

Smondays

Teachers' significant others are good sports. They help put up bulletin boards and prep art projects. They put up with dining tables, car trunks, and garage shelves full of teacher supplies. They put up with all the school talk at parties too. They accept when things go missing from home because they were needed at school. They understand that Friday nights won't be much fun anymore because the teacher they love is sound asleep on the couch by eight o'clock. And they understand that every Sunday they will have to be extra nice because that same teacher will come down with Sundayitis.

Sundayitis is the slow-creeping dread and sinking sense of gloom that hits all teachers when they realize that their forty-eight hours of weekend freedom is coming to an end. Teachers use a thesaurus of synonyms to describe this down-in-the-dumps state: the Sunday Night Syndrome, Sunday Scaries, Monday Eve, a Case of the Sundays, and Smondays—when your Sunday stops feeling like a Sunday, and you start thinking of everything you have to do on Monday. A few former colleagues referred to themselves as members of SNAC (Sunday Night Anxiety Club). One of my friends who teaches history calls his Sunday blues "the Great Depression."

Sundayitis strikes at different times. For some, it kicks in at sundown. For others, it turns up right after their favorite Sunday night shows are over. One teacher I know says his arrives in the second half of the NFL game on TV. Jill says she gets it the minute she wakes up Sunday morning. My Sundayitis would emerge right around the time *60 Minutes* came on the air. I used to hate hearing the show's loud ticking stopwatch that plays before and after every commercial. It always felt like they were ticking down to Monday.

How do teachers shake these blues away? Below you'll find a few tips that helped me shake away mine and will help you reclaim your Sunday too.

Plan Monday on Friday

Before you leave school on Friday, get everything ready for Monday. Set out your plans and materials. Post your Monday schedule on the board. Knowing everything is ready will alleviate a lot of stress and allow you to enjoy a cup of coffee on Monday morning while your colleagues are lined up at the copier. If, on Friday, you just can't bring yourself to do anything but stare blankly at a wall, prep everything for Monday on Thursday.

Get It Out

This isn't a new strategy, but it worked for me. Before going home on Friday, make a list of what you need to do the following week. There is something about getting your to-dos out of your head and onto paper that helps calm the mind. After you make the list, put it aside. If it starts to creep into your thoughts on the weekend, mentally put it back in the Monday box. It can wait.

Try to Leave Work at Work

One afternoon in my first year of teaching, I was leaving school with my correcting basket in my arms when I ran into Frank, my principal. He asked what I was holding, and I told him. Frank pointed at the building and told me to put it back. Then he said, "And I'm going to stay right here to make sure you don't try to sneak anything past me."

I understand that sometimes you have to bring work home and that if you're a new teacher, there's no way out of it, but when it's possible, try not to. Get as much prep and correcting done during your release time as you can. If you do take it home, guard your time by setting working hours. Give yourself a certain amount of time, and that's it. And don't put the work off till Sunday night. That's a sure recipe for the grumps.

Keep School Email at School

In today's world, one can literally be "at work" 24/7. You can check work email while eating, relaxing, and walking the dog. Many of us check our email first thing when we get up in the morning and right before we turn out the lights at night. Being plugged in has its advantages, but it can also be suffocating. I know it's tempting to check your school email at home, and it might feel like you're getting a head start if you do, but the reality is that it is counterproductive and adds to your stress. Reading work email at home keeps you amped up and doesn't allow you the break you need. Log out of your school email on Friday and don't look at it again till Monday. It's easier said than done, but your peace of mind is more important. If you do check it, do not answer parent email on the weekend. The weekend is your time. You need it.

Flip Saturdays and Sundays

I used to joke that Sunday was my day of rest—the day to do the rest of the things I hadn't gotten to during the week. On Sundays, I'd do chores and pay bills, but this wasn't helping my state of mind. So I moved my Sunday routine to Saturday mornings. It took some discipline, but it made a huge difference in my mood. This one change made me much less of a Sunday hater.

Plan Something to Look Forward To

If you're dreading the start of the week, plan a bright spot for Monday. Eat lunch with a friend. Instead of treating yourself to Starbucks on Friday to celebrate the end of the week, change it to Monday, so that you have something to look forward to. And think about saving Mondays for teaching something that you enjoy. If there are certain skills that you don't find particularly fun to teach, hold off on those till Tuesday.

Set Out Your Clothes on Sunday

I realize this suggestion is simple, but it was a game changer for me. After years of scrambling on Monday mornings to get my clothes together for the day, I finally decided to start setting them out on Sunday morning instead. Never again did one of my students announce that my socks didn't match because black and navy blue look the same at six in the morning.

Give Yourself a Pep Talk
If you find yourself fretting about the upcoming week, remind yourself that worrying today will change absolutely nothing about tomorrow. Monday will bring whatever it's going to bring anyway. You'll take care of it. You always do. Your teaching does not get any better if you stress out about it.

Find a Happiness Booster
Somewhere I read that the brain cannot process negative and positive thoughts at the same time, so fill your Sunday night with positives: Walk the dog. Light a fire in the fireplace. Watch old episodes of *The Dick Van Dyke Show*. Play a board game. Make your significant other a nice dinner. If you do, though, don't be surprised if he or she acts shocked by your behavior. Remember, your good sport of a partner is not used to seeing you act this way on Smonday.

Frozen

I was out on yard duty one morning after a heavy rain when I stopped dead in my tracks. On the blacktop, a first-grade boy was chest down in a giant puddle doing the breaststroke for all of his friends. As I stared at the child completely dumbfounded, I was experiencing a teacher freeze. The teacher freeze occurs when a student does or says something so shocking that the whites of your eyes double in size, your jaw drops, and you stop blinking. For a split second, you are utterly speechless, and your body experiences complete paralysis until you shake yourself out of it. If you have ever said "Please don't lick your friend," "Markers are not lipstick," or "Let's get this straight: You're wearing only one shoe because your other one got stuck in the toilet?" chances are these comments were preceded by a teacher freeze.

Some teacher freezes are short—like when a child pulls out his dad's shot glass collection for sharing, but your students don't really know what shot glasses are, so you're safe; or the moment you open a Tupperware container of birthday cupcakes for the class and discover that the frosting on one row has already been licked clean; or when a child refuses to eat her cupcake because it was delivered on a Spider-Man napkin. Other freezes last longer, like the time I took my students to the zoo and stood with my entire class in front of two zebras "being natural," or the time I observed one of my third graders banging himself against the classroom wall, falling onto the floor, then getting up to do it over again. As I stared at him, he announced that he was a bat and his echolocation (essentially, bat GPS) had broken. I assumed a freeze of similar length earlier that year when I witnessed the same child butting his head into some chairs, claiming he was a billy goat.

After you come out of a teacher freeze, the challenge always is: How the

heck do you respond? One way is to ask the child a question, like the time
Melissa asked me what *bosom* meant, and I replied with, "Why do you want
to know that?" Her answer: "I'm reading *Anne of Green Gables*. It says *bosom
buddies*." Another response is to just shake your head, which is what happened the day I was playing hangman with my students, and the word they
were trying to guess was *classroom*. The kids had given me an *A* and an *S*,
and the incomplete word on the board looked like this: _ _ ASS _ _ _ _. You
also could choose to act like nothing unusual is happening, which is how a
friend of mine responded while teaching her second graders virtually during
the pandemic. Throughout the lesson, one of her students drank grape juice
from his "special glass": a tall, broad-bowled wineglass with a long, thin stem.
And sometimes you have to quickly change the subject, which is what I had to
do one Monday at our morning meeting.

"And what did you do on the weekend?" I asked Evyatar.

"I went to a bris," he answered proudly.

My eyebrows shot to my hairline.

"What's *that*?" Carlos asked.

Uh-oh.

"That's a party you go to when a baby gets circumcised," Evyatar answered matter-of-factly.

"Circum-*what*?" Kelly called out.

Evyatar turned to her. "Circumcised," he repeated.

I felt the blood rushing to my head. My eyebrows had not come down yet.

Then Evyatar began to explain. "It's when they cut . . ."

Cut him off at the pass! "I'm so sorry, Evyatar. I'm afraid we're running
out of time. I'm sure it was a very nice party." I pointed at the next student.
"And how was your weekend?"

There is one teacher freeze that is forever branded on my memory, perhaps
because *I* was the one who caused it. It took place when I was teaching in
Hungary. My fourth graders and I were brainstorming some of their favorite
things. They'd soon be writing about them. We started by listing some common
foods that children love. I wrote them on the board as the kids called them out.

"Pizza!" István shouted.

"Hamburgers," Kyung Min volunteered.

"Spaghetti," someone chipped in.

"Pierogi!" Adam offered brightly. He was Polish.

I looked at him and said, "Adam, I'm not sure that's a common enough food. Not everyone knows what those are." He frowned, so I added it to the list anyway. Frown gone.

After finishing up with foods, I switched gears. "Okay, what about some of your favorite drinks?"

"Orange juice," Khaled called out.

"Diet Coke," Brittany broke in.

A smirk shot across István's face. "Wine!"

I gave him a questioning eyebrow.

"Shirley Temples!" Dmitry exclaimed.

"Shirley *Temples*?" I said, surprised. "You're from Russia. How in the world do you know about Shirley Temples?"

Dmitry shrugged. "I just do."

When our drink list was pretty long, I started a new one. "Now let's think of some desserts and sweets." The words came quickly, and I wrote as fast as I could.

"Cake!" Sofia jumped in.

"Strudel!" Emil shouted. I smiled at his very European answer.

"Brownies," someone added.

"Candy," another tossed out.

Eventually, I stepped back and looked at the list. "Well," I said, "I can think of one sweet that you're all forgetting. I can't believe no one has said it yet." I waited a second, then told them. "Cookies!"

"Oh yeah!" a couple of kids said.

Immediately Máté, István, and László started giggling. All three were Hungarian.

"What's so funny?" I asked the gigglers.

None answered.

As I wrote "cookies" on the board, I heard more snickering. I turned and looked at István. "Okay, István, why are you laughing?" He wouldn't respond. I threw his buddy a look. "Máté, *what's* so funny?"

He and István exchanged glances. Then Máté spoke up. "Mr. Done," he said hesitantly, "you shouldn't say that."

"I shouldn't say what?"

He looked at István, then back at me. "Cookie."

László nodded in agreement.

"Why not?"

István started snickering again.

"Because," Máté said, "in Hungarian, it means this." Then he made a giant pointing motion below his belt.

As the room erupted with laughter, I stood there in a perfect teacher freeze: eyes wide, eyebrows up, chin down to my Adam's apple. *A cookie is a willy?* I looked at László, then István, who was now covering his mouth, smothering a laugh. His shoulders were shaking. "Is that *true*?" István nodded, his mouth still covered. I tried to think of something to say, but all I could get out was an embarrassed "Well . . . okay then."

I turned around and erased "cookie" off the board. Then I started to chuckle to myself at the fact that I had just added a penis to our list of favorites. With my back still to the kids, I continued erasing the clean parts of the board so the children wouldn't see me trying not to laugh.

Later that day, I was in the staff room, where I told my friends Roxanne and Janet about the cookie incident. They burst out laughing. Roxanne was in stitches.

"Are you . . . are you *sure* it means that?" Roxanne asked, wiping tears from her eyes. "What if the kids are just fooling you?"

"The Hungarian teacher confirmed it," I said flatly. "A cookie is a boy's little . . ." I let out a defeated sigh. "You know what."

Janet shook her head. "I've never heard of this before."

"Neither have I," said Roxanne.

"Wait!" Janet shouted out, slamming both hands on the table. "Does it just mean a little willy or *any* willy?"

I covered my face and cried, "I DON'T KNOW!"

Spark

When the noon bell rang, a new teacher in my district excused her lively group of fifth graders for lunch, then left the campus to go have hers. But when lunchtime was over and her students stood in line, the teacher did not pick them up. The boys and girls waited, but she never returned. Eventually, a few kids went to the office and reported that their teacher hadn't come to get them. The principal got ahold of her on the phone, and she told him that she was never coming back. She'd had enough. She had taught for three months.

Sadly, many highly qualified and talented teachers are leaving the profession. It's a growing and serious problem. One Gallup poll showed that half the teachers in the States say that they are actively looking for a new job or watching for opportunities. The average new teacher doesn't make it five years. In my teacher training, I took most of the courses with the same group. One of our instructors told us to take a good look around. Half of us, she said, wouldn't be teachers in five years. At the time, we refused to believe it, but when I looked back five years later, she was right.

The issues driving teachers away from the profession are many: low wages, large class sizes, a lack of autonomy, increased demands, toxic work environments. A colleague of mine claims that teachers need the following things on their side in order to stay in the game: a supportive boss, supportive parents, and supportive coworkers. She says that if you don't have at least two of these, you'll wither. Some get out of the profession because they feel that teaching is no longer about teaching. It has become more about raising test scores, digging into data, appeasing parents, and jumping on the newest trends than it is about educating kids. As one friend of mine who retired early told me: "It just wasn't fun anymore."

Some call it quits because they are being asked to wear too many hats. Today's teachers are expected to be child psychologists, social workers, dieticians, health professionals, and disease control experts. And many teachers decide to leave because they are just worn out. I know a respected veteran teacher, a former Teacher of the Year in her district and someone who always gave it her all, who quit midyear. Needless to say, a teacher's job brings a huge amount of stress: beginning of school stress, parent stress, principal stress, new curriculum stress, misbehaving kid stress, performance review stress, colleague stress, marking stress. When the pandemic hit, virtual teaching stress was added to the list. On top of all this, many teachers work side jobs to pay the bills.

I remember one school year—it was my seventh year of teaching—I had a really tough group. Several kids had special needs. A large percentage were reading below grade level. And I had a number of challenging boys because the previous year's teachers felt that they needed a male influence. It seemed like every other week I was in another Student Study Team meeting, where teachers can bring up children that they are concerned about. Every day I arrived at school before it was light out and went home in the dark. I worked all weekend long too. By the end of the year, I was emotionally and physically wiped out. I was losing my spark.

All teachers begin their careers with teacher spark. Teacher spark is what ignites the smile in our eyes and animates our expressions. It's what creates the enthusiasm in our voices when we read a story, give a lesson, or comment on the tub of Polly Pocket dolls that a child has brought in for sharing. Teacher spark is what stirs up our excitement when we get a new idea to try out with our kids. It's what motivates us to sort through food drives, chaperone car washes, and make fools of ourselves at school assemblies so that our students will laugh. Teacher spark is what drives teachers to wear onesie unicorn pajamas on the day our little ones are learning the letter *U*, to come to school as hundred-year-old grandparents on 100th Day, and to dress up with your teacher buddy on Halloween as a coffee and a donut or Play and Doh. It spurs us to make classroom trees out of brown grocery bags so that children can hang construction paper apples with their names on them every time they finish a book.

It's when one's teacher spark begins to dampen that burnout can creep in. Feeling burned out is an awful place to be. Like the rubbed-out pink erasers on top of yellow pencils, burned-out teachers feel like there isn't anything left in them either. Like correcting pens that have run out of ink, teachers who are burned out feel that they're also running on empty. Like the crusty orange tops of glue bottles that won't open and staplers that are jammed, they too feel stuck. And like the Out of Order sign taped onto the copier, burned-out teachers feel like they should be wearing one as well.

Not all burnout is the same. Sometimes it goes away after a restful summer, and sometimes it never leaves. Severe burnout doesn't get better by itself, and it can get worse if you don't take steps to curb it. What follows are a few antidotes to help you keep burnout at bay and protect your teacher spark—a few spark plugs for the teacher:

Don't Try to Do It All

New teachers come out of Teacher School like racehorses raring to go. They are trained in the ideal way to teach the subjects but quickly learn that it's impossible to do it all. Disillusionment sets in pretty fast. If you're a new teacher who teaches multiple subjects, I recommend that the first year, you focus on one of them—say, reading—and do the best you can. The next year, tackle math. The following year, maybe writing. They say that it takes seven years to really learn a grade level. This could well be true. But be ready. Just when you feel that you've got your grade level down, your principal will move you to another one, and you'll get to start all over again.

Let Go of Perfect

Your car will become your second desk. It will be cluttered with books, papers, teachers' manuals, and empty coffee mugs. Your laundry will pile up. Your treadmill will be lonely. Lurking on the bottom of your teacher tote will be stray pen caps, old receipts, food wrappers, and sticky notes with your students' names, but you forgot why you wrote them. The week your report cards are due, you will eat microwavable meals, and your own kids will eat too much McDonald's and take-out pizza. All this is normal. You are not alone. You are human. Remember: You don't have to be perfect to make a difference.

Once, I worked with a young second-grade teacher named Sharon who tried to be a superteacher. Every day she would leave school with a giant tote bag full of correcting, and every night she'd stay up late, marking every paper. Yes, you could often see the bottom of Sharon's Finished Work basket (unlike mine). And, yes, Sharon received lots of praise from parents for being so on top of things. But she had no life. There was no joy in her expression. She was twenty-five, with dark circles under her eyes. Sharon was quickly approaching burnout, and I was worried about her. She needed a principal like Frank.

One day after school, I ran into Sharon in the parking lot. She was carrying her tote bag. I told her that I'd give her twenty dollars if she left it at school.

She laughed.

"Fifty bucks," I offered.

She shook her head.

"A *hundred*!"

She wouldn't do it.

Avoid the Morning Scramble

When teachers get to school in the morning, most hit the ground running. Before the kids arrive, they are touching base with colleagues, collecting supplies, responding to email, setting out materials, attending meetings, reviewing the day's lessons, and standing in line at the copier, hoping that the teachers in front of them don't have a lot to do. One way to avoid the morning rush is to get to school early. If you do, you'll have fewer distractions and will finish your work quicker. I understand that arriving at school earlier isn't possible for everyone, but if you can, even by just a half hour, it can make a world of difference. Added bonuses: The copier will be all yours, and there will be room in the fridge to put your lunch. Also, before you pick up your students, give yourself a breather. Don't work all the way up to the first bell. Grab a coffee. Sit at your desk for a few minutes and gather your thoughts. B-r-e-a-t-h-e.

Have a Friend at School

Just like kindergarten teachers have their young ones hold hands with a buddy when walking around the campus, teachers need their buddies at school too. To help beat burnout, it is tremendously beneficial to have a friend with whom you can be honest, someone who totally "gets" it, a teacher to talk with when a colleague is being difficult or a parent is driving you nuts. A friend at school will alert you when the copier is working again and cover your class when you desperately have to use the bathroom. This teacher can also be a sounding board, a listening ear, and a shoulder to cry on. If you already have a best friend at work, count yourself very lucky.

Give Yourself a Cutoff Time at Work

When teaching children, you need to be on your best game. In order to do this day in and day out, teachers need to recharge. So don't stay at work late. Doing so doesn't give you the time you need to recuperate from a long day and reenergize for the next one. There will always be more to do at school—after that extra hour or five. Set a time to leave the building and stick to it. At the end of the day, go home to your family. Your school can replace you, but your family can't.

Get Out of Your Classroom

A change of scene now and again can help brighten your mood. During your breaks, go sit in the staff room or the library, if it's quiet. If the weather is nice, eat your lunch outside. One high school teacher I know actually runs the track during his lunch hour. I don't recommend this for elementary school teachers, though. If we ran around the blacktop at lunch, we'd be followed by dozens of munchkins.

Take Your Lunch Break

Early in my career, I taught with a woman named Doris, who always worked through lunch. She'd been doing this for decades. One day I was surprised to see her in the staff room at lunchtime. "Hi, stranger," I said. "What brings you here?" Doris confessed that she was on three tranquilizers a day and that her blood pressure was through the roof. She said she needed to make a big change, or she wasn't going to make it.

A lot of teachers work through lunch. The problem is that doing so can wear you down. I understand that sometimes you have to, but try not to make it a habit. You need your breaks. Getting out of your classroom for those thirty minutes can help get you through the rest of the day. Also, in order to stay in the profession for the long run, you have to pace yourself. If you can't afford to take your whole lunch, at least take a break for part of it. You don't want to end up like Doris. Sit in the teachers' lounge at lunchtime. Chew your food. Talk with grown-ups.

Practice Companion Teaching

Gardeners have long known that certain plants can help and support each other when planted side by side. Garlic bulbs help repel rose pests. Beans attract insects that prey on corn. Herbs invite pollinators for melons and squash. It's called companion planting. And some plants do not do well together. Sunflowers, as an example, emit a chemical from their roots that prevents nearby plants from growing and competing for nutrients. Walnut trees are not good garden companions either, as they can be toxic to nearby plants. At school, plant yourself near those who support you and build you up. Sit beside *them* in the staff room. And avoid the walnut trees. You know who they are. Walnut trees like to complain and are often negative. Negativity saps joy and kills teacher spark. Be kind to the walnut trees, but spend as little time with them as you have to.

Release Those Endorphins

One day at school, I was hanging a piece of construction paper on the whiteboard with a magnet when the paper slid down the board. My third graders started giggling behind me. I pushed the paper up, put on another magnet, and watched the paper slide right back down again. Chuckles. I tried it a third time, and the paper slid again. More chuckling. Finally, I grabbed the rest of the magnets and slammed them onto the paper. It stayed. When I turned around and faced the laughing children, I couldn't help but crack up with them.

When something funny happens at school, don't try to keep a straight face. Enjoy a good laugh. A hearty chuckle lowers stress, helps restore balance, and triggers the release of endorphins. Kids like seeing their teacher laugh. It relaxes them and shows that you're human. Shared laughter between students and teachers also helps build relationships. These are the moments kids remember. Research suggests that laughter can even help us to live longer. If this is so, then it makes sense to me that laughter can help you enjoy a longer life in the classroom too.

Don't Make Education Your Hobby

Teachers are always looking for new ideas and reading books about teaching. Be careful, though, not to make your profession your hobby. Don't be a full-time teacher outside of work. Your brain needs a break. Do something completely unrelated to teaching in your downtime. It will help you stay fresh. And don't read those teacher books in bed. In fact, if you're reading this one in bed—put it down!

Take Summers Off

When I was a young teacher, I used to fill my summers taking classes. I'd teach summer school too. But by the time the new school year rolled around, I was already beat. Starting the year off tired is an invitation for burnout. If possible, I recommend that you take summers off completely and do not teach summer school if you don't have to. When we have trouble with our phones or computers, they will usually work again if we unplug them for a while. The same is true for you. Also, if you want to take classes toward an advanced degree, don't jump into it right after you start your first teaching position. Give yourself a few years to settle into the profession.

Pay It Forward

I once had a dear friend named Louise who would use *happy* as a verb. Whenever Louise was pleased about something, she would say, "That *happies* me." Louise believed that since we can say that things "sadden" us, we should be able to say that they "happy" us too. I agree. It's common knowledge that when you do something nice for others, it makes you feel good. So, if you're feeling burned out at work, go "happy" someone by doing something nice for them. It will get your mind off of yourself, and you'll feel better in the process. Let a colleague who's waiting behind you at the copier cut in front of you. When there are treats in the staff room, bring one to a coworker who is stuck in the classroom. Leave a hope-you're-feeling-better note on a teacher's desk when he or she returns from being out sick. Once, my friend Sandy was having a hard week at school. Report cards were due soon, and conferences were coming up. Sandy had two young sons at home. She was overwhelmed. I noticed on the duty wheel that she had playground supervision all week before school, so the next morning, I walked out to the blacktop where Sandy was standing and said, "Good morning. I'm here to cover your duty for you."

"*Really?*" she said, surprised.

"Yep. Go get some work done." I grinned. "Or give yourself a pedicure before the kids come in."

She laughed.

Later, Sandy came into my room to thank me. She said that my covering her duty had made her day. I told her that it "happied" me too.

Tune It Out

When I was studying music in college, one of my professors was a woman named Irene Dalis. Before becoming a professor, she'd had an incredible career as a mezzo-soprano with the Metropolitan Opera for twenty-five years. When Miss Dalis's students asked her for advice, she would say, "Tune out the noise. Focus on the voice." When I think of her words, I'm reminded of how perfectly they apply to teachers: Tune out the noise. Focus on the teaching. There's a lot of noise in education: school politics, staff room gossip, policy changes, negative news about the profession. All this noise can distract you from doing your best work with children. Heed Miss Dalis's words and try to tune it out.

Focus on the Small Wins

Teachers certainly don't bring home the big paychecks. But we get other rewards. Ours are the small wins that occur in our classrooms. Every school year consists of thousands of little victories: watching hands rocket skyward when you ask who'd like to share their writing; hearing kids laugh as they work together; listening to a child tell her classmates to hurry up so that story time will start sooner; seeing a student look up at you with big eyes and a bright face when something finally clicks, then watching him scurry off to work on it some more; hearing a child say she hopes that you will be her teacher again next year. Being able to recognize these wins is important. They help sustain us. But recognizing them doesn't just happen, though. You have to be on the lookout.

Talk with a Veteran

One day during my seventh year of teaching—the one that nearly did me in—I went next door to a fellow third-grade teacher named Ardis and told her how I was feeling. Ardis was a veteran with only a few years left till retirement. In the back of her cupboard, she had thirty-five plan books all lined up. On her desk sat number thirty-six. Ardis and I had worked beside each other since I started teaching. I was often in her room, running things by her, asking advice, and talking about kids. She knew all my students. Ardis was a true mentor to me. Every year on her Christmas card, she signed it: "Mom #2."

As I spoke with Ardis that day, I told her that I was considering taking a leave of absence and wasn't sure if I was coming back. I let her know that I'd started to fill out the leave papers from the district. Ardis listened and nodded. She didn't say much. She let me talk. The following morning, this letter was in my mailbox at school:

Dear Phil,

Thank you for sharing with me yesterday. I'm sorry to hear that you are considering leaving. I wanted to let you know that I understand. I, too, wanted to leave teaching early in my career. More than once, I considered taking a different job. I'm glad that I stayed. I'm writing to remind you of some of your students.

Do you remember when you had Corinne? She struggled in reading so. But you worked with her before school. You started your little book club at lunch. And do you remember Victor? Remember how he would line up on the blacktop before the bell rang just so he could stand close to you? Every day you met him with a giant smile. His home life was in shatters, but you made school a safe and happy place for him.

Do you remember Dustin? Remember how he cried when he had to write. He had such a fear of it. During writing time, he sat with you at your desk, practically in your armpit. You were so patient with him. And do you remember Jered and how he loved to perform? Remember how he sprained his ankle the day before the school play? His mom told you that the first thing he said after learning that he'd sprained it was, "Can I still be in the play?" And that year your Tin Man walked down the yellow brick road on crutches.

Do you remember Felicia? Remember how she cried the first week of school because she didn't speak English and couldn't understand? You worked with her every day, and in a short while, those tearful eyes turned into smiling ones. Remember how proud her parents were when she recited her poem for the whole school at the assembly? I remember how proud you looked too. And do you remember Rachel? She was not a happy child. She had few friends. But then one day you heard her singing and invited her to sing for the class. After that, she sang every week. Remember that?

The world will always be full of Corinnes and Victors, Dustins and Jereds, Felicias and Rachels who need teachers like you who will believe in them, love them, and light up when they see them in line. You've learned that teaching is one of the hardest jobs in the world. Yes, there are days when we don't want to be around kids. Yes, we have days when we don't want to "seize the day." I've had plenty. But you will never find a more rewarding profession. You will never find a more fulfilling life. Please stay. We need you.

Love,
Mom #2

When I finished reading Ardis's letter, I closed my eyes tightly to hold the tears inside. Then I rubbed my fingers over my eyelids to wipe away the ones that had escaped. After a couple of deep breaths, I folded the letter and put it into my love box. A few days later, I walked into Ardis's classroom with my leave papers and stood in front of her desk where she was seated. I held the papers up and tore them with one giant rip. "I'm staying," I said. Ardis only smiled. Then I pointed at her and said, "And it's all your fault."

Closing Thoughts

The Last Day

It was my thirty-third last day of school. I found it hard to believe. When I got dressed that morning, I took extra time to choose my socks. This class liked the green ones with pink flamingos on them the most.

All around the campus, there were signs that it was the last day. The end-of-school countdowns on the corners of classroom whiteboards all said "0." The custodian was looking shell-shocked, and the secretary's desk was loaded with gifts and cards. The return box in the library was overflowing with books. Above the box hung a poster of Batman with the caption "Batman returns his library books. Have you?" The kindergarten teacher had sent out an all-school email saying she found a summer home for the turtle. The sign on the fridge in the staff room reminded teachers to clean it out. The first graders were wearing badges that said "Second Grader in Training." The letters on the marquee in front of the school had been changed for summer. It said "Dear Parents, Tag. You're It."

My classroom had that end-of-the-year look too. The backpacks were bulging with work to go home. The wire that strung across the classroom for student artwork was empty, save for a few clothespins. On my desk sat a few gifts from the kids and some good-bye cards, including one that read "Mr. Done I'm going to miss you so mush!" When my students cleaned out their desks, one child proudly announced that he'd found thirteen pencils. Another returned my teacher scissors with the words "Do Not Remove!" on the handle. The stickers were off the cubbies, the blue tack off the walls, and the shelves were covered with butcher paper. In the Completed Work basket lay the kids' last writing assignment. They had written letters to next year's third graders with advice: "Do your homework." "Follow directions." "Listen to the teacher." "You'll like it here."

My classroom looked different than it usually did on the last day. Normally, I'd leave the faded butcher paper on the boards to replace in August, but now the boards were bare: no more construction paper beach balls and sunglasses and sand pails with bucket lists waiting to start. It felt strange not to see anything on my teacher board. I'd taken off all the photos of my students, my travels, and my dog. My teaching certificate and my second-grade paper that said "Someday I want to be a teacher" weren't there anymore either. My desk and file cabinet were empty now except for a few supplies and some sticky notes with messages that I'd left for the teacher who'd be replacing me, so she'd know where things were. For weeks, I had purged files, cleaned out cupboards, and taken things home. Every couple of days, I had delivered materials that I didn't need anymore to the new teachers at school to see if they wanted them. I would laugh whenever I stepped into their classrooms with an armful. Before I even opened my mouth, they'd cry, "Yes!"

The last day continued on as last days do—a class party, extended recess, more cleaning up, and constant requests to sign yearbooks even from kids I didn't know, because for children, getting a "Have a good summer!" and a funny happy face from any teacher is special. Eventually, it was already after eleven, almost time for early dismissal.

I asked my students to join me on the reading rug. Behind them stood a couple of moms. I had invited the parents in for our last few minutes together. The children and I shared our favorite memories of the school year. Heather's was the class play. Spencer's was a field trip. Jimmy's was when I couldn't get the old pull-down map back up. I asked the children what they felt they had improved in most during the year. Lots of kids said reading. Several said math and writing. Erin, who rarely spoke, said, "I learned not to be shy." I glanced up at her mom, who had clutched her heart.

Next, I began my end-of-the-year talk. Every year, I felt compelled to give it—one last set of reminders, a few final words of encouragement: "Be good," "Obey your parents," "Make wise choices," "Be considerate of others," "Choose what is right and honest and true." I knew that the kids had other things on their minds, but I needed to tell them. Then I asked the children a few questions: "What's eight times seven?" "How do you spell *because*?" "What's the contraction for *will not*?" so they would shout out, "That's easy!"

and I could point out that in the beginning of the school year, these questions weren't so easy for many of them. Ordinarily, in my final talk, I'd say, "Come by and visit your old teacher next year." But I couldn't say it this year. It felt strange not to. As I sat there, it hit me that this could well be the last time I would sit on a reading rug surrounded by children. I could feel my eyes watering up and pressed my lips together tightly the way people do when they don't want to cry. A crack in my voice gave me away.

Finally, the kids and I sang some of the songs they had learned that year: "Oh, What a Beautiful Morning," "Zip-a-Dee-Doo-Dah," "My Favorite Things." Our last song was "Edelweiss." I ended with this on purpose. My students knew why. Throughout the year, I had often told them that *they* were my edelweiss. The song lyrics describe the edelweiss flower as small, bright, and happy—just like children. Like edelweiss, my students had also bloomed and grown. As we sang together, I looked out tenderly at the children singing back to me. When we finished, I took my glasses off and wiped my eyes. "That's okay," Gina whispered, rubbing my shoe. I smiled at her. When I looked up, I saw a couple of moms wiping their eyes too.

Soon it was just about time to let my birds out of their nest. The kids put on their backpacks and set their chairs on their desks for the last time. I reminded them to make sure they didn't leave anything behind. At one minute before noon, I directed the children's attention to the clock, and we watched the second hand circle the numbers. In the last ten seconds of the school year, the kids started counting down. When the second hand reached the twelve, everyone cheered. I announced that they were now officially fourth graders, and the children cheered some more.

After one last good-bye, I excused the kids, and they bounded out of the room, excited for the start of summer. A few stayed behind for a hug. A couple of them cried. I followed the children outside and watched them run to the bus and the bike racks, their backpacks bouncing on their backs. After a few minutes, I stepped back inside and closed the door. Then I sat at my desk and wiped away my teacher tears. Last days of school are not easy for teachers. For nine months, you give everything you have to your students, and then all of a sudden, just like that, it's over. *Poof!* They're gone. You will have little if any contact with most of them again.

For a while, I lingered in the room, picking up things off the floor and putting up more chairs. A few teachers stopped by to say so long and wish me well. I had said good-bye to my colleagues earlier in the week. I didn't want to do so on my last day with the kids. Eventually, I grabbed my bag and the box of cards and gifts from the children and started to leave. Danielle had woven me a pot holder. Jayden gave me a plastic key chain that he'd baked in the oven. It had his name on it.

When I reached the door, I turned and gave one last look around. In just a few months, the room would be full of new faces. As sure as the tides and the seasons, the pattern that is school would continue. Finally, I turned off the lights, stepped outside, and locked the door. After dropping off my key with the secretary, I walked to my car. The last sound I heard was a child shout, "Bye, Mr. Done!"

If you are a teacher or are planning to become one, know that you have chosen a noble profession. Never forget that you walk into your classroom each morning for a reason. Actually, for *many* reasons. Each one has a desk, a chair, and a cubby. Delight in your students and laugh together. Build relationships and seize those teachable moments. Read to your kids every day and sing with gusto. Share your stories with your charges and be grateful that they turn to you for your storytelling. Be committed, compassionate, and creative. Provide a learning experience that children will be eager to be a part of. Take good care of yourself. Protect your spark. And most important of all—love your edelweiss.

Afterword

Two years have passed since I retired from teaching. I still have all my teacher socks and teacher ties. I can't bring myself to get rid of those. It's funny what you miss after you retire from the classroom. I miss hearing my name called hundreds of times a day. I miss walking down the hallway by the art room and seeing rows of painted sunflowers in September, snowmen in January, and surfboards in June. I miss the out-of-the-blue things that kids say, like when a child announces in the middle of a lesson that her tooth came out—and then the rest of the class claps. I miss those moments when the reading rug suddenly swirls with merriment, or the room whirls with laughter. I miss seeing children hug their parents as they drop them off at school. I miss watching kids stand on the blacktop when the school day is over, scanning for their moms and dads and then exploding into giant smiles when they spot them. And I miss the sounds of a classroom: that wonderful mix of children's chatter, the shuffling of chairs, the opening of binders, the tapping on keyboards, the grinding of pencil sharpeners, the *clonk* of a stapler, the squeak of whiteboard markers, the zipping of backpacks, and the *wham* of a beanbag chair after it has been flopped on. Classroom music.

When I retired, I wondered if my new year would still begin in August. It does. I wondered if I would still check out the new school supplies in the summer and look at the new children's books too. I do. Once a teacher, always a teacher. It never leaves you. When I'm out and about, I find myself smiling if I drive by a playground and see kids out on recess. I also miss that sound. And whenever I drive by a long line of children walking with their class on a field trip, I always look for the grown-up in the back of the line and say to myself, "God bless the teacher."

Acknowledgments

My heartfelt thanks to my agent Janis Donnaud, Piotr Konieczka, Heidi Fisher, and the entire team at Avid Reader Press and Simon & Schuster: Jonathan Karp, Jofie Ferrari-Adler, Carolyn Kelly, Ben Loehnen, Lauren Wein, Jordan Rodman, Alexandra Primiani, Meredith Vilarello, Jonathan Evans, Rafael Taveras, Annie Craig, Katherine Hernández, Caroline McGregor, Alison Forner, Sydney Newman, Carly Loman, Philip Bashe, Ben Wiseman, Dominick Montalto, and Alicia Brancato. With sincere gratitude to my balcony people: Ronald and Mary Done, the Konieczka family, Ann Rutherford, Debbie Reynolds, Mathilda Done, Irene Dalis, Carol Velazquez, the Scheidt family, the Guillet family, Rose Ranada, Adeline Greco, George Jacobs, Mae Murayama, William Smith, Monica Roben, William Stretch, Karl Kirschner, Robert Duncanson, Aldin Peterson, Robert Farrington, Charlene Archibeque, Charlene Chadwick, Barbara Barrett, Zoltan Karaszy, Ardis Gonzales, Frank Pelkey, Tommy Kay Smith, Eva Schinn, Vicki Garson, Linda Searl, Elaine Saussotte, and Sarrie Paguirigan. My deepest appreciation to Audrey Sager, Joyce Fox, Virginia Phillips, Stacy Molnar, Carla Beuchler, Lambert Dolphin, Mischa Nee and family, Judit and Francisco Papp, Giulio and Geraldine Valerio, Malgorzata Palimaka, Teresa Cavanaugh, Karin Farrell, Olivia Jorasch, Barbara Parks, Mary Jo King, Lisa Wilson, Marion Beach, Diana Schuster, Gábor Vodics, William Lane, Steve Grizzle, Troy Lapham, Deanna Aiello, Kathleen Arreguini, Patsy Timothy, the Bódi family, Judi Cotant, Debbie Wilson, John Wiley Jr., Jessica Cotant Fether, Dennis Schroeder, Marilyn Berger Kanes, the Grude family, Cindy Toland, Rick and Sandi Detwiler, Heather Crupi, Erika Nemes, Shelley Ganschow, Phillip Irwin Cooper, Henrietta Kígyósi, Mary Little, S. D. G., and Roxanne R. Colbert. A warm thanks also to the many families and colleagues I've had the pleasure of working with over my career.

Index

craft of teaching, *see* teaching
creating things, 295–97
creative dramatics, 198, 207–14
  acting out words, 209–10
  bringing lessons to life with, 213–14
  hot seating, 210
  science and, 214
  tableau, 211–12
  Teacher Reader, 213
  Wax Museums, 212–13, 228
creativity, 208, 261–66, 295
  inspiration and, 265–66
  and learning how things are made,
    265–66
  nature and, 262–63, 265
  notebooks and, 264–65
  observation and, 263–64
  solitude and, 265
  thinking time and, 264
  see also art
Cricket in Times Square, The (Selden), 120
Crow, Sheryl, 223
Crumple & Shoot game, 275
Crystal, Billy, 223
Cumberland Band, 205–6
cumulative folders, 331–32
curiosity, 266, 285, 286
curriculum
  art(s), 92, 195–206, 265
  attending performances, 203
    cursive as an art, 188
    dance, 196, 200–202, 218, 247
    encouraging the artists in your class,
      204–5
    funding for, 196, 205
    giftedness and, 218
    importance and benefits of, 195–96
    integrating into other subjects,
      197–98
    language of, 200
    measuring practice and, 155

museum visits, 199–200
music, *see* music
online classes on, 199
putting on a play, 215–16
tableau and, 211–12
teachers' ability to effect changes in
  teaching of, 205–6
teachers as artists, 223–26
teaching one artist a month, 197
visits from artists, 203–4
see also creativity
changes in, 4–5, 86
creative dramatics and, 198, 207–14
  acting out words, 209–10
  bringing lessons to life with, 213–14
  hot seating, 210
  science and, 214
  tableau, 211–12
  Teacher Reader, 213
  Wax Museums, 212–13, 228
cursive, 187–89
enrichment programs, 217–20
geography, *see* geography
grammar, 121, 172–74
  beginning a sentence with me (or him
    or her), 173
  can vs. may, 173
  good vs. well, 173
  prepositions and pronouns, 173–74
  of teachers, 174
math, 137, 148–60
  abstraction in, 149
  calculators and, 86, 189
  concrete objects in, 149–50
  edible, 157
  Five a Day strategy, 153
  measurement, 154–56, 158
  mental, 156
  movement and, 157–58
  multiplication, 149–51
  numbers, 91–93, 95, 157–58

curriculum; math (*cont.*)
 real-world, 160
 review in, 152–53
 scripted programs for teaching, 159–60
 smartness in, 91–93, 95
 technology and, 158–59
 textbooks for, 150, 153–54
 vocabulary, 151–52
 word problems, 153–54
 worksheets, 151, 153–54
music, *see* music
putting on a play, 215–16
reading, *see* reading
smartness and, 91–95
talking and, *see* talking
words and vocabulary, *see* words
writing, 103, 132–47
 art and, 198
 assignments, 112, 117, 127, 264
 authors' tea event and, 144–45
 balancing two schools of thought on teaching, 141
 brainstorming ideas for, 135
 "chunking" of, 142–43
 conferences, 138–39
 different types of, 136–37
 drafts and rewriting, 137–38, 140, 311
 explaining process of, 137–38
 how-to papers, 70
 lists, 103–7
 love of, 142
 modeling process of, 145–47
 out loud, 146, 147
 with a partner, 137
 place for, 137
 practicing, 136
 proofreading, 138
 and reading aloud, 121–22
 remembering your audience when assigning work, 141–42

 of research reports, 141
 scaffold supports in, 142
 sentence starters for, 143–44
 sharing your own, 140–41
 students sharing with classmates, 139
 supporting reluctant writers, 142–43
 as talking on paper, 142
 Writing the Room exercise, 139
 writing versus typing, 140
cursive, 187–89
custodians, 337–38
cute factor, 20–23

Dahl, Roald, 102, 280
 The BFG, 102
 Charlie and the Chocolate Factory, 198, 211
 James and the Giant Peach, 102, 114
 Matilda, 122
Dalis, Irene, 412
dance, 196, 200–202, 218, 247
da Vinci, Leonardo, 264, 265
Da Vinci Code, The (Brown), 223
death of a student, 383–85
devices, *see* screens
Didion, Joan, 264
difficult students, 29–31, 252
discipline problems, 253
discussions, class, 164, 167
 guidelines for, 166–67
 maps as springboard for, 179
Disney parks, 182–83, 197
ditto machines, 86
Doan, Andrew, 390
Docter, Peter, 295
Dollar Tree, 232–33
door, greeting children at, 70–73
dopamine, 282, 290, 390
drama
 creative dramatics, 198, 207–14
  acting out words, 209–10

About the Author

PHIL DONE is the recipient of the prestigious Charles Schwab Distinguished Teacher Award, was honored as a Teacher of the Year in California, and was nominated for the Disney Teacher of the Year Award. He is the author of the highly acclaimed *32 Third Graders and One Class Bunny: Life Lessons from Teaching*, *Close Encounters of the Third-Grade Kind: Thoughts on Teacherhood*, *The Charms of Miss O'Hara: Tales of* Gone with the Wind *and the Golden Age of Hollywood from Scarlett's Little Sister*, and *The Ornament Box: A Love Story*. Phil lives in Europe with his family.